THE SOCIAL MEDIA BIBLE

W9-BVF-848

THE SOCIAL MEDIA BIBLE

THIRD EDITION

LON SAFKO

TACTICS, TOOLS & STRATEGIES FOR BUSINESS SUCCESS

WILEY

John Wiley & Sons, Inc.

For general information on our other products and services or for technical support, please contact our Customer Care Department within the United States at (800) 762–2974, outside the United States at (317) 572–3993 or fax (317) 572–4002.

Wiley publishes in a variety of print and electronic formats and by print-on-demand. Some material included with standard print versions of this book may not be included in e-books or in print-on-demand. If this book refers to media such as a CD or DVD that is not included in the version you purchased, you may download this material at http://booksupport.wiley.com. For more information about Wiley products, visit www.wiley.com.

ISBN 978-1-118-26974-9 (paper); ISBN 978-1-118-28345-5 (ebk); ISBN 978-1-118-28478-0 (ebk); ISBN 978-1-118-28723-1 (ebk)

Printed in the United States of America.

10 9 8 7 6 5 4

CONTENTS

theSocialMediaBible.com

CONTENTS

PART II
Strategy: The Five Steps to Social Media Success

This project was the largest and most passionate undertaking of my career, and using social media to create a book on social media was by far the most enlightening.

When I first created the plan to write a book on social media, I thought it was going to be another typical business book: 250 pages, 20-plus chapters, 50,000 words, the typical business book formula.

Then I realized that it was not only in my best interest to use social media, but also in a way, that I should use social media to create this book. I knew that if I asked the business community what they wanted in a book and wrote it that way, the book would be successful and it was. What I didn't know at the time was the magnitude of the journey I was about to undertake.

We brought the initial concept of the book on social media to more than 1,000 people. They were mostly professionals with annual incomes over $100,000; most had college degrees, from associates up to PhDs.

Of more than 1,000 surveyed, 66.4 percent said that they could not define what social media is, while 99.1 percent said that they knew social media would have a significant effect on them and their businesses. Let me restate this: Two-thirds of these professionals didn't know what it was, but nearly 100 percent knew it was going to affect them. This is whom this book is dedicated to.

By using user-generated content and feedback, I also learned that the business community didn't want just another vertical business book; they wanted something much more comprehensive. They asked for a book that first explains: What are all of these things we keep hearing about? What's a blog, a vlog, a podcast? What is a *trusted network* and *wisdom of the crowds?* What is LinkedIn, MySpace, Flickr, and YouTube? So this became the blueprint for Part I, Tactics and Tools, which in itself is a business book on the tactics of social media.

Finally, they wanted a book that could pull all of this together answering the questions: How do I use social media in my business? How can

 theSocialMediaBible.com

I incorporate this in my business plan? How do I make money using social media? Where's the ROI? How will this change the way I do business? This became Part II of the book, Strategy.

During the past year, I have had the opportunity to speak with such companies as NCO, Levi Strauss, Nike, United Airlines, PepsiCo, Coca-Cola, Dial, Intel, Scott's, Frito-Lay, General Mills, L'Oréal, Kraft, Dannon, Omaha Steaks, Unisys (Burroughs), La Quinta, Lilly, and dozens of entrepreneurs, governmental agencies, and nonprofits. The one run-on question they had in common was: "How do I put together a strategy that includes my conventional media, integrates social media, determines what social media tools I should use, find the resources, and measure my success?"

So in this edition, the Part II, Strategy, section has been completely rewritten. In this new section, I give you "The Five Steps to Social Media Success," which addresses all of the questions asked earlier in five easy steps. This new section is down and dirty and in the weeds, and what you will get out of it is what you are willing to put into it. I ask you to look at things most marketing, PR, and upper management people never want to discuss: The cost of customer acquisition and the actual ROI of each of your existing marketing campaigns and efforts.

Once you determine your ROI, and cost of customer acquisition on your existing marketing, you can now better reallocate existing resources, both human and financial, to marketing that is significantly more effective: social media.

I approached John Wiley & Sons, Inc. with a concept of multiple full-sized business books (two business books in one). They trusted the wisdom of the crowds and the result is *The Social Media Bible*.

The remaining change that has taken place with this third edition is *The Social Media Bible* is now 75 percent of its original size. Now that people are beginning to understand the fundamentals of social media, I decided to reduce the size of the book and, while providing the history of all of the technologies, focus more on the state of the art of how social media is being used.

The Social Media Bible is an aggregation of ideas, thoughts, and my own experiences from blogs, vlogs, podcasts, videos, books, wikis, e-mails, and conversations. As Francis Crick, the Nobel Prize winner for his discovery of the double helix, said during his acceptance speech while quoting Sir Isaac Newton, "If I have seen farther than others, it is because I have stood on the shoulders of giants."

Thank you to Jimmy Wales for creating Wikipedia and the Wikimedia Foundation and to all of the people from around the world who have contributed to Wikipedia, providing such a valuable resource of cumulative human knowledge.

I want to personally thank all of the corporate partners who shared their expert insights in both the book and their executive conversations at www.theSocialMediaBible.com,

the 23 technical editors, and the 26 ROI of Social Media vignettes authors.

Thank-you also goes to Evo Terra for his *Podcasting For Dummies* book; blogger David Risley, for his top 50 blog tips; and to my friend and colleague Joanne Zimakas for her incredible transcription skills and attention to detail of the more than 24 continuous hours of executive interviews available on www.theSocialMediaBible.com.

I also want to sincerely thank Tiffany Coates, who was the project manager on this edition. Tiffany's attention to detail and people skills made it possible to pull together up-to-the-minute, highly technical, and sensitive information from more than 80 different contributors in an amazingly short time. Tiffany, thank you for all of your hard work and dedication.

My personal gratitude also goes out to the staff of John Wiley & Sons, Inc. for all of the wisdom of that crowd, and especially to Peter Booth Wiley for his support and contributions, without which this book would have never been published. Also, thank you to: Matt Holt for believing in and fighting for this unusual book; Kim Dayman for really putting the polish on the design; Shannon Vargo for her incredible author-wrangling skills, which allowed the book to be published; Christine Moore, for her insightful and meticulous editing talent, which made this book intelligible; Elana

Schulman for pulling it all together to make the book complete; and Lauren Freestone for making this book look good!

And I want to mostly thank my amazing wife, Sherrie, for working so hard both at work and around the house, for without her painting the deck, trimming the bushes, skimming the pool, and just taking care of business, I never would have been free from distraction and able to write. So Sherrie, "Forever and for always. . . ."

I hear the orchestra beginning to play, signaling that my time is up. So . . . THANK YOU EVERYONE WHO CONTRIBUTED TO MAKE THIS A COLLECTIVE SUCCESS!

—Lon Safko

P.S. In the 1980s and 1990s, I had the pleasure of working directly with and be inspired by a very special man who left his mark on me as he did with millions of others. For that, I wish to say "Thank you, Steve!"

Steve Jobs
1955–2011

www.LonSafko.com/TSMB3_Videos/Introduction.mov

Welcome to the third edition of *The Social Media Bible.* As you can see from the size of this book, I have done everything possible to include the latest up-to-date information and all of the tools used throughout the entire world of social media. This has been a daunting task, to say the least.

If you think the content of this book might not be as fresh or relevant as possible because social media is constantly reinventing itself, you will find that not to be true. This book presents all of the tools and techniques that social media has to offer while also discussing the reason these social tools are so effective.

Why a vlog (video) is the most effective form of marketing will never change. The psychological impact on your customers and prospects watching and listening to you on video is at the core of human nature. The techniques you use to create a podcast will be the same five years from now. The importance of building trusted relationships that result in sales will be the same long after you retire. Maybe some of the tools might change, but the rest of the content will still be relevant decades from now.

This book is truly a product of social media, user-generated content, and wisdom of the crowds. Literally, more than a hundred people directly

participated in the creation of this text. Some by editing the grammar, some by creating original content, some by adding their content to wikis, blogs, web pages, news articles, and some by editing my content with new technologies and a different perspective. This truly was a collaborative effort by experts from around the world.

Even the actual design of the book was user generated. Before embarking on this project, I simply asked my audience, you, what you wanted in a business book on social media. After surveying nearly a thousand people, you told me you didn't want just another business book on social media, you wanted three different books. Three different business books in one: Tactics, Tools, and Strategies for Business Success.

Part I—Tactics and Tools

The first book you asked for was a book on the tactics and tools of social media that explained what a *vlog*, a *podcast*, a *blog, lifecasting, followers, flaming, tags, SEO* and *SEM*, and *pass along* are. You asked that the book describe where it came from, where it is, and where the technology is going. You asked for the features and benefits of every type of social media marketing, what tools you should use, type of content, and the psychological benefits of each.

The second book you wanted was the tools, a guide, or a list, of all of the major tools of the trade. You wanted a list of the companies that provide the software, the apps, the websites, the text messaging, the virtual worlds, the game platforms, the mobile marketing insights, e-mail marketing providers, and content-sharing sites.

Then you asked for a third book, a book on strategy. You told me that once you read the second book and understood all of the different ways you could perform social media marketing and now that you've read the second book showing the top technology and service providers, you wanted to know how can you apply all of this newly gained knowledge to develop a successful social media marketing strategy.

You asked that this third book be comprehensive, but in a simple-to-implement, step-by-step process of developing a successful social media marketing plan. While this process needed to be easy to follow and easy to implement, it also had to be applicable to the one-person entrepreneurial company as well as to the Fortune 500. It had to be effective when applied to B2C (business-to-consumer) and also to the B2B (business-to-business) companies. It had to be pertinent if being used to develop a strategic marketing plan for an individual and a corporation. And, it had to apply equally to both for-profit and nonprofit entities, including governmental agencies. And, finally, the plan needed to work for marketing and public relations, but also for customer service and for the internal customers, your employees.

That's what this delivers . . . two books in one.

Part II—Strategy

In the Part II, Strategy, section of the first edition of *The Social Media Bible*, we took a more academic approach to developing a strategic marketing plan for you and your company. We discussed the age-old SWOT analysis, the four pillars of social media application, and gave the reader exercises to perform. While all of that information and that type of approach is completely valid and useful, you asked that I get down and dirty and give you exactly what you need to develop a successful strategy plan; no more, no less. In this edition, the entire third book has been replaced with The Five Steps to Social Media Success. While it looks like there are only five steps to developing a successful strategy, there is still quite a bit of homework you will need to do to ensure the success of your strategic plan. The amount of work you wish to put into developing your plan will determine the level of your plan's ultimate success. Like most everything else, you will get out of it what you put in to it.

The Five Steps to Social Media Success

The Five Steps to Social Media Success are synergistic, in which the total is greater than the sum of its parts, or the success you will realize is greater than the work necessary to complete your plan. This is true because the plan is comprehensive and because social media is incredibly effective.

The Five Steps to Social Media Success include:

Step 1: Analyze Your Existing Media—In this step, I ask you to list every marketing plan, strategy, and campaign you are currently executing. I want you to look at expenses and the number of new customers that that strategy generates. Then divide to determine your "Cost of Customer Acquisition."

Step 2: The Social Media Trinity—This step asks you to push aside all of the social media noise and hype and focus on the three most important categories of social media: blogging, microblogging, and social networks. Get into the weeds with these three. I'll show you the payoff.

Step 3: Integrate Strategies—Step 3 discusses how you need to completely integrate The Social Media Trinity into your existing marketing strategy, in detail.

Step 4: Resources—"Where do I find the resources to implement this totally new strategy?" is the most-asked question I get at my keynotes from the one-person shop all the way up to the Fortune 500. I'll show you the answer.

Step 5: Implement and Measure—This final step is how you can implement your successful social media strategy plan and includes a very important part of the step that is most often skipped, measurement. They say, "You can't manage what you don't measure." This is true.

If you don't measure your marketing campaign's success, how will you know what the ROI (Return on Investment) or what the CCA (Cost of Customer Acquisition) is? How will you know what you should keep doing and what you should stop doing? How will you know where the most effective use of your limited resources is? I will show you that also.

Social Media Experts

Since the first edition of *The Social Media Bible* came out, I have been amazed and equally appalled by the vast number of people calling themselves "social media experts" or "social media gurus." Please beware of anyone calling himself an "expert." It took me years and more than 600 pages to develop a comprehensive overview of what social media is.

It was the exercise of having to create a book as comprehensive as this for me to understand social media as well as I do. If not for the book, I might have focused on two or three of the hundreds of tools social media has to offer and called myself an expert.

When I first began creating this book, I quickly realized that I was not an expert and that no one could be, not in every category of social media marketing. That's when I realized I needed to reach out to the social media community, identify all of the vertical experts, experts in their respective fields, and ask them to teach me what they knew and to share their personal expertise and knowledge.

I identified nearly 50 different experts who covered the entire list of social media genres. These names ranged from Biz Stone, the inventor of Twitter; to Matt Mullenweg, inventor of WordPress; to Gary "V," social media marketer extraordinaire; to senior vice presidents of YouTube, MySpace,

Flickr, Google, Microsoft, and Yahoo! This list even included such dignitaries as Peter Wiley, the chairman of the board at John Wiley & Sons, Inc., and Vint Cerf, the real inventor of the Internet.

I called each of these extraordinary experts and spent 30 to 45 minutes with each of them, having them explain why they invented their technology, why they are passionate about what they do, and how businesses are profiting from the use of their social media tools. These are what I call "Expert Insights."

I have taken excerpts of those conversations with the industry's greats and placed them throughout every chapter in both Part I and Part II of this book. There is a lot more to the conversations than I had room for in this book. For the entire conversation transcripts, go to www.theSocialMediaBible.com.

If you prefer audio, there are the actual recorded conversations for you to listen to and download to your iPod or burn to a CD to listen to on a CD player in your home or in your car. If these interviews were played back to back, they would run for more than 24 continuous hours. As the owner of this book, I'm making all of them available to you for free.

The ROI of Social Media

The next most-asked questions at my keynotes are "Where's the ROI in social media marketing?" and "How much should I be spending on social media marketing?" My answer is always, remove the term *social media* from those questions and ask them again: "Where's the ROI in marketing?" and "How much should I be spending on marketing?"

Social media isn't a toolbox of silver bullets given to us by aliens, it's just a new set of technologies and concepts that we need to add and integrate into our existing marketing strategy. And, there is always a ROI to marketing.

In this third edition of *The Social Media Bible*, I went back to you, my audience, and asked for user-generated content. I asked for your stories of how you have used social media and have realized a positive, measurable ROI.

In each of the chapters in both Part I and Part II, I have included what I call "The ROI of Social Media," 500-word vignettes, or brain candy. These stories are of actual people just like you and me, who have used social media effectively, sharing stories in small, bite-sized examples of the power of social media marketing. They range from small nonprofit organizations trying to raise money all the way up to the PR team at OfficeMax. Here's actual proof of social media effectiveness.

International Perspective

Social media is a worldwide phenomenon. People and companies around the globe are experiencing their own successes. They are using not only the tools that we in the United States are familiar with, but social networks and tools you may not have ever heard of.

In most of the chapters in Part I, I have included stories, essays, and examples of how companies outside of the U.S. are using social media. Many or perspectives and most are actual examples, similar to the ROI stories above, but with an "international" perspective.

Chapter To-Do Lists

In each of the chapters throughout Part I of this book, I conclude with a To-Do List for that category where appropriate. These To-Do's include tips, how-tos, and do's and don'ts when using that category of marketing tools. These are helpful, quick lists that can make you more proficient using social media and help you avoid the pitfalls of this often-unintuitive form of marketing.

As I discussed earlier, the techniques, strategies, and concepts in this book will never become obsolete or outdated; some of the tools and companies providing those tools, however, might. As I also mentioned, we could not physically deliver any more information in a single book; three books and more than 800 pages are our limit. I still want to give you more than I can deliver in this format. TheSocialMediaBible.com is designed to be a resource that will allow you to access as much additional information as your brain will allow.

As an owner of this book, you will have access to the transcripts and podcasts mentioned earlier, clickable links where you can read about an example in this book, see the web link to the example, and either type the link in yourself, or just go to the website, select the chapter, and all of the links printed in the book are there for you to click on.

I have also provided you with direct links and discounts to many of the companies mentioned in the book along with access to all of the major booksellers where you can find the many books mentioned in the text.

This website will be an ever-changing, ever-evolving source for you to access the very latest news, products, services, and resources for the worlds of social media.

The entire content of this tome is focused on using these social tools to market you, your company, your products, and your services, by identifying where the conversations are happening, listening to those conversations, and participating in those conversations, which leads to building connections, relationships, and trust, which ultimately leads to sales.

This third edition of *The Social Media Bible* was designed and developed by your direction. My philosophy is, ask your customers what they want, deliver it with excellence, and your product will sell. I asked, I listened, you spoke, I delivered. Enjoy, grow, and profit!

—Lon Safko

www.theSocialMediaBible.com

www.ExtremeDigitalMarketing.com

www.LonSafko.com

TACTICS AND TOOLS

Part I of this book is all about the tactics and tools of social media. I discuss in these chapters what all of the many components of social media are: What a blog is, a podcast, virtual worlds, lifecasting, mobile marketing, photo sharing, and more.

It is important to understand the terminology, the technology, the application, and the companies providing those services. While this section is not a how-to, it does explain a great deal of the details and techniques to becoming proficient at each application.

Let's start with the basics: "What Is Social Media?"

theSocialMediaBible.com

What Is Social Media?

www.LonSafko.com/TSMB3_Videos/01WhatIsSM.mov

Social media is the media we use to be social. That's it.

That really is the short answer. The story is in the tactics of each of the hundreds of technologies, all of the tools that are available for you to connect with your customers and prospects, and the strategies necessary to use these tactics and tools effectively.

Ask Your Audience

When I began writing this book, I wanted to hear what my audience wanted in a book. I have written six previous books and I knew there was a standard formula for writing a typical business book: 250 pages, 23 chapters, 3,000 words per chapter. But I wasn't sure if this book should follow that formula. Did the audience for a bible on social media want a typical business book? I didn't know, so, I asked them.

I knew that if I asked my audience and delivered what they wanted, it would be a success. Go figure, ask your customers what they want in a product. Then, you told me some interesting facts. First, you didn't want

another typical business book on social media. You asked for three books in one: Tactics, in which everything is explained; Tools, with which you can find a comprehensive list of all the companies providing social media services; and Strategy, with which you can apply all that you have learned from Part I and Part II.

This approach of listening to my customers obviously worked. *The Social Media Bible*, first edition, sold out in the first four days across the country, has been among the top 10 best-selling books in America, and has hit the number one best-selling book spot in both "Business" and "Marketing" categories on Amazon.

The second fact I learned was from the first two questions on the survey, "Can you define social media?" and "Do you believe that social media would have a significant impact on you and your business?"

What I learned by asking my audience these two questions was that 66.4 percent said that they couldn't define social media and the remaining third lied. If it takes me nearly 26 chapters and more than 600 pages to define social media, they didn't know, not even the social media experts and gurus.

The second really interesting fact I learned was that 99.1 percent, nearly everyone, said they knew social media was going to have a significant impact on them personally and their businesses.

These two statistics told me and the publisher that two-thirds of everyone interviewed didn't know what social media was, but that it was coming for them.

So What Is It?

The first part of the terminology, *social*, refers to the instinctual needs we humans have to connect with other humans. We have been doing that in one form or another since our species began. We have a need to be around and included in groups of similar like-minded people with whom we can feel at home and comfortable sharing our thoughts, ideas, and experiences.

The second part of that term refers to the *media* we use with which we make those connections with other humans. Whether they are drums, bells, the written word, the telegraph, the telephone, radio, television, e-mail, websites, photographs, audio, video, mobile phones, or text messaging, media are the technologies we use to make those connections.

The application of the term *social media* in this book is about how we can use all of these technologies effectively to reach out and connect with other humans, create a relationship, build trust, and be there when the people in those relationships are ready to purchase our product offering.

What social media is not is a box of silver bullets given to us by aliens that will instantly solve all of our marketing woes and create instant wealth for all involved. Too many people are viewing social media as a foreign and strange set of technologies that they may or may not want to use to market themselves, their companies, their products, and their services.

In my keynotes, two questions always asked are, "Should I be doing social media marketing?" My answer is "Remove the term *social media* and ask it again. Should I be doing marketing?" See how ridiculous that sounds. The second question is, "How much should I spend on social media marketing?" I reply with "Remove the term *social media* again. How much should I spend on marketing?" And, of course, the answer to both is "Yes, and as much as you can!"

Social media is only a new set of tools, new technology that allows us to more efficiently connect and build relationships with our customers and prospects. It's doing what the telephone, direct mail, print advertising, radio, television, and billboards did for us up until now. But social media is exponentially more effective.

Why Social Media?

The reason social media is so much more effective than the conventional marketing that we've done for the last 6,000 years is that it's two-way communication, not pontification. Since we've been selling goats in the desert, we would stand on a rock and shout out the features and benefits of owning a goat. And, if we chose our words correctly and hit enough of the audience's psychological hot buttons, our prospect would become a customer. Nothing has changed in 6,000 years. Until now.

There is what I call "A Fundamental Shift in Power." It's a shift from pontification to two-way communication and it's a shift about which we no longer control our corporate message. No longer does the consumer trust corporate messages. They don't trust and don't want to hear our commercials any longer. They want their information from people they know, have a relationship with, and share a bond with through trust. They want to be educated by, hear their news from, and get their product reviews by people they know and trust. They want to share their experiences, both good and bad, with people who trust them.

With this Fundamental Shift comes a new way to communicate. The new way to sell is not to sell at all. In fact, if you use social media to sell, you will get flamed. Social media marketing is all about listening first, under-standing the conversation, and speaking last.

Social media marketing is like going to a networking event, a party, a trade show, sporting event, church, or anywhere that large groups of people gather. When you enter, you will see small groups of three to five people huddled together. Let's now suppose we use our conventional marketing approach.

You walk up to the group, interrupt everyone, announce your name, and start telling everyone what you do for a living, what you sell, and that they should buy from you! It's the radio car commercials that yell at you from their echo chamber "Sunday! Sunday! Sunday!" You've heard them. What will happen?

You probably will make everyone angry at you, everyone would walk away, and you might get slapped in the lips. Because that type of behavior in a social situation is completely inappropriate. Let's rewind and try the new marketing approach.

You enter the room, choose a group, walk up to that group and say nothing. You listen first. You understand what is already being said and when you have something of value to contribute to that conversation, you wait for a break, and politely share your ideas. The reaction to this approach is significantly better. At that moment you now become part of that group, that network, and you instantly have credibility and trust.

Then as the conversation continues, someone will eventually ask you, "So, what do you do?" Bingo! Now you can share what you do, a little about your product or service, and pause. Someone in that group will more than likely ask another question about your company or its offering, and if someone in that group is in the buying part of the *sales funnel*, he will ask for your card and you have made your sale. If he isn't in the *buy* part of the funnel, he will remember you when he is. Isn't this why you go to network-ing events? Marketing using social media is exactly the same. More on the sales funnel later.

Whether it's a social network like Facebook or LinkedIn, Twitter or blogging, it's about participating in that conversation and being there with a relationship when your prospect is ready to buy.

As you can see, social media is completely different from standing on a rock and shouting your message, but it is really a more natural and more comfortable way to sell. By building relationships through social media, you build a more lasting trusted relationship that will result in more sales, fewer returns, and greater word of mouth.

Remember the statistics from my Customer Concentric 101 presen-tation? Studies have shown that: An angry customer will tell up to 20 other people about a bad experience. A satisfied customer shares good experiences with 9 to 12 people. It costs five times as much to get a new customer as it does to keep an existing one. And customers will spend up to 10 percent more for the same product if they have an existing relationship.

Word of Mouth at the Speed of Light

The statistic that "An angry customer will tell up to 20 other people about a bad experience . . . ," that's face to face. With the use of social media like blogs, Twitter, and Facebook, those 20 people can quickly become 20,000 or even 200,000!

Here's an example about Dave Carroll, a country and western singer and songwriter who had an unpleasant experience with United Airlines and used a video on YouTube to "tell a few people." At the time this chapter was written, Carroll's telling of his story to "a few people" through social media had grown to 8,380,000!

On March 31, 2008, Dave Carroll and his band, Sons of Maxwell, were flying on United Airlines from Nova Scotia to Nebraska when just after landing in Chicago O'Hare, a passenger sitting behind Carroll noticed the baggage handlers throwing his guitar around the tarmac. Carroll immediately notified three flight attendants, but "was met with indifference." When Carroll arrived in Omaha, he found his $3,500 710 Taylor acoustic guitar smashed.

Over the next several months, Carroll called United representatives in Chicago and India (go figure), who told Carroll that United wasn't responsible and would do nothing to help Carroll. Carroll spent $1,200 to repair his guitar, bringing it only "to a state that it plays well but has lost much of what made it special."

The last straw for Carroll was when a United representative, Ms. Irlweg, sent Carroll an e-mail denying Carroll his claim because he didn't file it in the right place or at the right time. United even refused to compensate Carroll by giving him $1,200 in travel vouchers.

Carroll told Ms. Irlweg that he would create a music video with his band and take it to the people using social media. Carroll then created a 4-minute–37-second complaint video called "United Breaks Guitars." Irlweg was unimpressed. The video was posted on YouTube on July 6, 2009, and within 24 hours received more than 500 comments and 24,000 views. To date, Carroll's first of three videos has been viewed by more than 8,380,000 people, while his three videos have had more than 9,500,000 viewers!

Here's Dave Carroll's website where you can view all three videos and hear the story in his own words, www.davecarrollmusic.com.

That's what I call "Word of Mouth at the Speed of Light!"

Not all social media is used for complaints. Here's a personal story I have about airline customer service I experienced myself.

I was traveling with my public relations assistant while traveling back to New York last year on a press tour before this book was released. We had different flight times for the same day.

My flight was on time and uneventful, while hers was late leaving the gate. The gate attendant for Continental Airlines announced that her flight was running 15 minutes late, but they would board the aircraft as soon as it was serviced. My assistant immediately took out her cell phone and Tweeted a tweet: "Continental Airlines, 15 minutes late. What else is new?"

They serviced the aircraft and began boarding. As she entered the aircraft, a flight attendant stepped up to her and asked, "Are you Ms. Vega?" When she replied yes, the attendant handed her a glass of Champagne and apologized for any inconvenience. OMG! That's customer service.

This never became a music video, but I have told more than 10,000 people, and I am sure that they have told their networks, who told their networks, and on and on. Just by mounting Twitter and listening to their customers, Continental received positive press that was exponentially the cost of the one glass of Champagne.

These are examples of two-way communications, listening to your customers, the power of peer-to-peer, Word of Mouth at the Speed of Light, and the Fundamental Shift in Power.

Other Customers

The most obvious use for social media is for marketing, sales, public relations, and communications. Remember, social media is about communicating with your customers. Social media is a set of highly effective tools for customer service, business-to-business (B2B), and internal communications.

Marketing and sales is in part responsible for prospects converting to customers, but in many cases it's what happens after the sales that encourage existing customers to purchase again and, as you read earlier, encourage prospects to become customers. An angry customer will tell up to 20 other people about a bad experience. A satisfied customer shares good experiences with 9 to 12 people. If you are in customer service, social media is a must. It's the perfect tool for staying connected with your customers after the sale.

B2B

If you are a company that sells B2B (business-to-business), then social media has to be an integral part of your strategy. I have been in marketing for nearly three decades and while many insist that B2B is significantly different from B2C (business-to-consumer), I disagree. There are some subtle differences, but in B2B, the second B is still a C. The reseller is still a consumer or customer.

I agree that there is some information that should be between you and your reseller such as pricing, training, and customer support, but the majority of your conversation would benefit your end user. Set up a password-protected website and direct SMS text messaging for that content and freely distribute the rest.

Internal Customers

Don't forget about your internal customers, your employees. They want to feel like they are connected and part of the organization. Social media is an amazing set of tools that allow you to communicate directly to and with your employee base. Use Yammer as an internal, behind-the-firewall Twitter for text messages only your employees can read. Use Jott for team collaboration. Use video sharing for messages from the corner office, the C suite. Use photo sharing for all of your employees to exchange photos, ideas, memories, and a sense of team. Use audio podcasts in human resources to give employees updates on benefits, retirement, and their 401(k).

15 Social Media Categories

Another innate human characteristic is to put items in categories; the more items there are, the more there is a need to organize them. You can see my attempt to categorize the entire world of social media in Table 1.1. This was not an easy feat, but I think you will agree it works.

Table 1.1 The 15 Social Media Categories	
Category Title	**Tactics and Tools Chapters**
Social Networking	Chapter 2
Photo Sharing	Chapter 8
Audio	Chapters 9 and 10
Video	Chapters 11 and 12
Microblogging	Chapter 13
Livecasting	Chapter 14
Virtual Worlds	Chapter 15
Gaming	Chapter 16
RSS and Aggregators	Chapter 17
Search	Chapters 18 and 19
Mobile	Chapter 20
Interpersonal	Chapter 21

Social Networking

Social networking is as old as humans have been around. Just as in nearly every other species, humans have an instinctual need to be with, communicate with, and share thoughts, ideas, and feelings about their daily lives. Only the tools with which we communicate have changed over the millennia.

This category discusses the many platforms we use today in social media to connect, share, educate, interact, and build trust.

Photo Sharing

Napoleon Bonaparte is sometimes credited with having expressed the idea that "A picture is worth a thousand words," and if that's true, then Flickr's photographs are worth, well 4,000,000,000 × 1,000 . . . way too many zeros for me! Flickr now houses more than 4 billion photographs, and that doesn't count Picasa, SmugMug, PhotoSwarm, or the many other photo sharing sites.

Ever since there were photographs, people were sharing them with each other. Sharing photos are a way of capturing moments in time, which captures the emotions that we can share with others. Simply by looking at a photograph we get a rush of emotions, memories, and a recollection of that very moment that we can share.

Audio

Audio is a very powerful medium. It's easier to digest than text and to evoke mental images that video doesn't allow. Do you listen to the radio? Have you ever heard a book on CD? Have you ever heard Edgar Allan Poe's work read aloud?

Audio allows us to sit back and allow the author or orator to slowly spoon-feed us content with inflection, dramatic pauses, and human nuances of him being right there in the room speaking to us. While we listen to the cadence of the words being formed into sentences and thoughts, we can imagine the associated images and watch them play out in our minds to form the story the author is trying to convey.

Video

If a picture is worth 1,000 words, then at 25 frames (pictures) per second, video adds up to 1.5 million words per minute! That's why everyone loves video!

Video is the preferred medium of choice for relaying information overall. After a hard day at work, do you pick up a book, turn on the radio, or settle down in front of the television for a good movie or uplifting sitcom? Most likely we turn to the television to coast through some nightly brain candy.

People love video because it's the next best thing to being in the same room with someone who is sharing his or her knowledge and experiences. You can hear the words, imagine the images she is conveying, and also watch and become involved in the video that is taking place at that moment. We can see what the author is explaining, and become emotionally involved in the scene. We can hear the actors' inflections while experiencing their facial expressions and body language. It is estimated that 55 percent of all communication comes from body language, while 38 percent from voice, and only 7 percent from the words themselves.

Microblogging

Microblogging is no more than text messaging on steroids. With the demise of Pownce, for the most part we're talking about Twitter for open text communication and Yammer for internal or behind-the-firewall communication. The reason for Twitter's success was best put by Samuel Clemens (Mark Twain), when he said in the late nineteenth century, "I apologize for the length of my correspondence. Given more time, it would have been shorter."

We love the 140-character bite-sized messages because we can read and comprehend them in about five seconds. In that short amount of time, we can fully understand what the writer is trying to convey. With text messaging, you don't have the opportunity to drone on and on as we do in our e-mail correspondence. With Twitter, we read it, comprehend it, and move on.

Livecasting

Livecasting isn't for everyone, but those who livecast are passionate about it. My friend Jody Gnant livecasted her life for nine full months, 24/7. Chris Pirello has been Ustream'n his livecast of himself for years. Both have built a tremendous following and skyrocketed their music and careers.

Livecasting is broadcasting video live. It could be 24 hours a day or just for a simple one-hour television show. Livecasting is the ultimate in reality television and it's available for free to everyone. So if you've always dreamed of creating and starring in your own television show, the companies in this chapter can help you realize your dream.

Virtual Worlds

When organizations such as the American Cancer Society, CNN, Dell, Disney, Harvard, IBM, MTV, Reuters, Starwood Hotels, Sun Microsystems, Toyota, and Wells Fargo are all participating in virtual worlds, there must be something to it.

The American Cancer Society has actually raised $650,000 in real dollar donations during their time there. IBM holds their monthly engineers' meetings at their headquarters in Second Life, where engineers from all over the world meet, talk, exchange ideas, and watch presentations.

I have some oceanfront land and a two-story Mediterranean mansion in Second Life (http://slurl.com/secondlife/pinasrtri/215/8/21)

in which the first floor is a virtual store where you can purchase three-dimensional Internet advertising (paper models). My three developers meet me there from time to time to discuss projects and design ideas. They are in the Ukraine and I have never met them face-to-face other than our time in Second Life.

Gaming

Online gaming may seem like an odd category for *The Social Media Bible*, but it really isn't. Did you know that 17 million people are playing Halo 3 or an additional 17 million playing World of Warcraft? Any time you can measure a target audience in the millions, you need to be there.

Many Fortune 1000 companies have participated in gaming as a way to build brand recognition. Hewlett-Packard puts up billboards in auto racing games. An author friend of mine had a game developed for his website for the release of his new book that cost only a couple of thousand dollars, but now has an 18 percent conversion rate on buying his book. And mobile phone game apps is one of the fastest-growing app categories for smartphones.

RSS and Aggregators

RSS, or Really Simple Syndication, is the name of the technology and also the name of just one of the technology providers. An RSS feature on a blog or website allows you to sign up and automatically get notified whenever there is an update to the site including a new blog or news. Rather than having to go from site to site every day checking to see if new content has been posted, RSS notifies you when it has. RSS automatically feeds you new content from only the sites you want it from, and only when that content is new.

Try RSS by clicking the RSS button on your favorite blog site or try the Google landing page that aggregates RSS feeds from blogs, web pages, airlines, weather, or any changing information of interest to you.

Also in this chapter of the book, I highlight aggregators, websites that allow you to choose what type of content you want to see, where you want it to come from, present it to you all in an organized page, and do it automatically all of the time. Aggregators allow you to see all of the new blogs, web pages, news, audio, photo, and video updates all in one convenient web page location. This is like having an automated worldwide web clipping service and news agency at your fingertips. And, it's free.

Search

Internet search is one of the most important functions of the Internet. How else would you be able to find the one page you are looking for out of the one trillion Google-indexed web pages? SEO, or search engine optimization, is as important as ever. And, as the number of web and blog pages grows, search will become even more important to your Internet experience and to your customers and prospects.

If you want your customers and prospects to be able to find you and your company, you have to make it easy for them. SEO, tags, fresh content, external reputable links (Link Love), and keyword density, all add to your company's web and blog pages' Google Juice.

Mobile

Mobile marketing is the fastest-growing segment of technology-driven marketing. Kakul Srivastava, the general manager for Flickr, told me that there are three cell phones for every man, woman, and child on the planet. With that kind of technology penetration, you and your company need to be participating.

Mobile phones are less expensive than laptops, desktops, and broadband, and are completely portable. Not many people in Third World countries can afford to have an Internet-connected PC, but they can all afford a mobile phone. It's through this technology that people from around the world are staying in touch with one another, accessing their e-mail, sending photos, audio, video, blogging, and surfing the web.

Interpersonal

This is another category of seemingly unrelated technology. The common thread, however, is that they are all tools that allow you to connect and communicate with your customers and prospects. Some companies provide the means to host a meeting for your employees or perform a webbing for 1,000 people. Some allow you to use the Internet like a free telephone service. Others allow you to convert your voice into text messages to be sent to your e-mail and other team members.

The ROI of Social Media

Pioneer's Holiday Promotion Achieves 60 Percent Click-Through Rate (CTR) Using Forums to Target Influential Automotive Enthusiasts

Background

Advertisers face the same dilemma every holiday season: how to be visible when consumers are inundated.

Strategy

Pioneer Electronics (USA) Inc. overcame that hurdle with room to spare. A holiday-themed rebate offer for Pioneer In-Dash Navigation models achieved a 60 percent click-through rate by using PostRelease to target automotive enthusiasts in online forums.

Implementation

PostRelease provides an automated way to insert sponsored posts into relevant forum discussion threads.

Pioneer Electronics turned to PostRelease to help promote its holiday rebate offers for its new flagship AVIC-Z110BT and AVIC-X910BT navigation systems. The two companies crafted a sponsored forum post that included product images, direct links to the product web pages, and the rebate page on Pioneer's website.

The campaign ran as a sticky post—meaning the post remained in the lead position—in relevant audio-related discussion categories in 55 automotive-themed forums, from November 2 to November 9, 2009. The post was clearly marked as from PostRelease and Pioneer and, once unstuck, moved down the page as a regular forum post would. It remains part of the forum content for the life of the forum.

(continued)

(continued)

Opportunity

People on product-related online forums are ripe audiences for product-specific messages and offers. Consumers visit these types of forums expressly to discuss products, so they're open to relevant sponsored messages and they're more likely to respond.

Conclusion

The one-week campaign continues to drive traffic even after completion, because PostRelease posts remain archived and accessible for the life of the forum.

In fact, sponsored forum posts, clearly marked as advertisements, increase in their ability to drive response over time—by an average of more than 100 percent one year after a paid campaign has ended, according to an analysis conducted by PostRelease. After 60 days, the total number of click-throughs increased by an average of 40 percent, and after 180 days, they increased by an average of 77 percent.

The reason for this residual traffic: Forum posts contain content that can be discovered in search engine results, driving traffic to the ad not only from the audience of the forum in which it appears, but also directly from organic search listings.

Consumers don't have to be browsing a particular forum to discover an advertiser's message there. If a post offers useful content, it's likely to show up when it is relevant to a consumer's search for information—boosting traffic to the ad and to the forum. The click-through rates increase over time because posts are discovered by people who are actively searching for that content, and therefore are highly motivated to click through.

See one of Pioneer's posts here: http://g35driver.com/forums/g35-sedan-v36-2007-08/313580-200-rebate-pioneer-navigation-holiday-rebate.html#post4671215; http://bit.ly/xyju6p.

The top five forums to generate the most clicks and reads for Pioneer's holiday campaign were ClubFrontier.com

CamaroZ28.com

DuraMaxForum.com

Z06Vette.com

(continued)

(continued)

And 300CForums.com

No other online medium gives advertisers as precise a target as forums do.

—Justin Choi
www.PostRelease.com

Justin Choi is president of PostRelease (www.PostRelease.com) and author of the white paper "Online Forums: Social Marketing with Proven Results." He can be reached at justin@postrelease.com.

Expert Insight

Peter Booth Wiley, chairman of the board, John Wiley & Sons, Inc., www.wiley.com

Peter Booth Wiley

Not only is this book about social media, but the creation of the book is a form of social media. . . . This is a pioneering piece of work. It's been a little more than a year since we last spoke, and in that short period of time, things have changed radically. You could say we spoke pre-Kindle and now we are post-Kindle and post-iPad, and Wiley is doing things today that we were only talking about just a few years and months back. . . .

. . . I am a member of the sixth generation of Wileys involved in the publishing business; our company is 203 years old. There is a seventh generation, including two of my sons, both of whom are working in social media at Wiley. I've been the chairman of the board since 2002. Prior to joining our board of directors in 1984, I was a magazine publisher and a newspaper reporter and columnist, a writer of articles for magazines, and the author of five books. I am currently working on the revision of my last title, a guide to the architecture and history of San Francisco. Once the print version is completed, my daughter and I—we're coauthors—will work on a website through which people taking the walking tours in the book will be able to access additional information and visuals about the buildings they are looking at. In the spirit of social media, we are giving our readers the ability to comment on what they are reading and seeing, which we can later add to our content. . . .

. . . Back in the 1800s when our company was founded, social media was writing a letter, which was handed to somebody on a horse or stagecoach. It would take roughly four days for a letter to go from, say, Virginia to New York; and in the wet, muddy seasons, it probably went by ship. . . . Sending a letter and getting a response was a very tenuous interaction. Now we've got

(continued)

(continued)

information and creative ideas flying through the air at the speed of electrons with the ability to interact immediately. . . .

. . . In the 1950s, we began experimenting with introducing computers into the business. Twenty-five years ago, we tried to understand and experiment with computers and networks really aggressively, and our ideas about what we should be doing as a business came from our authors, our customers, and our technical advisors. We listened very carefully to them about new ways of accessing and shaping information and what they thought was going to happen. . . .

. . . We also continue to create a culture internally at Wiley that permits our colleagues to build products and related capabilities, including what we now call social experiences, or social media. We're working on capabilities that help authors share the necessary content with our customers and capabilities that help our customers find exactly the information they need in the format they want. We are helping our intermediaries (brick-and-mortar stores, online print and e-book resellers, wholesalers, et cetera) deliver the content to our customers quickly in the appropriate format. We are also building capabilities that help us internally to work collectively and that help our authors and partners interact with us and with members of their communities. . . .

. . . We use social networks (electronically, before we used them in an interpersonal way) to understand who you are and what you are capable of. So, in our initial conversation when you told me of your history in the world of technology, I was very impressed. And so Step One is: "Okay, I recognize that this guy is somebody who has been right on the cutting edge himself." Step Two is to use our social network to evaluate your capabilities and your proficiency in whether you are going to be able to deliver a manuscript that we'll be able to sell. . . .

. . . We built responsible risk-taking into the organization quite a while ago. The progression to where we are today in terms of digital media has not been in a straight line, and we've made mistakes at times by being ahead of the curve. I think what we've learned is it's best to be on the leading edge, rather than the bleeding edge, because we've spent time on the bleeding edge. . . .

. . . With the rapid rise of new forms of social media, we're thinking more about how we market our products. Traditionally, we talked about our author's "platform.". . . What's Lon's platform? By which we mean: "Does he speak regularly at conferences? How big are they? Is he going to get on *Oprah*? Is he going to get on *Good Morning America*? Will his books be reviewed in the *New York Times Book Review*? Sadly, the print newspaper book review is fading fast. Television, yes, it works to a degree. I think it's very effective at times. . . .

. . . We've also had experiences with other authors going on high-profile television programs and not selling a lot of books. Now we're looking more at networks, at an author's social media network, trying to understand the way in which an author creates his or her own community digitally and how we can communicate with that community to share with people what the book's all about. . . .

Another interesting thing is the understanding that the way in which an author writes his book, the connections he builds aggregating content and editing it, is creating his platform. No longer is it "Here's a book, write a marketing plan." The authoring and marketing experiences are interacting.

Of course, as a commercial publisher, we are interested in metrics. So we are interested in seeing the evolution of the effectiveness of marketing and the effectiveness of networks. And I think we are at an early stage with that, but I really look to the libraries and their interaction with publishers. They are able to measure usage. Say they license a hundred journals from us; they can look at which of those journals are being used. So the librarians are saying, "Okay, I've got these hundred journals and ninety-eight of them are used heavily. Let's review the two that are used less and decide whether to replace them with other journals or whether they should remain in the collection even though there is a low usage rate."

So, there are metrics being developed, and over time . . .

. . . But let's go back to what we were talking about earlier, about the way you are creating this book, because this tells us a lot about where publishing is now and what its future could be like.

I wrote my last book in 2000. An editor asked me to write it. I sent the manuscript to the publisher. The publisher reviewed it and edited it and sent it to production. Production designed it and laid it out. It went to the printer, then to marketing and sales, to the wholesale and retail intermediaries. And then it ended up in the customer's lap.

That's a very traditional print-on-paper model. Right now we are moving to a continuous process of content development and delivery. We have a favorite graphic that we use at a lot of meetings. It's about Frommer's. We're one of the leading travel publishers, and we've created this circle called the Travel Cycle, which illustrates how we interact with our customers at different points in their travel experience. So the first part of the cycle is when, you, the traveler, *dream* about where you are going to go. You look at travel newsletters, magazines, online forums, blogs; so right now we're publishing travel newsletters, online forums, and blogs about travel.

And then you *plan* your trip; and we are publishing guidebooks and travel websites with text, photos, video, podcasts, recommendations, interactive maps, and custom PDF guides.

And then you *go* on your trip; and when you're traveling, we continue to interact with you with audio walking tours, iPhone guides, and map and airport guide applications.

(continued)

(continued)

And then after you come *back* from your trip, you share with other travelers your experience via online trip journals and photo albums, and you post your reviews and ratings, all on Wiley travel sites. So there is a continuous process of interaction here, rather than the linear process I described earlier. And when you add to that what you are doing with *The Social Media Bible*, which is working with the community (your community) to develop content and review and refine the content, you have a completely different publishing model. . . .

WileyPLUS is our online teaching and learning environment that integrates the entire digital textbook with resources to fit every learning style. Instructors are able to choose and assign the material that fits their syllabus, and students who want more information have access to the full eBook and accompanying learning materials. . . . WileyPLUS provides students with immediate feedback and redirects them to specific areas for review if they don't understand what they are being taught.

. . . Equally important, particularly right now during a recession when institutions of higher education are packed with new students, WileyPLUS gives instructors an option to select only the materials they need, while keeping costs down.

To listen to or read the entire Executive Conversation with Peter Booth Wiley, go to www.theSocialMediaBible.com.

Credits

The ROI of Social Media was provided by:

Justin Choi, www.PostRelease.com

Expert Insight was provided by:

Peter Booth Wiley, chairman of the board, John Wiley & Sons, Inc., www.wiley.com

CHAPTER 2

Say Hello to Social Networking

www.LonSafko.com/TSMB3_Videos/02SocialNetworking.mov

What's in It for You?

A *trusted network* is a group of like-minded people who have come together in a common place to share thoughts, ideas, and information about themselves. These groups sometimes include hundreds of millions of registered users that host more than 10 billion photographs—as with social networking site Facebook (www.facebook.com).

A trusted network can also be as small as a single, influential person. These social networks develop the trust that ultimately creates influence among your consumers. By developing and cultivating networks, your

theSocialMediaBible.com

organization can create an opportunity to develop the trust that may result in more sales.

The desire to participate in conversation and influence prospects prompted the writing of a "Sales Manifesto" for a Fortune 500 client by James Burnes, vice president of development and strategy, Internet strategy, of creative services firm MediaSauce. The following excerpt showcases the need for embracing networks to drive business:

> Why do we sell the same way we always have? Because it's safe and reliable. Because it's what we know. Because we've become entrenched in thinking that what we have to say is what our customers want to hear. Because it has worked for the past (insert number) years!
>
> But the world is rapidly evolving. Advertising, messaging, and communication behaviors are changing more quickly than how we tell our story. Worse, our messaging is competing more and more with the noise that overwhelms our target customers every day/hour/minute/second of their lives. Customers are tuning out our old messages while social media and the Internet connect them with information that bypasses our expensive marketing communications strategies.
>
> The old tried-and-true tactics of the past (insert number again!) years, like our flashy direct mail pieces, our witty trade media advertisements or those well written, but terribly expensive brochures, aren't setting us apart.
>
> Worse, they aren't even being looked at. They're being ignored. And we're becoming irrelevant. We're becoming part of the noise.
>
> Can we stop being noise and become relevant again? Yes! Absolutely we can. But we have to have a new way of speaking to our customers. We have to differentiate ourselves from the rest of the world and be fresh and exciting.
>
> We need to transform the way we touch our clients, and integrate ourselves into the very fabric of what they do every day. We have to embrace social networks, digital connections, and the online experience and build an organization that embraces conversation and transparency.
>
> We need to take advantage of a new approach to selling, where we are problem solvers and the "go to" team for our prospects whenever a project arises that we contribute to. Everyone sells [product]. We have to be bigger than our [product]. We have to solve our client's pain points.

We need to get digital. We need to take advantage of the tools digital and social media can provide us to open up new channels and speak to prospects on the business issues and problems they are trying to solve.

We need to tell our story in a way that doesn't just interrupt our clients, but engages them and gives them a reason to pass it along. We need to be viral, innovative, non-traditional, and aggressive in how we seek out new business.

How will we do it? By embracing the opportunities that social media offer us to become connected to our customers. We're going to build a culture where communicating, engaging and embracing the feedback, positive and negative, make us a better organization.

Burnes's manifesto showcases the need for transformation, and how social networks and those connections play a critical role in your business.

You will see a common theme throughout the chapters in *The Social Media Bible* that discusses people's tendency to congregate around Internet technology to exchange information and grow into larger, trusted like-minded networks. By definition, the Internet *itself* was the first electronic trusted network. When ARPAnet (see Chapter 18, Spotlight on Search (Search Engine Optimization) for more information about ARPAnet) connected its first group of computers together to share files, everyone assumed that their fellow users would follow a certain protocol, respect each other's files, and share the same interests.

The social networking site phenomenon has completely and rapidly changed the way that people interact—in regard to personal and professional relationships. And any time there is a tool that millions of people in one place at one time, all with common interests, are clamoring to use, you, as a businessperson, need to understand it and be a part of it.

Back to the Beginning

Social networks have been around for as long as there have been humans to create them. When people were still living in caves and traveling in clans and tribes, those were the trusted social networks in which people banded together to cooperatively work, live, and protect one another. The words *society, tribe, clan, team, group, pod, school, flock, colony, troop, drove, clash, caravan, mob, pounce, band, quiver, pack, congregation, litter, bevy, gaggle, herd, Americans, Europeans, Latinas, family, caucus, pro ball teams,*

New Yorkers, Catholics, Presbyterians, and even a *business of ferrets* all refer to social networks with similar interests and a common bond—and most important, trust.

These are the groups that help people make life's most important—and not-so-important—decisions. If you are looking for a job, whom do you go to first? Most likely, your trusted network of friends and colleagues. If you are buying a new car, you go to trusted networks of fellow drivers and informational websites.

Any time a group of people with similar interests and collaborative trust gather in one place, businesspeople need to be participating. In fact, businesspeople also need to provide and *be* that very trusted network for the product or service. Understanding social networks is actually a twofold process that requires participating in other networks as well as becoming one for customers and prospects. In fact, the best way to understand social networks is to first participate in one. There are literally thousands of different kinds available today that you can join for free both on- and offline. But since the focus of social media is online, these are the groups upon which this chapter concentrates. The big two are the aforementioned sites Facebook and Twitter, with LinkedIn coming in as the largest professional network. These sites have amassed a great number of members, all with one common interest and goal: to socialize. Another emerging social media network concept is location-based social media, with Foursquare as front-runner for checking in, leaving reviews, and interacting with businesses and people from their mobile devices.

What You Need to Know

A social network, trusted network, virtual community, e-community, or online community is a group of people who interact through online networks, blogs, comments, sharing, checking in, reviews, and who use text, audio, photographs, and video for social, professional, and educational purposes. The social network's goal is to build trust in a given community.

Every social network has different levels of interaction and participation among members. This can range from posting and commenting on updates to Facebook, sharing tweets, adding comments or tags to a blog (see Chapter 6, The Ubiquitous Blog) or checking in from a smartphone to share with followers where you are, what you are doing, and whom you are doing it with, to watching videos of funny cats on YouTube.

Life Cycle

A membership life cycle for online social networks begins when members initiate their life in a community as visitors, lurkers, or trolls (see Chapter 5, The Internet Forum, for more information). After becoming comfortable, people become novices and participate in the community dialogue. Once they've contributed for a period of time, they become regulars; and oftentimes, these regulars will break through a barrier and become leaders. Members who have been participating in the network for a while and eventually depart are known as elders. The amount of time it takes to become an elder depends on the culture of the site. It can take only a few months or more than a year. This life cycle can be applied to many social networks such as Facebook, Twitter, YouTube, LinkedIn, blogs, and wiki-based communities like Wikipedia.

The following examples of each of the phases in the membership life cycle uses the photo sharing site Flickr:

- *Lurkers* observe the community and view photo content. They do not add to the community content or comments, and they occasionally visit the site to look at photos that someone has suggested.

- *Novices* are just beginning to engage in the community. They start to provide content and tentatively participate in a few threads. Such users make a few comments, become somewhat involved, and will even post some photos of their own.

- *Insiders* consistently add to the community discussion, comments, and content. They interact with other members and regularly post photos. They make a concerted effort to comment, rate, and participate with other members' material.

- *Leaders* are recognized as veteran participants. They connect with the regulars and are recognized as "contributors to watch." A leader would not consider viewing another member's photos without commenting on them, and he or she will often correct another member's behavior when the community considers it inappropriate. Leaders will reference other members' photos in their comments as a way to cross-link content.

- *Elders* leave the network for a variety of reasons. Maybe their interests have changed, or perhaps the community has moved in a direction that doesn't sit well with them. Their departure may be due to lack of time, lack of interest, or any number of other factors.

Contributing

There are many reasons that people want to contribute to social and knowledge-sharing networks like blogs, social media, and wikis (see Chapter 7, The Wisdom of the Wiki). In fact, the number of individuals who spend a great deal of time contributing to such social sites is pretty amazing. People usually become motivated to contribute valuable information to the group with the expectation that one will receive useful help or information and recognition in return. This kind of reciprocation is particularly important to many online contributors. Some individuals may also freely contribute valuable information because they get a sense of contribution and a feeling of having some influence over their environment. Social psychology dictates that people are social beings who are gratified by the fact that they receive direct responses to their input. Facebook is a good example of this kind of immediate acknowledgment, whereby readers can instantly comment on and participate in live content.

Dunbar's Number

In 1993, evolutionary psychologist Dr. Robin I. M. Dunbar of the Human Evolutionary Biology Research Group of the University College London anthropology department made an important discovery about the workings of social networks and human interaction. Dunbar proposed that the cognitive limit to the number of people with whom one person can maintain stable social relationships was 150. These are relationships in which individuals know who each person is, and how each person relates to every other person. The size of a typical social network is constrained to about 150 members because of possible limits in the capacity of the human communication channel.

Through the use of social media tools and social networking, however, this number has grown to maybe many hundreds. And by linking your network to each of your contacts' networks, your effective number of usable contacts can be in the millions.

Remember, social networking isn't about allowing everyone who requests to link to you be allowed to do so. It's not about the number of your contacts, but rather about the value that each one brings. Do you think it might be important to mention influencers in this case?

Social Network Examples

The best way to explain how a social network works is to describe a few specific social networks. The big three social networks are Facebook, with over 800 million members; Twitter, with over 200 million members; and

LinkedIn, with 120 million users. Facebook is by far the most popular and widely used social network.

Here are just a few statistics on Facebook:

- More than 50 percent of Facebook users log in every day.
- 206.2 million Internet users in the United States has a Facebook account.
- The average Facebook user has 130 friends.
- The average user is connected to 80 community pages, groups, and events.
- On average, more than 250 million photos are uploaded per day.
- 510,000 Facebook posts are created every 60 seconds.
- More than 4 million businesses have Like Pages.

Facebook

Facebook is currently the biggest and most popular social network on the Internet, and has more than 800 million active members.

Founded in February of 2004 in the dorm rooms of Harvard University, Mark Zuckerberg, Chris Hughes, Dustin Moskovitz, and Eduardo Saverin launched The Facebook as a way for students on campus to interact, share,

FIGURE 2.1 Facebook

and connect with their friends around campus. Initially exclusively for college students, Facebook is now available in more than 70 languages to anyone over the age of 12 with an e-mail address. This social platform digitally connects people's real-world social connections in a sage online environment.

Revenue Model As can be seen with many of the other social networking sites and social media tools, the revenue models are fairly simple: paid subscription, free with advertising, and free with paid upgrades (aka *freemium*). Facebook chose the free with advertising revenue model with no paid services. Facebook Ads use the information provided by the user in their personal profile to target advertising to the individual. Using the pay-per-click model, businesses are able to use provided information to advertise their service, event, Like Page or other external links to those who are interested.

How It Works Upon creating and setting up an account, Facebook users start by adding friends to share content or information with. Sharing information is really a matter of what is important to the individual users. Commonly, people share what is on their mind, what is happening in their day, and interesting links, articles, videos, and pictures that they come across. They are also able to comment on what their Facebook friends are doing by showing support, "Like"-ing their post, sharing what they have posted with their Facebook friends and, of course, read or watching articles, photos, and videos.

Facebook users are also able to interact with businesses and entities that they enjoy. By "Like"-ing a Facebook page, Facebook users are able to get information provided by those businesses and entities and interact with them. They are also able to comment on their pages with questions, stories, or comments.

There are many activities that take place on Facebook such as gaming, music, applications, events, messages; the list goes on and on. Facebook is about what is happening right now, what you are doing, what is going on in your life, and sharing it with those who care and want to know.

What's in It for the User?

Facebook users are creating their own online social community. Facebook users have been able to reconnect with old friends, find family, make new friends, and talk about life. This online community keeps people connected through sharing and informing.

What's in It for Businesses?

There isn't a business in the world that would turn down the opportunity to be exposed to and potentially talked about by over 800 million people. Every day hundreds of thousands of people talk about what is happening in their lives, and that includes shopping, spending, asking for advice, complaining, complimenting, and recommending, potentially about your business or industry. Why not be a part of the conversation?

Business pages (or Like pages) allow for businesses to share their professional information and engage with current and potential customers. Like pages are a great place to do your customer service, public relations, sales, marketing, and promotion. We recommend that you keep your page 85 percent informative and resourceful for "Like"-ers and 15 percent about your business.

Building an online community takes time, but will pay off when you have a valuable and supportive network of people that care about your information and actually want it.

Common Terms

- *Friend*—People who have connected in Facebook are called *friends*. Friends are usually people who users know personally, done business together, family, or those who just want to connect with them. Approved friends can see your posts, comment on your posts and activities, tag you in photos or posts, invite you to events, and add you to groups, and vice versa.

- *Like*—Button located on each post for Facebook users to show that you enjoyed the Facebook friend's post, link, video, or picture.

- *Like Page/Fan Page*—Pages are for businesses, products, company, organization, cause, entertainment, band, or artist to build their own community. These pages are separate from a friend or profile in that rather than accumulating friends (which are limited to 5,000), pages accumulate "Likes" (which are unlimited). When a Facebook user likes a page, she is showing support for the purpose of the page, she wants more information from that page, and she wants to be part of that community.

- *Tag*—This identifies a person in either a post, picture, or video. When tagging in a post, you must either "Like" the page or be friends with that person. Then using the @ symbol, type the person or page after it, making the name appear and be selected. To tag in a photo, you again must be friends with the person, turn on tagging for the photo, use your mouse to select that person in the photo, type in his name, and select him. By tagging, the person will be notified that he has been tagged, so he can also participate.

- *Notification*—Everything you do in Facebook comes back to the notifications. Every time a user posts a comment, likes a comment, shares a link or picture, or sends a friend request, it prompts a notification. These notifications let you know when people have interacted with what you have interacted with. Notifications can be: others liking your posts, photos, or comments, tagged you in a post or photo, commented on a post you made or also commented on, invited you to an event, recommended a page, accepted a friend request, commented in a group, and much more.

- *Comment*—Each post or status update made on Facebook can spark a comment from others. Comments are responses to what was said in the post.

- *Friend Request*—For users to become friends, they must be accepted. Users can search for someone by name and ask her to be a part of their Facebook network with the "Add Friend" button. When people have sent you a "Friend Request" you can either confirm or reply "Not Now."

- *Subscribe/Subscription*—The subscribe feature allows Facebook users to follow people whom they are interested in, but aren't necessarily acquainted with. This allows Facebook users to share their information with those who are interested in them and their information without having those people's Facebook activities in their news feed. Also, with the limit of 5,000 friends on Facebook, this allows for more sharing and engaging. Facebook users who have allowed others to subscribe to them are able to limit what information is shared with Facebook friends and subscribers with the "Update Status" settings in the bottom right-hand corner of the "What's on Your Mind?" box. This an ideal option for public figures, celebrities, and journalists.

- *Wall/Timeline*—The wall (or Timeline*) is the Facebook user's personal (or profile page). This is where all the individual Facebook user's posts and activities are seen. Previously, the news feed was referred to as the wall, as well.

---

*At the time this chapter was written, Timeline was not yet available to all users.

- *News Feed*—This is a continuous stream of comments, pictures, links, events, activities, check-ins, and all other Facebook activity that is constantly being updated by your Facebook friends. This also acts as your home page for Facebook.
- *Poke*—This gesture acts as a "Hey, I'm thinking of you." The Facebook user has the option to poke back, if willing.

Profile

Basics

- *Status*—This is where Facebook users share "What's on [their] mind." This is where the post happens.
- *Photo*—Sharing photos is one of the biggest features in Facebook. You can either share one photo or create an album with a series of pictures.
- *Place*—This is for Facebook places. See the "Location-Based Social Media" section of this chapter for more information.

About

- *Basic Information*—This is the general information about the Facebook user: sex, birthday, interested in (men or women), what languages you speak, and religious and political views.
- *Contact Info*—This is how a Facebook user or friends can get a hold of you; phone, screen names, website, e-mail, Facebook URL/vanity.
- *Relationships and Family*—Facebook users are generally friends with their family members on Facebook. This can show who your mom, dad, sister, or aunt is. Also, you are able to show what your relationship status is, whether it is single, in a relationship, engaged, married, widowed, or divorced.
- *Work and Education*—Tells where you went to high school and college.
- *About You*—This is where Facebook users talk about themselves. This can be a personal description, poem, or list. This is where the Facebook user defines who they are.
- *Living*—Where you have and currently live.
- *Favorite Quotations*—Facebook users are often inspired by many things that people throughout history have said. With favorite quotations,

Facebook users are able to archive what they feel are the most meaningful thoughts that touch and define them.

- *Cover*—Acting like a website banner, the Facebook cover is an image at the top of an individual's Facebook profile that she feels is most important to her. Sized at 851 pixels by 315 pixels, this area is where Facebook users shine, show off, brand themselves, and share significant moments.

- *Feature*—Each post made on a Facebook user's Timeline can be made into a feature so that it becomes a focus or highlighted moment on the Facebook Timeline. This generally is to highlight something of significance or importance to the individual Facebook user.

- *Life Event*—These are significant moments in your life that you feel are worth highlighting. With five options to start with: work and education; family and relationships; living, health, and wellness; and milestones and experiences, Facebook users are able to share their personal life events and highlight them for people to see on their Facebook Timeline. It is important to note that with Facebook Timeline, life events can be posted from before the Facebook user was on Facebook all the way back to their birth.

Facebook Interface

- *Messages*—This acts as an e-mail within Facebook. Facebook friends and users are able to send messages to each other that are private and not seen publicly on the Facebook user's wall.

- *Events*—Planning get-togethers, causes, or just sharing things that are to come can all be shared with Facebook events. Facebook users can provide all the details (where, when, why) and invite their Facebook friends to come with three options for response or RSVP: Join, Maybe, Decline. If you have created a Facebook event under a Facebook page, you are able to invite only your personal Facebook friends, not those who like your page.

- *Group*—This is for Facebook users who wish to connect and build a social network around a common interest, affiliation, location, and so on. Groups are different from Facebook pages, in that everyone who is a part of the group can know who is in the group. Groups have three settings: open (anyone can see the group, who's in it, and what members post), closed (anyone can see the group and who is in it, but only the members can post), and secret (only members see the group, who is in it, and what members post. You must be added to participate.)

- *People You May Know*—Social networking is all about whom you know and who those people know. People You May Know is generated by the Facebook algorithm based on places you have checked in, pages you have liked, and people you are currently Facebook friends with. This allows for Facebook users to connect with people they may already know or allow them to get to know new people.

- *Ticker*—Located on the left-hand side of the Facebook home page (aka the news feed), the ticker shows everything that your Facebook friends are doing right now on Facebook. Different from the news feed, which shows status updates, the ticker shows all the activity of your Facebook friends: when they like a new page, comment on another friend's post, or become friends with someone new.

- *Chat*—Your Facebook friends will undoubtedly be on Facebook at the same time you are at some point. Chat allows you to have a conversation with them inside of Facebook when your Facebook friends are also online when you are. In the lower right-hand corner, there is a box that says "Chat" inside a green circle. The green circle signifies that those Facebook friends are online. Note that when a Facebook friend goes offline, the chat then becomes a message.

- *Username*—The Facebook username, or Facebook URL or vanity, allows Facebook users to easily find people and pages on Facebook. To claim your username, go to www.Facebook.com/username

For Facebook Pages, you must have 25 likes to claim your Username.

- *Apps*—Apps allow for Facebook to have a more interactive experience on Facebook. Apps have an incredible reach with the variety of use; from games to contests to help tools to newspapers to Facebook Like Page tools, the use of Facebook Apps is monumental.

Privacy Settings

With so much information being shared on Facebook, it is important to make sure Facebook users are protected as much as they want to be. The privacy settings allow for Facebook users to protect their personal information like location, contact information, and so forth, and their personal brand (pictures, videos, posts, and so forth). Setting individual levels of privacy is up to the individual user. By default, Facebook makes accounts public, and it is the responsibility of the Facebook user to change the relevant settings to disclose only what they wish to disclose. Facebook does provide, however, very customizable and comprehensive privacy settings for their users.

The privacy settings can block people from seeing your information, Facebook wall, friends, prevent others from tagging you in posts or pictures, sharing apps, and even block unsolicited people or those harassing you. We encourage all users to modify their Facebook privacy settings to the level of privacy they are comfortable with.

The privacy settings can be found in the upper right-hand corner of the Facebook interface by selecting the upside-down triangle next to the word Home and then selecting Privacy Settings. For more information on Facebook Privacy, please visit www.facebook.com/about/privacy.

Child Safety

Child safety on Facebook is a top priority. To protect minors, Facebook has implemented safeguards, and limits what they can do on the site, for their own protection. Facebook also requires that Facebook users be at least 13 years old. There are so many options, features, and tools for safety on Facebook that we encourage you to learn more about Facebook security at www.facebook.com/safety

for a very informative and engaging explanation of Facebook safety for parents, teens, teachers and law enforcement.

Twitter

With a 140-character limit, Twitter turned microblogging into an information-sharing sensation. Started in March of 2006 by Jack Dorsey, Noah Glass, Evan Williams, and Biz Stone, Twitter has gained global popularity, with over 200 million users sending over 200 million tweets and 1.6 billion searches per day. Since its launch, Twitter is used by what seems to be most everyone, from celebrities like Ashton Kutcher and Lady Gaga to major corporations like Apple and Google. Even the president of the United States has an active Twitter account.

How It Works

The best way to think of Twitter is to think of it like sending a text message to a group of people you may or may not know who care about what you have to say. To get started, visit www.twitter.com

to sign up where you will need accessible e-mail address to get started. Follow the simple steps to get started.

There are three ways to use Twitter: on your computer, through a mobile app with a smartphone, or by sending a simple text message. With the desktop computer website and Twitter app, you are able to tweet, follow people, read and retweet information, and build your own Twittersphere, or community. If you use Twitter through text messaging, you can send your tweets only through text messages. For information on how Twitter text messaging works, visit https://support.twitter.com

and go to "Apps, SMS, and Mobile" for more details.

What's in It for the User?

Twitter is all about the right now! Tweets have a life span of about 24 hours before they are forgotten. Additionally, with only 140 characters to get your message across, thoughts must be quick, concise, and to the point married with abbreviations, hashtags, and *text speak* to deliver the message. And while spelling is often forgiven and it very common to use letters or numbers for words (for example: *for* is 4, *you* is u, and so on), it is important to remember that this is your online reputation we are talking about.

Tweeple use Twitter to stay up to date on what is happening in the world they have created for themselves around what they find most relevant and important. Each user's Twitter account is customized just for whomever, around the people, topics, businesses, and other information they are interested in. You can follow the *Wall Street Journal* for your news, *The Big Bang Theory* because you love the show, TechCrunch for all your latest technology information, your favorite author, movie, musician; the possibilities are endless, but it's all about what you care about.

Twitter also allows its user to have relationships with people and businesses that they never could have had before. Twitter users can now directly contact American Express, Target, JetBlue, or Pepsi to ask questions, get customer support, ask about deals, or to share an experience. A common way to use Twitter is for customer service; @Comcast is known best for this. When your Internet or cable service is out, Twitter users are able to contact Comcast through Twitter for support, find out what the problem is or get a call from Comcast directly to talk through the problem.

Twitter is all about what the Tweeple feel is important and what they want to talk about. There is no agenda, just conversation and sharing.

What's in It for Businesses?

For businesses to not include Twitter as a part of the marketing efforts would be like trying to bake a cake with no oven. Yes, you have all the ingredients, but no way to bake it. It's the same thing with Twitter. If you have a business, product, service, or nonprofit that you want to get out into the world, Twitter is where it will happen.

Twitter allows for businesses to follow other leading experts to learn from them and share their information, be part of relevant, industry-specific conversations, answer questions, share your information, generate a topic of conversation, and keyword search around the world or by city.

While building a Twitter community takes time (but tends to be easier and faster than Facebook), it has an incredible payoff. When you have a big announcement, sale, or product for sale, the community that you have built will respond to you with purchases, retweeting, and coming into your establishment. Keep in mind that businesses will only be able to build a quality community by spending time building Twitter relationships, not being spammy, pushy, or salesy. No one wants to be pushed on all the time; they want to build relationships with you and get to know you and your business.

Common Terms

- *Tweet*—This is the actual information that is shared or posted on Twitter. This is done in 140 characters or fewer.
- *Via*—This is sometimes said in a tweet instead of using RT.
- *Hashtag (#hashtag)*—When the # symbol is used in a tweet to allow highlighted parts of retweets for conversation so other Twitter users can follow or search the hashtag. These are often used for emotions (#excited), events (#SDCC), or statements (#BestMovieEver). A hashtag is created by Twitter users by simply typing the # symbol and tying a word or series of words with no spaces.

- *Trending Topics (Trends)*—Trending is what Twitter users are talking about most on Twitter. These topics are based on what is popular across the world, country, or city and allows for people to discover the "most breaking" news stories from around the world. Trends can be political (#occupy), people (Justin Bieber), conversation topics (#BestOfBothWorlds), inquisitive (#MyWeddingSon), or an event (#VMAs). Trends are constantly changing.
- *Tweeple/Tweeps*—Term used for Twitter followers who have become friends through regular conversation, sharing, and retweeting.
- *Twittersphere*—A group of people who tweet as a collective group.
- *Tweetup*—An event at which people who tweet or use Twitter regularly get together in person. These events are for people to meet who wouldn't normally get to meet or to put a face with a name (or in this case a Twitter handle.) Events can happen regularly and are generally planned with Twitter and by using hashtags (for example, #buzzcation).

Understanding the Tool

- *Profile (@TwitterHandle)*—This is who the user is. There are four parts to the profile:
    1. *Your name*—This can be your actual name (for example, Lon Safko) or your organization name (Walgreens)
    2. *Twitter handle*—This is what identifies you in Twitter. Starting with the @ symbol and a word or series of words (with no spaces) is how Twitter will identify you. You are not allowed to exceed 15 characters; for example, @LonSafko.
    3. *Website link*—Your website, blog, or best way for other tweeps to learn more about you, your business, or what you are about, for example, www.LonSafko.com. This can be left blank.
    4. *140-character description*—The description of you tells everyone briefly what you are all about. You can use hashtags, links, full sentences, and whatever else you wish to put in the description to describe who you are, for example, "innovator & author of *The Social Media Bible.*"
- *Followers*—These are the tweeple who have chosen to follow you based on who you are and what you have to share. These people are able to read your tweets and retweet your information.

- *Follow/Following*—These are the tweeple you chose to follow based on who they are and what they have to say. These people's tweets will be visible on your timeline after you hit the "follow" button on their Twitter profile.
- *Retweet (RT)*—When information is reposted in your Twitter timeline from someone else's.
- *Timeline*—This is on your Twitter home page and where all the tweets from the tweeple you have chosen to follow will appear.
- *Direct Message (DM)*—This is a direct message sent from Twitter user to Twitter user. DMs can be received only if both Twitter users are following each other. This message is not seen by the public or other Twitter followers. DMs can be found under "messages" in the Twitter interface.
- *Who to Follow*—Based on whom you have followed, Twitter makes suggestions as to who else you may wish to follow on Twitter.
- *Activity*—This shows you what the tweeple you have chosen to follow have been doing on Twitter; whom they have followed, lists they have made, and what they have favorited.
- *Favorites*—Used when a tweet is liked and you wish to save it for later. This can be found on each tweet with a star next to it.
- *Lists*—Similar to Facebook lists, this allows Twitter users to organize their Twitter following into categories. For example, social media, family, friends, coupons, companies.

Other

- *Bit.ly*—With a limit of only 140 charactes, URL links can eat up a lot of valuable character space. Bit.ly allows for users to insert their URL into their tool and it will compress the link to a fewer number of characters.
- *TwitPic.com*—Available to all with a Twitter account, TwitPic allows Twitter users to share media on Twitter in real time.
- *Instagram*—This iPhone app (only available for iPhone at the time this chapter was written) takes photos and applies a filter to make photos appear retro and then post to Twitter and other social networks. This popular app has changed how people share photos, shop, promote, and so much more.
- *Auto-Responders/Auto-Followers*—A lot of people believe that the number of followers is the most important thing in social networking.

Auto-followers and auto-responders are designed to find your followers no matter where they are. While these tools are normally free, they tend to be hit or miss. We recommend not using these tools, and focus on making sure your information is valuable and follow-worthy. Building an online community takes time, but is always worth it in the end.

Location-Based Social Media

More and more people are turning to their mobile phones for communication and engagement. In fact, 40 percent of social media users access their social media from their mobile phones. With the emerging culture of sharing what is happening right now, location-based social media (LBS) has grown exponentially with 5 percent of social media users with smartphones using LBS services to check in, share their activities, access rewards, and connect with friends.

How It Works

LBS is available as an application (app) from your cell phone provider's app marketplace. Once installed (and opened by you) the app uses the GPS hardware in your smartphone, and the LBS accesses a list of venues that are nearby. You select the venue you are at and check in. With each check-in, you have the option to say something; why you are there, whom you are with, or what you'd recommend from that place. Generally, you will also have the option to share with your other social networks like Facebook and Twitter.

What's in It for the User?

LBS users generally enjoy sharing multiple facets of their life, but they primarily do it for the rewards and incentives. When LBS users check in to participating establishments, they are rewarded for giving the business a shout-out and some free publicity. The incentives and rewards can be a few things, like a discount on purchases, a free something like coffee or appetizer (with purchase), or a donation to a cause can be made. These incentives are awarded to the person who has checked in the most (usually the "mayor" or "duke/duchess"), frequent visitor (checked in three times), or for specific shout-outs (Here for the #SuperBowl!).

What's in It for Businesses?

Business owners are always looking for simple and cost-effective ways to promote their businesses. LBS platforms are free to use, easy to set up, and businesses can offer the same things they offer in their print advertising. LBS allows for something that print advertising can't: word of mouth. Every business owner will tell you that marketing and advertising are necessary for any business, but word-of-mouth marketing will keep people coming back for more. Social media is all about word of mouth, sharing, and getting others to do it with you.

LBS also allows business owners to thank those who come in their stores and promote them. All business owners have that regular who is in there all the time, but with LBS they can know who they are, when they come in, and what they are saying. Is it really all that hard to say thanks with a discount or free something?

Common Terms

- *Check-in/Checking In*—When a user physically announces or shares his physical location to his friends and followers. This can be done upon arrival or departure.
- *Badges*—Digital rewards that are earned by users for checking in. These are unlocked by checking in to a variety of locations, doing activities, events (Super Bowl, 4sq Day, voting, etc.), days (Halloween, voting, New Years, etc.), frequenting locations, and unique check-ins (astronaut Douglas H. Wheelock unlocked the NASA Explorer badge for checking into Foursquare from the International Space Station).
- *Points*—Awarded for checking in. More points are awarded for different accomplishments, for example, checking in when "the mayor is in the house," adding new locations, visiting a first (your first coffee shop, movie theater, club, etc.), or earning a badge.
- *Rewards/Incentives*—Awarded by participating businesses when a user interacts with the location through a check-in. These awards can be a discount on a purchase or a free product. These are awarded or unlocked for being the mayor, checking in so many times (frequent visitor), or simply for checking in.
- *Geolocation*—When a user's real-world geographical location is tied to an object like a mobile phone. This service is accessed through the GPS in almost all smartphones.
- *Shout-outs*—Where the user shares what they are doing in the check-in.

Foursquare

Foursquare is the biggest LBS (as of the time this chapter was written) with over 15 million members checking in over 3 million check-ins per day. Launched at SXSW (South By Southwest) on March 11, 2009, by Dennise Crowley and Naveen Selvadurai, the New York City–based LBS company allows you to check in at the location you are at to share with your Foursquare friends, Facebook friends, and Twitter followers where you are and what you are doing.

Foursquare has an easy-to-use interface and a 140-character limit. Users unlock the world around them: what specials are near by (based on your geolocation), check into places to share your current activity, leave tips, know what your friends are doing and where, share pictures with your check-in (these should be related to the place you are at, such as food, artwork, performances, and so on), add new places, and identify different types of places that are in your immediate area.

Understanding the Tool

- *Activity*—This can be compared to the Facebook news feed or the Twitter timeline, where you see what your friends are doing, where, and how long ago.

- *Daily Deals*—Partnered with daily deal companies like Groupon and Living Social, Foursquare shares with users when local deals are near by.

- *Events*—With so many people creating new events for movies, concerts, parties, and other events, Foursquare added the events option so when users are at specific locations, they can check in to an event at that location rather than creating a new place in Foursquare just for the event. This can be seen as a red ticket in the Foursquare interface.

- *Explore*—Based on your geolocation, Foursquare finds specials, restaurants, shops, events, and outdoor activities that are nearby within a certain mile radius (the default is two miles.)

- *Friends*—Other users you have approved to share your location and their location with you. Their activity shows up in the "Activity" part of the Foursquare interface.

- *Following*—Businesses, organizations, and other entities can be followed by users to unlock extra tips at various locations as well as unlock sponsored badges and promotions. A few examples are *The Conan O'Brien Show,* the *Wall Street Journal,* and Walgreens.

- *History*—The last places a user has checked in displayed in order from most current to last.

- *Lists*—Based on tips left by other users and followed businesses, a to-do list is created by the user based on things the user wishes to do.
- *Mayor*—The user who has checked in the most to an establishment in a 60-day period.
- *SuperUser*—Foursquare has awarded power users to be able to edit and report venues in the Foursquare interface. These users help local communities with deleting and removing duplicate venues, report problems, abuse, and other Foursquare maintenance.

Other LBS

- *Facebook Places*—Launched in August 18, 2010, to rival Foursquare, Facebook Places allows for users to check in using their Facebook app. Users are also able to check in their Facebook friends (for those who have enabled the feature) and access Facebook deals. This feature is marketed as a loyalty card or digital coupon for checking in to participating businesses on Facebook. Deals can be discounts, coupons, or free merchandise.
- *Gowalla*—This LBS has a very similar functionality to Foursquare, but with a more artistic look. The biggest difference comes from the Trips feature. Trips allows users to create a trip or route of up to 20 locations and a pin (the equivalent of a badge) is awarded for completing your own trip or another user's. These trips can be pub crawls, nature hikes, or food tours. Gowalla also awards stamps, which are awarded for checking into places. Gowalla pins and stamps are easier to acquire than Foursquare badges and in more variety. A few pins and stamps include the Royal Gowallabies for the April 2011 royal wedding and Disney Parks, where you can check in to all rides to earn stamps or pins for completing the Disney Trip.
- *Yelp*—Founded in October of 2004, Yelp combines local reviews of businesses and social networking to create local online communities. Yelp is predominantly used to read and leave reviews of service-based businesses like restaurants, retail stores, clubs, and so forth. Users are able to access Yelp from their desktop or smartphone to find places to visit, read reviews, and check in. Yelp also offers Yelp Deals, which work similarly to Groupon deals, but with no time limit for purchasing a deal. Yelp also offers check-in deals and Yelp Royalty (to rival Mayorships) similar to Foursquare and can be accessed by the Yelp smartphone app.

The ROI of Social Media

Southwest Airlines Generates Top Sales and Website Traffic Days Using Social Media

Background

Southwest Airlines joined Twitter. Shortly thereafter, the airline began source coding all of the links it distributed in its tweets. Then something amazing happened. Southwest Airlines Emerging Media managers Paula Berg and Christi Day discovered that seven customers had clicked from Twitter through to southwest.com

and made a purchase that week. A whopping *seven!* Their excitement was quickly deflated when a colleague suggested that they *not* report their findings because the number "was so small." Technically, the colleague was right. Relative to the millions of people who book travel on southwest.com each year, seven didn't sound very impressive. But while the number was small, the potential was huge!

Strategy

Continue to engage with customers on Twitter, build a following, cultivate relationships, and monitor activity. In the meantime, bang down internal doors to make colleagues understand the revenue potential of Twitter and other social media channels, commit more resources and staffing power to the airline's social media efforts, and develop appropriate sale opportunities to test in said channels.

Implementation

Less than a year later, Southwest launched a 48-hour fare sale using nothing more than social media and public relations to promote it—no paid advertising—and achieved its top two sales and website traffic days in the airline's 38-year history. If anyone thought it was an anomaly, three months later, they did it again.

Opportunity

Inspire organizational change and drive revenue with increased investment in social media.

Conclusion

Anyone who works in social media sees its power and possibility every day. The ultimate challenge is finding ways to persuade peers and leaders to take risks, pursue new opportunities, and make the long-term investment required to succeed. Measurement and reporting can be powerful tools in gaining resources and support, but charts and graphs are just numbers on a page, and they don't predict the future. When measuring and reporting social media, it's essential to not just report past activity but to read between the numbers to spot trends, patterns, and possibilities. Reporting social media should, at times, be like reporting the weather—ignoring what the numbers were yesterday and focusing instead on what the numbers could be tomorrow—and then using that information to educate, inspire, and drive the organizational change needed to meet the needs and possibilities of the changing media landscape.

—Paula Berg, www.Southwest.com

International Perspective

China

With 1.3 billion people, regardless of what is going on now in China, it will continue to expand its presence in the ever growing area of social media!

So what are they doing? Well, as you may know, many sites such as Facebook are blocked by the "Great Firewall of China," but there are still plenty of local sites taking advantage of this and creating home grown powerhouses.

(continued)

(*continued*)

Currently there are approximately 400 million online users in China, many with multiple accounts. The leaders are:

Network	Members
Tencent	1 billion
Qzone	310 million
RenRen	200 million + 50 million Mobile
Kaixin001	75 million
51.com	160 million

But what are they doing? How well is the social in social media integrating into the business world?

The most popular site in China is QZone. A social networking site created by powerhouse Tencent (China's largest Internet portal) in 2005, it is used for blogs, diaries, photo sharing, and for listening to music!

What is interesting to note here is that in America, approximately 25 percent of the population create original content. In China, that number is over 40 percent! This makes things very interesting from a marketing standpoint. This could be because China has so many restrictions that the use of social media is a great way for people to spread their beliefs and views without repercussions. There is even an online currency, QQ, that is being used so widely across the country it is being taxed!

And although a lot of usage is IM and Chat, the main topics being discussed on these sites are:

Healthcare

Consumer Goods

Automobiles

Computers

Mobile phones

Sports

I think that China is taking the lead in using the web to do research and companies that ignore this are at risk. Especially when we consider that the average Chinese user will spend at least 5 hours per week on social media sites.

It should also be noted that China users are far more engaged in their online lives than Americans. It is typical for a China user to spend over 80 percent of his or her day online, compared to about 40 percent in the USA.

For many Chinese, they actually first hear about a brand online rather than in print or television. This means that your reputation online is critical if you want to make an impact on today's social media users.

So what should your company do in China? Research and more research!

In order to understand what is going on in China you need to understand all the channels being used online, what they are saying about your company and your competitors and what you can do to enhance your online reputation.

You also need to understand how Social Media users engage with other users and what their motivations are for using the most popular sites. From this you can make sure you are visible on the right channels!

As a resident of China, I am extremely excited to be here during a once in a lifetime evolution: 500 million users and counting. The future is looking to include gambling, two-way communication with users, location-based marketing, company discounts and promotions, and of course information sharing.

But all this activity still comes down to what I call the three pillars of success! Trust, Comfort, and Confidence . . . I wrote about this five years ago from a sales perspective but it still holds true today.

You need social media to build trust, create a comfortable user experience so they keep coming back, and finally, create a confident brand that users will know is in it for the long haul and will keep innovating!

So, keep doing research and listening to your customers and users. By the time you finish reading this article, the landscape would have changed!

Xie Xie!

—Anthony Solimini
Simitri Group
www.simitrigroup.com

Expert Insight

Gretchen Howard, director of online sales and operations, Google AdWords, www.google.com/corporate/execs.html

Gretchen Howard

. . . I'm a director at Google and I work on online sales and operations and I've been at Google for about two and a half years. I had a varied path before I landed at Google. I worked in financial services and also in consulting before that. . . .

. . . Sure, let's start with an acronym that you mentioned from the start, Search Engine Marketing, or SEM. Search Engine Marketing is really not intermixed with online advertising. It refers to programs that enable advertisers to run relevant ads alongside search results. So when users perform queries on a search engine, such as Google, online advertisement will also come up. . . .

. . . These onlines are featured advertisements that you're talking about; this is what we call AdWords. So AdWords is just Google's online advertising program. And we really like to describe AdWords as, it may sound a little corny, but I like to explain it as a matchmaking service that can match businesses and customers. They're really the tools that connect businesses to a product and services that sell and customers who are looking for those specific products and services, and online. And it's really done by matching relevant products and services to customers' search queries, and the thing that excites me most about AdWords is that it's highly targeted and cost effective. So it's a measurable system that helps advertisers, both large and small, find their customers online. . . .

. . . It's all about relevance, and so it's really easy to set up. One thing, just to take you quickly through how it works: When you go to www.google .com/adwords, you select "daily budget," [and] you create an ad. And you target your ad by choosing keywords and a geographic location, and then you let it run. So it's a cost-per-click model, which means advertisers only pay when users click on their ads. And then they are delivered to the advertiser's website.

So a click can be as low as one cent and you can modify your daily budget at any time. So you're not trapped into a large fee at any time. . . .

. . . It's a pay-per-click model, and that's why our philosophy is that all advertising should be relevant, targetable, and cost effective. And that's why the pay-per-click model comes in because it holds us accountable and not the advertisers with customers. . . .

. . . The other thing that it does is it really levels the playing field. And so it offers this powerful, measurable solution to the needs of both small and niche businesses, as well as large brand advertisers. So in some ways it really democratizes the web, which is just ground-breaking. . . .

. . . And it doesn't matter how specific. I mean the more specifically someone's looking for something, the easier they're going to find exactly what they're looking for. And so the user experience and the customer experience are both important to their business, and it helps both Google and the online advertisers, as well. So it's really a win-win situation. . . .

. . . So we have an ad traffic quality team and they're constantly at EQ. We have a three-stage system for detecting invalid clicks. The three features are (1) proactive real-time filters, (2) proactive offline analysis, and (3) reactive investigation. And this combined approach is really the essence of click-fraud management. The goal is to cap the net of invalid clicks efficiently, live, in order to have a high degree of competence so that actual malicious behavior is effectively filtered out.

So by proactively filtering these clicks, potentially worth hundreds of millions of dollars every year, we're able to provide a very effective protection against attempted click-fraud, and we take it very seriously. . . .

. . . Google has devoted significant resources and expertise to developing proactive and technically sophisticated measures to filter invalid clicks before advertisers are ever charged for them. We recognize that advertiser satisfaction from an advertiser's point of view is extremely important. So we investigate every click-fraud claim that comes in to us and we really try to respond to those advertisers' requests as appropriately and timely as possible. . . .

. . . And if we don't catch it proactively (and we do catch most of them proactively) we will absolutely credit advertisers retroactively because the last thing we want is for advertisers to be negatively affected by click-fraud in any way. . . .

. . . But I think this integrity is so key to the essence of our business that it's extremely important for our customer experience and our advertiser experience to be top notch. . . .

(continued)

(continued)

. . . AdWords actually is very easy to get started. I like to break it down into three main steps. First: As in any time you're creating an advertising campaign, especially an online marketing campaign, I think the first step and advice that I always give people is, "Know your audience; identify your goals." Precision is the key to search advertising. You want to reach the right advertisers at the right time.

Take a good look at the products or services you are selling and the customers who are buying them. You'd be amazed at how many people don't know who their target audience is, and this is an essential first step. Then, once you have a clear sense of your business, you need to focus on how to reach those customers and you'll need to understand and define what your ultimate goal is, so you can actually measure success.

Then you can look to target specific languages or geographic locations that your business serves, and that could be your region or that could be global. . . .

. . . That's one of the beauties of online advertising. You can change your geographic targeting at any time. So you can expand or contract or actually make seasonal changes based on geographic trends as well. . . .

. . . I think, you know, if you are someone in northern California and you're selling a snowboard, you can have a huge presence in the winter in northern California, but in the summer it's a slow time. So why not market those snowboards to folks in New Zealand where it's winter in your summer? So it's a great way to discount the seasonality of your business. . . .

. . . And that leads me to point Number Two and how to get started. It's the second tip that I tell people: "You really have to create effective campaigns." So the first step in that is choosing powerful keywords. Really start brainstorming and expand your list as broadly as possible, and then narrow your focus. Try to think like your customers do and use two- to four-word combinations instead of general words so you really target the audience that you're going after.

The other piece is that advertisers need to write what I call, "Got-to-Click" ads. So those are ads that users feel *compelled* to click on and learn more. Get to the point quickly, convey key product benefits, like free shipping or promotion; and then use "strong calls to action" such as "buy now" or "sign up today" and really direct users to the landing piece on your site that most relates to your ad. And not just to the general landing page, but make it as specific as possible so people get to the information that they are looking after and so they don't have to navigate further once they reach your website. . . .

. . . Keep the complexity out of the interaction and you will have many more sales than you ever dreamed possible. And I think that's a great point.

The third step is, "Track, test, adopt, and thrive." You really need to adopt an attitude where you're continually looking at the data that the online advertising provides you, and you continue to experiment. The online advertising environment is really dynamic and you can look at your marketing results and keep a close eye on statistics. And again, this is different from any other form of advertising.

You can leverage conversion-tracking software. Lots of people provide free software and at Google it's the Google Analytic product, but there's lots of tools like Google Analytic that provide data that will allow you to glean insight into your website and how to improve it and make changes so you can achieve your goals. . . .

. . . I think using two- to four-word combinations instead of general words . . . helps you become more targeted to reach that very specific audience, and it is usually much cheaper than a general keyword. . . .

. . . There are lots of other kinds of advertising we do. You can do print campaigns and you can do TV campaigns. . . .

. . . You can do audio campaigns, but I think that will take another whole session when there's time. But we're always looking at ways we can be innovative and, again, bring that targeted, measurable approach to general advertising. . . .

. . . AdSense is (and this is not my area of expertise) the team that manages our relationships with publishers. So they manage something called the "Content Network." The best example of this is to think about the *New York Times.* They have an online presence and they run AdSense advertisements on that page from various publishers that are relevant to the content in their stories.

So if you're online on the NewYorkTimes.com [site] and you're reading a story about dogs, there might be [an] advertisement shown from different pet food providers. And that's why we call these publishers, such as the *New York Times,* our AdSense publishers. . . .

. . . Anyone can put AdWords or AdSense ads on their blog, and basically anytime someone clicks through an ad from your published site, such as a blog, part of that revenue that's derived from clicking through that ad is shared with the publisher. . . .

. . . It's great for blogs and any type of publishers to actually have that relationship with Google, and it also provides valuable advertisements to their users based on the subject that they're writing about. . . .

. . . You can start at Google.com/Adword; you select a daily budget. That's how much you want to spend per day. You actually create an ad, you write a text ad, and then you choose your keywords and geographic location, and that's it! You let it run. So it's really quite easy to set up. You don't have to be tech-savvy to do it. There is a wizard that will take you through step by

(*continued*)

(continued)

step. But there are some common mistakes that people do when setting up an account that I'd be happy to walk through if that's an interest. . . .

To listen to or read the entire Executive Conversation with Gretchen Howard, go to www.theSocialMediaBible.com.

For additional Expert Insight excerpts on this subject, go to www .theSocialMediaBible.com:

- Chris Pirillo, geek and technology enthusiast
- Robert Scoble, famous blogger and author
- Kyle Ford, director, product marketing, Ning
- Stephanie Ichinose, director of communications for Yelp

To-Do List

- Create profiles and groups

  Go the most popular social networking sites—Facebook, Twitter, LinkedIn, and Foursquare—and create profiles and groups before someone else takes your names. Then create more profiles on lesser-known sites as well.

- Participate

  Start out by reading the comments on a few selected sites and listen to where the conversation is headed. Once you have an idea about how to appropriately respond, then participate.

- Build your own network

  Start building a following with your blog. Comment on other blogs and join in the conversation. Then consider building your own group or social network by using Ning or WordPress Group Platform.

- Check in

  Using your smartphone, find and download an LBS that you enjoy and find easy to use and start checking in. Share with your friends where you are and what you are doing all while getting great deals. Once you use it for personal use, implement it into your professional social media strategy.

Conclusion

The key to networking—as with all of the social media tools—is to participate. Go to the sites mentioned in this chapter—LinkedIn, Facebook, Twitter, Flickr, YouTube—and any other social network platform you can think of and create your profile and groups. If you don't, someone else will take your name or industry group—and it will be lost forever. Robert Scoble, famous Microsoft blogger, continuously says that to be successful in networking, first listen, then participate. It's like being at a social gathering.

So—join the party! You wouldn't walk into a party, step over to a group of people talking, interrupt, and immediately start telling them about yourself. (Well, maybe once.) But this is how people are currently marketing; and it's not really working that well. First, you have to actually be at the party. Then, you walk over, listen for a while, and then join in on the conversation with something valuable and appropriate to add. Social media marketing for businesses is exactly the same thing. To repeat, because it's important: You first have to be at the party, and then select a group, listen to them—and *then* join in with something valuable. That's how you build community, and that's how you build trust both offline and online.

To hear all of the Expert Interviews, go to www.theSocialMediaBible .com.

Downloads

For your free downloads associated with *The Social Media Bible,* go to www.theSocialMediaBible.com,

and enter your ISBN number located on the back of the book above the bar code. Be sure to enter the dashes.

Credits

Technical Edits Provided by:

Desiree Ford, subject matter expert

www.PinkMediaLLC.com

www.Facebook.com/PinkMediaLLC

The ROI of Social Media was provided by:

Paula Berg, Southwest.com

Expert Insight was provided by:

Gretchen Howard, director of online sales and operations, Google AdWords, www.google.com/corporate/execs.html

CHAPTER 3

It's Not Your Father's E-Mail

www.LonSafko.com/TSMB3_Videos/03Email.mov

What's in It for You?

Do you think you know e-mail? Probably—since most people have been e-mailing for about two decades now. Even before there was e-mail, companies were sending messages asking others in their trusted networks to look at their website or buy their products. And although spam (called by other names, such as *junk mail* or *rubbish*) had existed in bulletin boards (see Chapter 5, The Internet Forum, and Chapter 4, The World of Web Pages), it—and other commercial marketing messages—came to fruition in an especially strong manner through the birth of e-mail. After all, there isn't any other form of advertising that has a more reliable return on investment (ROI) than e-mail. What other marketing medium allows you to reach 5,000 to 50,000 of your potential customers for (nearly) free or a very inexpensive price with the help of an e-mail service provider?

When e-mail is used correctly, its conversion rate—the rate at which it turns potential customers into actual customers—can be phenomenal. It has the power to exponentially exceed the results generated by conventional direct mail, newspaper, magazine, and cost-prohibitive radio and television advertising. The Internet is one of the very few media formats that actually allows advertisers to count how many impressions, responses, conversations, and pass-alongs their ads produce, and thereby

theSocialMediaBible.com

determine *exactly* how many sales can be attributed to each e-mail campaign.

E-mail is one of the oldest forms of digital social media, and it is by far one of the most effective ways to stay in touch with your customers, transact with them, resolve their issues, recruit new customers, and develop your trusted network—oh, and by the way, it's *practically* free.

That's the incredible value of the Internet. Everything can be measured. Companies can test and perfect which image works best, which headline is more effective, and which offer drives the most sales. This is why major corporations are moving the majority of their advertising budgets to online ventures. According to the *Silicon Valley Insider,* newspaper ad revenue has been declining at an alarming rate. The prediction is that newspaper ad revenue will continue to drop from $42 billion in 2007 to only $10 billion by 2017. That's a $32 billion loss in offline advertising—and for good reason.

Back to the Beginning

The earliest form of e-mail goes back to the beginning of the 1960s. Single computer electronic mail—such as SNDMSG[1]—simply appended a file on an existing one on the same computer. Then, by opening that file, you could read what others had appended to it.

The first actual e-mail resembling present-day e-mails was sent around 7:00 PM in the autumn of 1971 as a test created by a programming engineer employed by Bolt, Beranek and Newman named Ray Tomlinson, who had been chosen by the U.S. Defense Department to build the ARPAnet: the first major computer network, and the predecessor to today's Internet. Ray was working in Cambridge, Massachusetts, on Network Control Protocol (NCP) for a time-sharing system called TENEX and CPYNET when he sent his first e-mail between two side-by-side PDP-10 computers. He addressed it to himself, and he recalls the message most likely contained the text "QWERTYUIOP," from the row of keys on his computer.

By the end of 1972, Tomlinson's two e-mail software packages—called SNDMSG and READMAIL—had become industry standards, right down to Tomlinson's first use of the @ in e-mail addresses. When Ray was asked why he chose the @ sign, he explained, "The 'at' sign just makes sense. The purpose of the 'at' sign indicated a unit price (for example, 10 items @ $1.95). I used the 'at' sign to indicate that the user was 'at' some other host rather than being local." And when he was asked about spam—well, he said that he had never anticipated that.

What You Need to Know

As mentioned previously, the overwhelming reason for the popularity and widespread use of e-mail is its ROI and effectiveness, and of course, the fact that it's nearly free. According to the Forrester DMA Gartner Group, e-mail marketing is significantly more effective than direct mail marketing. Some specific findings are in Table 3.1.

Table 3.2 shows some additional statistics from an industry survey of 2,700 marketers that states their primary goals for using e-mail in their marketing programs.

Table 3.1   Direct Mail versus E-Mail Marketing[a]

Measurement	Direct Mail	E-Mail
Development Time	3 to 6 weeks	2 days
Cost per Unit	$1.25	$0.10
Response Rate	0.1 to 2 percent[b]	5 to 15 percent[c]

[a]This doesn't mean that abandoning direct mail completely is the right choice for everyone. If you are selling RVs, for example, you had better keep sending direct mail pieces, since your typical buying demographic is older and not necessarily e-mail savvy. (However, an interesting note: The U.S. Census Bureau reports important changes for the coming years in the aging of the population. By 2050, one in five residents will be aged 65 or over, up from one in nine today. Refer to Part II of this book to determine which social media tool works best for your company, products, and demographics.)

[b]That's the same thing as taking 1,000 of your direct mail pieces, selecting one from the stack, and throwing the remaining 999 pieces into the trash.

[c]Some e-mail campaigns with which the author is familiar have reached as high as a 34 percent open rate.

Table 3.2   Primary Goals for E-Mail Marketing Programs

Build relationships with existing customers	60 percent
Acquire new customers	41 percent
Sell products and services	32 percent
Provide information	31 percent
Build the brand	25 percent
Drive traffic to a website	21 percent
Up-sell and cross-sell to existing customers	18 percent

Source: www.MarketingProfs.com e-mail Marketing Benchmark Survey.

These numbers are a surprise in that the highest usage of e-mail marketing isn't necessarily sales, but rather to build relationships with existing customers. The second-highest-rated use was to acquire new customers, and the primary use of e-mail for these marketers was to build and maintain their trusted network.

E-mail Terminology

Here are some important and often-used terms with which you should become familiar so you can maximize your e-mail marketing campaigns.

- *From line:* The sender of the e-mail is the first thing recipients look at. There are two components: What is displayed in the inbox and what is displayed when the e-mail is opened (see Figure 3.1).
- *Subject line:* The headline seen before opening the message gives a brief description of the subject of the e-mail. Recipients often decide whether to open an e-mail based on the contents of the subject line (see Figure 3.2).

Inbox	E-mail
The Wall Street Journal Online	WSJ@listserv.punchline.net [on behalf of Wall Street Journal]
Sony Electronics	sonyelectronics@sony.m0.net
E-nnouncements from T. ...	noReply@rps-updates.troweprice.com
Hewlett-Packard	[Hewlett-Packard] us-specials@your.HP.com

FIGURE 3.1   From Line

From	Subject Line
JCPenney	Home Sale: Redecorate with Savings
Quill.com	Look inside for sale offers selected just for you
Staples Newsletter	Regina, here's your July newsletter
Lands' End	DESIGN YOUR OWN JEANS

FIGURE 3.2   Subject Line

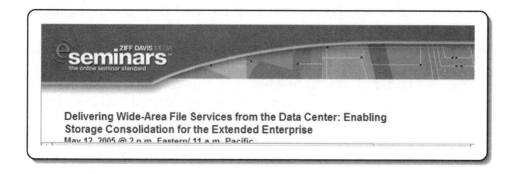

FIGURE 3.3   Preview Pane

- *Preview pane:* This element in many e-mail programs allows the recipient to view the first few lines of a message. This is also a big factor in getting the recipient to open the message (see Figure 3.3).
- *Open rate:* This statistic measures how many recipients opened the e-mail message, and either enabled the images or clicked on a link.

    This works only for HTML e-mails, because text-only messages have no images (unless, of course, you send a text-based message and ask your clients to click "receipt," which they are not likely to do). This is only the first of several necessary steps that you must take to convert readers of an e-mail message to visitors to your website, and ultimately purchasers of your product.

- *Click-throughs:* These measure the recipients who clicked on a link or an image in an e-mail, thereby opening the hyperlinked web page for additional content. Each link in an e-mail can usually be tracked separately.

- *Pass-alongs:* These are the number of recipients who forward your message along to a friend or colleague.

- *Bounces:* E-mails classified as *bounces* did not reach their destination and were bounced back to the sender.

- *Hard bounces:* These e-mails have been sent to a domain or e-mail address that no longer exists (or never did). You must have a system for deleting hard bounces immediately. Sometimes old addresses can be used as spam traps and hurt your delivery or get you blocked from future sending privileges with key service providers.

- *Soft bounces:* As opposed to hard bounces, soft bounces present a temporary condition that renders the e-mail undeliverable, the two main reasons for which are usually a full mailbox or a down server. You should resend soft bounces four times, and then delete the address from your e-mail list.

- *Opt-outs or unsubscribes:* These events occur when a user requests not to be included on your e-mail list. This can be done after receiving your initial e-mail, or by having a permission box prechecked. The number of recipients who ask to have their e-mail address removed from your e-mail distribution list is the number of opt-outs.

- *Opt-ins:* These occur when a user actively elects to receive e-mails or promotional messages by checking an opt-in box, which can also be prechecked.

  Be aware that, typically, less than 5 percent of customers will opt out of receiving e-mail messages, and less than 10 percent will opt in. An exception is the case of guest books, which typically have a 57 percent opt-in rate—and which can have a dramatic effect on responses to your e-mail.

- *Double opt-in or explicit permission:* Think of this as a double-dog-dare-ya. After the initial registration, a confirmation e-mail is sent to the user, who must reply (either by hitting reply, or clicking on a URL contained within the e-mail) before you can add this person to your e-mail list.

Spam with Your SPAM?

It's been estimated that e-mail users spend roughly 52 hours each year—that's about one hour per week!—sorting and deleting spam (junk e-mail) messages from their inbox. Cox Communications, the seventh-largest e-mail provider in the United States, estimated that almost 3.6 *billion* spam

FIGURE 3.4 SPAM

messages were delivered in 2007 alone. That number rose to more than 200 billion in 2011. Statistics like these prompted the CAN-SPAM Act.

The national CAN-SPAM Act went into effect in the United States on January 1, 2004. This law preempts all state laws governing commercial e-mail, and applies to both business-to-business and business-to-consumer marketers. (State laws are still in effect as they relate to fraud.) The law applies most specifically to commercial e-mail messages (the category into which most marketing messages fall), and not to transactional or relationship messages, which are those that are sent to complete a transaction; provide warranty, product updates, upgrades, or recall information; and notify users of changes in terms of subscription or service or account balance information.

The term *SPAM* originally comes from the meat produced by the Hormel Meat Packing Company in Austin, Minnesota, in 1937. Then-president J. C. Hormel created an amazing little recipe: a spicy ham packaged in a handy 12-ounce can (see Figure 3.4). He held a contest to give the product a name as distinctive as its taste. The winner was SPAM, for SPiced hAM. During its very first year of production, SPAM grabbed 18 percent of the market. Seven billion cans of SPAM have been sold since 1937, with 44,000 cans per hour rolling out of Hormel. A can of SPAM is consumed in the United States every 3.1 seconds.

How does this translate to online clutter, though? Well, when it comes to the Internet, you've likely seen, heard, or even used the term *spam* and *spamming,* which refer to the act of sending unsolicited commercial e-mail (UCE), which implies that someone has sent a message that has no value or substance inside for the recipient.

How might a company feel about its product being likened to something without value or substance? Hormel's official position on the term *spam* is as follows: "We do not object to use of this slang term to describe UCE, although we do object to the use of the word 'spam' as a trademark and to the use of our product image in association with that term. Also, if the term is to be used, it should be used in all lower-case letters to distinguish it from our trademark SPAM, which should be used with all upper-case letters."

The essence of the CAN-SPAM Act simply states that those sending e-mails have to be honest. It forbids the use of false header information, dictates that the "From" line must be real, demands that no use of deceptive or misleading subject lines occurs, mandates that all messages must give the recipient the ability to unsubscribe either through a link to a website or a valid reply to an e-mail address, states that the opt-out links must be clear and conspicuous, and must work at the time the message is sent for 30 days thereafter. It orders that opt-outs must be processed within 10 business days, that each e-mail must include a valid physical postal address (while the original CAN-SPAM Act said that a post office box does not suffice, the 2007 revisions of the Act said it was legal), that an ADV[2] warning label must be in the subject line only if a company does not have express permission (affirmative consent) from the recipient, and that one's mail servers must not have an open relay or allow others to send e-mail through their servers without their permission.

An important technicality to note: The law defines the sender as the party providing the e-mail's content—not the one renting the list, and not the list owner. Therefore, since any opt-outs are specific to the sender, you must obtain unsubscribe data from the list owner and add those names to your in-house suppression file. Remember: You have only 10 business days to process opt-outs.

The law also specifies that lists built with dictionary attacks, harvested e-mails, or randomly generated e-mail addresses are prohibited. A dictionary attack occurs when spammers connect to a server and ask to deliver mail to mailbox "A." If the server complies, then that address goes on their list. They then proceed to "AA," or "B," or any word or combination of letters that's in their automated dictionary. Randomly generated e-mails work the same way. Harvested e-mails require that someone search websites—either manually or automatically—to collect all of the e-mails without the recipient's permission. Both of these techniques are illegal and can get you blacklisted.[3]

The Federal Trade Commission and states' attorneys general offices can enforce violations with civil action, which can include jail sentences along with fines ranging from \$250 up to \$2 million per message. Also, Internet service providers (ISPs) can enforce the law with a civil action for damages or for fines ranging from \$250 to \$1 million per message. In the case of fraud, there is no upper limit.

Spam Filters or Content Filters

Spam filters or content filters are online tools that are used to constantly survey and identify spam, and trigger spam blockers upon finding any. Some phrases that often trigger these spam filters include: "Free __," "\$\$\$," "!!!," "Cash bonus," "ALL CAPS," "No Investment Necessary," "Satisfaction Guaranteed," "You Are a Winner," "No Purchase Necessary," "Social Security Number," and "No Strings Attached." How many times have you received an e-mail with one of these phrases in the subject line that actually offered any value? In fact, you're probably wondering why, if the laws in the United States are so tough, you still receive so much spam? Although the CAN-SPAM Act went into effect on January 1, 2004, most (if not all) of the spammers had moved offshore, mostly to Asian countries, in December 2003.

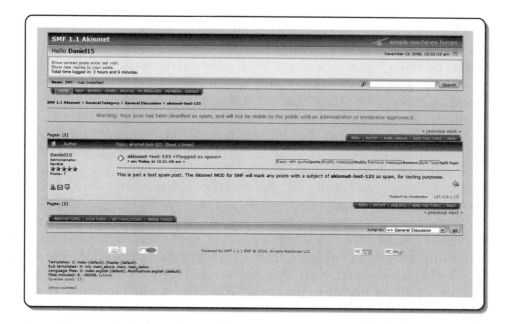

FIGURE 3.5   Spam Submit

There are resources available on different websites, but to spam-check your e-mail subject lines before you send them, go to one like www .programmersheaven.com/webtools/Spam-Checker/spamchecker.aspx.

Content Really Is King

Just as it is in your web pages, your brochures, and your direct mailer, content is king—the most fundamental part of your e-mail. It therefore requires the most significant amount of attention. The most important rule in all of marketing is the question of WIIFM: "What's In It for Me?" If you don't clearly and quickly convey the WIIFM in every marketing message, e-mail, and communication you have with your customers, then your work will be ineffective.

Think about how your customers perceive your corporate communications. Every time you want your customer to look at an e-mail, visit your website, or open a piece of direct mail, there is a transaction. It is very much like a sale, in that you are asking your customer to give you some amount of money (or attention) in exchange for you providing a service or product. The customer evaluates your offer and compares your product or service to the total cost of the transaction, which might include your customer going to a website, driving to your location, sending something in the mail, reading and comprehending your offer, filling out a registration form, and completing credit card information before even getting to actually pay you for that item.

Your potential customer subconsciously calculates all of these costs of inconvenience and adds them to the product's dollar amount to determine the overall cost—and decides whether your product or service is a good value. To hook your prospects into investing their cost of inconvenience before they actually decide to purchase, you have to convince them of their WIIFM, or you've lost them—and the sale.

Enticing your customers isn't a one-time event. There could be as many as a dozen occasions during which you have to convince your customer that your product or service is worth the total cost of inconvenience and money.

It's this very concept—believing that attracting customers is a one-time deal—that many companies too easily forget, and it therefore leads to poor conversion rates. This frame of mind leaves your e-mails unopened without ensuing click-throughs, pass-alongs, or visits beyond your home page, and usually results in shopping cart abandonment. Understanding the need to consistently woo your customers, however, will dramatically improve all of your marketing—in addition to what you do with e-mail.

Tips, Techniques, and Tactics

The 1.54-Second Rule/5.0-Second Rule

To understand WIIFM more clearly, take a more concentrated look at how people think, read, and evaluate these value propositions. Suppose, for some reason, that you really wanted to read the newspaper advertisements today. Your eyes are scanning over the pages of many ads, one of which catches your eye. You decide to not turn the page, but to look at the heading for that ad. How long do you think you are willing to spend to determine if the WIIFM is worth your stopping to read further? A study showed that people are willing to invest or spend only 1.54 seconds of time to make that determination.

If that headline doesn't convince the reader—in those 1.54 seconds—that there is a significant WIIFM and convey that value, then the reader is likely to move on to another ad or another page. Think about it. Isn't that true for you? If you are reading ads or flipping pages in a magazine, do you spend any longer than a second or two before either stopping to read more or turning the page? How about when you listen to an ad on the radio or are watching television? Does 1.54 seconds sound about right? What about when you are scanning down a list of Google Search results? Is 1.54 seconds still accurate? This emphasizes the great importance of that opening sentence—whether it's on television, radio, magazine, newspaper, search results, web page, or your e-mail message.

In a newspaper, it's called the headline; on your website, it's the header; and in your e-mail, it's the subject line. Your subject line has to convince your customer in roughly 1.5 seconds whether he should move on to the next stage of time investment. This is why the subject line is so important, and why segmenting is important, as discussed in the next section.

Only if you experience success in the first part of this transaction or value proposition of the WIIFM can you go to the next critical step—reading the newspaper ads. If a headline catches your eye and you subconsciously agree to spend or invest again in this next part of this transaction, how much time do you now give the ad before you determine whether to continue or turn the page? The answer is now five seconds. And while that may sound like a lot, by comparison, five seconds isn't much time to convey a second-level WIIFM. In fact, it's only about enough time to read one sentence.

The second part of this transaction in e-mail marketing is the opening line of your message. Within the first second of reading, your message has to convey a strong enough WIIFM message to keep your customer engaged—and has to do so in five seconds or less. If you are successful in these first two parts of the WIIFM transaction, your customer will continue to read your message to fully understand your value proposition and convert to purchasing your product.

The third step is conversion. If you have successfully convinced your customer that there really is something in it for them, then she will follow your e-mail message's call to action. In most cases, an e-mail's primary goal is to convert that message to a click-through to a web page. You might also define your conversion as a pass-along, a sign-up, picking up the phone, or just simply informing your customer. And your e-mail message is *always* about maintaining or building your trusted network by providing a WIIFM. Even if the definition of conversion for your message is only to inform, be sure that the value of that information is at least equal to the time your customer will need to spend to get it.

Segment to Maximize Conversion

By now, you should understand the importance of the 1.54-second and 5-second rules. The underlying message is that there isn't much time to hook your customers and show them your value proposition. So to help with this important step, the experts do something called *segmenting*.

Segmenting is no more than splitting your overall e-mail list into segments and testing the success of each of your e-mail components with your clients. One approach is to divide your total list into equal segments; you can also just pull a random sample from your list to test your message.

Splitting the total group into equal segments allows you to test your entire group in a more homogenous random sampling. Consider the following scenario. Suppose you have a total mailing list of 5,000 customers, a group that you split into five equal 1,000-e-mail segments. For each segment, you are going to craft five different subject lines. The word *craft* is important, because you will want to spend time and effort designing these subject lines and paying close attention to the nouns, verbs, and adjectives you use. Take your time. Create these five subject lines deliberately.

Now, send out your e-mail to all five segments. The important concept is to keep the rest of the entire e-mail the same. Make no other changes. By keeping all of the other e-mail message components identical, you are testing the effectiveness of only the five different subject lines. Give the e-mail a week or more, depending upon how your customers have reacted historically to your e-mails, and then look at the metrics. If the third subject line showed a significant rise in conversion, then look at what you did there and do it again. Look at which one of the subject lines converted the most poorly and stop doing that. It's that simple.

Your next e-mail should test your opening sentences while you keep the subject line consistent. Wait an appropriate amount of time, and then look at your statistics. The next steps are to segment and test your call to action and your use of images. You would be surprised to see that a stock photo of a man instead of a woman—or vice versa—can often make as much as a 20 percent increase in your e-mail conversion rates.

If you follow these steps over a roughly six-month time frame, you will have tested and perfected your e-mail message WIIFMs, subject lines, opening sentences, calls to action, images, layout, color schemes, and even HTML versus text. You will be able to determine that your e-mail campaigns can have as high as a 30 percent conversion rate. How's that compared to a 0.1 percent conversion rate for conventional direct mail? And all the while, you are building and reinforcing your trusted network.

Day Parting Will Get It Read

Another important component of e-mail marketing is a practice known as *day parting*. Most people have no idea of what that means, so if you don't either, don't feel bad.

The following example of day parting is one with which everybody is familiar. There is a time of day that is reserved for one particular type of television show on all the major networks. The time is Monday through Friday from 1:00 PM until 3:00 PM. What is it?

If you said "soap operas," then you answered correctly. Why are they called *soap operas*? You never see much soap (unless it's used during the gratuitous showering of a sexy star), and no one ever sings opera. These shows aren't really called soap operas by the TV networks; they are called daytime dramas. How did these shows come to be known by this name?

You're right: laundry soap. For nearly a half century, stay-at-home moms—and now dads—have been watching these shows. So what's the importance of 1:00 PM to 3:00 PM? That's when little Johnny and little Sally lie down for their naps—the first time during the workday that the stay-at-home parent can take an eye off the little darling to actually get some work done. And if you have ever had a child of your own, you quickly realize that laundry is a daily chore.

Can you think of any other hourly day parting on television—such as for news, prime time, and late night? Radio even has drive time, which is, of course, the time when the majority of listeners are traveling to and from work. These two time periods are traditionally from 6:00 AM to 10:00 AM and 3:00 PM to 7:00 PM, Monday through Friday, and represent the stations' highest listenership. Commercials cost significantly more during drive time.

Every media uses day parting for maximum marketing effect. Newspapers do it. What's Wednesday? Coupons and cooking (to sell more coupon products). This gives the reader Wednesday evening and Thursday to cut them out for Friday's shopping (most people get paid on Fridays, and therefore do their shopping that day). What about Thursday? Out on the town! Friday is too late to make plans, and Wednesday is too early. How

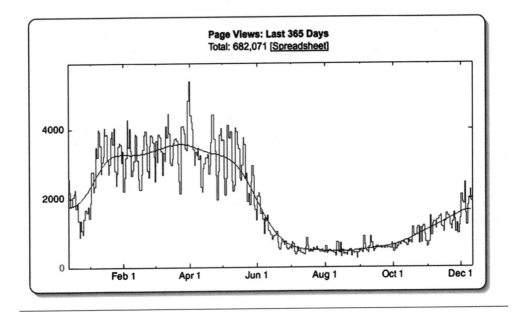

FIGURE 3.6 Seasonality

about Saturday? Real estate and home repair. Sunday? Ads, ads, ads! This is the day during which the reader has the most time to read the advertising and to shop.

How about monthly day parting? Do you or your customers have more money in the beginning of the month or at the end? And what if you take day parting to the yearly interval, often called *seasonality*. Every company has seasonality. What do you think the slow time of year is for a construction company? It happens to be the same as the peak season for ski resorts.

Understanding your customers' psychology, day parting, and season-ality will dramatically increase your conversion rate. Let's look at when you send your e-mails. Is it at night? Over the weekend? What are your customers doing when your e-mail arrives? When does the highest amount of Internet (e-mail) traffic occur? It's Monday through Friday, 8:00 AM until 5:00 PM, then 8:30 PM until midnight, and all day Saturday and Sunday. No surprise there, right?

If you sent your e-mail at night, your customer is most likely to receive it first thing in the morning. Is this good? Isn't this the time the mailbox is filled from the night before with spam? Isn't this the time she just came into work and is getting yelled at by six different people, preparing for meetings, and running around? How careful do you think your customer will be in determining whether she hits the delete button on your e-mail? Wouldn't around, say, 11:00 AM be better? Wouldn't she have had time to go to those early-morning meetings and deleted all of her spam and other unwanted e-mails by then?

How about that weekend send-off? Is first thing on Monday morn-ing really the best time for your customers to get your value proposition that they will use just 1.54 seconds or less to determine if they will read or delete?

Statistically speaking, Tuesday through Thursday from 11:00 AM until 3:00 PM is the best time to send your message, although it might be differ-ent for your particular customer. You need to test it. Now that you know about segmenting, try dividing and sending your e-mail message at differ-ent times of the day and different days of the week. See which one works best—and keep doing that!

A conference attendee once asked, "What if I sold canoes? What would be the best time to send an e-mail for that?" The answer for that year was, "Thursday, March 21, at 9:00 PM." Why, you ask?

If you are selling canoes, you most likely have people's home e-mail addresses, as some companies are getting cranky about using the Internet at work for personal business. Customers for recreational items are often in front of their computers on a weeknight at around 8:30 PM. Allow 30 minutes to clean out their junk e-mails and have an empty inbox. So around 9:00 PM the canoe e-mail will arrive, and they will have plenty of time to look at it—and not simply dispose of it.

Thursday is the best day of the week, because a customer who is looking for a canoe is probably younger and possibly fit—and is therefore likely to be out of the house instead of in front of the computer on a Friday night. But the e-mail should arrive as close to the weekend as possible, so that the customer remembers to buy it on Saturday morning.

Considering seasonality, an e-mail for camping and other outdoor products should go out near the end of March. That's when people are thinking about spring and summer activities. In the fall, their thoughts go to, "Oh, man, how am I going to store all this stuff over the winter?"

See how a few rules and a little common sense can make e-mail marketing fun, challenging, and most important, rewarding? And by the way—it's almost completely free.

The ROI of Social Media

Atkins Taps Powered to Cultivate Brand Activists through Its Branded Online Community

Background

Up until the beginning of 2008, Atkins had supplied a simple forum solution that allowed some interaction between Atkins loyalists, but engagement was low. Without the brand truly engaging with the community, users were left with unanswered questions and would actually find other places on the web to commune.

Strategy

Because users were not engaged directly with Atkins on the web, the company teamed with Powered, Inc. to launch an ambitious strategy to provide an open community for free (all of their competitors charged for online community access at the time) with expert content, including a blog by Atkins's vice president of nutrition.

As part of this strategy, Powered was tasked with building an online community that would activate Atkins users to the point that they become evangelists for the brand. Here are the first strategic steps that are considered the community's foundation:

- Audience acquisition and opt-in to the Atkins.com database
- Engagement to drive consideration of Atkins products
- Drive brand loyalty and retention
- Replace the Atkins.com message boards with a full-community solution

Implementation

Atkins and Powered started out by targeting current opt-ins to the Atkins newsletter and prospects who had indicated that they were interested in learning more about Atkins and how to get started with the nutritional plan. The developed online community features were built out in addition to the existing forums and provided the following engagement outlets:

- Community where visitors access advice, tools, resources, and support from other members
- Places for members to rate or review Atkins products, chart progress, and interact with a licensed nutritionist
- Professional, easy-to-navigate content, including courses, notebooks, checklists, and videos
- Encourage "Atkins Advocates" to reach out to new members and answer questions

Opportunity

The community has allowed members to come together to get advice from peers and Atkins nutritionists, share stories, and learn about the company's approach to weight loss and weight management. Community members have quickly learned that Atkins is committed to helping people succeed in their weight loss goals. As a result, Powered and Atkins have created a venue for loyalists to be supported and turned into advocates, driving acquisition, retention, and real-time consideration of Atkins products.

Conclusion

The impact of this richer community sent the number of registered members skyrocketing, and engagement with the brand by other users has also been impressive. Here are initial stats coming out of the 2008 launch:

- Over half a million registered members to date
- 78 percent increase in community registrations versus message boards
- 70 percent increase in total posts to the message boards and forums

(continued)

(*continued*)

Atkins is now using Facebook (www.facebook.com/atkinsdiet)

and Twitter (http://Twitter.com/atkinsinsider)

as touch points to direct users to its community. Engaging with users through popular social media outlets is important, but these outlets can also be used as additional touch points and gateways to attract customers to the next level of engagement: a branded home community with the goal of creating relationships in which customers become an extension and voice of authority for a brand. This approach has yielded impressive growth results and has continued to strengthen relationships between Atkins and its community members:

- Since the launch, registrations for the first year of the community quadrupled by over 400 percent when compared to the same period the year before.
- Registrations for the community increased by 97 percent.

—Aaron Strout, CMO Powered, Inc. http://community.atkins.com

Expert Insight

Eric Groves, Senior Vice President, Worldwide Strategy and Market Development, www.ConstantContact.com

Eric Groves

We challenge our customers to be writing content that is so valuable that those who receive them will set up a folder in their e-mail box just for that company. When they provide content that is so valuable that customers want to hold on to it, then they have really changed and revolutionized the way e-mail marketing is used by businesses. It's no longer just a, "I'm going to blast it out and try to drive immediate business." It's all about asking, "How do I send out a communication that builds my reputation with my customers so that they want to come back?"

And everybody's getting so much e-mail these days that it's important to rise above . . . sort of . . . the chaff and everything that's out there. The way to do that is to write really good content, and to demonstrate your knowledge. And, let's face it: small business owners go into business because they are experts. Sharing the expertise that they have with their customers turns out to be one of the most powerful ways that you can actually market your business.

For example, if you ask a business owner, "What are the three most frequently asked questions that your customers ask you?" and they write them down and then I say, "Okay, that's content!" "Oh, okay, I can do that."

And that the funny thing is that somebody asks you an interesting question, and you write it down and you use it in your newsletter, and you give them attribution and say, "Hey, Joey, my new customer tried to stump me with this one, and here's the answer to the question that he had. And, oh, by the way, if you want to try and stump me, submit your questions to me at this e-mail address."

Now all of a sudden you've got your readers, who are not only invested in reading your campaign, but also in giving you content ideas. So there're all kinds of great ways to come up with content that's actually engaging and fun. . . .

And if you think about why people turn to a small business owner, it's because they have a relationship with them and they trust them. Trust, in any relationship, is built over time by sharing of valuable information; and that's all you're doing. I mean, if you were a restaurateur, it could be as simple as sharing a couple of your recipes. . . .

(continued)

(continued)

On Spam

Well, the Can-the-Spam Act was enacted to really provide some peace to the folks in law enforcement to go after people who are sending fraudulent e-mail. And it does put forth a number of things that people who are sending e-mail legitimately need to be aware of.

A couple of those things are that you cannot falsify your sending address or use a bogus e-mail address to send from. And that's one of the reasons why, when you use Constant Contact, you have to verify the sending e-mail address you're sending from—just to make sure that you're in compliance of that.

Several other things that you have to do are to have your physical address embedded in the actual body of the message. And that's one other thing that we basically put on there for you. One of the other pieces is that you have to provide your recipient with the ability to unsubscribe. We have a tool called "Safe Unsubscribe" where with one click someone can remove themselves from the list.

Now, you have 10 days by law to remove these names from your list, but if you are using Constant Contact, you don't even have to worry about that. We take care of that for you. There are a couple other provisions within the Can-the-Spam Act, but those are the big ones.

On Granting Permission

Well, first of all, there are a couple of things you should know about permission. It certainly is perishable. If I say I would like to join your mailing list and I do not hear from you for six months, I'm going to forget that I gave you permission to join your list to mail to me. So it's really important that if you are going to be doing e-mail marketing, you are building a list of your customers that you do communicate with, at least on a quarterly basis.

To listen to or read the entire Executive Conversation with Eric Groves, go to www.theSocialMediaBible.com.

To-Do List

- Do not spam.

  You don't need to. As long as you're honest and understand the CAN-SPAM Act, you're good! If you are using your e-mail list to build and maintain your trusted network and your trusted community, then give them reason to trust you. Ask yourself this question: Are you informing your network that you really do have an offer that would benefit them if only they were aware of it? If the answer is yes, then send it.

- Provide a significant WIIFM.

  You always need to keep in mind that whether it's paper, electronic, e-mail, or website text, or a brochure or cover letter, you have to convey a strong WIIFM to prove to your customer that there is a good rate of return on your value proposition.

- Remember the 1.54-second and 5.0-second rules.

  Remember, you only have 1.54 seconds to hook your customers and convince them in the subject line that they should invest their time and effort in reading and comprehending your proposition. Remember, also, that even if you persuade your prospect to keep reading, you only have 5.0 seconds in the first sentence to get them to read the rest and not hit the delete button. Your messages have to be clear, concise, and understandable in these two allotted time frames.

- Segment to maximize conversion.

  This is really about testing. You have to test your WIIFM, your 1.54, your 5.0, your images, and your layout to see what works for your customers and what doesn't. It's about understanding how your trusted network thinks, and figuring out what motivates them. Segmenting is about trial and error with a short cycle to find answers that only a few years ago marketers spent millions of their clients' dollars and years to understand.

- Remember that day parting will get it read.

  By understanding how your customer thinks, and what he is doing during the course of his day, week, month, and year, you can send very effective e-mails. Appreciating your customer's larger monthly and annual cycles allows you to better allocate your e-mail and search engine marketing budgets. Day parting means getting your message to your customers when the timing is most right for them to receive it.

Conclusion

So what does e-mail marketing have to do with social media? *Everything.* E-mail was the original social media. Before there was Facebook, Twitter, Flickr, YouTube, and all the other sites, people shared content with each other by sending it in e-mail messages. And in many cases, they still do.

Also, social media is about two-way communication between you and your customers. If you aren't communicating effectively—or at all because a spam filter is stopping your e-mail—then you're not marketing. Social media requires you to build trust in your network, listen to what your customers have to say, and provide value and a strong WIIFM. That's the same with e-mail.

The more you understand the most effective way to communicate through e-mail, the stronger your relationships will be with your customers. Remember, any time you send an e-mail to your customer and she doesn't opt out, she decides to remain part of your network. If you can consistently provide value in the form of knowledge, information, resources, discounts, leads, examples, white papers, or even entertainment, your customers will continue to correspond with you. And like any relationship, the more they agree to converse with you, the stronger the relationship becomes. Remember the old adage, "The best compliment a customer can give you is a referral." Customers who trust you and buy from you will recommend that others do the same.

To hear all of the Expert Interviews, go to www.theSocialMediaBible .com.

Downloads

For your free downloads associated with *The Social Media Bible,* go to www .theSocialMediaBible.com,

select Downloads, and enter your ISBN number located on the back of the book above the bar code. Be sure to enter the dashes.

Credits

The ROI of Social Media was provided by:

Aaron Strout, CMO Powered, Inc., http://community.atkins.com

Expert Insight was provided by:

Eric Groves, senior vice president, worldwide strategy and market development, Constant Contact, www.ConstantContact.com

Technical edits were provided by:

Rosalind Morville, www.ConstantContact.com

Notes

1. The Send Message (SNDMSG) command was one instruction and function of Ray Tomlinson's mail program that was first used in 1971 for TENEX. Another component was READMAIL. SNDMSG was used to send electronic mail from one user to another.

2. ADV is a label that tells the recipient that an e-mail is an unsolicited *advertisement*.

3. A blacklist, or blocklist, is a list of IP addresses or series of IP addresses that Internet service providers (ISPs) create to block or to prevent the sender of e-mail messages from a server that is suspected of transmitting spam. The term *blacklist* dates to 1619 and refers to a list of persons who are disapproved of or are to be punished or boycotted. More information regarding the CAN-SPAM Act is available at http://business.ftc .gov/documents/bus61-can-spam-act-compliance-guide-business.

CHAPTER 4

The World of Web Pages

www.LonSafko.com/TSMB3_Videos/04WebPages.mov

What's in It for You?

According to Internet World Stats Miniwatts Marketing Group, there are an estimated 1,802,330,457 Internet users worldwide. This number breaks down as follows: Asia: 764,435,900; Europe: 425,773,571; North America: 259,561,000; Latin America/Caribbean: 186,922,050; Africa: 86,217,900; Middle East: 58,309,546; and Oceanic Australia: 21,110,490. These numbers show the staggering number of people who are participating in the World Wide Web.

Websites (measured by domain name) have been growing at a rate of 22 million per month, each with an average of 239 pages per site, totaling 526 million websites by November 2011. Even though no one knows for sure, or can even accurately guess, there were an estimated 126 trillion web pages as of 2011 (see Figure 4.1).

The sheer magnitude of these numbers is the force that drives e-commerce, while also making competition difficult. If you have some basic understanding of how web pages work, then you have the ability to outsell your competition—and thereby realize revenues and ROI that cannot be attained offline.

theSocialMediaBible.com

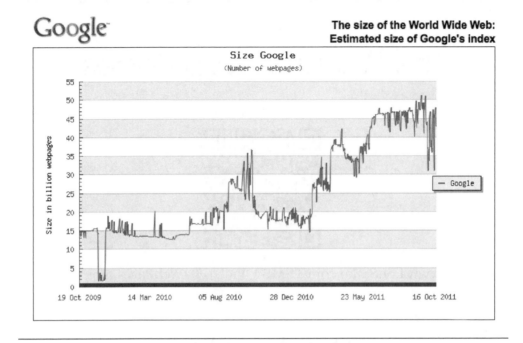

FIGURE 4.1   Total Sites across All Domains, October 2009 through October 2011

Source: www.netcraft.com.

Like any other process, once you realize some of the tactics, tools, and strategies, it's easier than you think to create highly visible, sticky web pages with a high conversion rate. *Sticky* refers to a web page that someone is willing to stay at for a higher-than-average amount of time before clicking the Back or Close buttons. The tactics are easy to understand, the tools are easy to use, and the strategies are easy to implement. But before discussing these tools and strategies, consider a brief history of the web.

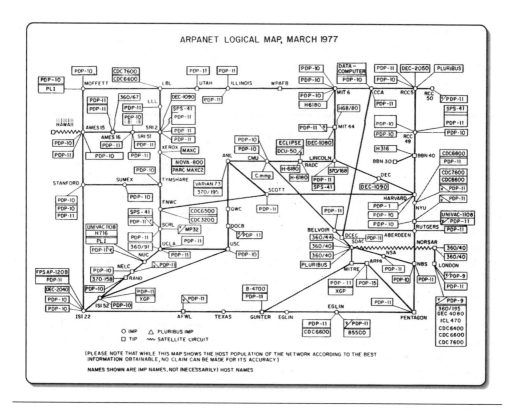

FIGURE 4.2 ARPAnet

Back to the Beginning

The very first website, web page, and web server debuted in the latter part of 1990. During March 1989, while working at the European Organization for Nuclear Research (CERN) in Geneva, Switzerland, physicist Sir Timothy John "Tim" Berners-Lee wrote a proposal blueprinting how computers could be connected to easily share information around the world by means of the Internet and the use of HTTP—or Hypertext Transfer Protocol, based on Vannevar Bush's work in 1945 and TCP/IP, Transmission Control Protocol/ Internet Protocol (previously created by Vint Cerf). Both HTTP and TCP/ IP are the systems used today to navigate across websites and web pages.

Robert Cailliau[1] became the staunchest supporter of connecting the Internet, HTTP, TCP/IP, and personal computers by means of creating the largest single information network on the planet. His goal was to help physicists share all of the information stored on each individual computer at the CERN laboratory, and hypertext would allow each user the opportunity to easily browse text on web pages using the HTTP links. The first examples of this were developed on Steve Jobs's NeXT personal computers.

NeXT Computer

After leaving Apple Computer in 1985, Steve Jobs went on to form a company that he called NeXT Computers—with products that were designed with all the bells and whistles available for computers at the time. This first prototype computer workstation was released in 1988, and had been developed specifically with the college student in mind (most likely due to Apple's early success in education—particularly in higher education). It was tested in 1989, after which NeXT started selling beta to universities. Jobs believed that if he could hook college students on his NeXT Computer during their college years, then they would want a similar model upon entering the workplace—and he would thereby be able to slowly push IBM and Windows out of the business market. However, the excessive amount of add-ons that were bundled with the base model at that time drove the price far too high ($6,500) for college students who didn't have that much extra cash on hand to afford one. Jobs sold NeXT to Apple in 1996 and he was soon back in the saddle again. Much of the current Mac OS X is based on the NeXTSTEP operating system.

Berners-Lee developed a browser-editor with the intent of creating a tool that would allow its users to build spaces to share information. The world's first URL address, website, and web server was info.cern.ch.

Many names were considered for this newly created sharing tool, and the creators settled upon the *World Wide Web,* or WWW. Cailliau became the first person to ever surf the web (*surf* having been derived from *Cerf*—a nod to co-creator Vinton Cerf's contributions).

The world's very first web address was info.cern.ch/hypertext/WWW/TheProject.html.

This page was set up to explain how this new Internet worked, what hypertext was, how to search the Internet, and even included technical data on how to create web pages.

To make their new web work, the team needed to create browser software that could run on the then-popular DOS-based IBM, Compaq, and Tandy computers, which paled in comparison to the sophisticated NeXT Computer. The team began testing the DOS-style browser to work with any personal computer or terminal. To operate on DOS, they needed the browser to eliminate all graphics and the mouse in exchange for just plain text, because Microsoft's DOS (Disk Operating System) could not recognize a graphic interface or the functions of a mouse.

By the end of 1991, web servers began popping up in other institutions throughout Europe. The first web server in the United States was at the Stanford Linear Accelerator Center (SLAC). Within one year of the web's inception, there were a total of 26 servers worldwide. By the following year, the number had grown to more than 200.

By 1993, users were able to access the web through Mosaic, a program released by the National Center for Supercomputing Applications (NCSA) at the University of Illinois at Urbana-Champaign. Within just two years, the Internet went mainstream with dial-up connections to companies like CompuServe and America Online (AOL). And now, with an estimated 1,802,330,457 Internet users surfing 206,675,938 websites containing more than 29,700,000,000 (est.) web pages, the World Wide Web has come a long way.

What You Need to Know

To understand how and why a web page is effective, it is important to first discuss a few basic marketing and psychological concepts. Although

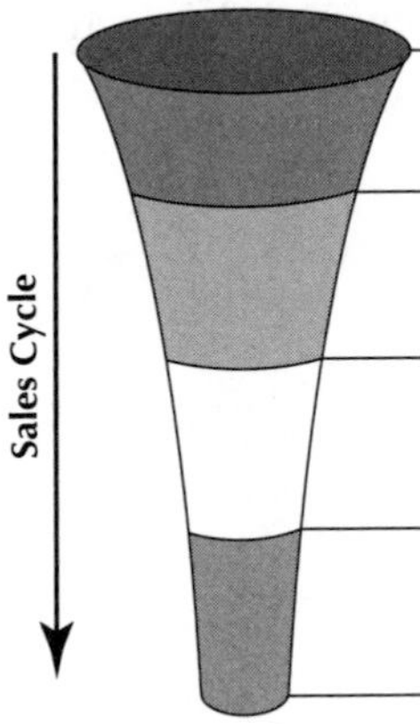

	Frame Of Mind	Goal	Conversion	Example
	Awareness	Build Brand Awareness	Very Low	Insurance
	Search	Frame Buying Decisions	Low	Car Insurance
	Research	Directly Compete	Moderate	Car Insurance Quote
	Purchase	Convert To Sales	High	New York Car Insurance Quote

FIGURE 4.3   Sales Funnel

The Social Media Bible is not intended to replace a book such as *Marketing For Dummies,* some fundamental understanding of the psychology of a sale is necessary to fully understand how to develop an effective web page. The first concept to discuss is called the *sales,* or *buying, funnel* (see Figure 4.3).

The sales funnel is a metaphor that marketers use to imagine what prospects and customers are thinking as they move through their sales cycle—from the moment they realize they need your product or service to the time that they actually purchase it. This cycle is especially critical with web pages, because it doesn't simply dictate the design of your home page. It requires that you have a web page designed specifically to accept and address the types of questions that your prospects have at any given moment during the buying cycle.

The stages that your prospects move through in their sales funnel are awareness, search, research, and buy. Let's take a look at these steps, using the example of an auto insurance salesperson in Phoenix, Arizona.

Awareness

Your (potential) client realizes that she is in need of car insurance. She begins to consider how she might get more information about auto insurance in her area, what she might ask about it, and what to type in the search engines to start her search.

Search

Your client will then begin to search the web, looking for information on car insurance. She's conducting a very general search at this point, since she doesn't yet know what companies offer it or even what type she is looking for. Her search would likely include only terms like "auto insurance" or "car insurance." Her frame of mind, however, is less general than it was during the awareness stage, as she has already begun to think about what she is looking for by choosing her key search terms.

Research

Once your client gets the chance to poke around and identify the companies that provide auto insurance, she then may drill down to searching with a term like "auto insurance quotes." Your prospect is now more knowledgeable, and her searches are much less general.

Buy

The last part of this cycle is the point at which your prospect is ready to purchase. She knows what company she wants to go with, she knows the type of policy she is looking for, and her search becomes significantly different. Now she is searching for "Travelers auto insurance quote Phoenix." Makes sense, doesn't it? Don't all online consumers go through this process at one time or another—whether they're looking for insurance, shoes, or vacations?

The length of this particular buying cycle could last anywhere from one night to a year or more. If the buyer's insurance policy isn't due to be renewed until next year, then the client might begin looking now, wait to learn more details when she pays her next premium, and not complete her final research until the policy is due for renewal.

Now, let's put ourselves in the mind-set of the prospect. If you were in the search mode—looking only at this point for companies that provided auto insurance—and were taken to a page for Allstate where you were asked to enter your personal information for a quote and a phone call from a salesperson—what would you do? You would probably leave that page, because the information provided therein wasn't appropriate for what you desired during your search mode of the cycle.

What if, on the other hand, the prospect was you, and you had completed all of the research necessary to choose an insurance company? You knew the type of policy you wanted, you studied the deductible, and you're ready to purchase. You search, you click, and you're taken to a specific insurance company's home page. Four clicks later, you still didn't find a place to get a quote; so what do you do? *You close the page.*

All that work the company did creating their site—optimizing their home page, paying for the pay-per-click just to get you there—and you leave. An ideal web page delivers the specific information your prospect is looking at during the appropriate time in her personal sales cycle. The lesson here: It's not about your home page; it's about everything that comes after.

Your Home Page Is Causing You Harm

People often judge a book by its cover. See: A Stanford study[2] involving 4,500 people over three years focused on how users determine the credibility of a website. The research isn't new, but savvy consumers today are spending less time evaluating a website than ever before.

Based on this research, here are some ideas you can use that still stand true:

> Show you're real—a real organization, with real people, offering real benefits:
>
> - Anyone can have a website. While it's great that a small company's website can appear alongside a big corporation's, this also pairs your legitimate company with less-than-reliable websites that may not represent a real company at all. A website doesn't provide any guarantee of an actual building, employees, or business experience. To single yourself out as a credible source, list your physical address prominently and include a picture of your office or feature memberships with local business organizations.
>
> Explain why the real people at your real company should be trusted:
>
> - Provide your credentials for visitors; this information can come in the form of business recognitions or awards, staff bios with experience listed, or testimonials from current clients.
>
> Make it painfully easy for visitors to contact you:
>
> - In addition to signaling that you're a real company, this tactic will help you get the leads you're looking for from your site. Give visitors several ways to contact you, so they can choose their preference—physical address, e-mail address, and phone number. If your company is larger, with several contacts, consider giving specific contacts for specific inquiries.

Include this information throughout your site, not just in tiny text at the bottom of your pages or on a contact page.

Signal you're still there—often:

- Be sure to keep your site up to date. If you're not watching your site, why should anyone else be? Regular updates show your business is active and responsive. And, updates can help your search engine rankings.

And, possibly most important—an unbiased opinion, of course . . .

Create a captivating, appropriate visual site design:

- One of the main ideas this research found was that people quickly evaluate a site on visual design alone. Layout, content, and images, as well as a design that matches your company's purpose, were all main factors used to evaluate the credibility of a design.

Most people, however, erroneously believe that the home page is everything. They operate under the assumption that it's the only page that needs to be optimized and advertised, and the only place to which traffic should be driven. This is a misconception. Driving your prospects to your home page is causing you more harm than anything else you could be doing on the web. Your home page is merely the cover of your book; it does not provide any of the information that your prospects are looking for.

Let's say a fellow worker who has read this book is holding it in her hand, and you ask her, "Where can I find the information in there about why home pages are bad?" Suppose that she responds by doing nothing but placing the book on the table in front of you, and pointing to the cover. How would you feel? Surprised? Confused? Angry? Wouldn't you expect her to open the book, find the chapter, turn to the page, and point to the paragraph? Well, that is akin to what your customers expect when they're looking for information on your website. Don't simply point your prospects and customers to the cover. Your home page is meant for branding, because when you're advertising—whether online or off, and when all else fails—you still always need brand recognition.

You need to develop a plan that addresses your prospects' mind-sets, and unearths what they are searching for through each step of their buying cycle. Each of the pages is easy to create, and must be simple to understand. The awareness page could very well be your home page. If you have more than one product, however, you might need a top-level page that must be generic and have general terminology along with high-level information.

The search page needs to be a little more specific, and perhaps mention all of your products with a description and some what's-in-it-for-me for each. Your research page needs to describe the distinct qualities of your products or services, so that your prospects can compare the value of your offering against all of your competitors. And the last page—the buy page—needs to only give your prospects the opportunity to review their order and, of course, to buy. Capture them when they are ready.

Designing a web page is unlike any other type of advertising you can do. Your website captures your prospects and customers at the very moment in time when they actually desire that specific information. No other advertising can accomplish this. Another key difference is that your prospects are always asking for your specific help on a specific topic on a web page, and they are doing so voluntarily.

Your customers will engage with plenty of advertising involuntarily. For example, how do you feel when you open your mailbox and find it filled with junk, catalogs, and coupons? What is your reaction when telemarketers call you during dinner? Or survey people come up to you in the mall? Are you offended? Has your privacy been invaded? Are you annoyed? Now, compare that to how you feel when you seek out someone's advice on a question—and they are immediately happy to help you. Web pages provide the same kind of gratification—*if* you design them right.

Comparing web page design to direct mail advertising, a web page would be like a psychic mailman. The keywords that your prospect uses—based on where he is in the buying cycle—are like very precise mailing lists. The search engine result wording is like an envelope, and the exact web page you take your prospect to is the material inside. The web page contents have been designed specifically for what that prospect is looking for, and is delivered at the exact moment he asks for it. A well-designed array of web pages can convert your prospects into your customers.

This concept also applies directly and powerfully to your blog page, the photographs you share, video uploads, and podcasts as well. Be sure to have something for everyone at every stage or frame of mind.

There is one additional stage in this sales cycle funnel: post-sale. Your prospects may actually be in the post-sale stage of the customer life cycle and are seeking support, engaging in loyalty, participating in your blog, uploading videos about your product, and engaging in other related activities. Be sure that you have a mechanism to capture and retain your hard-earned customers, so that they will come back and, most important, refer their trusted network to you to become new customers. (Be sure to read the chapter on blogs, as this is the most effective way to keep your customers—and your company—in the loop.)

To broaden the appeal of your web pages, consider that your target audience's efforts may extend beyond the obvious. You need to consider your prospects, customers, resellers, distributors, the press, industry analysts, investors, and even employees who may use your website as a resource or selling tool. Consider the needs and behaviors of all your important constituents. You may need to have specific web pages designed for each of them as they travel through their own sale (or thought) cycle.

Design Elements to Consider

The most basic concept to keep in mind when designing a web page is that this is where people tend to look *first* for information about your company or organization. Such design has essentially become a science. The *New York Times,* as well as many other major newspapers, are broken down into left and right pages, each of which contains six sections. The *Times* understands their customers' behavior so well that every story in their entire paper is specifically placed based on priority. The page split is designed to place important information where the eye looks first, and also takes into account how the newspaper will be folded by the reader when reading it on a train or other confined area.

(A great article about "NYC; How to Hold, How to Fold: A Lost Art" can be found at http://people.dsv.su.se/~jpalme/layout/.)

Madison Avenue advertisers never sleep (not a surprise, since Madison Avenue is in New York!). In their Landing Page Eyetracking Study (Figure 4.4), these advertisers showed that when bouncing low-wattage laser beams off the retinas of volunteers, people tend to look first at the *top left* of the page, time and time again. This comes as no surprise; after all, children are told to start at the top of the page on the left side. What does this say for web design? Put your most important message, image, or logo on the top left.

FIGURE 4.4 Eyetracking Study

Source: Go to www.theSocialMediaBible.com.

To read the full Marketing Sherpa report, go to:
http://www.marketingsherpa.com/exs/SMBGExcerpt_07.pdf

This study also showed that retailers that made their landing web page easy to read, provided a strong what's-in-it-for-me, and favored the top left section of the web page increased their conversion rate by as much as 64 percent.

Next, keep your message above the fold. While this term originated with newspapers, it refers to keeping your key message in the top window pane of your browsers; and don't expect your visitor to scroll down to find additional inspiration to stay on your page and hopefully convert. Keep in mind computer screen size. Your above-the-fold may not be the same as that of your prospects.

Psychological Marketing

Another effective tool in marketing on the Internet is psychological marketing, which requires that you go way beyond the traditional techniques of studying the demographics of your customers and try to get into their heads. You need to ask yourself, "What are they thinking when they reach my web page? What are they doing *right now?* Which adjective should I use to describe my product on this page? Which words will cause more conversions?"

As this isn't a psychology or marketing book, there is no room here to discuss this subject at length. However, if you go to www.theSocial MediaBible.com, you can use your password to download the "Psychological Hot Buttons" document (yours free as the owner of this book).

It's All about Conversion

What are you planning to do with all of the traffic you get to come to each of your specific web pages? Don't let any of it go to waste. You've worked hard to get every eye. The most important design element you can consider is your conversion message. Now that you have your prospects' attention, what do you want them to do next? You want them to convert. (And no, even though this is called *The Social Media Bible,* the word *conversion* does not refer to religion.)

The term *conversion* actually has a lot of different definitions in the context of web design. In fact, every different page you design—based on the preceding rules—carries a different meaning of conversion. The most common and easiest to understand of these is "Click Here to Purchase." There are many others. Wikipedia defines *conversion* as: "In marketing, a conversion occurs when a prospective customer takes the marketer's intended action. If the prospect has visited a marketer's website, the conversion action might be making an online purchase, or submitting a form to request additional information. The conversion rate is the percentage of visitors who take the conversion action."

If you have a pair of eyes on your home page, conversion means, "Read my message and click to another page." If your site visitor clicks to the next page that contains more detailed information and assists him through his sales funnel, you have a successful conversion. If you have someone land on a page that asks her to join your network and she signs up, you have a successful conversion. If either of them is asked to "pass this along to a friend" (referral) and they do, then your web page and call to action were effective and successful.

Accurately targeted traffic results in conversions—whether they are sales leads, large numbers of page views (visitors looking at pages), longer time on page or site (minutes spent interacting and reading: stickiness), brand awareness (because of immersion in the site and your marketing message), offline contact (consumers often change to offline contact through store visits or telephone calls), and pass-alongs (tell-a-friend referrals). Before you design the content of a web page, you must first consider its definition of conversion.

The most effective way to get someone to convert is to have a strong "What's In It for Me?" (WIIFM). Chapter 4, It's Not Your Father's E-Mail, went into detail on WIIFM. The first WIIFM's 1.54-second rule and the second with its 5-second rule will make the difference between your prospect converting and leaving. Be sure you've read and comprehend the section on the importance of selecting the right image to help convey that WIIFM message.

Each page should have only one definition of conversion stated by your WIIFM message. Once your prospects have found your page, you need to provide them with the exact information they are looking for and capture them with a strong WIIFM message that conveys that conversion. This is why a home page is harmful and ineffective: It has many conversions—probably every conversion your site has to offer. It's therefore somewhat confusing to your prospects. Refer to early comments about home pages.

Since Part I of this book is about tactics more than strategies (which are described in Part II), this section doesn't spend a lot of time on metrics.

However, whatever your definition of conversion is for each page, be sure to design the page in a way that allows you to measure it. If you don't gauge your conversions, then you can't manage them. If you don't set up Google Analytics or another way to assess your website's traffic, then you won't know if all of your hard work was successful. Determining what to measure is easy: How many visitors came to that page, how many converted (clicked through), and how many left.

If more people left your site than converted to the next step, then your conversion message was too weak, or it did not provide the call to action that your visitor was expecting. You need to constantly adjust and fine-tune your conversion message; test, measure, refine. Lather, rinse, repeat.

Here are a few other sample metrics to consider when quantifying your conversions:

- I want to increase the *number of orders* by 30 percent within one year.
- I want to increase the *click-throughs* on my page by 50 percent by next quarter.
- I want 25 percent more *visitors* who will look at *six pages* before leaving.
- I want the press to pick up our great *success stories*, resulting in *four trade articles* this year.
- I want to *reduce* the amount of tech *telephone support by 20 percent* this year by shifting it to *online support forums* (YouTube how-to videos, tech support podcasts, and company blogs).

Some metrics will be difficult, and some even impossible to measure. There still is a great deal of benefit to gain from your efforts, however. An immediate order (e-commerce) is easy to track, but a lagged order (whereby your prospect comes back later to purchase) drives prospects to a retail store (which applies to both business-to-business and business-to-consumer) or converts to a telephone order (Dell Computer has 5,000 separate 800 numbers for tracking). These are called *blended success metrics,* and one way to measure these is by incorporating extras like coupons, unique and trackable special offers, cashier questions, unique telephone numbers or extensions, promo codes, and unique URLs.

B2B Success Metrics

Business-to-business (B2B) marketers have an even more challenging time measuring their metrics. Consider tracking data like immediate lead generation, immediate order by phone, lead, or other phone contact, lagged order long after the site visit (consider their buying cycle), faxed Request for Proposal (RFP) or Request for Quote (RFQ) based on information learned on the site, catalog or brochure request, white paper download or request, newsletter, e-mail, or other registration and sales meeting request.

Testing Different Landing Pages

Keep in mind that you aren't limited to only one landing page per sales funnel category or conversion definition page; in fact, you can create many different pages that can each test different images, colors, backgrounds, fonts, headings, font sizes, layout, and WIIFMs (Figure 4.5). By testing multiple pages intended for the same conversion, you can directly compare the pages and determine which is converting most effectively. This is a lot like the practice of segmenting described in detail in Chapter 3, It's Not Your Father's E-Mail.

- **Conversions**
- *Man:* 33 sales, $72,795
- *No picture:* 32 sales, $67,435
- *Woman:* 25 sales, $54,120

The *man* picture sold 8 percent more than the *no* picture and 35 percent more than the *woman* picture.

The remaining design element you must always consider is the content. Search engines love good content—as do your prospects and customers. Above all, be sure that your web pages address your prospects' needs and desires, and always provide a strong call to action along with satisfactory value. Many experts interviewed for one of the author's podcasts—all of which can be found at www.theSocialMediaBible.com—had the same advice. To quote 2007 SEO World Champion Benj Arriola, "Content is king."

FIGURE 4.5   Landing Pages

Techniques and Tactics

The purpose of this book is not to teach you all you need to know about how to design an effective web page. It is more focused upon helping you understand the big picture, and imparting some of the little-known—and better-known—tips and tricks picked up along the way. If you really want to get into the technical side of web page programming, get books such as *Creating Web Pages For Dummies* by Bud E. Smith and Arthur Bebak.

Even so, some techniques and tactics help avoid many of the common errors that most people make. The first and most damaging relates to fonts. Never use serifs.

A *serif* is a term for characters that have a line crossing the free end of a stroke, sometimes referred to as *feet and hats* (see Figures 4.6 and 4.7). This style of typeface is thought to have been invented by the Romans. It is the most often used style of font and also one of the most legible styles in print, but *not* on the web. The popularization of this font style emerged in newspapers, where the font size was nine point or smaller. Because this made large blocks of text difficult to read, adding the serifs—or the short line segments—created a sort of top and bottom line for the eye to follow when reading. Remember the faint blue lines that teachers taught writing with in first grade?

This aid became so helpful to the newspaper industry—particularly to the *New York Times*—that nearly all printed words are done with serifs. This is why the most common serif fonts have names like Times (designed for the *Times of London* newspaper) and Times New Roman. The only instances in which a newspaper doesn't use a serif font is when the text is designed large enough to be easily read, such as a title of an article (in which case they often use Helvetica).

Here's an interesting test: Take a page from the newspaper and look closely at the text. See how the serifs almost create a line across the top and bottom of the text? Now, slowly turn the newspaper page away from you so you are looking nearly on its edge, but can still see the text. The serifs almost join to create the definitive lines.

This effect is fine if talking about print, which usually has dpi (dots per inch) greater than 300. Newspapers can be printed at 600-plus dpi, and many magazines can be printed at up to nearly 3,000 dpi. That's a lot of dots for every inch. However, reading a computer monitor is a completely different story.

The Internet is, by definition, viewed through a computer monitor (or worse, a mobile screen). No matter how much you pay for your high-resolution flat-panel monitor, the highest Internet resolution you are likely to see is . . . 72 dpi. This is a very poor quality compared to a printer. This is the case

FIGURE 4.6   Serif Font

FIGURE 4.7   Sans Serif Font

because the human eye can see only so many little bright lights—like those on your computer screen—per inch. At 72 dpi, serifs don't aid in reading; instead, they detract. The resolution of our monitors simply doesn't do justice to the fine detail of a serif. It just makes mud.

Web page and screen resolutions are rapidly getting better because of HD Video, ClearType fonts, and higher resolution monitors, but for now when designing a web page, be sure to always use nonserif, or what they call sans serif, fonts—like Arial, Geneva, Monaco, or Tahoma.

Trademark Sucks

Another effective technique is to use trademarks in your copy. This section is called "Trademark Sucks" because trademarks are a very effective tool for sucking or hijacking your competitor's traffic away from competitors and onto your website.

You can usually use another company's registered trademarks in your copy if comparing or contrasting different products or services. Comparative pages are generally considered fair use in the United States; Europe, however, views this differently. Trademark sharing is frowned upon outside of the United States, where content, editorial, and blog sites frequently leverage brands in content. Be careful when you do this, and always check which rules apply where—since there have been cases in which trademarks in hidden copy or meta tags have been litigated.

Keyword Placement

Question: Who shows up when you search for your brand? Is it you or your competition? Do a search, and find out.

As explained in more detail in Chapter 19, Spotlight on Search (Search Engine Optimization), the placement of your keywords can help with search engine rankings, and make it clearer to your prospects exactly what you're offering them. Start your content's paragraphs with keywords that make sense both to your prospects and search engines. Use nouns that describe the product or service accurately, and use them early. Use phrases that might be searched, and weave them into the copy. Make your copy unique to every page. You need to have a unique WIIFM.

Frames

Frames are programming techniques that create a grid of pigeonholes called *framesets,* wherein blocks of text from other web pages are inserted to create one visually pleasing page. Don't do this! Frames compile text from multiple web pages, and links to internally framed pages lead to dead ends—or pages with no text of their own. Frames will kill your site's search engine friendliness; even if you get the site indexed, the searcher's experience is very poor. Remember: no frames! For more information on Frames, go to www.useit.com/alertbox/9612.html or visit www.theSocialMediaBible .com for clickable links.

Flash

Embedding Flash into your site is okay, as long as the navigation and content are also available elsewhere in the HTML code and on the page. Flash is an animated cartoon or film usually seen as a website's home page introduction, created using Adobe Flash animation software encoded in a .swf file format. Full Flash sites are nearly unindexable (that is, they are practically invisible to search engines) because Flash isn't code that a search engine can read; it's compiled movie code with no HTML code of its own. Even Google and FAST, both of which claim to index Flash files, don't seem to rank them too highly. Flash may seem cool for your designers and marketers, but Flash misuse can kill your search engine optimization and anger your prospects. How many times have you been caught in a home page Flash demo and ran for the mouse to click "Skip Intro"? Your prospects feel the same way, too. Use Flash sparingly—and correctly.

Page Titles

Pick a page, any page . . . and look at your page title. It's even odds that your programmer never gave your page a title and that it's still called *untitled*— or it has the same name as all of your other web pages. Perhaps it's even just your company's name. You must have unique, descriptive titles on each page of your site, primarily for the search engines, and secondarily for your prospects. Be sure to use explanatory titles. These are the essence of each page, the WIIFM. Use titles that are unique and compelling for the searcher. Be sure to include phrases a searcher is likely to type (do some keyword research). Keywords in the title should be placed in web page copy as well. An accurate description of the page's content is much better than engaging in keyword stuffing—in other words, don't just add random keywords. Your title can be as long as 90 to 100 characters, but it's best to lead with your strongest keyword differentiator, not your site's or company's name. When titling your web pages, always consider plural and singular versions of a keyword.

Constructing Regional and Local Campaigns

It's important to understand the motivation behind the local searcher's query. If you are a local company, you must separate and differentiate your web pages by region or locale. Even if you are a national company, but sell and compete in different regions, localize your landing pages by using local state, town, city, county, and geographic names. This way, when your prospect is searching for a company in her area, your company will come up in her search—even if you are 1,000 miles away.

Offline Marketing Strategy

Before you had a web page, you likely had a conventional marketing strategy. What were the objectives of that strategy? And on an even more basic level, before you had this marketing strategy, what was the product or service that you wanted to sell? Your web page goals and objectives should align with your overall business goals and objectives. How close to your true goals and to your offline strategy can you get in online advertising and web page content? More about strategy is discussed in Part III of this book.

Affiliate Marketing

Many marketers rely on affiliates—or partners in branding and marketing—to generate sales on a commissioned basis. However, affiliate-marketing problems can and do arise. When you use this kind of sales program, you are essentially supporting someone else to compete with you for web page traffic. You need to ask yourself how your brand is portrayed, how much traffic you're giving away to your affiliates, whether you're fighting with an affiliate for your own traffic, whether your affiliates are escalating prices and costing everyone more—and, essentially, whether using affiliates at all is a good strategy. Affiliate marketing can be very successful for some companies; but it's not for everyone.

Website Platforms

The computer software framework and hosting technology underlying a website is known as the website platform. The different varieties of platforms upon which your website can be constructed are becoming more plentiful every day. The most popular include what is HTML-based—the old standby that's been used for more than a decade; Joomla, an easier-to-use, open-source platform; Ning, an easy-to-use, community-building platform; and WordPress, which is also a very easy-to-use, open-source, robust platform. You will have to research your options further as new ones are coming online every day. Find a website developer you trust, and ask him to explain the pros and cons of each platform so you can find what's right for you.

In-House–Out-House

Unless you want to learn how to program a website yourself, you should leave the programming to the web developers. If you choose what's called a high-level platform such as Joomla or WordPress, you should at least learn how to create and modify web pages and blogs. It's easier than you think; it could save you the time and money that it takes to go back to the developer each time you need a small change; and it can be fun to do.

The ROI of Social Media

Social Media Outreach Enhances Teen-Focused Cause Marketing Campaign

Background

Staples, the world's largest office products retailer and an expert on back-to-school retailing, worked with DoSomething.org, a national not-for-profit organization that empowers teens to take action in their communities, to create "Do Something 101," a national school supply drive. The inaugural campaign raised more than $150,000 for local charities to purchase back-to-school supplies for students who need them and generated more than 211.8 million media impressions. For 2009, Staples aimed to make the second Annual Do Something 101 National School Supply Drive bigger and better than the inaugural campaign. Staples and DoSomething.org wanted to inspire more teens to "do something" by collecting new school supplies for underprivileged kids, connect with teens in a unique and meaningful way, and increase donations and impressions over the previous year.

Strategy

The strategy was to conduct ongoing conversations about the need for school supplies for underserved youth, and how the Do Something 101 campaign can help. In addition to the traditional marketing tactics of in-store signage, customer e-mails, public service announcements, and media relations, Staples launched a social media campaign to reach teens where they spend the most time: Facebook. Staples recently launched its own corporate Facebook page geared toward its core audience of small business customers. Rather than trying to retrofit the Staples corporate page for teens, Staples developed a fan page focused entirely on the teen audience, as well as a new Facebook application, to raise awareness of the Do Something 101 school supply drive.

Implementation

Staples worked with a social media agency, Mr. Youth, to develop the Facebook fan page for Do Something 101, and create the new "Adopt-a-Pack" application. With Adopt a Pack, teens could tag their friends to fill virtual backpacks with school supplies to raise awareness for the cause and effort. With every backpack filled, teens could enter a sweepstakes for various prizes, including a trip to New York City to participate in a bag-stuffing event with the campaign's spokesperson, Grammy-winning Ciara. Staples spread the word about the fan page and application to cause-related and teen-focused blogs. It also worked with Mr. Youth's RepNation network to create a task force of students to spread the word through their existing online networks.

(continued)

(continued)

Opportunity

To connect with teens where they already lived online, allow them to show support for a worthy cause in a fun, unique manner, and build a foundation of teen engagement for future campaigns.

Conclusion

The Second Annual Do Something 101 national school supply drive raised more than $630,000 in customer cash donations, compared to $125,000 in 2008. Staples customers also donated thousands of items such as notebooks, calculators, and other supplies for students in need. The program received editorial coverage in outlets ranging from the *New York Times* to Seventeen.com, and resulted in 484.8 million media impressions, more than doubling 2008's results of 211.8 million media impressions. In addition, the Do Something 101 Facebook Fan page secured more than 6,000 fans who still continue to engage with the page well past the end of the 2009 campaign, and will serve as a base for the 2010 school supply drive. In addition, through the Facebook application, Staples achieved 211 million teen impressions (compared to 13 million teen impressions from a 2008 teen marketing program).

—Staples, Inc., PR team, www.staples.com

Expert Insight

**Vint Cerf, father of the Internet and futurist,
www.google.com/corporate/execs.html**

Vint Cerf

. . . Well, first of all, labeling me the "Father of the Internet" is not fair to an awful lot of people, especially to Bob Kahn, because Bob started the Internetting program when he joined the Defense Department in 1972; and then he came to me when I was at Stanford in early 1973 and said, "You know, I have this problem. How do I hook all these different nets together?"

So the two of us did the basic Internet design, descriptions of the design of the TCP protocol. As the design evolved, we split out the Internet Protocol from the TCP, producing what is now called the TCP/IP protocol suite. But there are many, many people, both before and after that stage, that have contributed to make the Net what it is today.

So, I'm just happy that I participated in it because it has been a lot of fun. . . .

. . . It certainly has been something of a surprise to me that the users of the Internet, the consumers of information, have now become the primary producers of information on the network. It's very widespread. It shows up in a number of different forms. It shows up as blogs, it shows up as video uploads in YouTube, tweets on Twitter, Facebook, blog pages, and other similar services. It shows up at social game sites. Things like World of Warcraft. It's showing up as people populate their own web pages, send e-mail, use distribution lists, and so on.

Some of those things have been around for a while. E-mail, of course, was invented in 1971, so it's an old medium in some sense but still very heavily used, as are distribution lists. There's chat and there are other kinds of more real-time things, including video now.

(continued)

(continued)

So all of these different ways of interacting have been very rapidly absorbed by the public. Mobiles, which only recently have come on the scene, now account for over four billion users, not on the Internet but in the mobile world. But the Internet interfaces to many of the mobiles and so people are beginning to do texting in the mobile world, they are doing instant messaging, they are doing e-mail exchanges, and they are searching the web from their mobiles.

What I'm seeing right now is a wide range of choices that people have in maintaining relationships and in interacting with people one on one, and in groups. I think this is likely to persist. Certainly, the sharing of information on the Internet has been dramatic. In the scientific world, equally so. Where scientists begin to build common databases that they can reference, such as the human genome database or astronomical information, or the geophysical information, we are finding that scientific results are achieved faster because people have reference to virtually everything that is known about some particular phenomenon because it's been codified in these shared databases.

So now we're seeing an increasing amount of collaborative work in the online environment and something, which Google, of course, is intensely interested in.

. . . [I]n these mediums, it's possible to be abusive, and I am very concerned about the side effect of cyber-bullying and things of that sort. Others have expressed a discomfort with the fact that anything and everything can be expressed on the Internet, including negative information . . . whether it's accurate or not, it sometimes has an impact.

So we have a potential for both positive and constructive and also rather negative kinds of interactions in this online environment. And I think we're still trying to discipline ourselves in how to treat these different media in a way that protects us from some of the abusive behaviors.

I am thinking not merely of the social media, but more generally speaking; things like viruses and worms and keyloggers that are looking for user names and passwords, or identifiers of accounts.

Those are all fairly pernicious abuses of this online medium, and I think we are still trying to learn how to cope with it socially and legally, as well as from the law enforcement point of view. . . .

. . . The FCC believes that it is responsible for all communications in the United States. It doesn't mean that it's responsible for communications outside the United States, but it has chosen to treat the Internet as a Title I Information Service. This is now in debate and the FCC has even suggested to move Internet services back into Title II (communication services). I think this might be beneficial if you are worried about the potential for anticompetitive behaviors among the broadband.

Internet service providers could abuse their control of the IP layer to ward off competing higher-level applications.

There are some side effects of that, which I think are not relevant to this discussion, although they're of concern to me; having a lot to do with "common carriage" and things like that; but the FCC has chosen to forebear to regulate, except in cases it considers to be anticompetitive practices. And you'll note that there was a recent decision by the FCC with regards to Comcast and its attempt to manage network use in the presence of BitTorrent and other kinds of peer-to-peer file sharing applications. That ruling is also in dispute at present.

The FCC censured Comcast for the way in which it undertook to do that management. There are other places in the world that are even more actively trying to control access to and use of the Internet. You're going to find that everywhere. The Internet is global in scope. It operates in virtually every country in varying degrees and countries have different views of what people should or shouldn't be able to do using this medium.

One of the biggest challenges, I think, is that no matter what position you take with regard to usage, you have the problem that if your position is different from some other countries' view, there is not much that you can do to enforce your view, and vice versa.

And so then you get into this question of, "Under my rules, my citizen was attacked by a person in another country and I'm looking for some kind of compensation."

You will not be able to deal with those problems unless there are more common agreements about what is or is not acceptable behavior on the Internet. And since the social views vary from one country to another, I think it is going to be hard for us to come to global agreements; but I think we will come to some agreements commonly.

For example, as far as I know, every country in the world rejects child pornography as an unacceptable form of behavior, whether it's on the Internet or otherwise.

So, maybe there are other things that we can agree are commonly unacceptable and, therefore, should be either prevented or punished if they are detected. It's going to take a lot of international work to make that a reality. Social networking is so wrapped up in cultural norms that applications in this domain, taken on a global scale, is almost sure to run into societal issues. . . .

. . . And, by the way, I would like to say something about China. When you talk to Chinese people on the streets, you discover that some number of

(continued)

(continued)

them actually appreciate the censorship. They claim to like it; they believe they are being protected; now whether that's true is independent of how they feel about it, or how they, at least, say they feel about it. So we shouldn't make the assumption that the First Amendment notion, which is powerful in our Constitution, is necessarily universally accepted as preferable.

There are cultures where, in fact, the citizens want this kind of control. . . .

. . . This reminds me of an interesting phenomenon that happened in the late 1980s. I had asked permission from the U.S. federal government to connect MCI, which is a commercial e-mail service, up to the Internet. And they reluctantly allowed me to do that. The reluctance came from the concern that we would be carrying, or using, government-sponsored backbones to carry commercial e-mail traffic.

After I put the MCI mail system up on the Internet, immediately the other e-mail service providers said, "Well, you know, the MCI Mail people shouldn't have an exclusive privilege." And so CompuServe came up and Ontyme came up and some of the other commercial servers also came up on the Net.

And the side effects of this was that they could suddenly interchange e-mail with each other through the Internet, which before they could not do. So it's this standardization that creates the possibility of interoperability. And this is why Google's OpenSocial, I think, is an important effort . . . because it potentially creates interoperability among those areas in social networks.

I think it will be very attractive for the users of those networks to be able to interact, regardless of which social networks systems you happen to be registered in. You know, we may see some interesting consequences of that interconnection as people begin to adopt it. There will be interactions that we might not have anticipated that are enabled by that standard. . . .

. . . I'm, of course, perhaps understandably, excited and feel positive about a lot of these new developments. The Internet was designed to be fairly insensitive to specific media, so it does not know if it is carrying a digital image or voice or video or some other digitized object . . . you know, part of a program or a piece of Web page. It just does not know, and that's very deliberate. It was intended to be a general-purpose transport mechanism, and the consequences of that is . . . every device that produces digital output potentially can be interfaced to the Internet and this output transfers around and delivers to other places. I think that we are going to see a very significant increase in the number of devices that are able to connect to and interact with other devices on the Internet.

There had been some discussion about the earlier phases of Internet being "Internet for everyone" and now it is becoming "Internet for everything?!" And I really do believe that. I think sensor networks, appliances, things at home, in the office, in the automobile, and that you carry around will all be Internet-enabled and this allows us to manage them better. These devices can report their status to us; they can accept, command, and control from third parties. You can imagine entertainment systems being managed over the Internet by third-party entertainment managers; you simply click here if you want this movie or that song, and it takes care of the details of getting it to the CD player in the car or the hard disc that replaced the CD player, or your iPod or some other DVR or whatever you have. All of these are possible once these devices become part of the Internet.

And, of course, mobiles are contributing to that because as they become more and more equipped with Internet capabilities, they too, will become remote controllers for many, many devices. . . .

To listen to or read the entire Executive Conversation with Vint Cerf, go to www.theSocialMediaBible.com.

To-Do List

- Understand your prospect or customer.

  Have a firm grasp on what's important to them, what they are looking for, and what they expect to take away from your site. Only then will you understand how to create content that will really draw them in.

- Understand the different sales funnel phases.

  By recognizing the different phases that your prospect or client undergoes, you can develop specific web pages—and corresponding titles—that address their particular needs.

- Implement metrics.

  Really, if you can't measure it, you can't manage it. If you don't look at the numbers, you will never know if something you are doing is effective or a waste of your time. Once you have some analytics in place, test different ideas, layouts, taglines, headings, bullets, images, colors, and copy. Go with what works, and remember that this is a continuous process.

- Understand the different conversion definitions.

  Understand the different definitions of conversion you have for each and every page, and design each page specifically to attain that desired conversion.

- Set specific measurable goals.

  Set realistic and measurable goals for your web pages. This way, when you track these numbers, you will know when you are successful.

- Remember that content is king.

  Whether it's search engine optimization, stickiness of your page, or how well your page converts, it's all about content. If your content is valuable and meets the expectations of your prospects, then they will become engaged and most likely convert to purchasers.

- Do not use serif fonts.

  Because of monitor resolution, fonts with serifs can become muddy and less appealing than a sans serif font.

- Use frames and Flash cautiously.

  Both frames and Flash make it difficult for search engines, and hence your prospects, to find you. Flash can also be annoying, so use it with caution.

Conclusion

Having a well-designed web page is probably the smartest thing you can do for your business. It certainly has the greatest return on investment. A cleverly designed site and page(s) will receive a high ranking on all of the search engines; be easy for your prospects and customers to find; provide valuable content for them; encourage them to stay longer on your site, thereby granting you a greater opportunity to convey your message; reduce customer service; expand your contact lists; build trust; and eventually convert them to a sale.

To hear all of the Expert Interviews, go to www.theSocialMediaBible.com.

Downloads

For your free downloads associated with *The Social Media Bible,* go to www .theSocialMediaBible.com,

and enter your ISBN number located on the back of the book above the bar code. Be sure to enter the dashes.

Credits

The ROI of Social Media was provided by:

Staples, Inc., PR team, www.Staples.com

Expert Insight was provided by:

Vint Cerf, father of the Internet and futurist, www.google.com /corporate/execs.html

Technical edits provided by:

Aaron Baer, Twitter: Aaron M. Baer

Technical Editors:

Ryan Parker, creative director, and Brian Murphy, chief of technology, www.XpleoMedia.com

Notes

1. Robert Cailliau, who worked at CERN, had independently proposed a project to develop a hypertext system, and partnered with Berners-Lee in hopes of getting the World Wide Web off the ground. He rewrote his project proposal, lobbied management for funding, recruited programmers, and collaborated with Berners-Lee on papers and presentations. Cailliau helped run the first WWW conference and became president of the International World Wide Web Conference Committee (IW3C2).

2. B. J. Fogg, "Stanford Guidelines for Web Credibility." A Research Summary from the Stanford Persuasive Technology Lab, Stanford University, May 2002.

CHAPTER 5

The Internet Forum

www.LonSafko.com/TSMB3_Videos/05Forum.mov

What's in It for You?

The (Internet or discussion) *forum,* or message board, was the name for one of the first Internet-based networking and online communication tools—and still is a great way to engage people in an interactive ongoing conversation on a particular subject. If you want to start a debate, solicit advice, share an idea, run a poll, or just participate in a conversation on your favorite subject, this is where you go—to the forum or chat room message board, as it's often called. (Message boards are more like forums; chat rooms are quite different, as is explained next.) A chat room differs slightly from a forum, however, because chat room participation requires the member to actively read and post to the conversation in real time, whereas in a forum, you can reply to responses days later. Either format allows you to log on, select a topic of interest, type your comments into a text box, and send them off, or *post* them, so that others can see your thoughts—or *posts*—and have them publicly reply to your comment (which was a comment on a previous comment).

theSocialMediaBible.com

The forum builds strong community ties, loyalty, and really exemplifies the notion of a trusted network. You can easily apply this trend to your business and create a company forum, so that people from all around the world who care about your subject matter will read, participate, share ideas and concerns, and build a community of trust. By participating in other people's forums, you can develop your own credibility and strong ties with that community. As with all social media, it's about trust, participation, two-way communications, user-generated content—and it's free.

 As an example, one forum website—aptly named the Forum Site (www.theforumsite.com), which was created in 2004—put forth the following statistics as a snapshot of its activity: 3,210 Forums; 60,188 Members with 47 online, 96 new today; Topics 194,731; 2,971,801 Posts with 1,519 today; 37,748 Journals with 238,520 replies; 50,267 Pictures with 113,500 replies; and 97,272 Ratings, 565 Reviews, and 4,738 Polls.

Back to the Beginning

Forums—often referred to as chat rooms, message boards, or bulletin boards—go back to some of the very first uses of the private Usenet in the 1970s, and some of the early public Internet forums started at the beginning of the Web's first public uses in 1995.

The forum was the predecessor to the blog (see Chapter 7, The Ubiquitous Blog, for more information). One of the author's own first experiences participating in a forum was in 1986, when Apple announced eWorld—its own online service for communicating with their Value-Added Resellers (VARs; see Figure 5.1).

A VAR, or Value-Added Reseller, is a company that takes an existing product and adds its own value, usually in the form of a specific application for the product—for example, adding a special computer application and reselling it as a new product or package.

A strong sense of community or trusted network develops around forums, most of which have a theme or a conversation in which members share a common interest. Some of these include computers, cats, dogs, pets, sports, a particular team, religion, fashion, video games, politics, hobbies, cars, questions, comparisons, debates, polls of opinion—just about everything you can think of that people want to talk about. A forum is intended to promote an ongoing dialogue on a specific subject, which differs from the idea of a blog, since the owner of the blog is the one who posts a thought and allows comments—and then moves on to another thought.

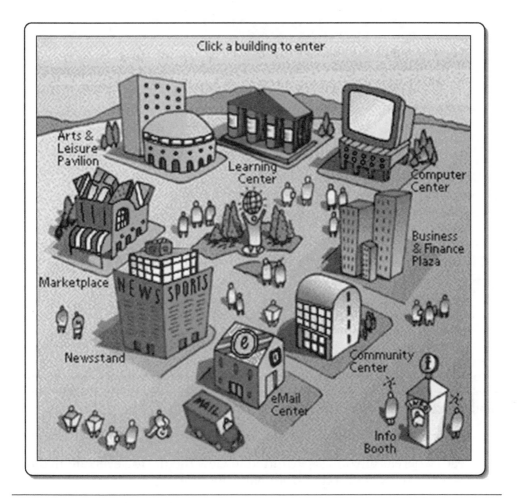

FIGURE 5.1 Apple eWorld Circa 1987

What You Need to Know

A forum is a website application that manages and provides a medium for ongoing online community discussion on a particular subject (see Figure 5.1). The users are a group of contributors or members, along with a moderator, who participate in the conversation. The moderator monitors the conversation to be sure that it adheres to rules and regulations set up by the forum owner(s). A member can begin a topic, which will allow others to comment on and add discussion to the previous posts or comments. This two-way communication is called a *thread*. In most forums, participants are required to register and sign in to participate in a conversation

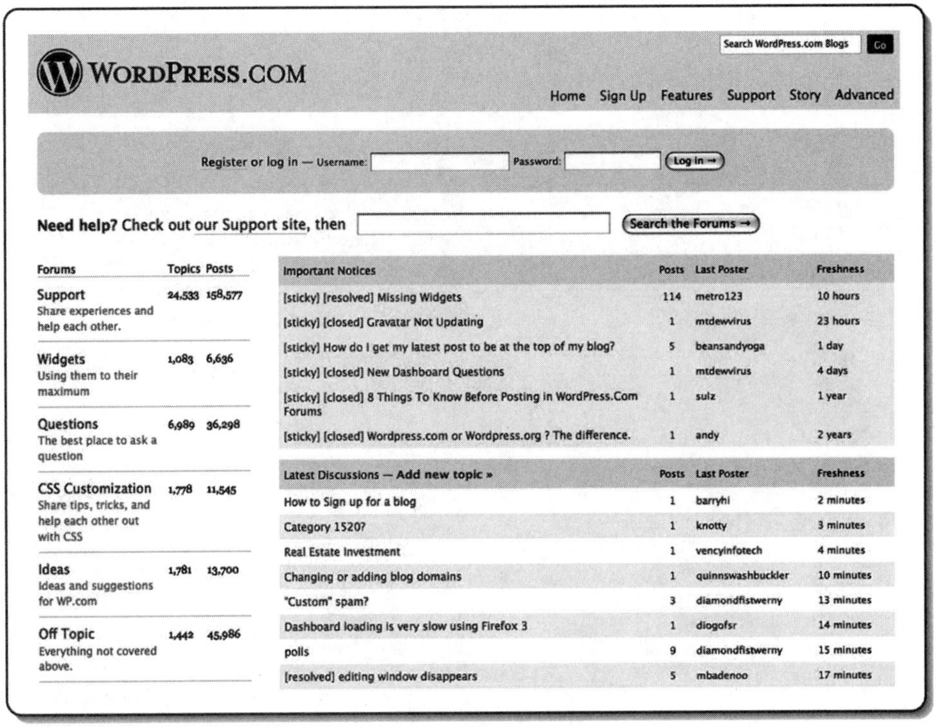

FIGURE 5.2 WordPress Forum

or thread, whereas anyone is permitted to view them. However, anonymous visitors are usually prohibited from participating.

Forum Rules and Regulations

Forums are created, managed, and maintained by an individual or group of individuals who are referred to as *administrators*. Guidelines for all forums are created, and all participating members are required to follow them. These regulations are often found in the Frequently Asked Questions (FAQs) section of the forum, and the rules are usually basic and apply to common courtesy. Behavior that is prohibited includes insulting, swearing, harassing, inappropriate language, advertising, selling, spamming, personal information posting, sexual content, having more than one account, and warez or other copyright infringements. (*Warez* refers to works that are copyrighted and traded in violation of the copyright law, such as cracked or pirated versions of commercial software.)

Forum Moderator

Moderators—or mods—read and have editorial access to the posts and threads. Mods usually come to hold this position by being promoted from within the ranks of the members. A moderator can have control over banning and unbanning, splitting, renaming, closing, merging, and deleting threads. The mods referee members' conversations to keep them free from rule violations and spam. Mods may also receive reports of guideline infringement from members, and then notify the offender when a rule has been broken in order to enforce the rules and, often, administer punishment. It is then up to the moderator to implement an action against, warning to, or banning of that member. First-time offenders are usually warned, whereas repeat offenders can be banned or banished for days—or even permanently. The offending content is always deleted.

Forum Administrator

An administrator (or admin) manages the technical requirements of the forum website. Administrators are responsible for promoting and demoting members to and from their positions as moderators, keeping the site running properly, and sometimes acting as moderators themselves. These are usually the owners of the forum or are appointed by the owners and have the ultimate say in the operation of the forum.

Forum Registration

To be able to participate in a forum, you most likely will need to register. Once you do so, you become a member of the forum and can participate in a thread, or start your own group or topic of discussion. Most forums require that a member be at least 13 years old; websites that are collecting information from children under the age of 13 are required to comply with the Federal Trade Commission's (FTC) Children's Online Privacy Protection Act (COPPA; see coppa.org).

FIGURE 5.3 CAPTCHA

Most forums allow you to create a username and password, ask for a valid e-mail address, and ask the user to validate their registration through CAPTCHA Code (see Figure 5.2).[1]

You've seen these verification codes (sometimes including numbers, symbols, and letters) on many different logins and registration sites. Blogs have them to prevent the blogs from being automatically spammed.

Forum Post

A post is a text message or a comment that a member types and submits. It is placed in a box that appears directly above the previous post box, and includes the member's user name, icon (or avatar), date and time submitted, and comment. In most forums, members can edit their own posts at any time after posting. This configuration of comment box upon comment box with more recent posts displayed in chronological order is called the *thread*. Once the original post has been made, subsequent posts will be placed on top of the previous one, continuing the conversation.

Most forum websites limit both the minimum and maximum number of characters per post. These numbers are generally set at 10 characters for the minimum, and at either 10,000, 30,000, or 50,000 characters for the maximum, based on the administrator's decision.

Forum Member

Once you properly register to a forum, you become a member (or poster) and are recognized by a username—or alias—that you choose. You can participate in posting threads to ongoing conversations, submit messages, and have access to all of the other features offered throughout the forum site. Members can use a signature (sig), photo, icon, avatar (see Chapter 15,

FIGURE 5.4   Avatars (left to right, top row): Lon Safko, John Adam, and Linh Tang; (bottom row) Chris Brogan, Jeremiah Owyang, and Jody Gnant

Virtual Worlds—Real Impact), or other image that represents them and their posts (see Figure 5.3).

Forum Subscription

Members can subscribe to a forum, like they can with a blog. Subscription is an automated notification that alerts you when a new comment has been added to your favorite forum thread. This is done through RSS—Really Simple Syndication—or Atom[2] feeds. (For more information on RSS, see Chapter 17, RSS—Really Simple Syndication Made Simple—for how these feeds can be aggregated into one easy-to-read web page.) It's automatic, and every time there is a new post or comment, you see it without having to go to the forum web page to check. You can also get e-mail alerts—it's not just RSS or Atom.

Forum Troll

A member of a forum who repeatedly breaks etiquette—or *netiquette*—is referred to as a *troll*. This person deliberately posts inflammatory remarks in an attempt to incite irritated responses. When a troll posts a negative comment that engages other members to respond, it can create a flurry of angry comments, called a *flame war,* or *flaming.* This activity happens often in forums, on Twitter (see Chapter 13, Thumbs Up for Microblogging), and even on social networking sites like MySpace and Facebook.

Flame wars take place when an ongoing dialogue becomes heated and its participants continue to post argumentative or inflammatory comments. It's especially frequent in forums that involve controversial groups and subjects like politics and religion. If a flame war breaks out, forum moderators will often warn the participants to stop the incendiary commenting. If this doesn't control the conversation and get it back on track, the moderator will then shut down the conversation thread—either for a finite period that is meant to give the participants ample time to cool off, or indefinitely. Excessive spamming can also cause flame wars and flaming.

Forum Spamming

Like flame wars, spamming is not appropriate or tolerated within forums, and it's also considered a breach of netiquette. A spam message or post is defined as "any unsolicited communication that is not transactional, such as a message to complete a transaction, warranty, product updates, upgrades or recall information, change in terms of subscription or service, or account balance information" (see Chapter 3, It's Not Your Father's E-Mail, for a full history and explanation of spam). Forum spamming can also include any posting that is willful and malicious—such as repeating the same word or phrase over and over to provoke a negative or aggressive response.

Someone on LinkedIn once sent out an obvious spam message to everyone on the network. The message read something to the effect of, "Hello, my name is . . . and I do consulting for . . . so call me for a free quote." The community went insane. Hundreds of backlash e-mails went to her and to other members reprimanding her for her inappropriate message.

Forum User Groups

A *user group* is a group of forum members that grows out of a specific topic of discussion. The group keeps the conversation topic focused to what members of that group wish to discuss. By participating in this type of idea sharing and opinion sharing, the group members' passion on a specific subject forms a bond between them, and this bond is what makes the trusted network as effective and as loyal as it is.

For example, say you participate in an antique car collector's forum. After a while, the members will get to know you from the many posts and contributions you make to their forum. Then say someone wanted a rec-ommendation on where to buy a hard-to-find part, and you suggested a resource; the members of that forum would trust you and your suggestion. You would have built their trust and friendship simply by participating. The same would hold true for a professional organization, a church group, or even a baseball league.

Forum Guest

A guest is an unregistered visitor to a forum site. Guests are generally allowed to access the entire site and read threads, but they are not permit-ted to participate and post comments in the discussions. To participate, they must be registered. A guest who visits a forum or group frequently without participating in the online conversation is referred to as a *lurker*. Lurking isn't necessarily bad; it's simply the way in which some people pre-fer to participate. It is somewhat like a blog; many people visit or subscribe to blogs and read them, but never comment on them.

Text Message Shortcuts

A lot of forum communication is done with text message slang or short-cuts. This is particularly popular in mobile text messaging, but is also used anytime you text in a manner that saves you keystrokes. (I'm no G9, but @ TEOTD, ALCON, whether it's your BF or just K8T, BM&Y, there's always a BDN of people texting, but DQMOT.) For more about texting and text shortcuts—and to decipher this message—see Chapter 20, The Formidable Fourth Screen (Mobile), and the downloads from that chapter for the com-plete Text Shortcuts Language Guide.

Emoticons

You've seen them. They're the little smiley faces that show up in your e-mail, in instant messaging applications, on a web page, or in the text of a com-ment. *Emoticons* are *emot*ional *icons*—a single symbol or combination of symbols that are used to convey emotions within the text message. Forums allow you to type a series of characters and symbols and have them auto-matically replaced and displayed as a small graphic or icon. A ":-)" will automatically convert into a ☺, or a ":-(" will look like a ☹. This also works in Microsoft Office programs like Word and Outlook. Microsoft's Messenger provides 70 different emoticons when you're messaging with friends to show them how you really feel. Emoticons are visual ways to express the way you feel when words alone just aren't enough. Try some emoticons in your next text message, e-mail, and Word document (see Figure 5.5).

Smile	:-) or :)		Open-mouthed	:-D or :d
Surprised	:-O or :o		Tongue out	:-P or :p
Wink	;-) or ;)		Sad	:-(or :(
Confused	:-S or :s		Disappointed	:-I or :I
Crying	:'(		Embarrassed	:-$ or :$
Hot	(H) or (h)		Angry	:-@ or :@
Angel	(A) or (a)		Devil	(6)
Don't tell anyone	:-#		Baring teeth	8ol
Nerd	8-I		Sarcastic	^o)
Secret telling	:-*		Sick	+o(
I don't know	:^)		Thinking	*-)
Party	<:o)		Eye-rolling	8-)
Sleepy	I-)		Coffee cup	(C) or (c)
Thumbs up	(Y) or (y)		Thumbs down	(N) or (n)
Beer mug	(B) or (b)		Martini glass	(D) or (d)
Girl	(X) or (x)		Boy	(Z) or (z)
Left hug	({)		Right hug	(})
Vampire bat	:-[or :[		Birthday cake	(^)
Red heart	(L) or (l)		Broken heart	(U) or (u)
Red lips	(K) or (k)		Gift with a bow	(G) or (g)
Red rose	(F) or (f)		Wilted rose	(W) or (w)
Camera	(P) or (p)		Filmstrip	(~)
Cat face	(@)		Dog face	(&)
Telephone receiver	(T) or (t)		Light bulb	(I) or (i)
Note	(8)		Sleeping half-moon	(S)
Star	(*)		E-mail	(E) or (e)
Clock	(O) or (o)		MSN Messenger icon	(M) or (m)
Snail	(sn)		Black Sheep	(bah)
Plate	(pl)		Bowl	(ll)
Pizza	(pi)		Soccer ball	(so)
Auto	(au)		Airplane	(ap)
Umbrella	(um)		Island with a palm tree	(ip)
Computer	(co)		Mobile Phone	(mp)
Stormy cloud	(st)		Lightning	(li)
Money	(mo)			

FIGURE 5.5 Emoticons

Forum Social Networking

With the convergence of all things digital—photos, audio, music, and video—along with the popularity of social networking sites like LinkedIn and MySpace and photo sharing sites like Flickr and Photobucket—forums have become much more social. Many of the forum platforms now allow members to include personal photo galleries, personal pages, and real-time member-to-member chat.

Create Your Own Forum Software

Ektron.com (www.ektron.com):

Ektron CMS400.NET is a resource that provides a complete platform with all of the functionality necessary for developers and nontechnical business users alike to create, deploy, and manage your website. Developers can take advantage of built-in server controls to launch a site out of the box, or customize this initiation using CMS400.NET's well-documented API. Businesses benefit from an intuitive user interface that is extremely helpful in managing their site's content and messaging. A comprehensive SEO (search engine optimization) toolkit ensures that potential visitors are able to find your site. Memberships, personalization, subscriptions, geomapping, and web alerts keep your site visitors coming back; and social networking and Web 2.0 tools (including wikis, blogging, polls, and forums) grow your online communities.

Forum Website

Yuku.com (www.yuku.com):

Yuku (Part of *Inform Technologies*)[3] is a site that allows users to create and participate in profiles, image sharing, blogs, and discussion boards all in one place. Your Yuku account can have up to five different profiles, because, although you don't always want to use the same profile, you *do* want only one account. Yuku's purpose is to help people connect and communicate online as easily and safely as possible. You don't need to download anything to use Yuku; all you need is an account, your profile, and your favorite Internet browser.

KickApps.com (www.kickapps.com):

KickApps is a web-based platform that makes it easy for you to add a wide array of social features to your website. Whether you are a one-person shop or a global corporation, the Kickapps.com suite of applications are designed to integrate seamlessly with your website and your brand.

Inform Technologies now owns Yuku: http://en.wikipedia.org/wiki/Yuku

Kickapps is now owned by KIT Digital: http://www.kitd.com/kickapps

While Kickapps is still considerd to be forum software, it is becoming more of a social network/community site builder similar to Ning.

The ROI of Social Media

Enabling Brand Advocates to Share Positive Brand Experiences with Their Friends on Facebook

Background

Multi-unit retailers are increasingly focused on driving "net promotions" or "intent to recommend" but are often at a loss on how to translate these customer intentions into actual brand recommendations. Empathica found that customers who frequented large retailers, restaurants, and financial institutions were willing to express their satisfaction with these brands online to their friends and family, but were not making recommendations because they lacked an easy and convenient process to do so. It is critical to not only understand the percentage of "net promotion" intenders of a brand, but also to marshal these customer voices into becoming active brand ambassadors.

As such, we recognized the need to create a tool to make it easy for brands to share their recommendations online. A Facebook application called GoRecommend was developed to address these aligned consumer and business needs.

Strategy

Research has shown that consumers are increasingly turning to online reviews and recommendations when making a purchase decision. The advent of social networking sites such as Facebook allows users to easily share recommendations and reviews with friends, colleagues, and family through their social network. These relationships add greater value to the recommendation,

(continued)

(*continued*)

as it is coming from a reliable source. Anonymous reviews and recommendations, though abundant, hold less value than those obtained from someone the consumer trusts. The social nature of Facebook makes it an ideal platform for GoRecommend.

If 1,000 satisfied customers were to recommend a brand experience using GoRecomend, and the average Facebook user has 130 friends, their personalized recommendations would be shared with 130,000 people.

Implementation

After a customer completes an Empathica retail experience survey, the GoRecommend engine prompts those who indicated a high intent to recommend their experience to share their recommendation with friends on Facebook.

The location-specific recommendation can be posted on the recommender's Facebook profile page, which exposes the personalized recommendation to all of the user's friends through the Facebook newsfeed. The recommendation can also be optionally posted to the brand's Facebook fan page.

These valuable recommendations can also include a coupon or an invitation for the recommender and his friends to join a brand's e-mail club or become a fan of the brand's Facebook fan page. These engagement tools easily turn the recommendation into an effective marketing tool that both drives traffic and extends the relationship between the brand and the consumer. By way of recent example, in just 60 days more than 15,000 satisfied customers recommended one large restaurant chain to their friends using GoRecommend. The program further generated over 10,000 e-mail club opt-ins and more than 1,000 Facebook fans for the brand.

Opportunity

GoRecommend is a true turnkey social marketing solution that fosters ongoing brand awareness by encouraging customers who have had a positive experience with the brand to make a recommendation. It is an automatic way the brand can use the social graph to generate positive, authentic, timely, and relevant communications about the brand.

It is cost effective and very easy to deploy, using an automated referral process that takes little to no effort from the brand itself.

Conclusion

Still in the early stages of deployment, to date GoRecommend has generated some 50,000 recommendations from satisfied customers that have been shared with over 7.7 million friends on Facebook.

—Dr. Gary Edwards, EVP Client Services
Julia Staffen, Director Product Management, GoRecommend
Empathica, Inc.

Web: www.empathica.com
Twitter: @EmpathicaCEM
Facebook: www.facebook.com/EmpathicaCEM

Expert Insight

Stephanie Ichinose, director of communications, Yelp, www.yelp.com

Stephanie Ichinose

(continued)

(*continued*)

. . . I am the director of communications here so I manage a bunch of differ-ent functions. Primarily it is media relations, analysis relations, and the like. I work closely with our management team and I have been with the company since April 2006. Prior to that, I was managing a public relations team for Yahoo!

. . . The interesting thing about Yelp and its approach to local search was that we recognized that there was this old model of word-of-mouth that existed. It is not even a model; it has just existed since the beginning of time, basically. Individuals would share a lot of interesting and valuable information between each other with these person-to-person conversations. Like, "Where can I find a great doctor? Who's the best mechanic in town for my small car that needs some work?" And the question at that point is how do we capture these conver-sations and bring them online?

Initially, we set out to solve that problem and were surprised to find that by building a community of individuals within a particular city we were able to really incite and encourage these conversations. On the back end, users were really passionate about sharing that information. Yelp started out spe-cifically only in San Francisco. And we focused our first year of operations to building up the site, supporting the community that existed in the Bay area, and trying to figure out what worked and what didn't.

And then in 2006–2007, we focused more on, "Okay, can we replicate this and push it out to other markets, with the same sort of conversation top-ics, in Chicago, in New York, in Boston?"

And we found, pretty quickly in 2006 that, that there was just some-thing universal about people wanting to share all of their great hidden gems, or wanting to rave about specific businesses, the "Mom and Pops" that they want to support. And so there was a really interesting dynamic of community (and local community), that really resonated across the nation. . . .

. . . I think it is interesting that when we watch some of our most active Yelpers, there is this notion that they are contributing right to the bloggers (or this community in San Francisco, or in their particular area, whether it's Dallas, Austin, or Chicago, or wherever they may live); there's this notion of being able to support local businesses, help share that information so that others who are out there that might stumble across the information would find it helpful; and just sort of become a part of the local community of indi-viduals who are passionate about sharing their experiences.

There is a network part of it, which happens when you sign up on Yelp. You plug into a community of people who are like-minded, but then the broader effect is that information is then seen by so many more individuals. We have had 14 million unique visitors to the site in the past 30 days. And that number contin-ues to grow and we are really excited about that. We currently have well north of 3.5 million reviews that have been written by Yelpers that contributed to the site.

Therefore, what that tells us is that there is a huge audience of people that are looking for this information and it is great that they are able to utilize this resource. In addition, we are then able to tap into the individual voices of the community.

. . . Actually, the cofounders really looked at the Craigslist model and figured out, "Okay, what did they do? What was part of their roll-out, and how did they achieve the success that they've achieved?" Therefore, there are some pages in this playbook. For instance, focusing and looking at individual markets and going deep, which is primarily what we did in 2005. . . .

. . . It has been interesting to watch our growth in continuing markets. We currently have 21 actively managed communities in major cities across the United States. But it has been fascinating to watch how each city ignites and how the communities are all very different and they all have different cultural tones. But underneath it all, there is the same common thread; "Wow, I am able to finally jump on my soapbox here and share all of my favorites." It is a little bit ego-driven, perhaps, but then the second part of that is about contributing back to the community in a meaningful way that is also heard by others. . . .

. . . I think what has been interesting to watch is that folks have made an analogy to Yelp as, "Oh, you are a social network?" And actually, we see ourselves more as a local community site. And that's because when you log in to a social network, you're effectively creating your account and inviting your social network to participate and engage, and finding folks who may already exist on that particular platform.

Whereas in Yelp, it's really more about joining a community of like-minded individuals who (guess what!) happen to live within the parameters of your geography, your city, and you all share a common interest. That is what Yelp is all about: local businesses and services. And so, we are defining what that community discussion is about.

There have been questions like, "Do Yelpers meet offline?" And they absolutely do.

It's probably because we all live within the same city; and very close people establish affinities, or interests. We are finding . . . that Yelpers will organize groups and then meet offline and get together. So there is a really interesting social element there. All of these things speak very strongly to the notion of communities, and we are designed to support that. . . .

. . . And that's what's illuminating. We've heard time and again that Yelpers are people who visit the site, perhaps more casually, just to find information. They may have lived in a particular city for all their life. Still they're finding new businesses that they never knew existed. In addition, Yelp (and the reviews they find on Yelp) is inspiring them to go out and try something

(continued)

(continued)

that is outside of their comfort zone. But they are exploring and they are discovering new businesses because they have a bit of a preview into that. The Yelp community is really saying, "Wow, this place is absolutely worth the 30-minute drive to (the next town over). You should check it out, it would be worth your while."

So we are finding that Yelpers write back in and say, "Wow, it's been extremely powerful in helping me find great businesses, and spending my money and dollars with locally owned operations is something I enjoy doing, and I now have the confidence to be able to extend myself beyond what I would normally do."

What I think you'll find over time, though, is that being able to then dive down in to the individual profiles of people who are talking about a business will even further refine those pick/sees.

Yelp is built entirely on this notion of community, and then individuals, as well, right? So my profile page has some general information about me, the light-hearted stuff (favorite movies, books, where I grew up, my interests in general). And so from there you immediately get a quick snapshot of what kind of person Stephanie is. And then you are able to look at all of my reviews, which serve in a way as lifestyle blogs. For instance, I like to go out to eat, and that for the five or six restaurants that I may try this week, I'll write reviews of those and you get a sense of that. Everybody has different preferences and tastes, and so if you are following my blog and you decided at some point, "Hey, you know I have a lot in common with this type of person, and she's rating and reviewing things similar in nature to what I would." I would want to select what should be one of my favorites, and I could almost follow that individual over time.

So now, it's you building a small set of preferences on Yelp. And that way when you are doing searches, when you're logged in, you'll be able to refine enough to tell that these same voices are pointing you to the direction of the business that they've tried.

We believe that's important because understanding what a profile or a person is all about really helps instill an additional layer of trust and value in the information they are providing. . . .

. . . As for myself, I use the site in two different manners just for the purposes of keeping in touch, but I will use my logged-in profile when I am doing searches personally. When I want to find something like a great seamstress, or whatever; and I have all of my favorites set so that the reviews of folks that I have been following for a while will pop up if these are businesses that they have rated and reviewed.

So it definitely helps out quite a bit. . . .

. . . And the interesting thing is that even when we take a look at Yelp overall, we look at all of the reviews and we look at our category breakdowns. What we are finding is that less than 34 percent of businesses reviewed on Yelp are restaurants. And 34 percent is a number that is a lot smaller than a lot of people would have guessed. . . .

. . . It is followed by the shopping category, which comprised about 23 percent of the reviewed businesses. Then there is beauty and fitness, which drops off at around 8 percent, entertainment at 7 percent, and local services at around 7 percent.

So the distribution of this type of review is really various and spans a lot of different categories. Where most people think we just judge restaurants, we actually have a lot more to offer. . . .

. . . So we find that Yelpers are truly passionate about showing everything that they consume locally, like the other local services offerings, spas, salons, manicures, and pedicures. And that's our goal, really. It is all about connecting people with great local businesses. . . .

To listen to or read the entire Executive Conversation with Stephanie Ichinose, go to www.theSocialMediaBible.com.

International Perspective

United Kingdom

By far the most predominant social network in use by UK marketers is Facebook. This is logical, because as they say "fish where the fish are" and Facebook has the highest usage and penetration in the UK. This is why a social network's only real currency is their user base, if you lose the user base, then you lose the brands and advertisers. Other popular platforms are Twitter,

(*continued*)

(continued)

Google+ and YouTube in that order. For B2B marketers, LinkedIn, Twitter, and self-contained social platforms have more prevalence. Social Commerce networks such as Groupon are gaining major traction due to their incredible reach and ability to drive direct conversions.

My strategy can be best described as "Discover and Engage." I see the benefits of third party social networks as broadly separated into two camps, amplification of content and user engagement.

Strategy	Amplification	User engagement
Tactic	Tweet this 'Like/Share' '+1'	Competitions, engaging with fans and followers, gaining their input into NPD
Benefit	Social Proof, traffic, discovery, SEO ranking and discoverability	Reduced costs, advocacy, loyalty, NPD insight, social proof at brand level (endorsement)

As the capability of social platforms becomes more sophisticated, so do the opportunities. No longer is it adequate for users to share a piece of content, but we can enable them to enrich their social profile and in the case of Facebook Timeline, their "digital autobiographies" with more information about themselves courtesy of brands. What cars they aspire to, what music they are listening to, and much more is the next stage in social networks becoming the glue that binds the Internet together.

For every piece of content shared on Facebook or Twitter, we receive on average 5.4 unique users in return through that link. Every fan or follower we acquire saves £5–£10 per annum in research costs and their visit frequency is increased threefold over a regular user who is not a fan.

—Ian MacDonald, Head of Consumer Marketing
Trader Media Group
www.TraderMediaGroup.com

To-Do List

- Search and participate.

  Pick a topic of your liking and search for a forum that has a group with an ongoing discussion on that topic. Begin as a guest, if it makes you more comfortable, and then register and participate for a while to see what you can learn from it. Think about the trusted network and loyalty that this forum is providing for you, and how you might be able to build that same kind of trust around your company or brand.

- Set up your own forum.

  Once you've participated in a few forums and experienced what it is like to build these kinds of strong connections, you might want to next consider building this type of community around your company, product, or service. Give it a try. Using Yuku is a free and easy way to see if creating a forum is right for you.

Conclusion

While the forum is one of the oldest technologies on the web, it is still a great way to easily create a trusted community around your company, product, brand, service, or subject matter. Try it! Set up your own forum, and invite a few friends, employees, customers, and prospects to engage in an ongoing conversation about your interests and what you do. It's free, and—as with many other social media tools—the ROI is unimaginable.

To hear all of the Expert Interviews, go to www.theSocialMediaBible .com.

Downloads

For your free downloads associated with *The Social Media Bible,* go to www
.theSocialMediaBible.com,

and enter your ISBN number located on the back of the book above the bar
code. Be sure to enter the dashes.

Credits

The ROI of Social Media provided by:

Dr. Gary Edwards, executive vice president for client services and

Julia Staffen, director of product management, GoRecommend
Empathica, Inc., www.empathica.com

Expert Insight was provided by:

Stephanie Ichinose, director of communications, Yelp, www.yelp.com

Technical edits were provided by:

Lynne Johnson, www.lynnedjohnson.com,

Stephanie Ichinose, director of communications, Yelp, www.yelp.com

Notes

1. CAPTCHA: Completely Automated Public Turing Test to Tell Computers and Humans Apart (see www.captcha.net)

is a program that protects websites against bots by generating and grading tests that humans can pass, but that current computer programs cannot. This term was coined in 2000 by Luis von Ahn, Manuel Blum, Nicholas Hopper, and John Langford of Carnegie Mellon University. At the time, they developed the first CAPTCHA to be used by Yahoo! For example, humans can read distorted text like that shown in Figure 5.3, but current computer technology cannot.

2. Atom is an XML-based document format that describes attributes of a file known as *feeds*. Feeds are composed of a number of items known as *entries*. Atom is used to syndicate web content such as blogs, podcasts, and news to websites and aggregation pages.

3. The KickApps-hosted, white-label platform puts social media and online video functionality directly into the hands of every web publisher who aspires to be a media mogul, and turns every web designer and developer into a social media rock star! With KickApps, it's now easier than ever for web publishers to leverage the power of social and rich media experiences on their websites to drive audience growth and engagement.

CHAPTER 6

The Ubiquitous Blog

www.LonSafko.com/TSMB3_Videos/06Blog.mov

What's in It for You?

Scientists, psychiatrists, psychologists, and counselors have known for a long time of the therapeutic benefits that accompany writing about personal experiences in a diary or journal. Blogs provide a convenient tool for writing about your individual thoughts and activities. Research shows that journaling improves your memory, sleep—and now, maybe even your bottom line.

In the twentieth century, professional reporters and publishers decided what the news was and determined how the public saw it. Though we might still have some professionals making these decisions in the twenty-first century, we now have personal reporters and publishers—more than 50 million of them—who bring our news to us on a daily basis.

Although communication is—and always has been—a two-way process, the methods of communication to prospects and customers has changed dramatically over recent years. The use of social media digital tools has allowed for less reporting and more conversation. The web log, or blog, is the easiest and most effective way to provide a conduit for this type of communication. Blogs create communication, and communication builds trust—and blogs are completely free to build and access. In fact,

theSocialMediaBible.com

bloggers and other contributors to user-generated content were the reason that *Time* magazine named their 2006 Person of the Year . . . "You."

Back to the Beginning

The term *blog* derives from *web log,* which is simply another word for an online journal. Peter Merholz then took the word *WeBLOG* and separated it into *We Blog* in a sidebar of his web page, www.Peterme.com.

Entrepreneur Evan Williams, developer for Pyra Labs' Blogger.com, first used the word *blog* as both a verb and a noun—in reference to posting to one's web log—and thus officially created the term *blogger.*

Before HTTP was in common use, a service called Usenet was the primary medium for communicating over the World Wide Web. Usenet featured a moderated newsgroup, which was either group- or individually controlled. Around this same time, Brian E. Redman—generally known as the first individual blogger—began posting summaries of other interesting information he found on the Internet, and thereby created his own blog called mod.ber (named for his initials, B.E.R.).

Back in the mid-1990s, there were online communities such as GEnie, BiX, EarthLink, Prodigy, and CompuServe, all of which were the earliest ISPs (Internet service providers) that provided bulletin board systems (BBS) and forums. Later, people would use this type of Internet software to create online diaries or journals to document daily activities of their personal lives. They called themselves *diarists, journalers,* and *journalists.*

An online diary called Wearable Wireless Webcam—which included text, photos, and video, broadcasting live using a wearable computer and EyeTap—is also credited with being one of the earliest blogs (see Chapter 14, Live from Anywhere—It's Livecasting). While this activity is referred to specifically as *livecasting* today, it was then considered to

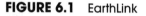

FIGURE 6.1   EarthLink

be a form of the earliest semiautomated blogging of someone's personal life in the form of a video journal. This type of livecasting is also referred to as *sousveillance,* a term that describes the recording of an activity from the perspective of a participant experiencing that very event.

The earliest blogs were simply continuous updates of a standard HTML website—a process that was difficult, and which required a certain level of technical knowledge to maintain the HTML code. However, more recent developments in browser-based blog platforms—enabling easy posting of articles in reverse chronological order and one-click editing features such as permalinks, blogrolls, and TrackBacks—made linking to other blogs and web pages easier (see Figure 6.2). The ability to blog finally became accessible to the average nontechnical computer user.

FIGURE 6.2   TSMB Dashboard

Blogs can be used on a hosted service—such as Blogger.com

or GoingOn.com

—or can be hosted on your own server with software such as WordPress, Blogger, MovableType, or LiveJournal. Nearly all websites in the mid-1990s—personal and corporate—had a What's New or News section on them, which was usually sorted by date. This was essentially the earliest form of news-based blog. One such web page—the popular Drudge Report—was created by Matt Drudge and began simply enough: through Drudge's e-mails to his friends. When this chapter was written, the number of blogs was approaching 200 million worldwide.

October 1998 brought the launch of Open Diary—a service that invented and introduced the reader comment, whereby readers could provide their own feedback to bloggers' posts. In August 1999, reporter Jonathan Dube of the *Charlotte Observer* published his own blog chronicling Hurricane Bonnie, which marked the creation of the first known use of a blog on a news site.

In August 1999, Evan Williams and Meg Hourihan of Pyra Labs launched blog publishing system Blogger.com,

which was later purchased by Google in February 2003. In September 1999, a site called Diaryland—which focused more on the personal diary community—was started.

But people weren't just blogging about their personal lives and daily activities. In 2001, several popular political blogs emerged in the United States. British political commentator and speaker Andrew Sullivan created AndrewSullivan.com;

attorney and journalist Ron Gunzburger launched his Politics1.com.

Blogging was beginning to go mainstream, and was becoming so popular that there were how-to guides and established schools of journalism that began studying and comparing blogging to more conventional types of journalism.

Blogging is often so timely that the mere term *blogging* has also come to mean *transcribed* or *editorialized*, as might occur during speeches or televised events. As an example, one could say, "I am blogging my reactions to speeches as they occur on television"—known as *liveblogging*. Many presentations are *tweeted* live using Twitter microblogging (see Chapter 13, Thumbs Up for Microblogging, for more information on Twitter). These snippets of

FIGURE 6.3 Blooker Award

information can be tweeted to a presenter's followers or to the user's blog—using the freshest, most current information available.

In fact, during a recent presentation at a PodCamp weekend, a small giggle ran through the audience in the middle of a presentation about social media. The speaker stopped and asked what the chatter was about, and someone admitted that another audience member tweeted that there was a spelling error in the presentation. The speaker stopped the presentation, corrected the error, and thanked the blogging audience. How fresh is *this?*

In January 2005, *Fortune* magazine listed eight bloggers whom business-people "could not ignore": Peter Rojas (www.crunchbase.com/person/peter -rojas),

Xeni Jardin (www.boingboing.net),

Mena and Ben Trott (www.sixapart.com), Jonathan Schwartz (www.blogs .sun.com/jonathan),

Jason Goldman (www.goldtoe.net),

Robert Scoble (www.scobleizer.com),

and Jason Calacanis (www.calacanis.com).

In 2007, media mogul Tim O'Reilly proposed a Blogger's Code of Conduct to enforce civility on blogs by being calm and moderating comments. The code was proposed as a result of threats made to blogger Kathy Sierra. Tim O'Reilly stated, "I do think we need some code of conduct around what is acceptable behavior. I would hope that it doesn't come through any kind of regulation [but that] it would come through self-regulation." See http://radar.oreilly.com/2007/04/code-of-conduct-lessons-learne.html; http://oreil.ly/AfULt.

All of these clickable links can be accessed through www.theSocial MediaBible.com.

What You Need to Know

A *blog*—or *web log*—is a website that is maintained by an individual with regular entries or posts that include commentary, thoughts, and ideas, and may contain photos, graphics, audio, or video. Posts are most often displayed in reverse chronological order. Most blogs provide news and content on a specific subject, while others operate as personal journals. Blogs usually have text, images, video, and links to other blogs and websites that relate to the blog's subject matter. One of the most important features of a blog is the reader's ability to interact with the author through comments. While most blogs are made up of text, many bloggers prefer to add art (creating an artblog), photographs (a photoblog), sketches (for a sketchblog), music (or musicblog), audio (creating an audioblog—see Chapter 9, Talking about the Podcast (Audio Create)), or a podcast blog. And just like podcasting can mean either audio or video, blogging refers to anyone who writes an opinion about something.

A blog can be personal- or business-related. Business blogs can be used for internal communication to employees, or designed to be viewed by the public. Blogs used for sales, marketing, branding, PR, and communicating with customers and prospects are often referred to as *corporate blogs*.

Blogs can fall into a number of different categories. One kind provides a feature called a Question Blog—called *Qlogs*—in which readers can submit a query through a comment, submission form, or e-mail. Blog writers and administrators are then responsible for answering these questions. A blog site that posts primarily video is called a *Vlog* (video blog website); then there are blogs that only post links to other blogs, called *linklogs*. Blogs that post shorter posts and a lot of mixed rich media are referred to as *tumblogs*; and blogs about legal issues and information are called *blawgs*. And of course, the not-so-legitimate spamming blog is called a *Splog*.

The entirety of all the blogs on the Internet is referred to as the *blogosphere*, while a collection of blogs located in the same geographical area is called a *bloghood*.

While most blogs are created and maintained just for fun, many are supported by advertising or product sales. Sites use resources such as automatic content-specific banners and other types of ad placements, like Google's AdSense. Some bloggers make money by promoting products and earning a commission for the referral. Most of the larger, more popular blogs that enjoy high monthly traffic are easily earning six figures in advertising income.

All of these different blogs spread out over the entire globe had to create the opportunity for blog-specific search engines. Besides the standard Google and Yahoo! search engines, other kinds each have a blog-specific option as well. There are online communities that help readers find the right blog for a particular topic or area of interest, such as BlogCatalog. There are also blog-only search engines like Bloglines, BlogScope, and Technorati, which is the most popular blog-specific search engine at the time this chapter was written. Technorati (www.Technorati.com)

actually provides lists of the most popular searches and tags used in posts (see Chapter 5, The World of Web Pages, for more information about tags).

A blog's popularity can be greatly enhanced by a high rating on Technorati, a site that was founded to help bloggers succeed by collecting, highlighting, and distributing information about the online global conversation. Technorati determines and assigns a ranking to each blog based on the number of incoming links (often called "link love"), and Alexa user hits. As the leading blog search engine and most comprehensive source of information in the blogosphere, Technorati indexes more than 1.5 million new blog posts in real time and introduces millions of readers to blog and social media content.

Maintaining a blog requires work and a moderate amount of dedication and effort. (While working on writing *The Social Media Bible,* the author updated his blog only half a dozen times and did not tweet as frequently. One of his loyal readers scolded him.)

The Gartner Research Group expects that the novelty value of the blog will wear off eventually, since so many people who are interested in the phenomenon create a blog just to see what it's like. Gartner further expects that new bloggers will outnumber those bloggers who abandon their blogs out of boredom, and estimates that more than 200 million former bloggers have already ceased posting to their blogs, creating a huge rise in the amount of *dotsam and netsam* (a play on the terms *flotsam* and *jetsam*), or unwanted objects on the Web.

There are currently more than 300 mainstream journalists who write their own blogs, according to CyberJournalist.net's J-blog list.

Many conventional bloggers have now moved over to more conventional media, including liberal media scholar Duncan Black (known by his pseudonym, Atrios; www.eschatonblog.com),

Instapundit's blogger Glenn Reynolds (www.pajamasmedia.com/insta pundit),

political analyst and current events reporter Markos Moulitsas Zúniga of the Daily Kos (www.dailykos.com),

American writer and futurist Alex Steffen of Worldchanging (www .worldchanging.com),

and Time.com

editor and author Ana Marie Cox of Wonkette (www.wonkette.com),

who have all appeared on radio and television.

Many bloggers have actually published books based on their original blog posts; these types of blog-based books are called *blooks*. Authors include Salam Pax, *The Clandestine Diary of an Ordinary Iraqi* from The Baghdad Blog; Ellen Simonetti, *Diary of a Dysfunctional Flight Attendant: The Queen of Sky Blog*; Jessica Cutler, *The Washingtonienne: A Novel* (washingtoniennearchive.blogspot.com);

and Scott Ott's *ScrappleFace* (www.scrappleface.com).

In 2005, the Lulu Blooker Prize was created for the best blog-based book. So far, the only winner who has made it to the *New York Times* bestseller list with a book based on his blogs is Tucker Max, who wrote *I Hope They Serve Beer in Hell*, or, as Max puts it, "My name is Tucker Max, and I am an asshole." Another example of a blogger becoming a book author is Julie Powell's The Julie/Julia Project, which became the movie *Julie & Julia* in 2009. This American comedy/drama film was written and directed by Nora Ephron and starred Meryl Streep as Julia Child, Amy Adams as Julie Powell, and Stanley Tucci as Paul Child, Julia Child's husband. This film won Meryl Streep an Academy Award nomination for Best Actress.

This film is based on the life of chef Julia Child and the life of Julie Powell, who cooks all 524 recipes from Child's cookbook over a one-year period, while Powell describes her experiences on her 2004 blog (http://en.wikipedia.org/wiki/Julie_%26_Julia).

The ROI of Social Media

Vistaprint Tweeting for Awareness, Reputation Management, and Revenue

Background

The Vistaprint public relations team began to notice buzz building around the company's brand in various social networks. While there was an overall positive tone, the team noticed that postings ran a gamut of emotions from truly positive to extremely negative and everything in between. Because social media was an apparently expanding marketing medium, the decision was made to research where it could have an impact, where to engage, and how.

Strategy

Knowing that the conversation about Vistaprint was happening with or without the company's involvement, the team decided that all mentions, positive or negative, warranted a response.

While the initial goal of interacting on Twitter was to increase the interaction level with customers and potential customers, the team also anticipated the impact the medium could have in regard to customer service and revenue generation. The approach toward revenue generation was to offer a soft sell rather than an aggressive offer (example: @jeffespo thanks for the plug @jaykeith; if you would like to give us a try, please visit www.vistaprint.com/twitter).

(continued)

(*continued*)

The initial customer service queries would be fielded by the PR team to get a baseline and establish if there was a need for true customer service department involvement.

Implementation

Before entering the space, the Vistaprint team spent three months monitoring where the conversations were happening. By looking at the commentary coming from all neighborhoods of Twitterville, the team established a framework for responses. In certain situations, the team will use a standard message but the majority of the time tweets are unscripted. These responses bring personality to the brand and avoid the feeling that the account is run by an automated tool, or bot.

The company began interacting on Twitter from the @Vistaprint account. This was done exclusively by the PR team. After 12 months, the team noticed an increase in customer service issues and created a second account for the company. The new handle, @VistaprintHelp, is now manned by Vistaprint's customer service team and handles all customer service–related questions.

The team selected Co-Tweet as a conversation-monitoring tool. The web-based application allows multiple users to log in to the company's accounts, assign workflow, and see the lifetime conversation thread with users.

Opportunity

As an e-retailer, Vistaprint is very conscious of the ever-changing landscape of the Internet. Without a brick and mortar location, the company is constantly looking for new avenues to reach and expand its customer base. With the continual growth of Twitter and its integration with mainstream society, Vistaprint's interaction will increase awareness of the brand and attract new customers.

Conclusion

With just the investment of time, the PR team's strategy has hosted over 12,300 conversations through the company's main accounts (@vistaprint, @vistaprinthelp). During the 2009 fiscal year, the company generated over $25,000 in orders from the targeted soft-sell URL.

—Jeff Esposito
www.vistaprint.com

Expert Insight

Matt Mullenweg, cofounder of WordPress, www.WordPress.org

Matt Mullenweg

For me, it was always that I wanted to have the means of personal expression. I always enjoyed writing and, so, publishing. It was pretty exciting. And I would say that it was really the *interaction* from the readers. So, although blogging is great, I blog for the comments. Because I know if I say something that's wrong or anything like that, the readers will let me know. . . .

It [provides] access to people all over the world that you would never meet otherwise, so what's cool is that sense, because my blog's very personal. It's people who are interested in the same things that I am. Maybe it's jazz or economics or photography or WordPress. So the answer to why I started blogging is I find it very, very rewarding. . . .

We probably do super-well on the search engines, and actually [they don't] try too many tricks or anything specific to target us at WordPress; [they] just create a really great user experience. Have the content well organized, have a permanent place for blogposts (which are often called a *permalink*). Just use proper HTML headings, tags, or the titles to the heading tags for the titles, for the posts. Some of these things get a little bit geeky, but if you create semantic, well-structured, frequently updated content, I think search engines . . . are just trying to serve their use by being one of the better resources on the web. . . .

The development is, you know, 95 percent user-defined; so from release to release we have a time schedule that we plan on a year in advance. But in terms of features for release, it's really defined by what our users are asking for. So, for example, in the last release we had, sort of, a *wiki*-like tracking feature, so every version of every post is saved forever. So if you make a mistake or go off-edit approach, you can go and see exactly what changed.

(continued)

(continued)

Things like that . . . some of our users don't even know it's there. It's a really powerful tool that your competitors haven't thought about yet. So we were able to get it early because we listened very closely to our community. . . .

I think what you really have to do if you're a leader of an open source process is something that inspires people, something that people can coalesce around and get them excited to work on, even though they are not getting paid. On the carrot versus stick, all you really have is the carrot! So, (laughter) you really have to make it fun and engaging, and I think people will come, especially since they will control it in such an amazing way that has impact.

To listen to or read the entire Executive Conversation with Matt Mullenweg, go to www.theSocialMediaBible.com.

International Perspective

Ireland

To say that Ireland has embraced social media would be an understatement. According to recent survey data, we are ranked the fourth largest user of social media sites within Europe and the largest business users internationally. Not only that but the Regus survey indicates that 64 percent of Irish businesses are utilizing blogs, boards, online forums, and social networking sites to connect and engage with existing customers as well as build customer loyalty and retention. When you consider that that the global average is 52 percent you now can understand my allusion to understatement. (An interesting aside here is that 90 percent of Irish Non-Profit Organizations utilize social media within their organization and communication!)

With 44 percent of the Irish business sectors utilizing social media for gaining more customers, we have steadily incorporated social media into our business strategy. This can be backed up with the fact that 52 percent of the surveyed companies actively encourage their employees to join online networking groups such as LinkedIn. In fact, Ireland has one of the world's highest penetrations of LinkedIn.

When we actual dig into active Irish business social media activity we have 53 percent of the business sectors utilizing it as an important resource for business information. With 48 percent of businesses following the same strategies as the rest of the world—customer awareness, gain, engagement, retention, and drive to online sale.

The main platforms for online communication are the holy trinity of social media: Facebook, YouTube, and Twitter and the clear market winners being those that are content consistent and creative.

The main reason for our success is the swift induction and incorporation of social media within the businesses marketing strategy. This was helped with the active online customer base engagement; competition, in the fact, that the majority of the individual business sectors are actively online and a growing social media savvy within the SME Irish business sector.

The majority of companies who are using social media successfully have a clear consistent content plan with inbuilt internal reviews and dedicated staff to their online social media brand. With the ease of accessibility, via smartphones, for picture and video posting and an online community acceptance and desire for unique bespoke reality digital posting we have seen the interaction grow on both sides. This is of particular interest to small businesses when you consider that 44 percent of them have gained new customers via a social media platform compared to 36 percent for medium companies and 28 percent for large businesses.

Facebook is by far the most current communication media for Irish businesses. The recent introduction of "Facebook Insights" has been a positive step toward driving internal management to a more professional and uniform approach to content and online posting.

With 75 percent of Irish businesses committed to social media to help grow their business and with businesses now actively engaging successfully with their customers online we have seen a positive shift to a new dynamic in customer service and professional practices.

—Jude Torley
www.judetorley.com

(continued)

(continued)

Source, Data and References

Survey Source: the EU Eurobarometer and the Regus Survey

EU's Eurobarometer: ec.europa.eu/public_opinion/index_en.htm

Regus survey: www.regus.presscentre.com/Resource-Library/Social -Media-1cf.aspx

NPO Data Source: The Wheel, the national representative and support body for community, voluntary, and charity organizations: www.wheel.ie /news/new-research-shows-non-profit-sector-leading-way-social-media

Reference material via articles in the *Irish Times* Finance Section and *Business and Leadership Magazine.*

To-Do List

While doing research for this chapter, the original intent was to take some items from David Risley's 50 Rapid Fire Tips for Power Blogging, paraphrase them, and turn them into a to-do list—but David's list had just too much good information to choose from. So here are David Risley's 50 tips in their entirety. *(Thank you, David!)*

50 Rapid Fire Tips for Power Blogging

I have been blogging for a living for many years now. I've learned a lot and, today, I wanted to throw out a bunch of quick tips in rapid succession. The goals here are (1) get lots of traffic to your blog, and (2) earn money with it. Okay, here we go (in no particular order):

1. *Use WordPress.* No other platform is as flexible with all the plug-ins, in my opinion.

2. *Post often.* Your blog will have more visibility if you post more often. These days, I usually post at least two times per week on my blog. On another of my blogs, it is twice per DAY. As a minimum, once a week or more is a good benchmark.

3. *Use catchy blog post titles.* Put yourself in the shoes of a person who is casually surfing the Internet, seeing your post along with hundreds of others. Will your blog headline stand out? Copyblogger is an awesome source for information on writing.

4. *Ask open-ended questions.* One of the best ways to invite commentary on your posts is to ask for it. Ask your readers questions and tell them to answer in the form of a comment.

5. *Comment on other blogs—often.* I actually maintain a separate folder in Google Reader for relevant blogs I want to follow more closely than others. And, on those blogs, I comment regularly whenever I have something to say.

6. *Use social media.* You need to be out there on Twitter and Facebook. LinkedIn is great if your audience is primarily professional. Google+ is newer, but we often find the most passionate crowds on there. So, definitely don't ignore Google+.

7. *Use Twitterfeed to pipe your latest posts into Twitter.* But, don't *only* use Twitterfeed. You've got to be a real person on Twitter, first and foremost. Twitter should not replace RSS.

8. *Make your RSS feed obvious*, above the fold, and preferably use the orange RSS icon.

9. *Provide an RSS-to-E-mail option* so people can subscribe to your latest posts without being forced to use an RSS reader. Many people still don't use RSS. FeedBurner provides a free RSS-to-E-mail service.

10. *Use images in your posts.* Images communicate on aesthetic wavelengths that words cannot. Ensure your image adds to the theme or meaning of the post and isn't just there for the sake of itself.

11. *Use header tags* to separate sections in your blog posts, where applicable: H1, H2, and H3 tags. And use good search engine keywords wherever possible in those headers.

12. *Structure your blog posts for easy scanning.* Use header tags, lists, and so on. Avoid long sentences and long paragraphs. People have short attention spans online. You need to work with it, not against it.

13. *Keep Things Simple.* What I mean by this is super *busy* designs with too much onscreen, animated graphics, and so on. These things make your blog truly suck and makes your content too hard to pay attention to.

14. *If possible, use a custom WordPress theme.* It is getting to the point where people can recognize cookie-cutter themes. It is okay to use one, but at least modify it so that you have a unique header design.

15. *Start your blog's mailing list as early as possible.* The sooner you start, the longer you have to grow your list and, trust me, that list can be used to make money later. Also, without a mailing list, your blog is simply reactive. It just sits there and you hope people come. With a list, you have the ability to reach out and bring them back.

16. *Research and choose your mailing list option correctly the first time.* I recommend Aweber. What you choose is up to you; however, moving a mailing list later can be a huge pain. I know from experience.

17. *When choosing a topic* to focus your blog on, two things should be considered: Your interest in the topic, and how marketable your topic is.

18. *Learn to sell.* The way to a full-time income by blogging is to learn how to *market* and sell things using your blog. Don't avoid being marketed to. Embrace it and learn from watching how they do it.

19. *Don't discount Facebook.* Facebook has over 800 million users. It simply can't be ignored.

20. *Create a Facebook page.* On Facebook, create a page for your blog or yourself and invite your readers and Facebook friends to become fans.

This page can be your blog's outpost on Facebook. Be sure to import your blog posts as notes.

21. *Don't be a me-too blogger.* You don't want to become a copycat news blog, where you type news-style posts about what is happening in a saturated market. In technology, this is common. Offer something unique that cannot be found everywhere else in your market.

22. *Learn to think about your blog as a business.* The blog is a promotional and delivery mechanism to your ultimate product or service.

23. *When writing your About page, pay attention to what you write.* Don't just rattle off some dumb, cookie-cutter facts. Your About page should tell a story of who you are and why your blog is worth reading. Step into the shoes of your new reader and convince them that your blog is worth their time.

24. *Do lots of videos.* Use TubeMogul to publish them in as many places as you can. And make sure your blog URL is not only in the video, but also in the text description that accompanies the video.

25. *When making videos, be real and be personable.* Your videos are an important component to your blog's brand. Don't waste the opportunity.

26. *Link to other, related blog posts regularly in your own posts.* Not only your *own* posts, but also the posts of others.

27. *Remember, blogging is a social business.* Be accessible to your readers and proactively get out there and talk with other people in your niche.

28. *If you can afford it, travel to blogging conferences.* Not only can you learn a lot, but also socializing with successful people often breeds so much motivation and success in yourself that it is simply beyond words.

29. *Write an e-book, create some videos*—whatever—but the idea is to create something that is of value to your readers on your subject, and have it available to *sell* to them on your blog.

30. *Get involved as an affiliate* and start linking to products relevant to your posts using your affiliate links. You are providing relevant links to your readers (valuable) while potentially making some money.

31. *Don't post low FeedBurner counts.* Do not show your RSS subscriber count unless you have a high enough number (at least a few hundred). A low number acts as social proof that your blog has no readers, and that's not good.

32. *Install a plug-in for popular posts,* which ranks your posts based on popularity. Whether you display this information in public on your blog or not, knowing which of your posts are most popular tells you

that that particular subject material works and you should probably do more of it.

33. *Put relevant keywords into your blog's title.* Use All-In-One SEO to have more control over the titles across your blog.

34. *Use a photo gallery.* People dig photos, so a photo gallery can be a great component to your blog. If you use Flickr, check out the Flickr Photo Album plug-in for WordPress.

35. *Create a video* gallery to bring your YouTube videos into your blog automatically. Check out the TubePress plug-in.

36. *Spend some time creating some killer posts for your blog,* then link to them somewhere so that new arrivals can quickly see your best work. It is your best stuff, which is going to sell them into becoming a subscriber.

37. *Make sharing easy.* Put options on your blog for your readers to share your posts across social media. Focus on the most relevant social networks only. I don't recommend using a plug-in that litters your post with tons of social media sharing buttons. When you give people too many choices, they likely won't do anything. Plus, it is just added clutter.

38. *Share and share alike.* If you submit your own posts to sites like Digg or StumbleUpon, be sure to also submit other posts. I might even recommend a 10-to-1 ratio of other people's posts to your own posts. You do not want to develop a reputation on these sites as somebody who submits only their own content.

39. *When you write a post for your blog, aim to be helpful.* You want your visitors to come away with a solution to the problem they arrived with. Chris Brogan does so well because his posts are truly helpful.

40. *Read other blogs often.* When starving for ideas to write about, go to your RSS reader and read related blogs. Often, your own post can be a response to a post on another blog. In fact, this is usually a good idea.

41. *Train your readers to do what you want, if needed.* If you're in a market where the people will not know how to use social media, RSS, and some of these other things that help promote your blog, *train them.* Write posts or do videos which show your visitors how to Digg a post, use StumbleUpon, how to use RSS, and so on. Perhaps you can educate them and they'll become part of your promotion army for your own blog.

42. *When starting a blog, decide on its mission.* Your posts should, for the most part, center on a specific theme if you want your blog to really take off. If you run a personal diary kind of blog, where you write about anything that comes to mind, your blog traffic will always be limited because your blog will never attract any particular segment of

people. Stay on topic. If you have no specific topic, that's fine, but realize your blog is going to be more a hobby than a business at that point.

43. *Don't overload your blog with JavaScript widgets.* These things slow down the load speed of your site. The more things you bring in from third-party sites into your blog, the slower it will be.

44. *Use Analytics.* I personally use Google Analytics as well as the JetPack plug-in (from WordPress) on [my] blog.

45. *Use Windows Live Writer.* It is the best blogging client program out there. Even though it is a Microsoft product and a Windows-only product, it is also better than any Mac blogging client I have tried. And it's free. If you're on a Mac, MarsEdit is pretty good.

46. *Be yourself.* I believe it is a good thing to show personality on your blog. Don't be a fake. People can see right through it. Chris Pirillo draws people to his blog and Ustream feed almost solely on personality alone.

47. *Don't write like you're writing for Britannica.* You want your spelling and grammar to be correct, but be colloquial. Talk to people like you would normally talk to people, not as if you're writing a PhD dissertation.

48. *Link to your social profiles on your blog.* Link your various social media profiles right on your blog so that your readers can connect with you outside the confines of your blog.

49. *Go where your readers are.* Every market is different. When I blog about blogging, I know most of my readers are pretty adept online and probably hang out in the social media space frequently. Your readers might be on Facebook. If they're Linux nerds, they may be in the Ubuntu forums. Regardless, you need to maintain a consistent presence in the spaces your readers congregate. Be an authority and be helpful, and traffic will be drawn over to your blog.

50. *[Spend] equal time reading and writing.* You should probably spend just as much time reading and learning as you do writing for your blog. This is how you expand your knowledge, become a better blogger, and get new ideas for your own site. Blogging isn't all about you. Remember that.

This list originally appeared on www.davidrisley.com.

Go to www.theSocialMediaBible.com for a clickable link.

Conclusion

Blogging is by far the easiest and most effective way to communicate with your customers and prospects. Starting your own blog is as simple as going to WordPress, creating an account, selecting the New Post button, typing your thoughts, and hitting Publish. That's really all there is to it. Please give blogging a try. It really only takes 15 to 20 minutes once a week, and is as easy as typing a half page in a standard word processor. By blogging, you create links through which your prospects can find you, you generate "Google Juice,"[1] you position yourself as an industry leader by providing the latest information in your field, you allow for a two-way conversation, and you build trust.

Once you have created a few posts, use all of your other forms of communication to promote your new source of information to your customers and prospects. Soon, the numbers will begin to grow, your "link love" will increase—and the industry will be waiting to hear your next insights.

To hear all of the Expert Interviews, go to www.theSocialMedia Bible.com.

Downloads

For your free downloads associated with *The Social Media Bible,* go to www.theSocialMediaBible.com,

and enter your ISBN number located on the back of the book above the bar code. Be sure to enter the dashes.

Credits

The ROI of Social Media was provided by:

Jeff Esposito, www.vistaprint.com

Expert Insight was provided by:

Matt Mullenweg, cofounder, WordPress, www.WordPress.org

Technical Edits were provided by:

David Risley, www.DavidRisley.com

Note

1. Google Juice is a term used to describe the results that follow when you search for your name, your company's name, and your product or service's name in Google or other search engines. The more listings and the more pages that a search engine returns to the searcher, the more Google Juice you have. The goal of this book is to squeeze as much Google Juice as possible out of your social media marketing and communications.

CHAPTER 7

The Wisdom of the Wiki

www.LonSafko.com/TSMB3_Videos/07Wiki.mov

What's in It for You?

The word *wiki* comes from the Hawaiian word for *fast,* or *quick,* and it alludes to the pace at which wiki content can be created. While some say wiki is an acronym for "*What I Know I*s," this came after the original naming and is rarely used within the wiki community. Wikis are websites that allow people to collect and edit their intelligence in one place at any time. These websites truly represent the social media foundation of user-generated content and the wisdom of the crowds.

A wiki is a browser-based web platform that lets volunteers contribute information based on their expertise and knowledge, and permits them to edit content within articles on specific subjects. Together, this material creates an encyclopedia-type knowledge base that is founded on the integrity of the contributor's additions. Wikis can either be open to the public or restricted to members or employees. Many companies today, such as Pixar, are using wikis to create knowledge management systems for retaining corporate information for collaboration and for training. By incorporating a company wiki, many firms can gather the collective knowledge of their employees on subjects such as policies and procedures, manufacturing and sales, company history, products—and even how to fix the fax machine's paper jams.

As wiki inventor and computer programmer Ward Cunningham puts it, "The wiki concept has become a study in what's now called 'social software.' With a wiki, I write the seed of the idea and I come back in a week and see how the idea has grown."

The wiki has become an extremely valuable, easy-to-use, free resource tool. It is as simple as write, edit, and save.

Back to the Beginning

Ward Cunningham came up with the concept for the wiki in 1994. Cunningham wanted to create a unique online site for programmers involved in a type of software development known as object-oriented programming, which allowed the user to drag and drop, and just click to make easy edits. The first website to be titled a *wiki* was Cunningham's own WikiWikiWeb (wikiwikiweb.com),

originally described as "the simplest online database that could possibly work." Cunningham gave the site this name upon recalling a Honolulu International Airport counter employee telling him to take the "Wiki-Wiki" shuttle bus in order to get from one airport terminal to another. Cunningham explained, "I chose wiki-wiki as an alliterative substitute for 'quick,' and thereby avoided naming this stuff quick-web."

Cunningham's initial design concept for his website came from Apple's HyperCard, an easy-to-use

FIGURE 7.1   Wiki-Wiki Bus

programming language that the education industry had widely adopted for the Macintosh computer in the late 1980s and early 1990s. HyperCard was a graphic metaphor of a stack of index cards that contained links to other cards.

On March 15, 2007, the word *wiki* entered the online Oxford English Dictionary.

As Apple phased out HyperCard from its software library, software company Silicon Beach developed a programming alternative called the SuperCard. From the early to mid-1990s, Safko International, Inc. was considered the largest SuperCard/HyperCard programming company in the country—with more than 150 programs and more than 1 million lines of code.

What You Need to Know

Cunningham and Bo Leuf—coauthors of *The Wiki Way: Quick Collaboration on the Web*—describe the wiki this way:

- A wiki invites all users to edit any page or to create new pages within the wiki website, using a plain vanilla web browser without any extra add-ons.
- Wiki promotes meaningful topic associations between different pages by making page link creation almost intuitively easy, and showing whether an intended target page exists or not.
- A wiki is *not* a carefully crafted site for casual visitors. Instead, it seeks to involve the visitor in an ongoing process of creation and collaboration that constantly changes the website landscape.

A wiki's ease of use lies in the fact that it allows documents to be collaboratively written using a web browser. While the wiki website is called the *wiki*, a single page is called a *wiki page*—which consists of user-generated content and hyperlinks to other articles, wiki pages, and external websites.

Editing and Creating

Wikis allow the users to easily generate pages with the click of a button from any web browser. The name of the wiki is condensed into a page title where spaces and some special characters are removed. This type of titling is called *Camel Case.* To see the Camel Case title of the wiki page called Matt Mullenweg—cofounder of WordPress—on *The Social Media Bible* website, go to the clickable link on www.thesocialmediabible.com/2008/08/29 /matt-mullenweg-founder-ceo-of-wordpress.

Simple Markup Language Tools

The system for creating and editing a wiki page is called SML (Simple Markup Language), or more often simply called *wikitext.* If you have ever created a blog, then you know what this is. (If you haven't created a blog, you need to read Chapter 6, The Ubiquitous Blog, to find out why you should!) SMP is easy to use and has the WYSIWYG (what you see is what you get) editing features of most common word processing software: bold, italic, underline, insert photo or video, center, right, left, and full justification, and so forth. Most wikis indicate who has made edits and when they've been made by keeping track of versions of the content, a feature that helps prevent mistakes and vandalism.

Security

Wikis are a very open set of documents, and are generally accessible to the public or an entire employee base—which only makes them all the more vulnerable to mistakes and vandalism. Wikis are designed to make it easy to correct errors, and they contain a useful "recent changes" page feature. This page lists all recent edits, when they were made, and by whom. In addition, wikis provide the previous unaltered version and what is called the *diff* feature—a tool that highlights the difference or changes between page revisions. This way, an editor can view the article before it was altered, compare it with the new page, and even restore the wiki page to its previous revision before the edit was made, if necessary.

While malicious vandalism can and does occur, a wiki's editors can easily catch it and revert to a previously stored edition to eliminate any unwelcome changes. Lars Erik Aronsson, a Swedish computer programmer, consultant, and founder of two Swedish websites—the free electronic book archive Project Runeberg and the Swedish language wiki http://en.wikipedia.org/wiki/Project_Runeberg

—summarizes the controversy as follows:

> [When] most people . . . first learn about the wiki concept, [they] assume that a website that can be edited by anybody would soon be rendered useless by destructive input. It sounds like offering free spray cans next to a gray concrete wall. The only likely outcome would be ugly graffiti and simple tagging, and many artistic efforts would not be long lived. Still, it seems to work very well.

Depending upon how openly a wiki is designed, it can be susceptible to intentional disruption. This is why most open wikis require that you become a registered member or user before you are allowed to edit the contents of an article. Any intentional disruption is known as *trolling*, or vandalism. (For more information on trolls, see Chapter 5, The Internet Forum.)

Deciding whether to have an open or closed wiki presents one with pros and cons. While a closed wiki provides more security from vandalism, its content grows very slowly. An example of the difference would be Wikipedia versus Citizendium. Citizendium, another wiki encyclopedia project, requires the user to provide a real name, a biography, and even recommendations from other Citizendium contributors before being allowed to make edits. While this makes the Citizendium wiki nearly vandalism free, it also hinders wiki growth. On the other hand, Wikipedia's open forum allows anyone with Internet access to edit capabilities to the articles—therefore permitting the site to grow quite rapidly. In fact, Wikipedia's English language version (en.Wikipedia.org)

has the largest user base among all wikis on the Internet, and ranks in the Top 10 traffic of all web sites. (See further on for more information on Wikipedia.) Other popular wiki web sites include WikiWikiWeb, Wikitravel, Wiki Answers, wikiHow, Uncyclopedia, Memory Alpha, and Erik Aronsson's Wiki, WikiHow.com

the Swedish-language knowledge base.

Wikis have gained such popularity that there are now three well-known annual wiki conferences: The International Symposium on Wikis (WikiSym) conference, which is dedicated to general wiki research, the Wikimania conference, which focuses on research and practices of the Wikimedia Foundation's projects, such as Wikipedia and Recent Changes Camp, a barcamp-style Unconference focusing on wikis. In several cities worldwide, wiki aficionados attend Wiki Wednesday meet-ups on the first Wednesday of each month.

Wikipedia

Wikipedia is a nonprofit organization that provides a platform for the world's largest online user-generated content encyclopedia. The site contains roughly 20 million articles, has been visited by 365 million visitors (at the

FIGURE 7.2 Wikipedia

time this chapter was written), and is by far the largest and most successful wiki there is.

The following was copied directly from the Wikipedia entry on http://en.wikipedia.org/wiki/wikipedia

Wikipedia is a free, web-based, collaborative, multilingual encyclopedia project supported by the non-profit Wikimedia Foundation. *Wikipedia*'s 15 million articles (3.3 million in English) have been written collaboratively by volunteers around the world, and almost all of its articles can be edited by anyone with access to the site. *Wikipedia* was launched in 2001 by Jimmy Wales and Larry Sanger, and is currently the largest and most popular general reference work on the Internet....

...[C]ritics of Wikipedia accuse it of systemic bias and inconsistencies (including undue weight given to popular culture), and allege that it favors consensus over credentials in its editorial process. Its reliability and accuracy are also targeted. Other criticisms center on its susceptibility to vandalism and the addition of spurious or unverified information, though scholarly work suggests that vandal-

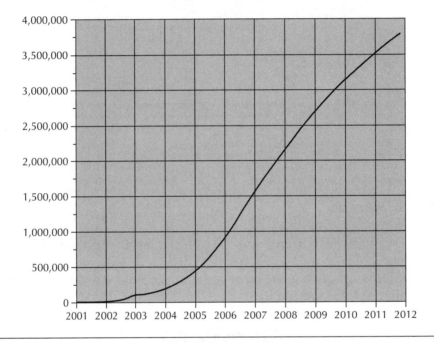

FIGURE 7.3 Number of articles on en.wikipedia.org

Source: http://en.wikipedia.org/wiki/Wikipedia:Modelling_Wikipedia%27s_growth;

http://bit.ly/ysMX4q.

ism is generally short-lived and an investigation in *Nature* found that the material they compared comes close to the level of accuracy of *Encyclopaedia Britannica* and had a similar rate of "serious errors."

Wikipedia's departure from the expert-driven style of the encyclopedia building mode and the large presence of unacademic content have been noted several times. When *Time* magazine recognized "You" as its Person of the Year for 2006, acknowledging the accelerating success of online collaboration and interaction by millions of users around the world, it cited Wikipedia as one of several examples of Web 2.0 services, along with YouTube, MySpace, and Facebook. Some noted the importance of Wikipedia not only as an encyclopedic reference but also as a frequently updated news resource because of how quickly articles about recent events appear.

The word *Wikipedia* was coined by Larry Sanger and is a portmanteau from *wiki* (a technology for creating collaborative websites) . . . and *encyclopedia.*

Figure 7.3 shows the number of articles on the English Wikipedia from its creation in 2001 up to the present.

Despite the criticism in regard to Wikipedia's potential bias and factual inaccuracies, many of the site's critics have agreed that the information contained within Wikipedia is actually quite accurate. Even though the Wikimedia Foundation repeatedly declined to participate directly in *The Social Media Bible,* the author agrees that web users should still be grateful for a resource like Wikipedia. This single site contains much information on so many different aspects of the tools of social media. Wikipedia was an invaluable resource for the aggregation of information in this book.

MyGads

A great illustration of a very simple, easy-to-use, and free mini-wiki is a site called MyGads (MyGads.com).

CommonCraft.com (commoncraft.com),

a company that does great, simple, and easy-to-understand explanation videos, did one for MyGads on soccer team parents who need to keep track of which ones were responsible for bringing snacks to each game. The team coach created a page (mini-wiki) or a *Gad* on the MyGads web site, where team parents can add information to the page by just clicking and typing. The page contains information on all of the game dates, times, parents, and snacks. Because it is a MyGads page, the users can access the page through text message, instant message, or the MyGads web site. For example, soccer mom Sherrie is at the grocery store, and she needs to know if it's her turn to bring snacks. She sends a text message to MyGads that says, "June 26 Snacks." Within just a few seconds, she receives a message back that says "Sherrie"; since she's in charge that week, she buys the snacks. It's as simple as that—and MyGads is secure, and always up to date.

Such a MyGads site would look like this:

Game Schedule		Snacks	
Date	**Time**	**Date**	**Snacks**
June 12	6:00 PM	June 12	Sheila
June 19	6:00 PM	June 19	Jenny
June 26	6:00 PM	June 26	Sherrie
July 3	6:00 PM	July 3	Vicki

MyGads is a useful resource for businesses as well; for example, let's say that you are a sales manager and need up-to-date inventory, price, and sales figures while on the road. MyGads works with most corporate databases, allowing you to keep the most up-to-date information on the MyGads page without any extra effort. You simply text message your MyGads page with "Medium Red Shirt," and you instantly get a message back: "247" in stock. And again, you can get all of this information through a text message or instant message or from the website. To watch the Common Craft demonstration video on YouTube, go to: youtube.com/watch?v=0S-WkhDygTA.

Go to www.theSocialMediaBible.com for a clickable link.

The ROI of Social Media

Self-Service E-Mail Marketing

Introduction

VerticalResponse, Inc., offers self-service e-mail marketing, online surveys, and direct mail service empowering small businesses to create, manage, and analyze their own direct marketing campaigns. Founded in 2001,

(continued)

(continued)

VerticalResponse is aimed at small businesses, and enables anyone to get an e-mail marketing campaign up and running within minutes, regardless of technical expertise.

Background

The target audience for VerticalResponse is small businesses with fewer than 100 employees. Because of the small staff size of their typical customers, there is often no dedicated e-mail marketing expert within the company. Also, small businesses may be fearful of social media tools, or be interested in implementing tools such as blogging, Twitter, and Facebook, if they only knew how.

Strategy

VerticalResponse believes that social media and e-mail marketing are complementary technologies and have similar fundamentals when it comes to using them for marketing purposes. By educating our customers on how to use social media with e-mail marketing, VerticalResponse can help make them more successful. Ultimately, when customers grow their business, this helps VerticalResponse, too.

After using webinars regularly to help educate small business customers, the company decided to create a Social Media Series webinar campaign. This webinar series would engage VerticalResponse customers and prospective sales leads by educating them about how they can use social media and e-mail marketing together.

Implementation

Given that VerticalResponse is an e-mail service provider, the company took the time to analyze its target customers and tailor the e-mail content to their specific needs. The seven separate e-mails in this series were sent to a total pool of several thousand people—however, this list was segmented for each e-mail according to their past social media preferences and which webinars customers had signed up for.

Opportunity

From a content perspective, the campaign was special because these e-mails introduced VerticalResponse customers to a free social media webinar series that they would not otherwise have access to. Small businesses are hungry for educational resources tailored to beginners that can teach them how to use other related tools such as social media to make them look like marketing gurus. VerticalResponse was positioned as a thought leader on e-mail marketing and social media.

Conclusion

The VerticalResponse Social Media Series webinar campaign highlighted the superior results that can be attained by integrating social media and e-mail marketing efforts. There were thousands of attendees and registrants for the seven-part series, made up of both customers and prospects. Of this group, approximately 50 percent were prospective customers—representing a huge sales and marketing opportunity for VerticalResponse. After listening to one or more of the social media webinars, these prospects were now warm leads for the company to advertise to.

The series was also a key initiative for the retention of existing customers. By educating customers on the benefits of integrating social media and e-mail marketing, VerticalResponse is positioned as a thought leader within both spaces—and the go-to resource for small business marketing topics that matter most to customers.

Further validating the success of the VerticalResponse Social Media Series, the campaign won MarketingSherpa's fifth annual E-mail Marketing awards—winning out against hundreds of competitive submissions. VerticalResponse took out Gold in the B2B category "Best Dynamic Content or Personalized E-Mail." The e-mails sent as part of this campaign achieved double the open and click-through rates of VerticalResponse's standard customer newsletters. For example, one of the e-mails in the Social Media Series generated an open rate of 53.49 percent and a click-through rate of 51.16 percent. This is a high engagement rate for busy small business customers.

—Janine Popick, CEO and founder, www.VerticalResponse.com

Expert Insight

Jack Herrick, founder of wikiHow, www.wikiHow.com

Jack Herrick

It's amazing—the variety, type, and quality of information we get using the wiki method. When I started wikiHow, I wasn't exactly sure what was going to happen. I wanted to build this how-to manual, and all its different topics. It's definitely veered away from the traditional how-to manuals at this point.

We have things about relationships, about . . . all the how-to topics you'd expect to find. . . . But we've got just totally different types of topics, really wild things. It's really expanding the definition of what a how-to manual can be. . . .

I've always really been interested in building a really big how-to manual. I owned e-How, which is sort of the Web One Point Zero version of the how-to manual. E-How got started in 1999 during the dot-com boom, and they raised a ton of money from venture capitalists. They had 200 employees, and they were writing this massive how-to manual; and at the time, I had nothing to do with that company. [But] I knew the founder of e-How, and always admired the company. Unfortunately, [e-How] went into bankruptcy and had to lay off all 200 employees; and basically, the company went into a deep freeze. It was bought out by another venture capital–funded company, called IT-Exchange, and they tried to nurse the site along and find a business model that would work; [but] they also failed to do that. They were about to shut the site off. So, a friend of mine and I got together and bought the site. We were both working full-time jobs . . . but we sort of brought the site back to life.

We hired a couple of writers and fixed lots of bugs on the old site—and it started to work; and on a very, very small cost basis we were able to get the site profitable. But while I was doing that, I became a little disillusioned with the e-How business model. We found that you cannot hire writers to cover all the world's topics in all the world's languages. For example, I could hire someone to write about mutual funds, Viagra, you name any high cost-per-click (CPC) keyword and it was very profitable to have someone write about [topics like this]. But I wanted to have someone write about the really obscure things—there is no business model for that. I really wanted to have a how-to manual to cover every single imaginable how-to topic, and in multiple languages. You just weren't going to get there with this professional writer model—[not] with high quality.

First, I was sort of puzzled about how we could accomplish this goal of producing high quality content across a broad range of topics. When I stumbled upon Wikipedia, I was just amazed at the quality [and] the breadth of information. So I started thinking if we could take the same wiki model and apply it to write a how-to manual. My engineer, Travis Derouin, and I sort of beavered away, and in late 2004, [we] tried to import the media wiki software and transform it to a how-to manual. And then we launched wikiHow.

I see my role as building a platform and enabling others to collaborate on a shared goal. There are a lot of people out there who want to do something, and a wiki allows you to put a certain [amount of information] together, and [give you] one place to do it. wikiHow attracts a group of people who are as passionate as [I am] about building a large, shared how-to manual; and it allows them to do that. When I first started wikiHow, the very first month—we had it up in January 2005—we had over two thousand people visit the site.

And those two thousand people may [only] be 5 or 10 people [who] actually wrote an article or edited something. And so there really wasn't much going on at the site in the very early days, but it works in a virtuous cycle where the next month you had these 5 articles, or 10 articles and those brought some people in from search engine traffic. And some of the people read the articles and said, "Hey, this article is not very good. I can do a better job." And they pressed "edit" and they improved the content; and then the content got better, and maybe moved up in the search engine rankings, [which] brought more people in . . . who've also said, "Wow, I can do better than this!" And *they* pressed "edit" and improved the content and the cycle keeps going. . . . Synergy! I think that it definitely happened in the case of wikiHow. It definitely happened in the case of Wikipedia, and I've also talked to people who are working at Fortune 500 companies and hearing those same sorts of stories. People within the enterprise are turning on wikis and finding that the knowledge in the organization is far more than people at the top would have assumed. I think more organizations are going to try and figure this out and protect it.

(*continued*)

(continued)

There are thousands of people who contribute to wikiHow over any given month; and within that group there is a much smaller and tighter group of people that will number in the hundreds—people who I call the "Hard Core wikiHow Contributors"—and they are responsible for making sure the quality stays high. Every edit that goes to wikiHow is looked at by another human . . . a volunteer who looks at "edits" and says, "It is good" or "It is bad," or "I'm going to check this . . . am I going to send it out, or am I going to edit this edit to make it even better?" That's happening all the time, all day long in real time. That's our first line of defense.

This really allows situations where you would think there would be complete chaos—where we allow anyone to edit. We do not even require people to log in or tell us any information about themselves whatsoever; and yet [by] allowing anyone to edit, wiki creates a high quality.

To listen to or read the entire Executive Conversation with Jack Herrick, go to www.theSocialMediaBible.com.

International Perspective

France

Vive le Skyrock, the number one social networking site in France!

Skyrock started off as a blog site called Skyblog, compliments of a French independent radio station SKYROCK Radio, 96.0 FM, in Paris. As its popularity grew, the site evolved gradually into a fully fledged social networking site.

The site has all the bells and whistles of other social networking sites. Members can create profiles, write blog entries, converse in chat rooms, and

FIGURE 7.5 Skyrock

send messages to each other. They can make friends and see what other people are up to. And this all takes place in a kinetic Web environment packed with features—there's not a square inch of Skyrock that isn't covered by pictures, profiles, animations, or video.

While the site is based in France, there are versions of Skyrock available in other languages including English, Spanish, Italian, German, and Portuguese. According to comScore, the site ranks in the top 10 social networking sites in the world. As of July 2009, Skyrock had over 39 million members.

—Jonathan Strickland, Senior Writer
HowStuffWorks.com
Discovery Communications

To-Do List

- Visit wikis.

  Go look at the most popular wikis. Look at Wikipedia. Do some searching. Find a subject that you are passionate about. Read some of the articles . . . and comment on them. Add some facts. Correct some typos. Google other wikis, and check them out. Visit wikiindex.org

  to learn about the many different types of public wikis out there. Most importantly: Participate and contribute.

- Create a company wiki.

  Try to develop an internal company wiki. Go to one of the providers, sign up for an account, and create a wiki. Encourage other employees to participate; get them to create topic pages. Get others to contribute to the content. You will be surprised how fast your content and loyalty will grow within your trusted network.

Conclusion

Wikis are a great way to collect the wisdom of the crowd—whether it's a public wiki on a sport, hobby, or other area of interest, or a member-only company wiki that accumulates the collective knowledge of your employees. Wikis are a fun, easy, and free way to create your own information management system.

Without wikis like Wikipedia, the research and aggregation of the content in this book would have been significantly more difficult. Thank you to all of the contributors to Wikipedia, and the many wiki sites on the Internet!

To hear all of the Expert Interviews, go to www.theSocialMediaBible .com.

Downloads

For your free downloads associated with *The Social Media Bible,* go to www.theSocialMediaBible.com,

and enter your ISBN number located on the back of the book above the bar code. Be sure to enter the dashes.

Credits

The ROI of Social Media was provided by:

Janine Popick, CEO and founder, www.VerticalResponse.com

Expert Insight was provided by:

Jack Herrick, cofounder, wikiHow, www.wikiHow.com

Technical edits were provided by:

Nicole Wilson, www.wikiHow.com/User:Elocina

CHAPTER 8

A Picture Is Worth a Thousand Words (Photo Sharing)

www.LonSafko.com/TSMB3_Videos/08Picture.mov

What's in It for You?

The most important feature of photo sharing is that it's fun! Showing pictures to others is about sharing your memories with family members, friends, and colleagues. It's fun to display and remember your Christmas party guests, your coworkers at your promotion dinner, your child's school play, or the birth of your new son. It's also enjoyable to recall those moments with your friends and family—wherever they are in the world. Additionally, there is something to be said about having all of your photographs organized into groups, sets, categories, events, and albums online where you can look at them anytime you wish—instead of having all of your memories stuffed in a shoebox in your closet or under your bed.

However, since this book focuses more on utilizing social media for business than for fun, let's play "What if?" What if a prospect you were trying to land was doing some research on your product and went to Google Images, Flickr, or Photobucket and searched for either your trademarked name or a generic description of your product—and he found photo after photo? What if your prospect was preparing a budget presentation and

FIGURE 8.1   Sedona, Arizona

needed photos of your type of product to secure funding, and his search consistently led him to your website or photo sharing site? Wouldn't you or your company be perceived as the best-in-class expert in the field?

Now, imagine that your prospects were conducting just a general search—as they might do during the research phase of their sales funnel—and your company's product photos continued to appear. (See Chapter 4, The World of Web Pages, for more information about the sales funnel.) What would your prospect think about your company and your product? And now ask yourself: What if this type of marketing opportunity were completely free?

This high quality and low-cost exposure is exactly what photo sharing brings to your business marketing and communications plan. By simply uploading your company's product photos for free, you are participating in an area of Internet marketing that is highly targeted, competitively advantageous—and completely free of charge.

When you are uploading your company's product or service snapshots to your photo sharing website, be sure to remember the other items you have in your corporate shoebox. What if that same prospect also saw images of happy customers or your design or sales teams? How about some great shots of your company's headquarters, customer service installation, or repairs in progress? Take advantage of the resources that you already have, and use them frequently to provide visual proof of your business's dedication to its customers. After all, if only one prospect per quarter sees your photos and becomes a customer, isn't it worth the free posting?

Back to the Beginning

The real rise of photo sharing websites grew with the popularization of the digital camera in the late 1990s. Digital cameras allow you to go directly from your camera to the web with only one step, and without any additional hardware or software. It is as easy as plugging your camera into your USB port and uploading your images. Of course, the next natural application of photo sharing that came about was through e-mail. Sending your brother photographs from graduation, or Grandma pictures of the kids, became increasingly popular—and increasingly demanding on the user to create an e-mail for each viewer. The desire for a one-stop personal photo gallery—with your own personal photographs available 24/7 forever—became an ever-more appealing concept.

The other trend that quickly emerged was the incarnation of web sites such as KodakGallery.com

(and others like it) that allowed customers to order prints made from their digitally uploaded photographs. As these sites developed greater capacity to store and view higher-quality (larger file size) photographs, thumbnails, and slideshows, their popularity amplified.

With the advent of desktop photo management applications such as iPhoto—containing photo sharing features and integration that allow direct photo uploading, e-mail, and drag-and-drop through predesigned templates—the task of organizing, uploading, and sharing photographs became simpler than ever. There are currently a plethora of online photo sharing websites that include online photo finishing, subscription-based sharing, peer-to-peer, peer-to-server-to-peer, peer-to-browser, and web photo album generators. Perhaps the simplest way to share photos is through a social media site you are already using, like Facebook. Also, the process of sharing photographs has now grown beyond the standalone digital camera and personal computer to include cell phones and smartphones, almost all of which include a high quality, built-in imager. Many of today's mobile devices will let you take a picture, crop it, adjust the color, remove red eye, and e-mail it to a contact or immediately post it to your blog, photo gallery, or Facebook page—all from within the device.

What You Need to Know

The first step in this process is obvious: Actually *take* a photograph. Since digital cameras (and smartphones) don't use film, you can take as many photographs as you wish at no cost whatsoever. So go out and click away, practice, try different angles, lighting, and camera settings, and take a lot of pictures. It's free!

As an alternative to using a digital camera, try your cell phone or smartphone. Many smartphones—such as Apple's iPhone 4S and various Android-based devices—can rival the quality of a good digital camera, and have as high as 10 megapixels, but they do lack other useful features, such as optical zoom and macro mode (for extreme close-ups). You can also use your digital video camera set to still photography mode.

Next, transfer your photographs from your camera to your computer. The cable (usually USB) and software, if you need it, will have been provided to you by the camera manufacturer. If you are using a film camera, then you can have your photo processor deliver your photos in a digital format or store them on a CD. If you want to share older photos that have already been printed on photo paper, then you will need to digitize them using a flatbed scanner. If you still have the negatives for those photographs, then you can save time and effort by having your photo processor print from the negative directly to a digital CD.

Once you've finished transferring, you can use a variety of software to crop, brighten or darken, sharpen, correct red eye, and otherwise enhance your photographs before uploading them to a photo sharing service. While Adobe's venerable Photoshop is one of the longest established and most versatile photo editing applications for both PC and Macintosh, at more than $150, it probably does more than you will need. A scaled-back version, Photoshop Elements, competes with Apple's Aperture at about $80 retail, while Pixelmator (for Macintosh)—widely heralded as a Photoshop replacement—is available for download from the Apple App Store for just $29.99.

For most of what you'll need to do, however, iPhoto (included with every Macintosh) or the free photo editing software that comes with most digital cameras will work just fine. Be sure to check the original CD that came with your digital camera for free photo editing software, since most camera manufacturers bundle such software with their merchandise.

You can also download free photo editing software from the Internet. Google's Picasa, for example will allow you to restore old photos with marks, water stains, and scratches to excellent condition, and even let you add text and watermarks.

Now that you have all of your photographs edited to perfection, simply upload them to your favorite photo sharing website. Many photo editing applications allow you to upload your photos directly to your photo sharing service. Once you have created an account, just follow the directions on how to proceed. This is usually as simple as selecting Upload, then Browse, locating your image, and hitting OK. Many photo sharing services also offer their own uploading software that allows you to simply drag and drop your photos onto the application to automatically upload them to the website. You can even send photos for sharing by your e-mail.

Once you've posted your images to a photo sharing website, you can organize them into sets and albums, and add captions, titles, descriptions, and meta tags (keywords). Choose keywords that you would use yourself if you were searching for a photograph like yours. (For more information on meta tags and keywords, please see Chapter 18, Spotlight on Search (Search Engine Optimization).) You can also have friends, family, prospects, and customers comment on your photographs, and you can comment on others' as well. Most photo sharing sites provide other services, like allowing you to order prints of your photographs, as well as create photo books or albums, and even custom calendars from your personal snapshots. And always remember to upload your photographs to the Flickr World Map or Google Earth. By selecting the user photograph layer, you can upload your photos and view those of others as well, based on geographic location.

Privacy versus Piracy

While some people believe that you should be less fearful of piracy than obscurity, others just don't want their photographs taken and used by the Internet community at large—especially for commercial purposes. Online photo theft and fraud have become critical issues with photo sharing websites and their members. Nearly every one of these sites supports the Creative Commons License, which allows users to designate their photos by the level of copyright protection they wish to have. All the sites take theft seriously. (For more information on the Creative Commons License, see Chapter 9,

Talking about the Podcast (Audio Create), or go to creativecommons .org.)

The Creative Commons License allows many photo sharing websites to grant those with copyrighted photographs access to use the site to sell licenses to their photographs. So, in addition to helping to protect the photographer, they are providing a system for the photographer to make money through their photographs.

Techniques and Tactics

Although this chapter acknowledges that uploading photos is largely focused on sharing with friends and family your images of birthday parties, bar mitzvahs, babies, and weddings, the purpose behind this book—and this chapter—is to show readers how to use photo sharing web sites to create additional revenue. Businesses are using these techniques to share images of their products, tech support, employees, assembly lines, inventory, and happy customers.

You can help this process along by uploading as many photographs as you can, and entering the best meta tags as possible. Be sure that you use product names, applications, and serial or part numbers. Also make sure that your company names, geographic areas, and service descriptions are part of the meta tags, captions, and even photo file names. Remember to approach this process from the mind-set of a prospect or customer who is searching the site for you and your product or service. What words would you use if you were they? What kind of images would you want to see, or would you find helpful?

Most photo sharing web sites allow you to create and participate in groups. Be sure to link your photos to the appropriate groups and communities on your photo sharing site. For example, the author presented with Matt Mullenweg, the cofounder of WordPress, at the Arizona Entrepreneurship

Conference. Twenty-one press photos of the event were taken. These pictures appear at www.flickr.com/photos/lonsafko,

FIGURE 8.2   Flickr

with a group for these photos named #AZEC. The conference founders created a larger group named 2008 Arizona Entrepreneur Conference. This
group pool combines 190 photographs from all of the other attendees. You
can look at just one smaller group of photos of the event or all 190.

Remember to install any free widget, gadget, or plug-in provided by
your photo sharing service on your company website or blog to pull photos
from your photo sharing website, and place clickable thumbnail images right
on your web page. This step will introduce your prospects to the concept
that you have photographs available for view on a photo sharing website and
allow them to hyperlink directly to your photo site. These external links can
also raise your site's standing with search engines.

The ROI of Social Media

PI Social Media Network's Hive/Cross Pollination

Introduction

The PI Social Media Network includes the Procurement Insights and *PI
Window on Business* blogs, the *PI Window on Business Show* on Blog Talk
Radio, and the PI Inquisitive Eye and TV2 Young Entrepreneurs Internet TV
channels. The *PI Window on Business* is a featured show on Blog Talk Radio.

The combined syndicated reach through affiliations with social media
sites such as Blog Talk Radio (which has more than 7 million listeners each
month), Evan Carmichael (500,000 visitors monthly) as well as various social
networking groups and forums has enabled the PI Social Media to connect
with an ever-expanding audience of readers, listeners, and now viewers.

Background

The PI Social Media Network's origins began with the launch of the
Procurement Insights blog in May 2007. The blog was created as a means of
providing various magazines and publications with a single site access to our
articles and reports.

Procurement Insights is today the top-sponsored blog in its industry
sector in terms of the number of total sponsors.

As a means of building upon and expanding the reach of the Procurement
Insights blog, the *PI Window on Business Show* was launched in March 2009.
Within three months, it was a featured show across the entire Blog Talk Radio
Network.

In June 2009, the *PI Window on Business* blog was launched as an adjunct support for the show. Within the first six months, the total number of site visitors cracked the 10,000 mark on a monthly basis.

Based on the cross-pollination between venues both within and external to the PI Social Media Network, the Procurement Insights blog realized an 1,100 percent increase in blog visitors in the past 30 days, while both the *PI Window on Business Show* and blog have seen equally impressive growth.

The PI Social Media Network recently launched two Internet TV channels as well as corresponding blogs.

Strategy

The hive/cross-pollination concept or theory is based on the observation that individuals will likely choose at most one or two primary social networks as their preferred platforms. That is, they will spend the majority of their social networking time interacting within these main hives.

While they may venture out into the vast social media–social networking world visiting countless other networks, similar to the honey bee, these forays are ultimately geared toward gathering information and insights to bring back to the hive to share with their established community of contacts.

Simply put, while static, single sites (regarding blogs, websites, and so forth) that limit their cross-pollination activities to providing somewhat passive links to other similarly myopic single site blogs or websites, have failed to recognize that market dynamics change, and that you have to connect with the audience through their preferred venue points.

Implementation

The PI Social Media and its service offerings provide our clients with an ability to transition from the traditional and largely ineffective broadcasting model of yesterday, to the relationship-centric conversational marketing world of social media.

Opportunity

The opportunity afforded the PI Social Media Network, through its services both in the present as well as in the foreseeable future, has been proven by the steady and sustained growth in readership, listener, and viewer base.

Through this expanded and diverse reach that leverages venues such as blogs, Internet Radio, Internet TV, and social networks, the company's increasing revenue base reflects the model's effectiveness—even during a slow economic period.

(continued)

(*continued*)

Conclusion

The following are the links to the various franchises within the PI Social Media Network:

Procurement Insights (blog)

http://procureinsights.wordpress.com/

PI Window on Business (blog)

http://bit.ly/9yJlmP

—Jon W. Hansen, http://bit.ly/mUex9b

Expert Insight

Tara Kirchner, head of marketing, Yahoo!'s Flickr, www.flickr.com

Tara Kirchner

Flickr, at its core, is two things. First and foremost, it is a photo sharing site, making it easier for people to share what is happening with their lives with their friends, their families, or potentially with the world. And it is really this last part—the second part of what Flickr is—a social media site.

When you think about traditional media businesses, you think about places where you find out about news and information. Flickr fundamentally is that. At the scale that we are today, we have 3 million photos and videos uploaded on a daily basis, and you can only imagine the sound of 3 million shutters snapping across the world on any given day. We are really capturing what is happening in the world and in people's lives for a very, very personal perspective. So we see our vision as being the eyes of the world and really making that possible. . . .

It [is] actually really easy. I think, to start with, you have to take a photo; and luckily, for us today, you can take a photo with almost any device out there. Camera phones, which everyone has; there is an average of three camera phones for every human on the planet that are being used now. That's a really incredible number! And almost all of them have photo sharing features in them, not to mention the huge adoption of digital cameras, as well, across the board.

So it is really easy to start taking photos, and then sharing them is the next step. That happens through the pervasiveness of Internet connections, not only through traditional devices like the PC, but again through phones and other devices as well. So it is actually pretty [simple] to get started. And then—[with] Flickr itself, for example—if you snap a shot with your camera phone, you just have to send it to an e-mail address here with Flickr, and it will be uploaded to your Flickr page. Then all of your friends and family can see what you are doing at that given moment. . . .

(continued)

(continued)

Yes, it is amazing and, of course, there is the mobile aspect of it, which is a really pervasive platform [wherein] you can just take it from any camera phone and share it immediately, including through a native Flickr app for the iPhone. Beyond that, we are integrated with almost all [of] the leading desktop photo applications, so you can go through any of the applications that people like to use and upload to Flickr from there. And, of course, the dominant way of sharing through Flickr is [probably] through our website and our uploading application. You can just drag and drop a bunch of photos—or video for that matter—and share it with your friends and family. . . .

It starts with something very basic—which is that "this is something in my life and I want to share it." And if you think about what people were really trying to hold on to in the early days of photography—it was a memory. This is an important day; this is a birthday, for example, and I am going to take photos and share those with people.

With digital photos, the ease of sharing—as well as the ease of capturing these moments—has really expanded—from uses beyond just, "I want to hold on to this particular moment" to "I want to document everything that's meaningful to me in my life." That can be everything from, "Here is an interesting piece of graffiti I saw at the bus stop I was waiting in," or "Oh my God, there is a protest going on down the street from my office. I can capture it!" or "I'm in Galveston, Texas, right now and there is a hurricane, and I think the world might want to see this."

So it is really, *really* amazing how people are capturing and sharing what they are seeing. But what is interesting about a site like Flickr (which is not just about this content, but [also] the way that communities form around this content) is that people start interacting with the content in a very interesting way. So you almost have this second-order community effect starting to happen. For example, one of the biggest groups on Flickr is something called "Squared Circle," and the premise of the group is really simple: people take a photograph of something circular and they crop it to a square and they upload it to this particular group. . . .

It has been just incredible to see how much meta-data and meaning our members have been able to find in some of this content. One of my favorites is [an] example of a photo of some dockworkers leaving the shipyard in the afternoon. One of the comments on the photo is by a Flickr member who says, "I remember as a kid; we lived down the street from this shipyard and at night we would see the light of the welding torches." And that's a really poignant moment that gives life to that photo in a way that it never would [just by] sitting in a library archive. So, again, the kind of things that people are starting to do with photo sharing is really tremendous; everything from the most banal thing of, "Here's what I had for my lunch today," to a deep and moving understanding of the world around us. It is very powerful!

One of the reasons that businesses come to Flickr is to actually engage with some of the customers who are using their product. If you search for pretty much any brand name on Flickr, you will find tens—if not hundreds—of groups where Flickr members are talking about the product or the brand and why it is interesting or helpful—or not helpful—to them. And that's an incredible way to have this two-way communication with your customers. . . .

The second aspect is advertising—also a known and loved model in traditional media—and [it] has very, very interesting implications with the social media side of the world with targeting, and with these rich two-way conversations that we were talking about.

The third here—and this is something more closely related to the photo sharing than the social media aspect of it—is that there are a lot of services that people want to have around their photos, whether it is standard prints or books or canvas prints of their photos, or canvas prints of other people's photos. There is a lot of incredible art that is being shared, so there is a rich business there.

And then the fourth—and probably the most recent, from a Flickr perspective—is a licensing business. You may have heard of our partnership with Getty Images that allows Flickr members to actually monetize their images by licensing them. [There is also] the Commons Project—which we were talking about earlier—which is a way for institutions like the Library of Congress to show their images on Flickr. That is actually a completely separate initiative than Creative Commons, which is a way to allow users to apply licenses to their images governing usage of how their content can be used. Our partnership with Getty Images lives right alongside our incredibly strong support for the Creative Commons. It is just another opportunity for people to choose how they want to license their image. . . .

You know, it is just a great, great field to be in. One of the things that we love about being here at Flickr, as part of Yahoo!, is we really are at the epicenter of some of the most interesting things that are happening. With social media on the Internet, Yahoo! has a deep commitment to the power of people and empowering people to do great things. You've probably heard a lot about Yahoo!'s open and social strategy, and this is what social media is really a key part of. So we are very excited about that. We spent a lot of time talking about photo sharing, but from our perspective, video is a key part of that as well. We launched video sharing on Flickr two years ago, and it has become a very important site of our community.

So I think overall, we are just really excited to be one of the leaders in social media, and we are looking forward to being part of the innovation that this industry is really bringing about.

(continued)

(continued)

To listen to or read the entire Executive Conversation with Tara Kirchner, go to www.theSocialMediaBible.com.

International Perspective

Canada

Canadians are famous for being friendly, and that reputation follows them into social media. While the average Facebook user around the world has 130 friends, the typical Canadian boasts 190.[1]

Yet businesses in Canada are embracing social media with much more hesitation than both tech-savvy Canadian consumers, and companies south of the border.

Although 45 percent of all online Canadians visit a social media site at least once a week[2]—only 17 percent of Canadian companies regularly post and monitor social media sites. Half the executives surveyed blamed a lack of resources for not engaging more.[3]

The most popular platforms for those companies on social media are Facebook (by far: 70 percent), LinkedIn (32 percent), and Twitter (31 percent).[4] Facebook's popularity among brands matches those of consumers, although LinkedIn and Twitter membership are steadily growing. Leading brands usually have a presence on all three networks; some are also rolling out Google Plus accounts.

One unique challenge facing many Canadian brands is engaging in both official languages—English and French. Some maintain separate accounts; others, like the Moncton Public Library, employ a bilingual team member to post and respond in both languages.

Those companies who do engage online employ a wide range of strategies.

Crowdsourcing. Before ING Direct Canada launched THRiVE Chequing, CEO Peter Aceto posted a YouTube video inviting clients to preview the product and send him their feedback. 22,000 fans responded with valuable ideas, the best of which ING incorporated into their product.

Customer Service. As planes were grounded in a massive snowstorm, Air Canada used Twitter to interact with thousands of customers who needed to find information on their flights or alternate travel arrangements. They responded in real time to help customers and share the latest information on how the stormy weather was affecting air travel.

Employee Performance. Toronto startup Rypple created a web-based social performance management platform. The platform helps companies improve performance through social goals, continuous feedback, and meaningful recognition.

Influencer Outreach. Quebec-based entertainment company Cirque de Soleil empowers their online community to be brand ambassadors by giving them access to insider information, special promotions and discounts, and tickets to the shows. They recently invited a dozen Las Vegas bloggers to attend their *Zumanity* show and post reviews of the performance.

—Bart Byl
www.Radian6.com

[1] www.techvibes.com/blog/are-canadians-the-worlds-most-extreme-users-of-facebook-2011-05-23

(continued)

(*continued*)

[2]http://bit.ly/nnDhvk

[3]http://bit.ly/ruvQPG

[4]http://yahoo.it/spxDlT

To-Do List

1. **Take a lot of photographs.**

   Get a digital camera or camera phone and start taking pictures. Because they are digital, there are no associated development costs. If you don't like the way the picture came out, you can simply hit Delete. If you are satisfied with it, then save it to your hard drive. Like anything else, the more you practice, the better you become.

2. **Edit your photographs.**

   While many photo editing software applications have a one-click photo enhance feature, try using the manual adjustment sliders and effects. It's fun, and there's always an Undo function. To play it safe, always practice on a copy of the original photograph.

3. **Upload.**

   Find as many photographs as possible that you already have. Combine them with the new photos you are taking, and upload them to the photo sharing site of your choice. Creating an account on a photo sharing site is easy, only takes about 10 minutes, and is free.

4. **Use meta tags and descriptions.**

   Take a few minutes to think about the words that you will use to describe each photo, and the words that your prospects would use to search for your products and services.

5. **Create and join groups.**

   Search your photo sharing website for groups that are similar and appropriate to the type of product or service you sell. Often, the best way to become part of a group or community is not to sell; a trusted network works *because* of the trust. Observe, participate—and *then* sell.

6. **Comment.**

   Participating means commenting. Comment on others' pictures, and encourage others to comment on yours. The more communication you have with one another, the more visibility your photographs will have.

Conclusion

Sharing your photographs with global communities, friends, family, coworkers, prospects, and customers and encouraging them to comment and communicate their feelings about your photos is the very essence of social media. Social media is all about two-way communication. Upload your photos, create communities, and start building credibility and trust with your clients and prospects.

To hear all of the Expert Interviews, go to www.theSocialMediaBible.com.

For your free downloads associated with *The Social Media Bible,* go to www.theSocialMediaBible.com,

and enter your ISBN number located on the back of the book above the bar code. Be sure to enter the dashes.

Credits

The ROI of Social Media was provided by:

Jon W. Hansen, http://bit.ly/mUex9b

Expert Insight was provided by:

Tara Kirchner, head of marketing, Yahoo!'s Flickr, www.flickr.com;
http://explore.live.com/windows-live-essentials

Technical edits were provided by:

Stephen Farrington, www.stephenfarrington.com

CHAPTER 9

Talking about the Podcast (Audio Create)

www.LonSafko.com/TSMB3_Videos/09Podcast.mov

Why do you suppose it is that automakers have been scrambling to make their cars iPod and iPhone compatible? It's because so many people who drive—especially those who spend long periods behind the wheel—use that time to listen to music, news, sports, weather, and other forms of audio information. In-car audio programming used to be the exclusive domain of radio, an industry that was built on finding ways to entertain or inform, and then to sell stuff to a captive audience of drivers during the highly lucrative drive-time hours.[1] But that was then.

As automakers today know, iPods (used synonymously here with all portable music-playing devices) have become so ubiquitous and indispensable that they are routinely played in cars. Now, you and your company can be there too, and in all of the other places people take their iPods. This is provided you know why, when, and how to make podcasting (producing audio for iPods) part of your business strategy.

theSocialMediaBible.com

What's in It for You?

Podcasting is an effective way for you and your business to be heard—to capture the valuable mindshare of customers, prospects, and employees. And, like nearly all of the social media tools in the ecosystem, *it's free!* Podcasting is quite easy to do and produces a medium that is much more psychologically desirable—and frequently more accessible—to your customers and followers than mere text. One report states that 75 percent of all journalists prefer rich media (see Chapter 4, The World of Web Pages), and education studies show that rich media is more effective for teaching. Almost all search engine optimization (SEO) people (see Chapter 18, Spotlight on Search) have known this for more than a decade. Even Confucius (551 to 479 BC) knew a picture was worth 1,000 words! A picture is worth a thousand words, an audio podcast is worth a thousand pictures, and a video is worth a thousand audios.

Back to the Beginning

The distribution of digitized audio recordings has been around—in one form or another—for nearly as long as the Internet has existed. The first audio files to commonly appear on the early Internet were based on the Resource Interchange File Format (RIFF). These files included *Audio Interchange File Format (.aiff)* on Macintosh computers and later *Waveform Audio (.wav)* files on Windows PCs. A typical $3\frac{1}{2}$-minute song at CD quality occupied an uncompressed file size of about 35 megabytes (MB). Because of its smaller file size and faster download times, a highly compressed audio format called *MP3* emerged and soon became the de facto standard for Internet audio. *MP3* stands for the Motion Picture Experts Group standard MPEG-1 Audio Layer 3, and is able to fit that same $3\frac{1}{2}$-minute song into roughly 3.5MB—a 10-fold reduction in size—with practically no discernible loss of quality. Podcasting, for the most part, is done in the MP3 format.

Note: Keep file size and download times in mind when creating your podcasts—a 20-minute session in CD-quality stereo could run more than 30MB. Fortunately, *bit rate* is a selectable parameter in most podcast recording software, and choosing a lower bit rate and monaural encoding can cut the size of a spoken language podcast by another factor of four while still sounding great.

The Birth of iPod

Apple cofounder Steve Jobs introduced the first iPod to the world on October 23, 2001. The iPod was not the first portable digital music player—SaeHan

Information Systems and Diamond Multimedia had both introduced models (*MPMan* and *Rio*) as early as 1998—but, with its sleek design and novel scroll wheel interface, the iPod quickly won the attention of consumers as the coolest MP3 player available. (A Diamond Multimedia marketing executive would later comment that he was too ashamed to reveal his newest *Rio* model to a fellow airline passenger en route to the product's introduction because the other guy's iPod, despite its use of (non-MP3) AAC encoding only and compatibility only with the iTunes music service, was still clearly a cooler product).

The iPod also benefitted from the use of a small hard drive, in contrast to the lower capacity flash memory systems of its competitors. And while the Recording Industry Association of America (RIAA) had been suing companies like Diamond Multimedia over their product offerings, Apple's iPod was tethered to Apple's legal downloading service, the iTunes Music Store (IMS), which remains the world's top-selling digital music service (now offering untethered MP3 downloads). On October 4, 2011, Apple reported that 300 million iPods had been sold and 16 billion songs had been downloaded from iTunes. According to Apple's CFO, Peter Oppenheimer, in 2010, IMS accounted for about 85 percent of all digital music sales in the United States (at about $1 each).

Later generations of the iPod were developed to accommodate MP3, AAC/M4A, Protected AAC, AIFF, WAV, Audible audiobook, and Apple Lossless formats. The iPod photo model can display JPEG, BMP, GIF, TIFF, and PNG image file formats, and iPod video can play MPEG-4 (H.264/MPEG-4 AVC) and QuickTime video formats. With the introduction of Apple's third-generation video-playing iPods, Apple began selling video content through iTunes. With video on the scene, the term *podcast* began to apply to both audio and video recordings, but since *vodcasting* is becoming an increasingly popular term for video broadcasting, we will use the term *podcast* to refer only to audio.

The Birth of Podcasting

Podcasting is an equally accessible and entertaining application of the iPod. The word *podcasting* comes from combining the terms *iPod* and *broadcasting*. Although systems that enabled downloading of serial episodic audio content onto portable devices for later playback had been around since 2000, the ability for anyone to produce and publish audio content as podcasts really took off after the first Bloggercon weblogger conference, organized by software developer Dave Winer and friends in October 2003. Winer is the author of RSS, a web-feed format used to publish frequently updated media, such as blog entries, and news headlines (see Chapter 17, RSS—Really Simple Syndication Made Simple).

At that first Bloggercon, Kevin Marks demonstrated a script to download RSS enclosures and pass them to iTunes for transfer to an iPod. Marks and early audioblogger Kevin Curry discussed collaborating, and following the conference Curry offered his blog readers an RSS-to-iPod script called iPodder. iPodder moved MP3 files from Winer's weblogging product, Radio Userland, to iTunes. Curry encouraged other developers to build on the idea, and thus podcasting became accessible to you and me.

Podcasting and You

Podcasts are ordinary MP3 audio files and aren't limited to the iPod or the iTunes Store. A podcast can be played on any MP3 player or right from your browser from any website that offers podcasts. Go to www.theSocial MediaBible.com

for nearly 50 Executive Conversations podcasts with social media industry leaders. You can listen to an audio recording live by streaming it into an audio player, or you can download and save the file to your PC. Podcasts allow anyone to create one's own talk show, interview, educational or training seminar, sermon, speech, presentation, or music file that can be distributed worldwide to literally thousands of listeners who can hear what you have to say . . . for *free*. You can create a following of colleagues, friends, and customers who care about what you have to say; and by podcasting, you've created a viral, entertaining, and informative medium through which you can be heard.

What You Need to Know

The more interesting you make your message, the more likely people are willing to hear it. Of all rich media—which includes video, audio, and animation such as Flash—audiences prefer video over audio, and audio over text. However, video—while the most desirable form—also requires the most effort and the greatest initial expense to create. Video requires a computer, digital video camera, and video editing software at the very least.

On the other hand, audio podcasting is a much simpler—and still great—expression of user-generated content, and all of the tools you need to create your own audio podcast are right inside your computer (or smartphone). From the audience perspective, audio files are smaller and download faster than video, can be played on more existing portable players, and can be listened to while driving, walking to work, or working out at the gym. So, for many, podcasting audio content is the easiest and most effective way to broadcast their personal message.

To create an audio podcast, all you need is your computer, the built-in microphone (or an external one, if your computer does not have a microphone built in), the free audio recording and editing software that came with the computer—and a little bit of creativity. Just hit Record, speak your message, hit Save, and upload it to a website like PodBean.com

for Internet distribution, and you are podcasting.

Podcast Components

An audio podcast can range from less than a minute to more than an hour in total length, depending upon the content you wish to include. The podcast can sound slick, as though it was professionally produced, or have a rough-around-the-edges homemade flavor to it. It can start with an introduction to the content and speaker, and even have a musical intro. Many podcasters find the easiest way to sound natural is to have more than one person speaking, like a radio interview or discussion. Whatever your choice of content, podcasts are effective, portable, and fun.

The Value of Podcasting

Creating successful podcasts on a given subject will allow you to build a loyal following, and convey to your audience that you are an expert in your industry or subject field. Your audience may include people interested in your subject area or in following what you do. Most importantly, they may be both existing and potential customers of your product or service.

As with all of the other chapters in this book, a strong "What's in It for Me?" is imperative. If your podcasts contain valuable takeaways, your listeners will continue to come back for more. They will also be able to provide user feedback—yet another benefit of podcasting. By allowing your listener the opportunity to give comments on your podcast, you can hear directly from your audience what you are doing right—and what you can do better.

Podcasts are like blogs in that they can be RSS-fed (see Chapter 17, RSS—Really Simple Syndication Made Simple, for more about RSS). Essentially, your podcasts can be syndicated or distributed, and made available worldwide for free. People who like your podcasts and want to share them and be alerted when you've created more content can be informed every time you publish a new podcast. You can also set up Facebook, LinkedIn, and other free services to automatically publish when you have added a new podcast episode.

Tips, Techniques, and Tactics

How to Create Your Own Podcast

Creating your own podcasts is easy, so don't be afraid if you've never created one. The process follows four steps: planning, recording, editing, and publishing.

A great resource for creating and distributing podcasts is *Podcasting For Dummies* by Tee Morris, Evo Terra, and Dawn Miceli (see Figure 9.1). Go to www.theSocialMediaBible.com

to download the *Podcasting For Dummies* primer e-book. It's free!

FIGURE 9.1   Podcasting For Dummies

Planning

It's best if you plan out your podcast ahead of time—gathering and importing information, and then writing the script. Although the goal of podcast production is to make it sound professional, it needn't be perfectly polished. What is right depends on your audience and your personal production style; many podcasters try to sound more relaxed and casual, while others go to great lengths to make their radio shows, audiobooks, and other recordings rival the production value of traditional media sources. Less than perfect is okay, even better. But be sure the audio quality is pleasing; your customers are more likely to listen to it all the way through.

The less-than-perfect maxim holds true for all social media you produce, and the reason is the audience's perception of the purpose for which the podcast was produced.

For the most part, when an audio or video has that polished, Madison Avenue, network production feel, it can safely be assumed that it cost a great deal to have it produced. It also stands to reason that if someone is writing a big check for the production, most likely there is an agenda for that media. And excluding public service announcements (PSAs), that usually means there is a commercial message behind all that professional-sounding media.

With social media, the content is by the people, for the people. It's ad hoc, fresh, spontaneous, unbiased, and noncommercial. Most commercial products and companies wouldn't want to be represented by anything less than professional quality. So, with decreased focus on production quality comes a perception of homemade, honest, truthful, and trustworthy.

Keeping this concept in mind, it's better *not* to strive for perfection— and to be very careful how self-promoting and commercial your social media message may sound. This holds true for your blogs, vlogs, podcasts, and any other form of media you might produce (excepting only your corporate web page). You can mention your product, or even have a quick introduction to it at the beginning of your vlogs for your sponsor, company, or yourself; just do it tastefully and keep it at a minimum. Otherwise, you will lose your listener's trust.

Introducing Your Podcast

The next step of planning is to sketch out the type of introduction that you want to have. It can include a verbal opening explaining who you are, what your subject matter is, and what you will be talking about in this episode. It can also be saved for future use as the introduction for your next podcast. Remember: Your intro is your persona, your audio image, and your brand for you and your content.

Your introduction can also include a couple of riffs or a few bars of music. Get an idea ahead of time the feeling you want your podcast to convey: serious, businesslike, entertaining, educational, or something else. Then pick about five seconds of music that conveys that feeling to your listener. Apple's GarageBand (assuming you own a Macintosh computer) is a great tool for this. In just a couple of minutes, you can select a few instrumental riffs (several seconds, or chords), and lay down a track (create a piece of music) that will really get your listener's attention. If you don't own a Mac, then you can capture a few seconds of music from any recording on the Internet that is copyright-free.

The best part of working with GarageBand is that *anything* you create is copyright and royalty free. Always be sensitive to copyrights and keep in mind: *If someone else created it, it belongs to that creator.* Rarely is any music you download from the Internet or rip from a CD free for you to use. To include someone else's music in your podcast, you will need written permission from the copyright owner. Otherwise, you could end up as Napster: The Sequel.

However—in terms of copyrighted music—there is the Creative Commons Project. Creative Commons (CC) is a nonprofit organization that has developed copyright licenses that grant certain rights to the public—rights that the owner of copyrighted material is willing to waive so that others may use those not-in-the-public-domain materials. The Creative Commons licenses vary, and can include dedication of copyrighted material to public domain or open content. For more information on the Creative Commons Project, please visit http://creativecommons.org/.

And, for more information on U.S. copyrights, you can visit www.uspto.gov

and select "Copyrights," or www.theSocialMediaBible.com

for clickable links.

Recording

When making your podcast, use a few bullet points or a slide show to convey your main ideas. You can then simply read a bullet and just speak spontaneously about that subject, without sounding too rehearsed or rigid. And if you don't want to plan out your podcast—then it's okay to just wing it!

Once you know what you want to say, it's time to record it. To begin, you will need to use your computer's built-in microphone or connect an external microphone for better quality. A number of high quality USB-compatible microphones are available from online retailers for as little as $30 or less. You will also need audio recording and editing software. Use Audacity, Sound Studio, GarageBand, or other inexpensive or free sound editing software. Some statistics suggest that nearly half of all of the creators of podcasts are either using or have used Audacity to record and edit their shows. It provides easy-to-use, high quality tools—and it's free! Audio recording software, including podcasting-specific features, sometimes also comes bundled with some of the USB microphones mentioned earlier. For straight-ahead no-frills recording, the latest release of Apple's Quicktime Player—a free download for Mac and Windows—will also record, allow you to trim, and save audio in the .mov, .m4p, and .m4v formats. Of course, you're also welcome to use more expensive and elaborate software.

Some audio editing software can import sound file formats such as .wav, .aiff, .wma, and MP3s, and record from a microphone as well as from the computer's sound card and auxiliary devices. If you want to record a talk-show format or telephone interview, and your guest or co-host is working in a different location, VoIP (Voice over Internet Protocol) software, such as Vonage and Skype—both also *free*—can record both sides of the phone call directly though the use of add-ins like VoIP Recorder (for Vonage) and Pamela (for Skype).

Starting with the release of the Leopard version of its operating system and continuing through Snow Leopard and Lion, Apple began shipping Mac OS X with an included utility called Podcast Capture (in the Utilities folder inside the Applications folder). According to the introductory screen, "Podcast Capture lets you easily capture high-quality audio and video from a camera or your Mac's screen and send your content to a Podcast Producer Server for processing." Podcast Producer is a Mac OS X Server application that automates the publishing of podcasts to blogs, iTunes, and iTunes U. Podcast Capture requires you to enter the address of your Podcast Producer Server before it will let you do any recording, editing, and tagging, and most people I know don't have a Mac OS X Server lying around waiting to publish their podcasts, but if you are on a university campus or in another enterprise that runs one, this may be a viable option for you. And while no Podcast Producer hosting services have popped up as yet to fill this potential market niche, in the near future, you may find Podcast Producer services for hire on the Internet—maybe even for *free!*

Signing Off

The last part of podcast planning involves writing or rehearsing your closing, or sign-off. During this part of the session, you should remind your audience of who you are and what your subject matter is, where they can find more of it, and perhaps mention your sponsor (if you have one). Your sign-off is perhaps the most important part of your podcast, because it is the last thing your listeners will hear each time they listen to you, and through repetition, it establishes your auditory brand identity. For a great example of a consistent sign-off, listen to podcasts from National Public Radio's weekly program *Talk of the Nation Science Friday* (http://sciencefriday.com).

Editing

You will need to edit your podcast somewhat. In most software packages— even the free ones that came with your computer or that you downloaded from the Internet—it's as easy as copying, cutting, pasting, and deleting. At the very minimum, you will need to trim the dead air at the beginning and end of your recording; and in most cases, you will want to paste together the music and verbal intro and your sign-off content.

Most audio editing programs include basic editing tools such as the ability to cut segments, mix tracks, convert formats, and split tracks (see Figure 9.2). Some incorporate advanced tools like automatic gain controls and recording volume sliders. Many programs also feature a variety of filters and effects such as reverb (discussed in the following "Special Effects" section). This all might sound a little daunting at first, but after playing with the software for a mere 30 minutes, you might consider yourself an expert. And lest you think you need to

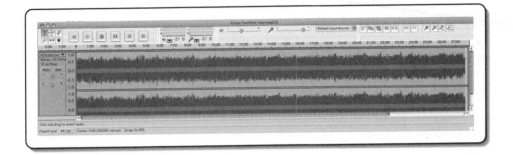

FIGURE 9.2   Audacity Sound Editing Software

be sitting at your computer, there are also smartphone apps now in which you can perform all the basic recording and editing functions you will need.

Publishing

The final step in podcasting is publishing. Because of podcasting's growing popularity, a lot of new software now has podcast publishing wizards built right in. This software fully automates your podcast tags or keywords (see Chapter 18, Spotlight on Search (Search Engine Optimization) for more information on keywords), and RSS feed creation (see Chapter 17, RSS—Really Simple Syndication Made Simple). You simply click to publish, and you're immediately able to share your material. Podcasts are meant to be shared; the more people who share your podcasts, the more people who are sharing your thoughts and ideas—and the bigger the following you will have.

Liberated Syndication (www.Libsyn.com)

is one of the largest media-hosting providers that podcasters use. Starting at $5 a month, they'll provide all the download bandwidth you need regardless of how popular your show becomes. Some people host their podcasts on their own server and have plug-ins to play the podcast directly from the web page, while most others upload it to podcast websites— such as PodBean and iTunes (RSS)—where it is easily syndicated.

Special Effects

Special effects, properly used, can enhance your podcasts. By adding a little creativity and a special effect here and there, you can keep your content exciting and entertaining.

If your software has features that allow you to do so, you should first boost your volume and your bass. Most microphones—especially the inexpensive built-in types—can make your recording sound shallow and tinny. Boosting the volume and bass will add fullness and fidelity to your recording. Another (free!) piece of audio editing software called the Levelator does all that boosting for you automatically (see Figure 9.3).

The Levelator (www.conversationsnetwork.org/levelator) also performs audio normalization—leveling out the volume of two people talking. This feature is very useful, since one person is usually a little closer to the microphone, or at the other end of the telephone.

FIGURE 9.3   Levelator

Software

Podcast recording and editing programs include GarageBand, Quicktime Player, WordPress PodPress Widget, Sound Studio, Soundtrack Pro, Audacity, Evoca, ePodcast Creator, Gabcast, Hipcast, Odeo Studio, Phone Blogz, Podcast Station, Propagan, WebPod Studio, and others. This may sound like a lot to think about, but remember, you need only one. Install a few editing applications, try them, and then stick with the one you like the best. It's that simple.

Hardware

Hardware can include your computer and accompanying microphone, desktop stand or lapel microphones, recording decks and mixers, telephone recorder interfaces (for recording directly off the telephone), headsets, and digital recorders. A $49 Overstock.com

digital recorder was a great purchase. It is approximately one-half by one-half by four inches, fits in a breast pocket, works with a lavaliere or lapel microphone, and will record up to 12 hours of continuous stereo digital audio (see Figure 9.4). Whenever making a new or unique presentation, on it goes—and a podcast is recorded without any effort. All that's left to do is add the intro and the sign-off, and it's ready to go!

FIGURE 9.4 Digital Recorder

Websites and Podcast Distributors

You can find a variety of different types of podcasts on the Internet today on a variety of topics that range from subject-specific, to informative and educational, to entertaining, to commercial, to the occasional rant.

Podcasts are everywhere. When the term *podcast* is googled, almost 93 million results are returned for sites like PodCast.com,

Digg, MSNBC, CNN, Yahoo!, *New York Times*, PodcastAlley, NPR (National Public Radio), PodBean, Grid7, iTunes, iTunes University, Scientific American, NASA, and CBS News.

For some great examples of podcasts and amazing content from 50 of the social media industry's founders, CEOs, and vice presidents, go to www .theSocialMediaBible.com

menu item Insights.

The ROI of Social Media

Crisis Overnight: How We Raised $160K+ in Three Weeks with Social Media

Background

A beloved and trusted crisis community center helping hundreds of abused individuals in Elgin, Illinois, was in desperate economic straits. The center had completely exhausted its monetary resources and was waiting for a drawn-out decision from state lawmakers to approve a budget and release necessary funding.

Approximately three weeks before the center's funding and cash-on-hand was officially drained, the center's leadership made a desperate plea for help. They acknowledged a brutal fact—they might have to close their doors.

Albeit impromptu, the right people came together at the right time, and the Crisis Center board and executive director trusted us to try something new. The decision to integrate social media and share the center's story publicly was agreed to unanimously.

Strategy

The idea for Crisis Overnight was born. In addition to traditional fund-raising efforts, an overnight awareness campaign would be held at the center, documented through social media with a call to action to encourage people to donate.

We had four days to develop a plan, create a donor website, craft our messaging, and implement.

The truth of the situation became the primary messaging of the campaign: "The goal is simple. We raise $150,000 by July 1 and the Community Crisis Center stays open. We don't, and they close." However, because social media was an integrated part of the outreach, it meant reaching more than just a local constituency. The team developed separate messaging and tactics for the local community, and a broader message was used to appeal to a national audience that could relate to the causes of domestic violence, economic issues, and sexual assault.

Implementation

To communicate socially with the local community and world, we used the center's LinkedIn profile and amped up their social media toolbox by creating a blog, a Twitter account, and social bookmarking accounts.

Nevertheless, developing a community and building credibility through social media platforms takes time—something that was not available. To maximize the center's online visibility, I donated my entire online presence, a platform of more than 40,000 followers.

The online communities we used during the campaign included Twitter, Facebook, Seesmic, PRsarahevans.com,

YouTube, and CrisisOvernight.org.

The campaign began as a one-night event and expanded into a three-week campaign, securing continuous donations, both in person and online. All online donors were populated on the Crisis Overnight website with their city and state to visually convey that people across the United States were fighting for one community's crisis center.

Opportunity

The opportunity was to generate local and national awareness of the crisis center's story, which would drive funding so that the institution could continue to support the abused individuals in the community.

(continued)

(continued)

Conclusion

All efforts related to Crisis Overnight raised $161,000, buying the center one month of payroll and the ability to pay off end-of-the-year bills.

—Sarah Evans (@prsarahevans)
http://PRsarahevans.com

Expert Insight

Evo Terra, coauthor, *Podcasting For Dummies*, www.podiobooks.com

Evo Terra

Well, there is a lot of information out there about starting a podcast, and the most common word that is given out is, "Just start, and figure it out as you go along." And that isn't bad advice for some hobbyist that just wants to play in the media. But for businesspeople—and for those who really want to get in to make a splash—I suggest they take a different route.

The very first thing I would suggest to people interested in podcasting is: do your homework. You know, find out if there are other people in the space that you are getting into. Most businesspeople are not going to say, "I want to open up an ice cream stand," without having some understanding of the ice cream market. You have to know what you are getting yourself into, even if you have no idea how to run an ice cream stand; you can, at least, know what the business is.

The same thing goes for podcasting. You can figure out what the competition is doing, if you want to think about it as competition. I don't. I use the word because we all understand it. But [you have to] at least understand what is competing with the topic of your podcast for people's time; and the other sorts of media that are doing the same thing, just not in a podcast form. Whether that's radio, or whether it's an audiobook, you know, understand what your listeners are likely to want to listen to. Do your [due] diligence. . . .

I could go on for days on what *not* to do. As I am often reminded myself, you know, there is no one right way to do things; but there are lots of wrong ways. There are lots of tip and advice books out there that will give you some suggestions; but one of the things I think I would caution people about is that, since we're talking about this user-generated content of podcasting, amateur people who have not had a lot of experience using the tools are getting into the space.

There are a lot of people out there advising that it's the content that's the most important, and I don't disagree with them. Content is *king*. You have to have something that is worth talking about and that is interesting to people. However, I think that oftentimes, this comes at the expense of quality. In fact, I have heard more than one person suggest that you ought to not worry about the quality of the show, because it's content that matters; and then discuss other reasons why quality does not matter. And I just . . . I have to disagree! And I have to disagree for one reason. I know how easy it is to make your podcast sound professional.

There are quite a few tools out there. I recommend that anyone starting out new in podcasting does not go out and spend crazy amounts of dollars. In fact, you should spend as little as possible. . . . I still use Audacity. It's free and it's simple and it does just about everything you are going to want to do at your level. . . .

There's another piece of equipment that I like to use called The Levelator. It is free software that you run your spoken-word audio through, and it magically (I don't mind using the word, because I have seen this tool work and I use it every day myself) brings up your audio level to a fantastic

(continued)

(continued)

level. It is not a perfect tool; and there are plenty of engineers who don't like to use it. But my recommendation to all new people and all podcasters today is . . . you should be using The Levelator. It is amazing what it can do to your sound. . . .

Now there are some specialty tools which come into play if you want to record telephone conversations. Or maybe you want to buy a library of prelicensed music, so that you don't sound like everybody else discovering the free stuff. There are those investments to make. But if it is your first time doing it . . . don't! Don't invest any additional money. Your computer most likely already has set up what you need to do to get started, even with a cheap, $5 microphone that it came with. I know many people that started out that way, but once they figured out what they wanted to do, [they] eventually graduate to bigger and better equipment. But start off with spending next to nothing. . . .

You know, quality has become very important—even though people don't recognize or realize it. I think one thing that's becoming easier to discern from the podcast listeners—as they have matured over the last four years—is the issue of authenticity. And I think you may be right [about sounding *too* good]. Early on in the process, if something sounded really slick and polished, you started wondering, "What's the underlying agenda? What corporate underwriting sponsorship is happening here?"

But I think consumers are becoming a lot more educated in that now. They're a little more sophisticated, and they are really able to get down to the message. If your goal is to try and sound like the guy who does the 10 o'clock news, then that's going to fail miserably. You know why? That's a terrible delivery. They have to do that in a certain way because they have a certain amount of time to get to people before they get to bed, and they drag you along and put the weather at the end. . . .

To listen to or read the entire Executive Conversation with Evo Terra, go to www.theSocialMediaBible.com

or www.podiobooks.com.

International Perspective

Mexico

(continued)

(continued)

As the fastest-growing social networking site in the world for the first half of 2008, Hi5 is the largest site of its kind that you may have never heard of. The site grew 78 percent in the first half of 2008 alone.

Based in San Francisco, Hi5 launched in 2003 and was turning a profit by 2004. By 2005, the site had 10 million members. While sites like Facebook and MySpace began to dominate the U.S. social networking scene, Hi5 began to look at other opportunities internationally.

In 2006, it launched a Spanish version of the site to great success. Versions of the site in other languages soon followed. This new focus paid off. Hi5 became the most popular social networking site in Mexico and many Latin American countries. Like many other social networking sites, members create profiles, share photos, play games, and post messages.

—Jonathan Strickland, Senior Writer
HowStuffWorks.com
Discovery Communications

To-Do List

- Podcast.

  Go forth and podcast, often. Go and be creative! It's easy and free! Just try it. You will surprise yourself how good you are.

- Do not covet thy neighbor's copyrights.

  Be careful not to take or use something that belongs to someone else. Creating a five-second song is really easy. There are even royalty-free sound bites and music you can use called *pod-safe* music.

- Experience sound editing.

  Sound editing sounds scary, but it is really easier than you think. Many good editing software packages either come free with your computer or can easily be downloaded from the Internet.

- Do not spend a lot of money.

  Unless you really want to get into podcasting, don't spend a lot of money doing it. Remember in this one case that "good enough" might actually be *good enough*.

- RSS feed your podcasts.

  By RSS feeding your podcasts, you are making them available to literally millions of potential listeners. You can learn more about RSS (Really Simple Syndication) in Chapter 17, RSS—Really Simple Syndication Made Simple.

- Upload your podcasts to iTunes.

  Be sure to upload your podcasts to iTunes. Tens of millions of people search iTunes every day looking for content that might be similar to yours. Be sure to follow their guidelines to ensure your podcast's success. And keep in mind that if your podcast falls into the educational category, you should upload it to the iTunes University.

- Keep your podcasts brief.

  Most people only have about a seven-minute attention span for audio. Taking any more time than that will lose your listeners' interest. If you have a 30-minute interview or a 45-minute panel discussion, leave it at that length. If your audio file can be broken into five- to seven-minute chapters, topics, or ideas, then break it up.

- Produce in the right file format.

  Be sure that when you link or upload your podcasts, they are in a usable file format. While QuickTime is great for Macintosh users to play, Windows and PowerPoint users have difficulties with it. Most people want your content in an MP3 format so that it is compatible with their digital music players.

- Be conscious of file size.

  While you may have a lot to say, a 53MB file is just too large for most people to download and install on their digital players. Most tunes run at about 3.5MB each, so try to keep your finished files in the single-digit MB range.

- Be creative.

  This, again, is the most important commandment. The more creative you are and the more "What's in It for Me?" you provide for your listener, the more people will download it, listen to it, pass it along to their friends, recommend it, and comment on it; and the more loyal listeners and followers and trusted network you will build. Remember to ask your customers to be collaborators of your content.

Conclusion

As long as your podcasts have a strong WIIFM, your listeners will keep coming back for more. The more you podcast, the more quality content and contributions you will provide to your followers, listeners, and customers. Keep podcasting, because it helps to build your trusted network; your customers and followers will perceive you as an industry and subject matter expert; and when it's time to buy, you will be the one they think of first. It's free, it's easy, it's fun—so do it!

To hear all of the Expert Interviews, go to www.theSocialMedia Bible.com.

Downloads

For your free downloads associated with *The Social Media Bible*, go to www.theSocialMediaBible.com,

and enter your ISBN number located on the back of the book above the bar code. Be sure to enter the dashes.

Credits

The ROI of Social Media was provided by:

Sarah Evans (@prsarahevans), http://PRsarahevans.com

Expert Insight was provided by:

Evo Terra, coauthor, *Podcasting For Dummies*, www.podiobooks.com

Technical edits were provided by:

Stephen Farrington, www.stephenfarrington.com

Note

1. Drive time refers to 6:00 AM to 10:00 AM and 3:00 PM to 7:00 PM Monday through Friday when the majority of radio listeners travel to and from work and significantly more commercials are run.

CHAPTER 10

Got Audio? (Audio Sharing)

www.LonSafko.com/TSMB3_Videos/10Audio.mov

What's in It for You?

Today, it is estimated more than 56 million people subscribe to podcasts, and that number is growing exponentially. Podcasts are essentially a vehicle for the many other types of media that individuals and businesses can use in the realm of social networking. You can add music, digital photos, animated company logos, colorful videos—anything that it takes to get your message across.

Audio is by far the easiest of all rich media to create and share. All of the tools that you need are in your computer already, and those that aren't are available for free from the Internet. You probably already have a built-in microphone and the recording software (see Chapter 9, Talking about the Podcast (Audio Create)) in your PC. While audio isn't as appealing as video, it is a lot easier to record, edit, and share, so the trade-off between convenience and high-tech appearance is well worth it. Also, audio files make for a quicker download than video, and listeners can safely tune in to your content while driving or working out.

No one is an expert on everything, and when it comes to social media, it's hard to be an expert at all because the industry is simply changing faster than most people can keep up with. There are, however, a great number of

people ahead of the pack, and hearing *their* insights is important. That's why this book and the associated website present the collected wisdom of nearly 50 founders, CEOs, authors, and experts in the social media field. (See the many impressive and detailed Executive Conversations at http://www.lonsafko.com/TSMB3_Videos/10Audio.mov.)

How does this apply to you and your business? Ask your customers and prospects what they would like to hear from you. The first step is to create some audio podcasts (see Chapter 9, Talking about the Podcast (Audio Create)) and share them. While *The Social Media Bible* is not intended to be a how-to book, an important topic is the basics of sharing audio. This chapter discusses two prime examples: iTunes and Podbean.

Back to the Beginning

As soon as a network became established, people began sharing the many different kinds of files they had—text, photos, images, video, and audio. Most of these "Back to the Beginning" sections are the longest ones in each chapter. Since the beginnings of audio sharing were covered in another chapter, the focus here is on some of the tools that have made audio sharing such an easy and successful approach to business promotion (see the previous chapter's "Back to the Beginning" for more information on the history of audio creation and sharing).

What You Need to Know

Every single day, your customers, prospects, and employees are inundated with information from e-mail, voicemails, junk mail, and memos. The important question for you to ask is: How do you get your important messages across to them in a way that doesn't get lost in all of that noise? The answer is podcasts.

As explained in the previous chapter, a *podcast* is an audio or video recording that a person can subscribe to, receive, download, listen to, or watch using a personal computer, iPod or iPhone, or other mobile device. Your customers and prospects can therefore listen to or watch this information whenever and wherever they wish—in their cars, during lunch, in the evening, at the office, at the gym, while jogging, or even on their day off.

A podcast is similar to a television program or radio show, but easier to create and distribute, and it's free to do so. The process of audio sharing requires that you first create an audio file, and then make it known and available. Chapter 9, Talking about the Podcast (Audio Create) describes in detail how to create an audio file podcast, while this chapter focuses on sharing it with others. A great book to help with this topic is Tee Morris, Chuck Tomasi, and Evo Terra's *Podcasting For Dummies*. For extremely helpful step-by-step instructions on how to publish your podcast using iTunes, go to www .mvldesign.com/itunespodcast.html.

Let's begin by discussing iTunes, the most popular audio and video solution for downloading, playing, aggregating, and publishing your podcasts.

iTunes

Apple Computer developed iTunes for both the Macintosh and Windows operating platforms and released it on January 9, 2001, at the Macworld Expo in San Francisco. iTunes is used for playing, organizing, downloading, and publishing audio and video files, and now iPhone, iPod, and iPad apps, through your desktop, laptop, mobile phone, and, of course, your iPod, iPad, or iPhone. iTunes enables users to connect to the iTunes Store through the Internet, where they can purchase and download music, music videos, television shows, iPod, iPhone, and iPad games, audiobooks, various podcasts, feature-length films, movie rentals, and ringtones. iTunes is available as a free download for Mac OS X, Windows 7, Windows Vista, and Windows XP from Apple's website (Apple.com). iTunes also comes bundled with all Macs, and some HP and Dell computers, and can be accessed directly from iPhone, iPod Touch, and iPad (through a Wi-Fi connection).

The original media player software that was iTunes's predecessor was developed in 1999 by Casady & Greene, a software publisher of shareware products, created primarily for the Macintosh and called SoundJam MP. Original developers Jeff Robbin and Bill Kincaid sold SoundJam to Apple in 2000, which gave it a facelift and the ability to burn CDs, and rereleased it in January 2001 with its new name: iTunes. iTunes was available only for the Macintosh line of computers until March 2007, when Apple released its Windows version. iTunes 64-bit versions for Windows became available on January 16, 2008.

FIGURE 10.1 iTunes

FIGURE 10.2   QuickTime Audio

By July 2011, Apple's iTunes App Store had provided more than 15 billion downloads of apps and currently advertises more than 500,000 titles. Ninety percent of the apps[1] are priced at less than $10, and thousands are available for free, including custom applications for staying plugged in to all your social media sites, from Facebook to LinkedIn to Twitter.

iTunes users can manage audio and video files on their personal PC, which is required for iPod operation and synchronization. Within the iTunes application, the user can engage in a variety of activities: Create playlists, edit file information, record CDs, copy files to digital audio or video players, purchase audio and video files from the iTunes Store, download free music and audio podcasts, back up their music and video to CDs and DVDs, display a visualizer graphic effects screen, encode digital files in a myriad of formats, listen to any of a larger number of Internet radio stations, and publish audio files and podcasts to the iTunes Store. iTunes organizes music and video by creating virtual libraries wherein it stores and keeps track of each song's attributes such as artist, genre, album information and cover art, lyrics, how often it's been played, the last time it was played, and the personal rating that users can give it. iTunes users can view their music libraries in one of four ways; as a list of songs by title; by the music's cover artwork; in an application called Cover Flow, which is an Apple-style slide-scrolling catalog of artwork; or a Grid View of the iTunes library that can sort music by artist, by album, and album by year.

iTunes can also rip or copy music from CDs, but not DVDs. Certain movie studios introduced iTunes Digital Copy in 2008—a bonus feature that is available on some DVDs, which provides an iTunes-compatible file for select films for otherwise copy-protected material.

iTunes can currently read, write, and convert between several types of files—including MP3, .aiff, .wav, MPEG-4, AAC, and Apple Lossless.

FIGURE 10.3   QuickTime Video

The application can also play any audio file and most video formats that QuickTime can play. QuickTime is a free application developed by Apple for both the Windows and Apple platform that allows the user to create and play videos in full screen, create movies for iPod, and download movies from the web (see Figure 10.3). The $29.99 Pro version of QuickTime includes audio processing features such as equalization, sound enhancement, cross fade, and Sound Check, which automatically adjusts the playback volume of all songs to the same level. iTunes can produce static, party, and new Smart[2] playlists that can be played randomly or sequentially.

iTunes added video playback and the ability to download and view video content in .mov, .mp4, .m4v, and .mpg formats from the iTunes Store and other sources, including both purchased and free content such as video podcasts—or Vodcasts.

It also saw the addition of built-in support for podcasting, which allows iTunes users to subscribe to podcasts for free in the iTunes Music Store or by entering the RSS feed URL. Once a user subscribes, any new podcast is automatically downloaded hourly, daily, or weekly, or manually. Users can listen to podcasts directly from the Podcast Directory, which is an index of user-generated content from commercial and independent podcasters. They can also browse podcasts based on their popularity, and even publish their own material through the iTunes Store. When discovery of podcasts was added to the mainstream and widely used through iTunes, many podcasters reported downloads of their podcasts increased by multiples.

iTunes was up to version 10.5 at the time this chapter was written and along the way has added the availability of song lyrics, CD liner notes and photos, sharing of media libraries within a home network, movie special features, and offers store categories dedicated specifically to music (including music videos), movies, TV shows, apps, books (including audiobooks and enhanced books), podcasts (including audio and video podcasts), and iTunes U (educational podcast content), as well as a new social network for music, called Ping, which allows users to follow their favorite artists and the listening choices of friends.

Because iTunes takes full advantage of podcasts' RSS features—for *podcatching*—it is considered one of the best in its class for providing downloadable audio and video. iTunes is also closely integrated with Apple's iWork and iLife software packages—providing you a complete podcasting production tool chain. You can, for example, create a podcast in GarageBand or edit a video in iMovie, export it directly to your iTunes library, and then embed it in your website using iWeb (Apple's web design software).

Beginning with its first version, iTunes has given users access to popular Internet radio services. As of November 2011, iTunes Radio provided users with built-in access to nearly 7,000 Internet radio streams. These stations make up every genre from music to sports to talk radio to more traditional radio stations as well. In recent versions of iTunes, the radio tab is disabled by default, but users can enable it through the iTunes preferences window, which is accessible through the iTunes dropdown menu. Users can also enter their own stream feed to listen under the Radio tab by selecting the dropdown menu option Advanced, and then selecting Open Stream. QuickTime Player also supports Internet radio, and you can find iTunes plug-ins from iRadioMast (www.iradiomast.com).

Now that you're familiar with the world's largest music sharing, upload, and download service, let's discuss a website called Podbean—one that hosts, syndicates, and distributes your uploaded audio files for free.

Podbean

Podbean (www.podbean.com, Figures 10.4 and 10.5)

FIGURE 10.4   Podbean

FIGURE 10.5   Podbean Skin

opened in July 2006, providing podcast publishing tools for users to begin creating professional-caliber podcasts. Podbean allows them to do so in a very short amount of time, with an easy point-and-click, bloglike environment—and requires no technical knowledge. The website gives users the chance to manage, publish, and promote podcasts with just a few clicks. Most importantly, Podbean hosts and serves up the actual media file that is your podcast's audio content (iTunes merely catalogs your podcasts—you still need to store them somewhere from which they can be downloaded). Podbean is used by a wide variety of podcasters—from education, religion, real estate, music, sports clubs, travel agents, government agencies, hobbyists, and entrepreneurs, to larger corporations.

Signing up for a Podbean account grants users a personalized podcast website with one's own URL for banding. Users can even select themes, or *skins* (see Figure 10.5) with different colors, fonts, and layout for their pages. Podbean also provides users with website traffic reporting and analysis tools, so that they are able to measure their podcasts' success and know exactly how they're performing. Podbean provides an in-depth, multidimensional view of a site's visitors, subscribers, hits, and geographic location distribution, and even lets users download these data.

All of the Podbean pages have full RSS feed generation for RSS2, iTunes, and Atom integrated right in. Podbean supports RSS 2.0 and Atom feeds (see Chapter 17), as well as the extended Apple iTunes podcasting tags. Podbean also provides a Web 2.0–based podcast player that can be embedded directly into your website, blog site, and other social networks. The more podcasts you create—and the more popular your podcasts become—the more regularly your files will be downloaded, the more storage and bandwidth you will require (see Chapter 11, Watch Out for Vlogs (Video Create), for more information on bandwidth). But no matter how popular your podcasts become, Podbean provides the storage and bandwidth you need for free. It also allows users to earn revenue through advertising, paid subscription, and merchandise sales. In fact, Podbean has a full-function online e-commerce tool provided to users for free.

Most of the social media tools covered in this book work on the freemium business model—meaning that most of the service that the providers give to individual users is done completely free of charge, while enterprises or premium users pay a modest fee for additional services.

The ROI of Social Media

Social Media in Focus

Introduction

Nicole Walker Photography is a small family portrait photography start-up based in Glendale, Arizona, that focuses on providing high quality portraits to families that cannot afford to pay high studio prices.

Background

We consciously chose to leverage the power of social media to quickly create awareness to a targeted customer base without investing a significant amount of working capital on marketing-related expenses.

In an industry that is extremely competitive and with hundreds of direct competitors in a very small space, we needed to find a way to differentiate ourselves and consistently keep the brand active and relevant in the eyes of consumers.

Strategy

Our strategy was to be active in a space where our customers already were. Our primary target consumer group is 21- to 40-year-old mothers and mothers-to-be within 25 miles of Glendale, Arizona. Many social media platforms allow for this specific level of search and filtering capability so we could easily create introductions, become visible, and interact with existing and potential customers.

Instead of being in constant sell mode, we chose to share our photos, start discussions, create content, and exchange ideas that add value to our communities of target customers that they would feel compelled to participate in and pass along to their friends and family.

Implementation

We created a blog using Blogger [a Google-owned blogging tool], as well as branded pages on Facebook, MySpace, and CafeMom. We have found that these are the spaces in which our target customers regularly interact with friends and family, and inserting ourselves into their daily interactions was extremely simple.

Opportunity

The opportunity is to showcase our talent to thousands of mothers and mothers-to-be by attaching the samples from each of our recent sessions to our various social media pages while discussing parenting and other family issues with a community of like-minded individuals.

Conclusion

Since launching our social media pages, we have generated thousands of unique visits to our website with little push or hard selling. We have seen

(continued)

(continued)

a consistent doubling to tripling month over month in new unique visitors (1,360 percent total increase in the past 10 months). For many of our key search terms, we are now found within the first five pages of Google, Yahoo, and Bing. Additionally, we have improved our advanced booking pipeline from one to two weeks to two-plus months (even the slow summer season).

—Chris Walker
www.NicoleWalkerPhotography.com

Expert Insight

Alan Levy, founder and CEO, Blog Talk Radio, www.blogtalkradio.com

Alan Levy

Well, we have two parts of the network. The main network is the network which we launched in October 2006, which we launched from scratch. I mean, we created this idea. . . . I came up with the name, *BlogTalkRadio*. We had no content. We invented this technology which, essentially, incorporates using the phone, or any kind of phone, into the web. And to date we've broadcasted about 110,000 segments . . . maybe about a 115,000. Each day, we broadcast 500 new live shows. You can see them all at BlogTalkRadio.com.

They all appear here in our programming guides.

We have had everyone on the network, from John McCain, who has been on three times, to Yoko Ono, Brad Pitt, Brian De Palma, Salman Rushdie, famous authors, actors, and of course, thousands and thousands of bloggers. Anybody, really, who is looking to communicate a message and promote an idea or promote a book can come on *BlogTalkRadio* for free. All they have to do is create a profile, set up a show on when they would like to broadcast, and they can dial in and be on [the] air in a matter of minutes. . . .

We found that . . . I'm either very crazy or very smart; I don't know which one yet, but we realized that a lot of people that had been coming on *BlogTalkRadio* were being asked to pay hundreds, if not thousands of dollars to have their own radio show. And we figured out a way to keep it at a very low-cost point by using the phone. That's my background, in phone technology. And by doing that, we are able to provide the service for free. And I think that when you create a platform that is open and available, you look into democratizing the medium, much like blogging did for bloggers and tech space communication.

BlogTalkRadio is doing the same for audio and, soon-to-be, video. . . .

Yeah, we are very pleased with the quality. You know, when I first came up with the idea, the podcasting . . . and this is, you know, podcasting was something that I really did not know much about. . . . I did not set out to create or become another podcasting company. I set up BlogTalkRadio because I created a blog for my dad, who was ill with lymphoma and cancer, and I wanted to . . . and I learned about blogs, and I realized that there were 75 to 80 million of them. And everyone's talking about "conversation," and I

(continued)

(continued)

could not hear any. So I created it. We created a platform that allows live, interactive conversation using the phone, of course, as I mentioned . . . and we achieved it. That's the easy part of it.

So, for us, I do think we're more like a broadcast medium as an alternative. If you look at our audience, the guests that are on, [there is] such diversity. It is incredible the type of content, and then it's archived for the long run, which we can then modify. . . .

We did build it from scratch, so we are . . . we have people looking at the site and our own internal customer service people and feature editors, and the like, and very often . . . you know . . . we'll get an e-mail from one of the hosts and it will say, "You know, we've got to call the FCC." And we say, "Fine, call the FCC."

I mean, they have no mandate here. This is a collection of conversations and it's all . . . it's monitored, it's run by us on our site. So there is no FCC. There is . . . but we do ensure that the quality is good, and we double up the best content, and the platform is not being used to facilitate hate or conversations like that, for example. . . .

Yeah, well, it is self-policing also, in a sense, because the hosts know that when they come on this network . . . they sign a form and they're responsible for content, and there's clearly terms and conditions; things they can and cannot do. And if they're in breach of those terms and conditions, I mean, they'll get a warning. But then, they'll be removed from the network. And there are no other places for them to go. . . .

So, you know, they're not going to go to podcast, or they're not going to go to a podcasting platform because they don't even know how to create this podcast. We take care of everything from the broadcast, the live interaction, all the way through iTunes and the RSS feed. So, it is self-policing, and it's very exciting to see it grow and evolve. And many times the listeners become hosts. You know, they're getting involved and they say, "Why not! I could do one of these things."

To listen to or read the entire Executive Conversation with Alan Levy, go to www.theSocialMediaBible.com.

International Perspective

Cyprus

Cyprus Tourism Organization (CTO), www.visitcyprus.com, has been utilizing social media since early 2009. The main social media channels being used are Facebook, Twitter, YouTube, and Trip Advisor. CTO's first steps for social media utilization were made by monitoring user generated content in the above channels. After realizing the real potential of social media, CTO engaged in more active participation by creating branded Cyprus pages in Facebook, Twitter, and YouTube. The main objective of these pages is to provide subscribers with travel related content, news, and updates on Cyprus.

"Our experience with social media utilization aids our learning process towards providing valuable content for our subscribers, which facilitates their engagement with the travel destination Cyprus. The enthusiasm that characterizes our subscribers' communications on our social media channels and their positive sentiments, provide the feedback we seek on customer satisfaction. As we consider our subscribers' communications to be very important for improving the quality of our offered products and services, we monitor their comments very closely." Dr. Haris Machlouzarides, CTO's eMarketing department.

Tourism is one of Cyprus's main industries and social media utilization is one of the main electronic marketing activities performed by CTO for promoting the island as a tourism destination worldwide. Social media enable Cyprus to reach its global audience in a cost effective way and establish a dialogue with people, attending to their needs and providing answers to their questions.

During the period of utilizing social media, CTO ran several promotional actions toward triggering subscribers' interest for active participation and engagement on CTO's channels. These actions had positive results on the number of subscribers on these channels as well as the virility of content disseminated through channel subscribers. For instance, CTO's Facebook page which is hosted under www.facebook.com/LoveCyprus has around 10 percent of its subscribers talking about the content published under this channel.

Yet, the most amazing statistic of all on the above CTO's Facebook page is the subscribers' demographics. More than 50 percent of total subscribers are adults aged 45+, while youngsters aged up to 24, count only to 20 percent of total subscribers. Finally, adults aged 25 to 44, count to around 30 percent of total subscribers. The above numbers encourage CTO's efforts on social media marketing, as it seems that the provision of valuable content to target

(*continued*)

(continued)

markets yields positive results. Moreover, the above numbers prove that CTO's target markets are moving to social media.

As the above information suggests, successful communication with CTO's social media subscribers facilitates nurturing existing relationships with them, and encourages customer loyalty. CTO's social media subscribers expect to get useful and interesting content that will have a positive appeal to them. They are eager to share such information with their friends and family, promoting in this way the destination. The more interesting and appealing the published content is the more viral is expected to become, facilitating CTO's marketing objectives in maximizing customer reach.

CTO will continue investing in social media marketing activities as it has realized the potential offered by social media channels in engaging with its customers worldwide.

—Haris Machlouzarides, E-Marketing, IT Officer
Cyprus Tourism Organisation
www.VisitCyprus.com

To-Do List

- Try iTunes.
  Go to www.Apple.com,

and download iTunes for your Mac or Windows platform PC. Try it, even if you don't plan on buying and downloading music. See how the interface works. Refer to the previous chapter on podcasting, create a podcast, and try to upload your new podcast to iTunes. Get in the game. It really is here to stay, and the more you know, the more you can participate.

- Try a podcast hosting site.

  Try using a podcast-hosting site such as Podbean. It really is easy to use; RSS syndication is just a one-click process, it's compatible with iTunes—and best of all—it's free! Just use your PC's built-in mike (or buy one for $8), open your sound editing software, and record your thoughts on your profession or other subject matter of interest to you. Think about the WIIFM (What's in It for Me?), from your customers' and prospects' point of view. What can you tell them in 10 minutes or less that is important to them? This way, they come away from listening to your podcast message with something of value. If you can give them that, then they will keep coming back, refer you to trusted colleagues, and perceive you as an industry expert. All this builds trust, loyalty, and revenue.

Conclusion

It's truly worth your effort to take some time to understand how easy and effective it is to download audio podcasts and music. You'll find that there is great ROI to uploading your podcasts, so that others are exposed to your professional thoughts, and can respond in kind.

Creating your new podcast is one thing, but making it available to your customers, prospects, and employees is quite another. It doesn't do you any good if you have captured your best ideas on audio but no one gets to hear them. So, share your ideas with the world. Upload your podcasts to iTunes and Podbean, and get your material out there. Embed your podcasts on your website and blog site. Simply by creating a library of audio files with a great WIIFM content value will allow your customers and prospects to view you as an industry expert.

Consider your own reaction when you type an individual or company name into a search engine like Google, and see page after page of search results return. You immediately know that this person or firm has a widespread presence on the web. Seeing these dozens of pages of results—including web pages, blog pages, photographs, audio podcasts, and YouTube videos—prompts you to view this party as an industry expert. Now, isn't that how you want your customers and prospects to see *you*?

To hear all of the Expert Interviews, go to www.theSocialMediaBible.com.

Downloads

For your free downloads associated with *The Social Media Bible*, go to www .theSocialMediaBible.com,

and enter your ISBN number located on the back of the book above the bar code. Be sure to enter the dashes.

Credits

The ROI of Social Media was provided by:

Chris Walker, www.NicoleWalkerPhotography.com

Expert Insight was provided by:

Alan Levy, founder and CEO, BlogTalkRadio, www.blogtalkradio.com

Technical edits were provided by:

Stephen Farrington, www.StephenFarrington.com

Notes

1. Applications, or apps, are small software applications that are designed to be installed in smartphones to increase the device's utility and for fun. Apps typically exploit the device's multitouch user interface, camera, accelerometers, rate gyros, GPS, and other hardware features in creative ways, and include web-enabled services such as Google Mobile Search, Maps, Gmail, YouTube, and hundreds more.

2. Smart playlists can be set to automatically filter your music library based on a customized list of selection criteria, similar to a database query. The Genius Feature is another tool that automatically generates a playlist of 25, 50, 75, or 100 songs from the user's library that are similar to a selected song.

CHAPTER 11

Watch Out for Vlogs (Video Create)

www.LonSafko.com/TSMB3_Videos/11VideoCreate.mov

The audio podcast chapter mentioned that a video recording can also be considered a podcast since the iPod and other digital playback devices display photographs, audio, and video. This book differentiates audio recordings as a *podcast* and video recordings as just *video* or a *vlog*. As the word *blog* stands for weB LOG, *vlog* comes from Video web LOG.

What's in It for You?

Human psychology is such that the more robust or stimulating the experience, the more engaging it is, and the better we comprehend and retain that experience. An engaging video also ensures that your viewer will watch it to its conclusion. This is why people often prefer watching a good movie at the end of the day as opposed to reading or even listening to an

audiobook. The more senses that are involved in gathering information, the more compelling the process becomes. This accounts for the overwhelming popularity of YouTube.* Creating video, vlogging, and video posting are all about using this human trait to better educate and communicate with your network and with your customers.

The human being evolved to communicate first through facial expressions, and then through speech. Verbal communication is a relatively new human trait, and the written word is even more recent. Writing can be traced back only a half dozen millennia, while communication using facial expressions and voice tones is the oldest method that any living being has used. Nearly every species on earth that can share information does so in this way.

When two humans want to express an idea, thought, or concept, 55 percent of the communication comes from body language, 38 percent from voice, and only a mere 7 percent from the words. Letters and e-mails clearly don't contain inflection and body language, which is why writing can be so easily misinterpreted or misconstrued. Watching and listening to someone while he speaks allows us to study facial expressions and tone so as to help build trust and make it easier to recognize when someone isn't being sincere. For this reason, vlogs can be the most effective way to communicate with your customers.

All it takes to create a vlog is a digital video camera, some free editing software, and—most important—*creativity*. Companies such as BMW, Quiznos, and Nabisco are using video to grab huge audiences and increase their market share (see Figure 11.1). Even a blender company can get over a million views of its product video in just 24 hours by using off-the-shelf technology and a little creativity (see the "Will It Blend" example at www .theSocialMediaBible.com).

---

*In the time it took you to read these first two paragraphs (60 seconds), more than 4 hours of video was uploaded to YouTube!

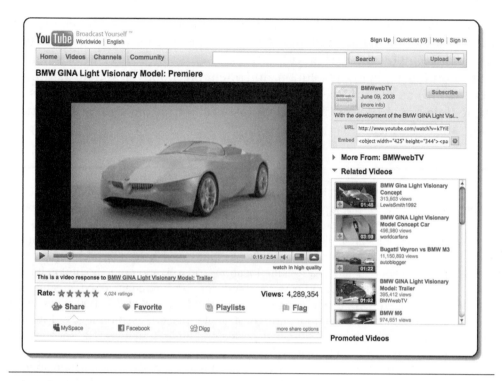

FIGURE 11.1 YouTube BMW

Back to the Beginning

People have always tried to push the limits of this new medium by providing more and more rich media: midi, music, audio, images, virtual reality images (QTVR), and video. The early constraints were CPU speed and bandwidth.

What Is Video?

The technical measure of video content is *frames per second,* which means the number of still images every second. For standard film, the frame rate can be 32 frames (or images) per second, while video frame rates can range from 25 to 30 and even 50 to 60 frames per second for high definition (HD) video, which means that for a standard video that is running at 25 frames per second, there are 1,500 separate images every minute. Based on the dimensions of the video screen, that can add up to a lot of data per frame (image), and a huge amount of information every minute. Getting all of those data through the earliest 300-baud modem (300 bits per second), or even today's 56K-baud modem (56,000 bits per second) is a monumental task. This is why the earlier videos (and even some today) were small in size, short in length, low resolution, and often ran choppy (less than 32 frames per second) as the Internet tried to serve those data to the user. And as all those data came in, the CPU tried to assemble it into a continuously running, smooth video.

The *bit* is the most fundamental piece of data that a computer or any digital device uses to communicate, store, or display. A bit is a single 0 or 1, which represents either the presence of an electrical charge or the absence of such a charge. These digits of 0 and 1 are why today's electronics are called *digital*. Eight of these digits in a stream make up a single byte. Depending upon the computer, it takes as many as 4 bytes (32 bits) to represent a single pixel on your screen in a specific location—on, off, and color. So, if you have a 350K image, it would be 350,000 bytes (*K* stands for 1,000 in engineering, creating the term *KB* for kilobytes). That one image (frame) would consist of 350,000 bytes times 8 bits—or 2.8 million bits of information for a single image. Based on this, a 3-minute video would be 350K bits times 32 frames per second times 3 minutes (180 seconds), or more than 20 billion bits of information!

As the Internet grew, so did *bandwidth,* which is the size of the information conduit and the ability to push more bits through the wire or air—and, consequently, the amount of data that could be displayed. In the early days of the Internet, text was the first type of data because it could be transferred and displayed quickly because of the small number of bits (32 bits per character) involved. A full page of single-spaced text can be as small as 2K (2,000 bytes). A standard color image can be 350K, a 3-minute small-size video can be 20MB (million bytes), and a full-length movie can be more than 4.5GB (4.5 billion bytes)!

With present cable technology, a residential cable Internet connection can provide you with download speeds as high as 4 to 6 Mbps (million bits per second; M stands for million). High-speed cable Internet compared to a 56K dial-up connection can run up to 70 times faster. For an additional fee—and assuming it is available in your area—most major cable providers, such as Cox Communication, Comcast, and Time Warner, also offer premium packages with speeds as high as 8 to 10 Mbps.

Yay for Apple QuickTime!

The first major breakthrough in video for the computer was Apple's release of QuickTime in 1991 (see Figure 11.2). For the first time, users were able to view reasonably good quality color videos on their computers. QuickTime was mostly about compression rate. The less information that needed to be sent out per frame, the more frames that could be transmitted, assembled, and played. Compression is about finding patterns in the data, creating a kind of shorthand for that pattern, and transmitting the shorthand data and rules, which represent much less overall information. Later versions of QuickTime maximized the video file size and allowed users to transmit very small videos through still-restricted bandwidth and play them on slow computers, but it worked!

Microsoft also released Windows 3.0 in 1991, along with their version of a video/audio player called Media Player. This eventually became Windows Media Player, which is now the Windows-based computer's standard file format for audio and video files.

FIGURE 11.2 QuickTime

With small-file-size compressed video available on the computer and distributed over the Internet, it was only a matter of time before people created websites dedicated to sharing their thoughts through the use of video. Steve Garfield launched his videoblog in 2004 and announced that it would be the "year of the video blog." In June of that year, Peter Van Dijck and Jay Dedman started the Yahoo! Videoblogging Group, which became the first—and to this day, most popular—community of vloggers.

In July 2006, YouTube became the fifth-most-popular web destination, with over 100 million videos viewed, and more than 65,000 new video uploads every day. As of 2011, YouTube's members are uploading 48 hours of video every minute and more than 1 billion video downloads per day!

Bandwidth and Storage

Up until the advent of websites like YouTube, video distribution was still somewhat of a problem. The video files were larger and longer, and with more and more people watching them, the total amount of data transmitted from one's website could be quite huge. Also, downloading all of the data before you watch a video is time consuming and impractical. No one wanted to wait until a file was completely downloaded to start watching a video. As a result, video streaming was introduced. Streaming takes place when the ISP spoon-feeds the data to the computer at a slightly faster rate than is needed, so that the modem downloads the video without interruption while the user begins to watch it.

Along Comes YouTube

You can't discuss video creation without discussing video sharing; after all, it's what you do after you've created your video. (For additional information on sharing content, refer to Chapter 12, Got Video? (Video Sharing).) With more people being connected to the Internet with broadband (high-speed transfer rate), such as DSL, Dish, and cable modems, the amount of data a person could download and view became less of an issue. CPUs became much faster, and the cost of disk storage plummeted. Then along came websites such as Google's YouTube. YouTube, a video sharing website allows users to upload, view, and share video clips. In February 2005, three former PayPal employees created YouTube. In November 2006, YouTube, LLC, was purchased by Google Inc. for US $1.65 billion and now operates as a subsidiary of Google.

In October 2006, the BBC launched its first official video blogging site for its children's television series *Blue Peter,* with video asking children to name a new puppy character on the show.

FIGURE 11.3   YouTube

Early employees of PayPal Chad Hurley, Steve Chen, and Jawed Karim activated the domain name YouTube.com on February 15, 2005. They developed their website over the next several months, and YouTube was presented to the public in May 2005.

For more information on video sharing and video examples, please read Chapter 12, Got Video? (Video Sharing) and be sure to visit www.theSocialMediaBible.com.

Lifecasting

Vlogging is so appealing because it removes geographic boundaries and creates a truly global community through personal interaction.

What You Need to Know

Again, the most important thing to know is to *just do it!* The sooner you start vlogging, the sooner you will begin seeing results.

Uploading Your Videos

For more information on uploading video, please read Chapter 12, Got Video? (Video Sharing), on video sharing.

Tips, Techniques, and Tactics

Creating Your Own Video

Vlogging can be as easy as using a cell phone with built-in video capabilities. However, while you can certainly use your cell phone, as famous blogger Robert Scoble does occasionally, starting with this level of quality is not recommended.

Buy or borrow a video camera, and just start shooting some video. While shooting a comprehensive video is more involved than recording your voice in an audio podcast, getting something worth watching is not that hard, especially if there is good content—a valuable takeaway for your viewers.

Script Your Thoughts

It's always best to script your thoughts, or at least organize them as a list of bullet points. One suggestion for recording a video is to first create a Keynote presentation (PowerPoint, for non-Apple users). Position the monitor behind the camera or print the slides and tape them where you can speak to them while recording. Directly reading a script is the *worst* thing you can do.

Don't attempt to record too much at one time. If you can get through a slide, say "cut," take a deep breath, and start fresh with a new slide. If you are one of those people lucky enough to be able to just start talking, then by all means, do that. The bottom line is to do whatever you are most comfortable with; you will come across as confident in the video. Your audience will mirror whatever your emotions are. If *you* are having fun, they will have fun as well.

Be sure to remember to record your introduction: who you are, your subject matter, and your website address. Keep in mind that you must also record your conclusion, which will consist of a summary and a reiteration of who you are and your website. The introduction and conclusion can also contain some music, and even titles.

Editing Your Video

Once you have created some raw digital video, it's time to edit. Select a video editing application such as Apple's iMovie and import your video (see Figure 11.4). Pick out some theme music, still photos, and other additional video clips you might want to include. You can also do a voice-over by recording directly from the microphone over your still photos or video clips.

Your video editing software will allow you to create tracks, which will enable you to place your video in as the main track, insert your introduction in front of it, and even lay down a separate music track that will play simultaneously. You can, of course, control the track volume, so that the background music remains in the background.

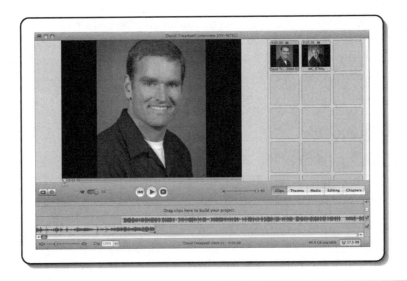

FIGURE 11.4 iMovie

There are many choices for video editing software; the one you use will depend on your computer's operating platform, be it Apple or Windows. Macintosh aficionados use iMovie to create and edit videos, benefitting from the drag-and-drop features of Macintosh software. You could also use Adobe Premiere or Final Cut Pro on the Mac OS. If you are a Windows user, you can use Adobe Premiere or ArcSoft's ShowBiz.

Once you have your video ready for prime-time viewing, it's time to decide how to distribute and otherwise make available your motion picture work of art. The easiest and most effective website is, of course, YouTube. The process is simple: you set up an account, select Upload Video, enter a description, answer a few other questions about your video, and hit Upload. Wait a few minutes, and your video is now available for viewing anywhere in the world, 24/7, for free!

Keep in mind that just because your video is on YouTube doesn't automatically mean that others will watch it and you will become an overnight success. It is now your responsibility to drive traffic to your video. You do this through RSS, blogging, e-mails, commenting, and the use of other social media tools, so read on. See the chapters on RSS, blogs, and e-mails for more information.

Many open-source content management systems, like WordPress, Joomla, or Drupal, have integrated widgets and capabilities that allow you to post your video content. This permits vloggers to host and distribute their own video blogging, right from their own websites.

Note

The convergence of mobile phones with built-in digital video cameras allows users to capture and publish video content to the Web almost as it is recorded.

Expert Insight

Patrizio Spagnoletto, senior director of marketing, Yahoo! Search Marketing, http://advertising.yahoo.com/

Patrizio Spagnoletto

. . . I have been with Yahoo! for about seven and a half years, and in my current role I manage the marketing team for the search-marketing product, which is basically the product where small and medium-sized businesses (or businesses of all sizes) can be listed in Yahoo! Search results. . . .

. . . To be more specific, it's the marketing part. So our team focuses on the awareness of the product, customer acquisition [and] retention, and just making sure that our customers, overall, are getting the most out of their investment with us once they start participating in this "Sponsored-Search world," and that happens through education, communication, and innovation of products that we provide for their products or features of the current search product. . . .

. . . When somebody goes to a search engine on Yahoo.com and searches for, let us say, cars (more specifically a used Honda), what the user has just done is show an explicit intent that he is looking for and willing to purchase that specific product. Now if you flip that and put your advertiser hat on, that is probably the single most qualified lead that you will ever be able to receive. And that is because unlike other marketing media in Sponsored Search, it is the user that tells us that they are interested in buying our products and services. And this all happened because of the search engine results page. . . .

. . . And in fact when you think about it in context of direct response (meaning that a business wants to increase their sales), I really do not think there is any other marketing medium out there that is as effective as Sponsored Search. And we are doing a lot of research to justify a statement like that.

Having said that, marketers have multiple objectives. You know, whether it is *response* (and Sponsored Search does a great job there), or if it's *awareness* (or other mediums like television and the offline world; or graphical ad display, which I was a major player in), it is really the combination of the two that makes a business be really successful. Where the sum of the two is much greater than the individual parts.

Yahoo! is really in a unique position in that it is truly the only business that can offer the two products on an own-it–operate-it site. On the Yahoo! site, you can buy banners and you can buy Sponsored Search; and therefore, really create what we call a 360 Campaign where you can surround the user with both graphical and Sponsored Search. . . .

. . . Banner advertising is what most of us see when we go on pretty much any site. It is those graphical advertisements, sometimes they are video, or what we call *rich media,* or sometimes they are just static images. But it is a graphical way for an advertiser to convey their message. And Yahoo!'s invention is a leader in this and has been since the inception of Yahoo!. And we are very good at targeting users through some of our own proprietary data on the back end. This is done in the way that we are able to target (whether it be demographic, behavioral, or graphic), or just some of the ways that we are able to match graphical advertisements with the users. Because online search is where you have the benefit of the user actually telling you what it is that they are looking for. With *graphical,* it is really about the more general persona of a person that is visiting the site. . . .

. . . What we typically ask our small-business customer is, first and foremost, what is your objective? If their objective is really that they want *direct response,* that is a clear signal that they should really be investing at least their first trunk of money to Yahoo! Sponsored Search. And that is because it is by far the most effective medium to garner more sales. And for Sponsored Search, [it] is very easy to sign up for it on Yahoo! You can do so online through a simple process, or you can, literally, just call in. We have reps that can help you go through this final process, the latter honestly being very unique to Yahoo!.

One of the things that we pride ourselves on is really helping our prospective customers by being, literally, just a phone call away from them. . . .

. . . And when you phone in for the sign-up process, what they will do is walk you through the actual online sign-up form, but with the advantage of just giving some of the best practices of thinking through. For example, what keywords to choose or how to write an effective description. So that is available right now. . . .

. . . We think it is extremely valuable because, as you probably know, small businesses are experts at what they do, but they are not necessarily experts at advertising, let alone Sponsored Search advertising. And so we feel it is almost *our* responsibility (and to be honest with you, it is in our best interest) to make sure that these customers get set up correctly the first time around so that they can start receiving the best results right off the bat. . . .

(continued)

(*continued*)

. . . Actually, you can trace it all the way back to a company that was called GoTo.com, which started in the late 1990s. That company that we branded to Overture, which subsequently was purchased by Yahoo!, and then rebranded to Yahoo! Search Market. So we are, quite honestly, the pioneers of paid search. We are the ones who invented the category that represents more than half of online spending. So it is something that is a good thing for us to think back on. . . .

. . . So our model is what we call a *pay-per-click model,* frequently referred to as PPC. So the first comparison is to all other mediums, so let's say you are buying a newspaper ad or anything that is offline. There is a fixed cost to those purchases, which you may or may not recuperate, depending on how many people actually purchase your products. So in a newspaper, you will buy a half-page for, say a thousand dollars (I'm making up these numbers, of course), that is a stock cost, and you are going to try to make it up.

Whereas with Yahoo! Search Marketing, in a PPC model, you only pay when somebody actually clicks on your listing on the Yahoo! Search results. And the price is not set by us; it is actually set by the advertiser. And this is what you are referring to as a bidding mall. If you think of every *keyword marketplace* as exactly that (a marketplace), advertisers will bid to be listed in those search results. It is important to know that it is not just how much you bid that determines your position. There are other factors in there, including the quality of the listing, and that is because we want to make sure that the experience for the users is optimal. So *quality of the listing* means we want to make sure that it creates a *relevant result* for our user. And we reward or we penalize if the listing is not good. . . .

. . . If all listings are created equal, meaning that the quality of each of the listings is exactly the same, then the amount you bid is really what will determine who shows off first, if you will, and second and so on and so forth. But I put that caveat of the listing quality because it is a really poignant one. So let me give an extreme example.

Let's go back to our used Honda car. If I was an advertiser and my listing says, "Buy the best car ever, at my site now" and by contract, your listing said, "Quality used Honda cars at reasonable prices," my guess is that your listing is of a much higher quality than mine is because it speaks specifically to what the user was looking for. . . .

. . . And as a result, even if I am bidding, say 60 cents per click and you are bidding 20 cents per click, you may actually show up higher than I may because of the quality of your listing. And, again, all the numbers are completely fictitious. . . .

. . . It becomes even more important when you combine it with our display advertising because the user sees multiple impressions. So if you imagine a banner that talks about your used Honda car sale, and then actually apply it finally to a search query, and then a searcher sees your listing and recognizes the name of your company because they have seen it on a banner. That's what I was referencing, the two pieces really working hand in hand to increase not only the awareness of the brand, but ultimately in a product like that, the click-through rate and, obviously, the sales that follow. . . .

. . . Sure, so if you go to Yahoo.com, there are a couple of links that will take you to a sign-up process. The easiest one is at the bottom of the page. It is Search Marketing, so very descriptive. And at this place, you will go through a couple of pages that will help you understand what the product is about, as I have done for you now. There are, at the core, really four steps.

The first one is *targeting*. So it is understandable whether you want your listing to appear to the entire nation or a specific geographical component, or area.

The second one is *choosing your keywords*. The used Honda is a perfect example of what we mean as a keyword.

The third is determining *how much you want to bid*. So back to your example of your pay-per-click, and we refer to that from the advertiser perspective "as your bid."

And then last, but not least, obviously, is the usable budget, the marketing budget.

In addition, with Yahoo! Search Marketing, you can start your campaign for as little as $30. Although I will be honest with you, we encourage advertisers *not* to pay down at that limit, not because we want them to spend more, but quite honestly, it is because in many categories today they have become fairly competitive. So we want our advertisers to make sure that they have enough money in their accounts so that their listings appear and getting enough "click-through-ing" so that they start to get the returns that they are looking for.

So, it is one of those models where you have a little bit of efficiency of scale, and if you spend a little bit more you actually see a lot more return. And by the way, when I say a little bit more, I do not mean in the thousands of dollars. For most advertisers, a couple hundred dollars is more than enough to get the feel of how this process works and then start deciding if they want to invest more in it. . . .

. . . So let us go back to our example. If somebody types in the keyword *car,* that is an extremely broad word; and if I am selling used Honda cars

(continued)

(*continued*)

where if I put my listing under the keyword *car,* I am going to get all sorts of people and not necessarily all of them will be looking for what I have to sell.

However, if I choose as the keywords *used Honda cars,* then almost by default I am limiting the queries (or the users) to the ones who are looking for exactly what I have to sell. Now there are two benefits in doing so.

The first is (what I just mentioned) a much more qualified prospect for you. And the second is, from the planning perspective, terms that have two or more words in a keyword phrase are, generally speaking, a little bit less expensive than what we call *head-turns to our cart.*

Therefore, if you combine the two, you are getting better-qualified leads at a lower cost, and that is really the best of both worlds for advertisers. . . .

. . . So if an advertiser knows what they are doing (and I really emphasize that) because there are a lot of advertisers who come in with the expectations that they can set up an account in 10 minutes, and then all of a sudden see sales fly. That is not going to happen, I will tell you that right now.

But if you know what you are doing (and by that I mean really taking the time to learn the account and the interfaces, and the teachers are there at your disposal) and take the time to manage it, then you will see the returns that you are designing. We have countless advertisers who see those on a daily basis, which is, quite honestly, why they stay with us.

And going back to the objectives of our team, this is to make sure our advertisers really do, clearly and simply, understand how to optimize their account. . . .

To listen to or read the entire Executive Conversation with Patrizio Spagnoletto, go to www.theSocialMediaBible.com.

International Perspective

Switzerland

The Social Media landscape in Switzerland is not easy to map for several reasons: the country is not a member of the European Union, it has three language regions and, in the absence of a localized URL (.ch), it is not always possible to allocate social media channels.

The latest statistics published by "Internet World Stats" for Switzerland, at the end of June 2011, show that 80.5 percent of the population were Internet users and 43.17 percent of those were on Facebook, and by the end of December, according to Facebook that percentage had climbed to 47.52 percent. According to "Relax in The Air," social networking in Switzerland in dominated by 5 sites: Facebook, YouTube, Twitter, LinkedIn, and Dailymotion. Only Facebook and most likely YouTube have a percentage of reach in double digits, the other three are below 5 percent. As Google do not publish data for their own brands' usage in the Swiss market—there is no youtube.ch—YouTube's ranking is presumed. The second tier is made up of Flickr, Xing, Orkut, MySpace, and Vimeo with a reach around 2 percent.

Out of the 18 European countries that ComScore track in their statistics about social networking reach, Switzerland is one but last with a percentage well below the average and the second lowest growth rate in 2010 at 1.5 percent. The low statistics can be explained by mobile usage, including access to social media using smartphones. Like other European countries, information and media consumption in Switzerland is changing, mobile usage is increasing rapidly.

In their report on business and social media, Howald & Partner PR note that more and more Swiss companies would like to use Social Media and are taking their first steps in that direction. They deplore that social media activities are still based on trial and error with no clear strategy or are utilized as a traffic bringer without any definite concept. They contrast corporate and private usage underlining the possible existence of untapped opportunities.

A study of the landing pages of the 10 largest Swiss companies listed in the Fortune top 500 in 2011 show that only two, Novartis and Credit Suisse, have links to their social media pages. A link to Facebook is buried in the ABB's contact page. The table below lists the 10 companies and the social media their home page links to.

(continued)

(continued)

Company	Industry	Social Media Links (in the order of display)
Glencore	Commodities	
Nestlé	Nutrition, health and wellness	
Zurich	Financial services	
Novartis	Pharmaceuticals	YouTube, Facebook, LinkedIn, Flickr, Twitter
Credit Suisse	Banking	Twitter, Facebook, YouTube, Flickr
Roche	Pharmaceuticals	
UBS	Banking	
Alliance Boots	Pharmaceuticals, health and beauty	
ABB	Power and automation	Facebook
Xstrata	Mining	

Further study of the social media pages for the Novartis, Credit Suisse, and ABB show a low level of users, never more than a few thousands.

The companies listed above are large international groups not necessarily familiar to the ordinary Swiss people. Howald & Partner PR have examined social media usage by popular Swiss brands. They note that employees of the Rail Service, in their own free time, use Twitter to distribute information about connections and delays but the feeds are not an official information feed from the Swiss National Railways (SBB). Victorinox, the famous Swiss manufacturer of knives is present on Flickr with an extensive photo stream but there is no link from the company website to Flickr, the content is probably not official. It is interesting to note that financial services and banking groups have a mobile link on their home page.

Sources

Howald & Partner PR / Namics (2010). Everything you need to know about social media but were afraid to ask/Switzerland.

Relax In The Air (2011). "Defining Social Networks in Switzerland."

comScore (2011). Europe Digital Year in Review 2010.

—Claudette John, Rice MBA
Faculty, Glion Institute of Higher Education
Les Roches Gruyere, University of Applied Sciences
Glion.edu

To-Do List

- Look at some of the most popular videos shared.

  Go look at the most popular videos posted on YouTube and other video sharing websites. See what they have in common. Notice the strong entertainment value (entertainment is a very strong "What's in It for Me?").

- Create a video.

  Go out and create a video. Try it. Keep it light, and keep it short (three to five minutes). Try to have the highest WIIFM you can for your customers. Give them a takeaway in the form of information, such as an "I didn't know that," or a "You can use it that way," or just plain have fun.

- Do not spend a lot of money.

  If you have a digital video camera, start shooting. If you don't own one, borrow one first and try it to see if you like it. Download free software from the Internet, and have some fun editing.

- Comment.

  Start building a community around your videos, products, services, hobbies, or other subject content. (See Chapter 2, Say Hello to Social Networking, for more information on how to build networks and communities.)

Conclusion

Creating your own video is a lot of fun. It is a little more technically challenging than an audio podcast or a simple blog, but the rewards are well worth it. Video is almost always the best medium for communicating with your customers. Being able to share your expressions, inflections, and body language builds much greater trust and conveys sincerity to your viewers. Watching someone deliver a message is powerful. Just look at how television influences lives.

Don't be afraid of trying to create your own video. Don't spend a lot of money to start out. Use your existing camera or borrow one from a friend and start videotaping. The best way to experience vlogging—to borrow a sport shoe slogan—is to "Just Do It!"

To hear all of the Expert Interviews, go to www.theSocialMediaBible.com.

Downloads

For your free downloads associated with *The Social Media Bible,* go to www.theSocialMediaBible.com,

and enter your ISBN number located on the back of the book above the bar code. Be sure to enter the dashes.

Credits

The ROI of Social Media was provided by:

Sherry Heyl, www.concepthubinc.com

Expert Insight was provided by:

Patrizio Spagnoletto, senior director of marketing, Yahoo! Search Marketing, http://advertising.yahoo.com/

Technical edits were provided by:

Ira Rosen and Corey Sanchez, Mojo Video Marketing, www .mojovideomarketing.com

CHAPTER 12

Got Video? (Video Sharing)

www.LonSafko.com/TSMB3_Videos/12VideoShare.mov

If you can get 43 million views of your video because of its entertainment value—as did a 23-year-old in Korea—or you can get 93 million views—as did one comedian who posted a six-minute segment of his comedy act—then wouldn't you? Especially if it was free?

Read on for more information.

Video sharing is the easiest and fastest way to start building your social media portfolio. You and your company already have a box of VHS tapes or video on a hard drive somewhere. You need to locate that video, identify the best representation of your company, and start uploading it to video sharing websites. If you don't have good video, start making it. Uploading is free, it makes your message accessible to all of your prospects and customers, and it helps build your Google Juice![1]

As mentioned in the previous chapter, while video recordings can also be considered podcasts—since the iPod and other digital playback devices can display photographs, audio, and video—for the purpose of this book, audios are treated as *podcasts*, and videos are referred to as either *videos* or *vlogs*.

What's in It for You?

A blender company called Blendtec, which is located in Orem, Utah, uploaded a funny in-house product demonstration video to YouTube. Within the first 24 hours, more than one million viewers watched its video; within the same 24-hour period, the company sold out of its $600 Blendtec Blenders.

What would you pay to have your product or service's 90-second commercial viewed by more than one million potential customers in 24 hours? You most likely couldn't afford this kind of media exposure. The Blendtec video has now been viewed more than 3.5 million times (see Figure 12.1). (To watch Blendtec president Tom Dickson blend a brand-new iPhone on the day they came out—and other video examples—go to www.theSocial MediaBible.com;

or go to YouTube and search for "Will It Blend.")

FIGURE 12.1   Blendtec

http://www.youtube.com/watch?v=WvDedo8r1Fk

   Can anyone guarantee that the phenomenal success that Blendtec has enjoyed will happen for you? No, but when you already have the video or can produce it easily as Blendtec did—and it's free to upload—then what do you have to lose?

Back to the Beginning

As with several of the other chapters that have both a Sharing and a Creation chapter (such as this chapter and Chapters 9 and 10 on Audio), the creation and sharing history of video sharing has been interwoven into the same story. And since video sharing's history is only a very small part of the larger video story, you can find this information later in this chapter.

What You Need to Know

The most important thing you need to know is to *just do it!* You have to start sometime, and the easiest way to do so is to gather all of the videos you currently have on hand and start uploading them to YouTube. It's actually simpler than you think. Set up your account (it's free), select Upload Video, follow the instructions, and there you have it. (For more information about creating your own video, see Chapter 11, Watch Out for Vlogs (Video Create).)

   Examples are the best way to explain why uploading videos to a video sharing website can give you such a great rate of return on this investment of your time. Three videos in particular discussed in this chapter have been extremely successful for their owners. One is a personal video, while the other two are business related. Remember, there's no guarantee that you will have the same success, but who knows?

The first example is one of the earlier and more popular videos on YouTube called "Guitar" (youtube.com/watch?v=QjA5faZF1A8;

see Figure 12.2). This video of Pachelbel's *Canon* played on an electric guitar was created by a 23-year-old from Korea named Jeong-Hyun Lim who recorded his video himself in his bedroom in his mirror. The video "Guitar" has had more than 54 million views to date—simply because it's entertaining.

You can go to YouTube and type in "Guitar" or go to www.theSocialMedia Bible.com

to click on the link in the chapter section for a clickable link.

Another example of how popular a self-made posted video can become comes from the comedian Judson Laipply, who posted a six-minute portion of his comedy act, which he called "Evolution of Dance," on YouTube (youtube.com/watch?v=dMH0bHeiRNg; see Figure 12.3).

FIGURE 12.2   YouTube "Guitar"

FIGURE 12.3   YouTube "Evolution of Dance"

To date, this video has had more than 109 million views—and has been the record holder for most-watched video on YouTube until recently, when a video for a music group has surpassed it.

You can go to YouTube and type in "Evolution of Dance" or go to www .theSocialMediaBible.com

to click on the link in the chapter section for a clickable link.

Imagine having to invest nothing more than 10 minutes of your time uploading a video you already had in order to have 93 million people watch your six-minute commercial. While it doesn't happen often, there is an audience for a variety of works. How about that as an extraordinary ROI?

Uploading Your Videos

The only prerequisite for uploading videos is that they need to be in a digital format and not exceed the host's maximum file size. If you have made your videos relatively recently, they are probably already in a digital format. If your videos are still on VHS, then you will have to convert them.

You can buy some VHS-to-DVD recorders for under $100. Put the VHS video in, put in a blank DVD, hit Play, and when the video is at the end, you have a digital video on DVD. LG, Samsung, Sony, Toshiba, and Panasonic make some really good units. You can also find service providers that will convert your VHS videos inexpensively. Many services offer to accept your VHS tapes by mail and return them in a digital format recorded on a DVD. An example of this is Home Movie Depot, a company that charges anywhere from under $20 to more for damaged tapes.

You can also buy a VHS player made by Ion that connects directly to your computer through the USB port. Another alternative is to buy a converter box for about $250 that connects your VCR to your computer, such as the **ADS PYRO A/V Link**, Analog to Digital Video Converter that ships free with Adobe Premiere Elements 4.0 for around $160.

Once you have gathered all of your videos in a digital format, you can go to YouTube or another video sharing website and start uploading. That's all there is to it. Make sure you have your tags picked out ahead of time. (See meta tags in Chapter 18, Spotlight on Search (Search Engine Optimization).)

Once you have a list of your tags or keywords and a short description, then you're ready to upload. And, like the shampoo bottle says, lather, rinse, repeat: load, tag, repeat.

Keep in mind that simply uploading your content to a video sharing website doesn't create a post with an RSS feed. The video has to be included as an enclosure in an RSS feed, similar to a podcast, to allow your followers to subscribe to your chronological posts. This is a distinction that can be important if you are building a community and a following. By building your video into an RSS feed, it is easy for your video to become a viral one that is posted to the Web and passed around by word of mouth. Video posted to your blog is also video that isn't enclosed in the RSS Feed (see Chapter 17, RSS—Really Simple Syndication Made Simple).

Another advantage of posting a video to YouTube is the ability to comment back and forth and respond to comments the video posts have generated. In comment marketing, this kind of feedback is considered almost essential. Many videobloggers still feel that YouTube misses the main point, because their subscription model isn't RSS-based. So, although you can subscribe to favorite users in YouTube, that subscription can't be accessed in a video-enabled RSS reader such as FireAnt or iTunes. (For more information on RSS, see Chapter 17, RSS—Really Simple Syndication Made Simple. For more information on comment marketing, see the interview with Amanda Vega, from Amanda Vega Consultants.)

Peer to Peer

Another form of file sharing for music, video, e-books, movies, software, and other digital data is known as peer to peer (or P2P). P2P takes place when many computers on a network, connected through the Internet, all share digital data in the form of files. For example, if you want the latest music from your favorite band, you can download that copyrighted material by connecting to a peer-to-peer network, selecting the file, and downloading that file to your computer. All the while, your computer is being used to transfer digital bits of another file that someone else has requested. Once all of the bits have been downloaded to your computer, the file is put back together or assembled into the original working data file.

BitTorrent

BitTorrent is a type of peer-to-peer file-sharing protocol used to distribute data such as movies, music, photos, software, audio, and other digital data files. One computer starts as the initial distributor of the complete file. Each peer-to-peer (or individually connected) PC that downloads data also uploads data to other peers. This provides a significant reduction in the original PC's hardware and bandwidth costs. It provides redundancy against system errors and reduces dependence on an original distributor. BitTorrent also reduces the liability of the original computer's distribution of copyrighted materials, as the system actually passes around the data from machine to machine and compiles the completed files that have been transferred from many computers on the system.

Programmer Bram Cohen designed the BitTorrent protocol in April 2001, and it debuted on July 2 of that year. The original BitTorrent is now maintained by Cohen's company, BitTorrent Inc. This system is widely used to distribute copyrighted games, music, and movies that are sometimes still playing as first-run showings in theaters.

The ROI of Social Media

Chemistry Creates Mom-Pleasing Campaign for Steaz

Introduction

A $100K social media campaign created by Chemistry, Pittsburgh, for organic tea company Steaz, [in] Newtown, Pennsylvania, yielded a $500K monthly sales increase, and solidified and expanded retail distribution.

Background

Before October 2009, Steaz was sold in health food stores only. When Target's 1,500-plus stores began carrying the brand nationally, Steaz's total shopping audience quadrupled overnight—a huge opportunity for the fledgling brand, and also a challenge. The unfamiliar brand's shelf-presence within Target would be tiny, and if it didn't sell, it would soon be discontinued. Steaz needed a national promotion to generate awareness and trial, and quickly, within a two-month window.

Strategy

Chemistry estimated that, before social media, an outdoor and couponing campaign might have met those goals, at a $2M budget—far beyond Steaz's means. But because 72 percent of women online now learn about new products through social media, Chemistry figured a moms outreach program, focused on healthy ingredients and value pricing, could be implemented for $100K.

Implementation

Sample kits and e-mail went to 72 leading mom bloggers and 130 couponing bloggers. A real time, sample-supported, Twitter tea party of sorts generated 2,800 tweets in one hour. Ongoing Facebook and Twitter presences were developed, offering BoGo and free, one-per-computer couponing. The campaigns yielded 6,000 blog mentions or reviews, 30,000,000 total impressions, and most importantly, *250,000 coupons downloaded over eight weeks.*

Opportunity

Target sales were directly affected, jumping 350 percent, from $6K to $21K, in one week. Three weeks in, the opportunity was nearly lost when sales matched total production and shelves emptied. (Production was ramped up.) At promotion's end, Steaz's $1M total December sales were *double its previous best month ever.*

Conclusion

Post-promotion, weekly sales settled at 200 percent of their pre-promotion level. Steaz remains in Target. And Kroger, with nearly double Target's locations, will soon carry the brand.

—Rob Pizzica, Chemistry
www.visitthelab.com

—Dan Barron, Conroy Barron Public Relations
db@conroybarronpr.com

Expert Insight

George Strompolos, content partnerships manager, YouTube, www.youtube.com

George Strompolos

I am the content partnerships manager here at YouTube, and that's really a fancy way of saying that I reach out to content creators and help them engage on YouTube and to distribute their content and connect with audiences around the world. And so YouTube being an open platform, those content creators can take on many shapes and sizes. They can be someone as small as a video blogger producing videos in their bedroom, up to what we call a *broadband studio* or a *digital studio,* which creates original content just for Internet distribution. And this goes all the way up to traditional media companies and premium content providers that we are all familiar with: CBS and the National Basketball Association, Discovery, ESPN.

So, at its core, YouTube is a website where people can upload videos to share them with the world. It's also a great place to watch videos. It's actually an interesting fact that YouTube currently receives 48 hours of video uploaded to the site every minute! In fact, more videos have been uploaded to YouTube in the past three months than ABC, NBC, and CBS have aired since 1948. It's staggering.

What you'll find is that people upload videos to YouTube for different reasons. Some of them just want to share pictures of their baby, or their vacation footage. We are certainly happy to support that. However, it's becoming more and more common for amateur and professional content creators to produce content for YouTube and make a living out of it.

The way that they do this is they become a partner through my team, or by applying online at YouTube.com/partners.

They basically tell us, "Hey, we're producing original content and not only do we want to share it with the world through YouTube, but we want to give you the ability to run ads against that content.". . .

And then we will share the majority of that ad revenue back to the content creator. So I call it a *performance-based* model. In other words, you can become a content partner, and if you upload video and it gets zero views, well, there's clearly no ad revenue there, so nothing is being shared. But if you upload a video and it gets one million views, for instance, we put an ad on every single view. And so that ad revenue starts to accrue and, in many cases, can become significant for a lot of the content partners we have. . . .

The main format of advertising that you'll see on YouTube when you are watching a video (if you're watching a video from a partner) is what we call *in-video* advertising. And it is, essentially, a transparent overlay that shows up toward the bottom of the video window; and it's cool. It can be animated, and a cool example is when *The Simpsons* movie was premiering, the studio behind that movie ran an in-video overlay of Homer Simpson chasing a donut across the bottom of the screen. It goes pretty quick, you know, and it's usually relevant. I think they targeted that against comedy and animation content, so to that audience it was probably actually a nice surprise. And as a user, you can click on Homer Simpson and see, maybe, the movie trailer, or you can choose to close that overlay out, or just wait a few seconds and it will just disappear. We also run other industry standard ad formats such as pre-roll and companion banners.

So, creating original content and sharing in ad revenues is one way to approach YouTube, and that's more from an entertainment perspective. But from more a marketing perspective, I've just been amazed at the way that companies actually think of clever ways to use YouTube. "Will It Blend?" is one of my favorite examples.

I should defer to them, of course, but I did read an article at one point that their sales actually went up 300 percent as a result of their presence on YouTube. . . .

This is from a marketing effort that essentially cost them nothing: Create a YouTube channel, no cost; set up a guy on camera with a blender (they make blenders so it cannot be that expensive for them), and blend a couple of cool things. And they were smart enough to blend things that are kind of hot and in the news. So the new iPhone comes out and they buy one on the first day and they blend it. And of course, people are searching for the iPhone video and things like that, and just the controversy of destroying something in a blender that is so sought-after is something that translates to a lot of video views. . . .

Here you have this tremendous marketing tool in YouTube, and for a company like Blendtec. What's interesting is that I read a blog post a few months ago from a well-known guy in Silicon Valley who said, "I see a future

(continued)

(*continued*)

where your marketing can become a profit center." And if you look at "Will It Blend?," that's a perfect example. So their marketing is clearly driving sales, but also they are providing original content.

So they are certainly welcome to join our partnership program, and if they are comfortable having other ads running against their videos, they can actually make money off those ads. So it's kind of an interesting situation there. . . .

You know, one of my favorite examples is a young guy named Lucas who has a character that he does on YouTube called "Fred." Lucas is about 16 years old, and he plays this character named "Fred" who is a six-year-old, and the shtick is that he is a six-year-old with anger management problems.

YouTube "Fred Frigglehorn."

It's one of these things that are really made for kids—like a lot of Pixar Films, for instance—but it is also funny to adults. It's kind [of] a bizarre thing, and you can see it at YouTube.com/Fred;

and it's really just taken off like a rocket.

I think it's actually the fastest-growing channel in YouTube history.

And Fred is a partner, so we traffic ads against his videos and we share the majority of that ad revenue with him. He's at a point where he'll post a video, and within a matter of days, that video will have at least 3 million views, I guarantee . . . sometimes as high as 8 to 10 million! So that is about one video every week, sometimes more. There are cable programs, even network television producers that would die for those numbers.

Absolutely an impressive feat, and if you look at someone like Fred who uploads a video and gets 3 million views at a minimum. All he has to do is post 10 videos and he's going to achieve viewership on par with shows like *American Idol.* But don't forget that people are constantly watching Fred's older videos, too. It's really a powerful thing, and I won't get into the details of this partnership, but he's making decent money off of YouTube, substantial . . . and he's, naturally, being approached by all kinds of brands, because he's really hitting that tween audience. Fred actually has a feature-length movie coming out this year—talk about a YouTube success story!

To listen to or read the entire Executive Conversation with George Strompolos, go to www.theSocialMediaBible.com.

International Perspective
China

While many social networking sites strive to create global communities, others look to cater to very specific audiences. In the case of 51.com, the audience was a nation: China. In 2008, the site had 120 million members.

(*continued*)

(continued)

In other words: More than half of the 210 million Chinese citizens with Internet access at that time had a member account on 51.com. According to comScore, China has passed the United States in overall number of users on the Internet but the percentage of Chinese citizens with Internet access is still very low. In the United States, nearly 73 percent of the population uses the Internet. In China it's closer to 22 percent.

Members of 51.com can create personalized profile pages, upload photos, and write blog posts. The site has a reputation for pretty exceptional user engagement; most members visit the site multiple times each month.

The site plans to launch a major game project, with an investment of more than 100 million yuan (about $14.6 million US) would only enhance this engagement. Investors in 51.com include Intel Capital, Sequoia Capital China and Redpoint Ventures, the company that invested in another well-known social networking success: MySpace.com.

—Jonathan Strickland, Senior Writer, HowStuffWorks.com, Discovery Communications

To-Do List

- Convert any VHS videos to digital format.

  Take all of your useful VHS tapes and either convert them or have them converted to digital format. Get your product videos, your service videos, your company party video (use discretion!), your happy customer videos, and get them ready for posting.

- Upload.

  The highest ROI comes in finding all of the videos you currently have and getting them uploaded to a site. Your customers can't see them if they aren't there. Get any existing video you have, figure out its keywords, and upload. It's free!

- Post everywhere.

  Once you are comfortable with one video sharing site and have it loaded with all of your videos, consider posting your videos to a second or even a third video sharing website. Post them on YouTube, and on several of the other free video sharing websites. Don't forget to post to some of the lesser-known websites such as Blip.tv, VideoEgg, and Daily Motion.

- Comment.

  Start building a community around your videos, products, services, hobby, or other subject content. (See Chapter 2, Say Hello to Social Networking, for more information on how to build networks and communities.)

- Do not post copyrighted material.

  If you're going to post it, be sure you own the rights to it. Don't post something that belongs to someone else, *especially* if someone else owns the copyright.

- Become familiar with the Creative Commons Act.

  Go to www.theSocialMediaBible.com to find out more about the Creative Commons Act to find out what you can and cannot use when posting to the Internet.

- Be sincere and have fun.

  The most important step in this process is to be yourself, be sincere, and have fun. If you're not enjoying yourself when you are creating a video, it shows.

Conclusion

The common theme in this book is "Just Do It!" Video sharing is a great way to get your company and product names out there. The more "What's in It for Me?" value that the video has, the more it will be watched and passed along. Get your videos, pick out a few video sharing websites, and start posting. Be sure to mention the videos in your blogs and e-mails. Be sure that you have chosen the proper meta tags, so that when someone is looking for your content, it can be found. And be sure to use RSS feeds whenever possible. Look at other people's videos and descriptions, and be inspired by their style and content.

To hear all of the Expert Interviews, go to www.theSocialMediaBible.com.

Downloads

For your free downloads associated with *The Social Media Bible,* go to www
.theSocialMediaBible.com,

and enter your ISBN number located on the back of the book above the bar
code. Be sure to enter the dashes.

Credits

The ROI of Social Media was provided by:

Dan Barron, Conroy Barron Public Relations, db@conroybarronpr.com

Expert Insight and technical edits were provided by:

George Strompolos, content partnerships manager, YouTube, www
.youtube.com

Note

1. Google Juice is a term used to describe the results that follow when
   you search for your name, your company's name, and your product
   or service's name in Google or other search engines. The more listings
   and the more pages that a search engine returns to the searcher, the
   more Google Juice you have. The goal of this book is to squeeze as
   much Google Juice as possible out of your social media marketing and
   communications.

CHAPTER 13

Thumbs Up for Microblogging

www.LonSafko.com/TSMB3_Videos/13Microblog.mov

What's in It for You?

American author Mark Twain once paraphrased French mathematician Blaise Pascal's famous comment by saying, "If I had more time, I would have written a shorter letter."[1] The character limitations on microblogging force us to communicate in a more succinct manner. The content of our text messages is written completely differently from our e-mails. This is why they are read.

If only Pascal or Twain had been writing during the dawn of microblogging. This increasingly prevalent trend's value lies in its portability, immediacy, and ease of use. It's simple to post a microblog for your friends, family, coworkers, clients, and prospects. Your complete thought must be conveyed in 140 characters or fewer!

Microblogging is text messaging and a little more. It can be as effortless as sending a text message from your cell phone to a select group of friends. Anyone can microblog as often as they like, and can promptly read posts from other like-minded bloggers. Microblogging includes the ability to send messages, audio, video, and even attached files; it empowers users to make friends; get directions; give and receive advice; review books, restaurants, and movies; obtain up-to-the-minute news; identify, research, and

theSocialMediaBible.com

purchase products and services; update customers; inform clients; send calendar and event notices and news; and more. Or—in the particular case of *The Social Media Bible*—get advice on the book's chapters, the design, the content, interviews, and technical support.

Microblogging lets those who participate create small, intimate communities that are centered on topics such as politics, technology, or medical issues. You can read posts about cancer treatments and chemotherapy effects. You can send or read play-by-play updates from a conference or event happening at the moment you're reading. Microblogging lets your friends know where you are and what you are doing, and allows you to tell them things like, "I am at Twenty-fourth Street and Camelback Road. Anyone want to meet me for dinner?" With global and local, nearly real-time, mini-to-mini conversations; many-to-many IMs (Instant Messaging); two-way communication being sent and received on any computer, BlackBerry, PDA, or cell phone—microblogging is the epitome of social media two-way communication. For example, at a conference featuring musician, community marketer, and participant in the famed "One Red Paper Clip" story Jody Gnant (whose Executive Interview can be heard at www.theSocial MediaBible.com),

she informed the audience that on the way to the presentation, she needed directions to find the venue. Within moments, she had 15 people microblogging her back with turn-by-turn directions. That's a powerful network, or, as Twitter puts it, "A global community of friends and strangers answering one simple question: What's happening?"

Back to the Beginning

Microblogging began with the advent of the blog. After some time spent writing lengthy, detailed accounts, people began to post more condensed, convenient, portable, personal versions of their conventional blog posts into something that was termed a *microblog*. Microblogging was immediately hailed as conventional blogging's easier, faster, and more immediately accessible cousin. One of the very first providers of the microblog was Twitter, essentially providing technology that offered a simplified blogging service. Twitter was born in March 2006 as the result of an R&D project at the San Francisco–based start-up company Obvious. It was initially used by the company's own employees to communicate internally, and launched to the public seven months later on. On March 19, 2007, Twitter's official debut took place at the annual South by Southwest (SXSW) meeting in Austin, Texas. Twitter is a microblogging and social networking service that allows its users to send and receive brief (140 characters or fewer) text-based, micropost instant messages that are referred to as tweets. These text messages are displayed on the user's technology of choice—be it a text-messaging cell phone, website, PDA, Twitter website, RSS (see Chapter 17, RSS—Really Simple Syndication Made Simple), SMS,[2] e-mail, or an application such as Facebook, Hootsuite, Tweetdeck, or a web page aggregator. These messages are also delivered to anyone who has signed up and been accepted to follow your messages, and the same is true of any tweets that you have requested and been approved to follow.

What You Need to Know

While Twitter is the most popular microblogging platform, it certainly isn't the only one. Other platforms gaining recognition are Jaiku—which started in Europe and has since been acquired by Google—Pownce (now defunct),[3] and PlaceShout. However, for the purpose of this chapter, microblogging is discussed primarily in the context of Twitter, since the company had the first-to-market advantage at the time this chapter was written—with 100,000,000 active users and more than 250 million tweets per day, up from 100 million tweets per day in January of 2011! To give you an idea of how aggressive some tweeters (Twitter users) are, at the time this chapter was edited, tweeter and musician Lady Gaga was following 141,100 other tweeters, and had 15,556,937 people following her. In November 2011, Justin Bieber was running a close second to Lady Gaga, with over 14 million followers each. Katy Perry is ranked third, with Kim Kardashian and President Barack Obama ranking thereafter.

In April of 2009, actor Ashton Kutcher challenged CNN to a Twitter popularity contest, in which Kutcher edged out the news giant to become the first Twitter user to reach 1 million followers. The media outpouring during his race to 1 million certainly shed light on Twitter and made the platform more mainstream.

FIGURE 13.1   Would It Kill You to Update Your Twitter Status if You're Going to Stay Out So Late?

Then there's the famous blogger, Robert Scoble—another Twitter fanatic. Robert is currently following 32,530 people and has 217,048 following his tweets.

As your presence on Twitter or any microblogging service grows, people you don't know will begin to follow you. This is kind of like people reading your blog or visiting your website. The number of people whom you follow will be significantly less because there are only so many messages you can read, just as there is a finite number of blogs you read or web pages you visit. Some experts, such as Guy Kawasaki, suggest following every person who follows you. With more and more helpful platforms making their way to mainstream and the integration of Twitter lists, it's possible to follow hundreds of thousands and still stay a part of the conversation. While it's impossible to truly stay connected with each and every one of your followers, it's possible to follow many and stay connected.

Tweeting and following constitute the two-way communication and trusted network that drive the microblogging community. Any time someone you are following ceases to deliver relevant "What's in It for Me?" content, you can simply decide to unfollow that person. This is the power of permission-based marketing, whereby you choose who is allowed to market and communicate to you. Opting not to follow someone is like having your own built-in, user-controlled spam filter.

While microblogging started with the early adopters, it is currently a primary way that thought leaders, technophiles, Millennials, Gen Y's, and technologically savvy users keep in touch with one another. It has moved into the mainstream and is now widely used throughout the United States. For example, Democratic presidential candidates Barack Obama and John Edwards both microposted details of their runs for office while actually on the campaign trail. Also, the *New York Times,* the BBC, and many other traditional media organizations have begun using microblogging to post headlines and links.

While many give credit to Twitter for being the first microblogging platform, some believe that the microcontent trend has been around for a while—depending upon your definition of the term. In fact, many think that regular blogging should be considered microcontent or user-generated content, while others contend that posting a small note or adding to StumbleUpon, or typing some text on a photo posted on Flickr or Facebook, or creating a review on Yelp is also considered microblogging. The purists of this movement still give Twitter credit for creating the first intentional interactive microblogging/micropost network.

The popularity of microblogging can be attributed in part to the ease of creating a micropost. While blogs are considered fairly simply to write and maintain, a two-sentence update is still easier. Microblogs are also significantly less complicated to digest than conventional blogs, especially when you are following several hundred or more tweeters. This makes the tweets more desirable, more current, and more likely to be read. Commenting on tweets spurs an entertaining rapid-fire exchange of conversational tweets from other tweeters. And—like so many other social media technologies discussed in this book—Twitter and other microblogging platforms are free.

Since microblogging requires much less effort than conventional blogging, many people find it more entertaining. You simply send out a tweet whenever you have a moment; there is much less pressure to regularly update your thoughts. Unlike your web page, blog page, Facebook, and other networks you can post on, there is no blog-roll showing visitors how frequently (or infrequently) you blog. Many people are using microblogging to supplement their main blog by publishing short descriptions of their latest blog post—along with a corresponding link to create attention and drive traffic to the web or blog site.

Twitter and microblogging aren't just U.S. phenomena; microblogging is widely popular around the world. Twitter announced in October of 2011 that Twitter is still growing in popularity internationally. Growth in countries like Japan have led to the ever-increasing number of users around the world. While the popularity of the microblogging site has increased in the most recent past, countries like China continue to block the microblogging site from the entire country. Twitter creator Jack Dorsey stated in a 2010 New York panel discussion on social media, however, that in due time the Chinese should have access to Twitter.

The Microsphere Is Not All Good

Trivial Pursuit

The most common criticism of microblogging is the trivial nature of most posts (see Figure 13.2). Most people perusing the Internet really don't care if someone is about to eat their dinner or is currently waiting for a plane. The ease of use and the lack of cost encourage people to become tweeting maniacs, and people tend to lose a sense of responsibility by continuously tweeting about the most mundane occurrences in their day-to-day lives.

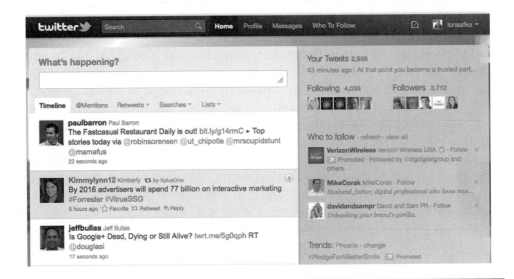

FIGURE 13.2   Twitter Tweets

When you are following 500, 1,000, or 5,000 tweeters—as well as receiving mobile telephone text messages, voicemails (home, office, and cell), news aggregators, snail mail, junk mail, and spam—it can create social media overload. Some people who thrive on social media are so fanatical that they've essentially overloaded themselves with too much data. They are receiving information as a steady stream of noise that has made it nearly impossible to contact or communicate with them. Their e-mail is full and won't accept any more memos; their outgoing cell phone message asks that you "please don't leave me a voice mail, because I don't retrieve them anymore" (and the recording is full anyway); and they no longer respond to their tweets.

In March of 2010, a study by *Retrevo* revealed our true social media obsession. *Retrevo* reported, "We were not surprised to learn how many people appear to be, shall we say, obsessed with checking in with their social media circles throughout the day and even the night." The study reported that users under the age of 25 were more likely to interrupt activities such as eating, going to the bathroom, or even having sex to update microblogging sites such as Twitter. The trend, of late, is a growing obsession and dependency with microblogging and social media in general.

Microspam

When the first edition of this book was published, microblogging spam was not prevalent on microblogging networks. In August of 2009, Twitter reported to have seen a massive increase in spam, equivalent to 8 to 11 percent of overall tweets. On March 23, 2010, Twitter reported that the overall spam on the microblogging site had decreased significantly from its height in August of 2009, reportedly falling to as little as 1 percent. As discussed in Chapter 6, in forums there is flaming, or flame wars, in which other users will respond to a spammer with pretty nasty replies, which keeps spamming at a minimum in normal circumstances. This reaction also happens in professional networks such as LinkedIn. On Twitter, however, even flaming or flame wars have not kept spammers at bay. Experts suggest that while Twitter may claim to have as little as 1 percent spam, the level of spam is still high even if the proportion is small.

Microadvertising

The inevitable question often associated with microblogging sites comes back to "How can they make it profitable?" The developers at Twitter have been trying to figure that out for some time. Twitter, and many other microblogging sites, have little, if any, advertising. For sites that in essence are free, advertising is the largest way for them to generate income, for which Twitter has yet to release.

In 2010, Twitter rolled out their advertising, which consists of promoted tweets, promoted trends, and promoted accounts. Promoted tweets are more than just a tweet—they're a tweet broadcast to a much wider and more relevant audience. Promoted trends are an exclusive and expensive option, placing a business at the top of a trends list with massive exposure. Promoted accounts are shown to new users and recommended to others. Your account is recommended to similar followers.

Apart from their usual ad offerings, Twitter is looking to enter the world of politics in the 2012 elections as part of their advertising expansion. After raising $800 million in investment funds, Twitter was valued at a whopping $8.4 billion in 2011.

The Fail Whale

Only a year after Twitter was launched, it began experiencing outages with its user base. Because of its overwhelming popularity, the folks at Twitter still haven't been able to avoid server overload from the sheer volume of traffic to its site. The Twitter website and service can sometimes be completely shut down for several hours. In August of 2009, the site experienced one of its longest outages because of a DDOS attack (distributed denial-of-service attack). While DDOS attacks are nothing new, the outage caused quite a stir online not only for Twitter, but also for Facebook, LiveJournal, and others.

This isn't the first time a DDOS attack has affected hundreds of thousands or even millions of people. In the beginning of 2000, e-commerce sites like eBay, Amazon.com,

and even Yahoo! were affected by a massive DDOS attack estimated to have cost a collective $8 million in damages and lost revenue.

On the occasions when the site is experiencing problems, tweeter attempts to tweet or visit the website are met with the all-too-familiar Fail Whale (see Figure 13.3). This character created by Yiying Lu—an image of a happy cartoon whale being lifted by a multitude of small red birds using nets to hoist him from the ocean—has become somewhat of an industry icon for monumental failure. Because of their high-pitched twitter, the Beluga whale is known as the "canary of the sea." Not surprisingly, the message on the image reads, "Too many tweets! Please wait a moment and try again."

When people become dependent on a particular technology—like e-mail, iPhones, or blogs—and that is taken away from them for even a short time, they become paralyzed. The social media industry as a whole has been too slow to sufficiently monetize its efforts. If this trend doesn't reverse, Fail Whales of all kinds will be appearing with more and more social media technology.

A good example of this is Pownce. Pownce is similar to Twitter without a really distinct competitive advantage. People in the social media world knew it didn't have a sustainable business model, either. Pownce didn't place unwanted advertising in your messages and didn't offer the industry fallback revenue model of freemium products that could be purchased in

FIGURE 13.3   The Fail Whale

addition to all of the free services Pownce offered. As a result, Pownce and its whale went belly up.

On the Lighter Side of Microblogging

Some Twitter Jargon

Twitter is the most prevalent microblogging technology used today.

- A *tweeter* is a person using Twitter to send out posts or *tweets*.
- A *tweet* is a post or text message sent from one twitterer to another.
- A *retweet* (RT) is reposting someone else's tweet
- The tweeting community is called the *Twittersphere*.

Much like e-mail, once you hit Send, the tweet is out there. A regretted tweet is called a *Mistweet*. (Never tweet after a bottle of Chardonnay.)

Google Maps has a mash-up called *Twittervision,* which shows users the geographic location of twitterers. The list of Twitter jargon goes on and on.

Corporate Tweeters

Small, medium, and large companies alike are beginning to adopt social media tools into their marketing, public relations, communications, and customer service approaches. Like any early adopters, these companies will have a significant advantage over those who wait until social media becomes mainstream. Here are just a few of the many large companies that have incorporated microblogging into their corporate culture:

- Southwest Airlines regularly tweets as one of its standard customer service tools. The following is an actual tweet from Southwest Airlines: twitpic.com/1bzrxh

—Today, SW Employees donated these Easter Baskets to DAL Ronald McDonald House & Children's Medical Center Dallas 10:22 AM March 30, 2010" (a TwitPic is a clickable link to a posted picture on TwitPic .com).

- The somewhat controversial Dave Winer—who calls himself the "original blogger" and inventor of RSS—tweets his followers on a regular basis about his River project at the *New York Times*. The project is what Dave calls a "river-of-news format," wherein a stream of short text messages about the latest breaking news from the *Times* is sent to followers by cell phone, PDA, or web page aggregator to create a news roll of top stories. Dave explains, "I created the site because I wasn't getting enough news about products. It's that simple. I'm interested in the other stuff too, the finance, trends, parties, puppets—the River Project allows readers to prioritize and aggregate their news in one website."

- Bill Gerth is part of Comcast's digital care initiative in Philadelphia's Center City region. Bill has the daunting assignment of monitoring blogs and tweets for unfavorable posts aimed at Comcast. Bill and his team offer immediate and personal customer service on Twitter, which sets companies like Comcast apart from their competitors.

- Chief blogger at Dell Computer Lionel Menchaca was immediately on top of things when Dell's laptop computer batteries began exploding. Lionel got tweets from customers and the media asking for information about the problem. He kept tweeting and blogging, and continuously updating his customers with the latest updates he had. The industry—as well as Dell's customers—were shocked to see a company that big taking such personal care of its customers. This provided a huge public relations advantage at a time when Dell needed it most.

- Large businesses such as Cisco Systems and Whole Foods Market use Twitter to provide product or service information to their customers through tweets.

- The Los Angeles Fire Department put the technology to use during California wildfires since 2007 to get up-to-the-second information of where the fires were breaking out, where people were trapped, and where their help was needed most.

- NASA used Twitter to break the news of discovery of what appeared to be water ice on Mars by the Phoenix Mars Lander. Other NASA projects, such as Space Shuttle missions and the International Space Station, also provide updates through Twitter.

- News outlets such as the BBC have also started using Twitter to disseminate breaking news or provide information feeds for sporting events.

- Several 2008 U.S. presidential candidates—including Democratic Party nominee Barack Obama—used Twitter as a publicity mechanism. The Nader/Gonzalez campaign used Twitter and Google Maps to show real-time updates of their ballot access teams across the country.

- The College of Golf at Keiser University is using Twitter to relay information to students such as school announcements, golf weather updates, and even encouraging students to ask questions through the online platform. They have also utilized Twitter to answer third-party questions about the sport of golf, and encourage the golf community to support each other through the platform.

- Westwinds Church in Jackson, Michigan, uses Twitter as a part of its weekend worship services, and actually introduced the concept of Twitter Church. Westwinds runs training classes for Twitter and encourages members to bring laptops and mobile devices to church. On occasion, the Twitter feed will be shown live on the screens in the auditorium, and everyone is encouraged to give their input, make observations, and ask questions to encourage an interactive worship format.

Microblogging clearly has widespread global appeal, and it can play a vital role in keeping people safe during disasters and tragedies. During the August 2011 hurricane, Irene, Twitter users started flooding the web with images and stories. The microblogging site was also used by the government and FEMA to inform people of the path of Irene and safety precautions. Nonprofits were able to raise money on Twitter as well.

Twitter has become the communication tool of choice by many emergency services around the world, and has been used by activists and journalists during other natural disasters.

Twitter is also credited with doing a better job of getting information out during emergencies than the traditional news media or government emergency services, as was the case with the Virginia Tech shootings in April 2007. In the Virginia Tech case, the news media and family members were getting real-time updates through Twitter while it was actually happening.

Tweets in the News

The *Wall Street Journal* Digital Network Twittering the US Airways Plane Crash Landing

Shira Ovide

Notch Another Win for Citizen Journalism

Janis Krums, a guy with a camera and a penchant for social media tools, posted one of the first and most remarkable photos today of US Airways Flight 1549 after it crash landed in the Hudson River.

"There's a plane in the Hudson," the Sarasota native wrote on the microblogging site Twitter just as reports began to break of the plane hitting the water off Manhattan's west side. "I'm on the ferry going to pick up the people. Crazy."

The photo, which Mr. Krums posted online using a Twitter photo sharing site, has been viewed more than 43,000 times.

Social media tools like Twitter—which allows users to tap out 140-character status updates—have changed how breaking news events are recorded and covered. They made for on-the-ground reports from the Mumbai terror attacks in November [2008], for example.

After he documented the Hudson River crash landing, Mr. Krums then became a minor celebrity in traditional media, too. He conducted an interview on MSNBC and says on his Twitter profile that he's preparing for even more interviews this evening.

(continued)

(continued)

Source: http://on.wsj.com/5NoB.

For a clickable link, go to www.theSocialMediaBible.com.

Microblogging beyond Twitter?

A number of services exist that have a similar concept to Twitter's, but have country-specific versions of their services, such as www.frazr.com.

Other sites—such as Jaiku and Friendfeed—combine microblogging with other capabilities like file sharing and allow the Twitter user to attach a file to posts.

Plurk is another microblogging platform that has been gaining in popularity. This service launched in May 2008 and gained considerable acceptance in Silicon Valley during its first 30 days. While the number of Twitter users are far greater than Plurk's users, Plurk's horizontal time line and group conversations create a more robust interface and adds a spatial dimension to microblogging that make it a good alternative to Twitter.

Other services include Yammer, which launched on September 8, 2008, at the TechCrunch50 Conference and is marketed as an enterprise version of Twitter. Yammer asks, "What's happening at your company? With Yammer, you can share status updates with your coworkers." The service is currently used at over 100,000 businesses worldwide.

Prologue is a microblogging tool created by Automatic—the makers of WordPress—that was released in January 2008 and allows its users to "post short messages about what they're doing" in a secured environment. Later in 2008, a new and improved version of Prologue, dubbed P2, was developed and made available to the public.

Then there's the Enterprise Social Messaging Experiment (ESME) created by Demo Jam at SAP Labs, which allows you to create new groups instantly by clicking on cloud tags or word frequency. For more information, see www.youtube.com/watch?v=y1dPAV8C0Tw

or go to the www.theSocialMediaBible.com and click on the link.

Social Cast is a FriendFeed and Twitter tool for the enterprise, and Laconica is considered an open microblogging tool—an open source application (one in which software source code is available to the general public without a license that restricts or limits its use, modification, or redistribution) that can be installed on corporate servers and used behind the firewall.

And then there is OraTweet, created by Oracle—the world's largest enterprise software company—as a microblogging tool for internal employee and external client use. OraTweet allows companies, universities, and organizations to run their own in-house microblogs that keep their communications private and secure and that encourage the development of internal communities. OraTweet operates the same way as e-mail and instant messaging, but allows enterprises to broadcast messages safely within their own environments.

Some other sites include:

- *Status:* A lighter communication tool that displays an update of your team's progress on a single screen at one time.
- *Trillr:* A small group service intended for coworkers, partners, and customers to communicate. Trillr allows users to stay connected with quick, frequent exchanges of data, and answers the question, "What's on your mind?"
- *I Did Work:* A task-based update tool that provides teams with the ability to leave short status messages. This site creates a work log that keeps a history of your progress and shares it with your team.
- *Joint Contact:* A collaboration tool that incorporates microblogging features and connects Twitter to your project status to inform your followers of upcoming events. With Joint Contact, you can link your tweets to your project management system.
- *Blue Twit-IBM:* Launched in 2007, an internal Twitter client that has been providing IBM employees with an alternative to e-mail.
- *Present.ly:* A micro-update communication tool that gives employees the ability to instantly communicate their current status, ask questions, post media, and more.
- *Mixin:* A service that spans both internal and external corporate communications and "lets you share your daily activities and intentions to get together more often with your friends."
- *Spoink:* A multimedia microblogging service that integrates blogging, podcasting, telephony, and SMS text messaging. Spoink supports all major mobile audio, video, and picture formats.

And then there's identi.ca,

Jaiku, FriendFeed, Dodgeball, tumblr, and TWiT Army—and all of the most popular social networking websites such as Facebook, Google+, MySpace, and LinkedIn, which have their own microblogging feature called a *status update*.

The ROI of Social Media

Twitter for Business. You're kidding . . . Right?

Background

As an executive and entrepreneur, I don't have time for toys and fads. So back in March of 2006, when Robert Scoble stood on the stage of the First Arizona Social Media Conference and said that "Twitter was the next *big* thing," I turned to Francine Hardaway in horror and whispered, "You're kidding . . . Right?" Later, like many other new Twitter users, I signed up for an account and then promptly forgot about the whole thing. After all, it was just a fad. It wouldn't last.

Strategy

It was quite a few years later that I again took a serious look at Twitter as a business communication tool. And this time, I looked at it more strategically on the odd chance that maybe, just maybe, it was not a fad, after all. After checking in with the "experts" (it's in quotes since the people who know the

(continued)

(continued)

most about this stuff *hate* to be called experts), I got a few tips, tricks, and
tools, and started to experiment. I started off slow. One Twitter ID (@joankw)
and two blogs with the exact same content (http://jkw.typepad.com

and www.joankoerber-walker.com

on WordPress). The test was simple. The TypePad blog would be promoted
on Twitter. The WordPress blog would use standard SEO. I would try it for 90
days and see what impact Twitter had on traffic to the blog and for its acceptance by readers. We set the two up on FeedBurner and started gathering data.

Implementation

After 90 days, the results were not bad. We were running a traffic ratio of
10 to 1 on the TypePad (Twitter-promoted) blog compared to the WordPress blog,
according to FeedBurner statistics. With this small level of success, and due to
a tweet frequency that was annoying to some, we moved to the next step and
experimented with segmenting the company's potential Twitter audience into
new categories through targeted profiles in the areas that were our corporate
focus, creating @CorePurpose for the company as well as @JKWleadership,

@JKWinnovation, and @JKWgrowth, since as a company, we believe that Leadership plus Innovation equals Greater Growth. We were very transparent in our strategy, posting not only the Twitter IDs but also our strategy *and* the tools we were using right on each of our blogs (for example: http://jkw.typepad .com/corepurpose_joan_koerberw/my-profiles-on-twitter.html).

Opportunity

CorePurpose is a thought leadership organization that provides solutions to *big* problems for large companies and organizations. We also publish, through our CorePurpose Publishing division, books for universities, trade associations, and business readers. Our advertising and marketing efforts target both potential customers and potential partners in key business areas of expertise. If Twitter, as a tool, would allow us to connect with that audience so that we could demonstrate our expertise and convert them to customers or partners, our business would increase.

Conclusion

And now for the big question: Was there a return on investment? One year later, I had an opportunity to speak to the Society of Women Engineers, and shared some results. You will find the video on YouTube here: www.youtube .com/joankw.

(continued)

(continued)

By reinvesting marketing resources on Twitter, CorePurpose has had the opportunity to connect to both potential partners and customers on Twitter across *four* continents. Relationships developed using Twitter as a business communication tool have allowed us to make connections, share and exchange information, and most importantly, convert contacts to customers and partners at a higher rate in one year than traditional marketing strategies did in our first seven years of operations. We have expanded our social media tool set to YouTube, LinkedIn, and numerous blogs. I sure hope Twitter is not a fad. You see it is working! And that ratio of RSS feeds is now 131:1!

—Joan Koerber-Walker
www.corepurpose.com

Google Profile: www.google.com/profiles/jkoerberwalker

Expert Insight

Biz Stone, cofounder, Twitter, www.twitter.com

Biz Stone

I'm the cofounder of Twitter, and before that I helped start a service called Xanga.com,

which is a social journaling service that we started in 1999 in New York City. They are still there, but I left and I ended up working at Google. I was specifically on the Blogger team for a couple of years before I left there, and sort of got back in to the start-up world with a project called Odeo. This is an audio on the Internet, a podcasting service, and it was actually when I was at Odeo that Twitter was actually a side project that we were working on that we fell in love with. This ultimately turned into its own company that just grew and grew and grew. That's where we're at today. . . .

Yeah, it's really just a short messaging service, at the simplest level, but a communication utility. What it becomes now that we have so many people using it, it really becomes the pulse of what's happening with the people and the organizations that you really care about most. So, on the one hand, you

(continued)

(*continued*)

use it to just communicate; on the other hand, you look through it to find out what's going on. . . .

Twitter is the name of the service, and it comes from the idea of the word that you can look up in the dictionary which is a "short trill, chirp, or burst of information," referencing a bird call. People are tricked into calling it *individual updates*. Every time I give an individual update on Twitter, I actually get saved and archived on Twitter. It becomes its own individual web page, and people have been referring to those individual updates as tweets. This is the axis of twittering, or sometimes I say "tweeting," because they are fond of that word *tweet*.

It is nothing that we officially stated. People starting using it, so it works out well for us. . . .

Yes, it's a short message, a short text message. . . . One of the key things about Twitter is that it's agnostic when it comes to what sort of device you prefer to use to interact with the system. So if you prefer to use SMS and mobile texting on a mobile phone, Twitter will work that way for you. But it also works over the web and it also works with several thousand right now (more in the future), third-party independent pieces of software that you can either download for Mac or a PC, or use with Slash. Basically we opened up our infrastructure; we created an API so that smart developers around the world can create custom interactive software to interact with Twitter. . . .

I mean, we did it early on just to, sort of, scratch an itch. One of our very early developers wanted to be able to interact with Twitter a certain way, so we created a very simple HI; in fact what happened was the service is simple and the API was so simple that even a beginner API developer could jump in and build something on Twitter that worked very quickly. So it became popular to build on top of Twitter, and what it did for us is that it created so much variety out there (of ways of interacting with Twitter) that it ended up just creating a lot of traffic and creating a lot of opportunities and options for people, which is great. . . .

Yeah, and it's really that mobile aspect that we were trying to get at early. Twitter was basically inspired by the away messages on IM, so if you ever used an IM tool, you see that your coworkers or your friends are in a meeting, out for coffee, or whatever. You can look at a group of 12 people and get a sense of what everyone's doing, what everyone's up to; but that's related to the computer and what they are doing on the computer. So when we took that idea and we just broke it out and we made it more mobile by adding the ability to interact with SMS. We made it more social by building in more features.

Then we created, basically, new kinds of communications—a kind of real-time group communications that really didn't exist before. And it's something that turned out that can be very useful for people. . . .

To listen to or read the entire Executive Conversation with Biz Stone, go to www.theSocialMediaBible.com.

To-Do List

- Begin microblogging.

  Don't be afraid of microblogging. It's easy, it's free, and it's fun. It's a great way to stay in direct and immediate contact with whomever you choose—whether it's friends, family, club members, church groups, coworkers, prospects, or customers.

- Tweet.

  Tweet! The technology isn't any good unless you use it. Tweets are only 140 characters, and are as easy to send as a text message. When you receive a relevant thought, text it out to your followers. And remember to always have that "What's in It for Me?" content value.

- Follow tweeters.

  Follow other tweeters. Find people with similar interests, good ideas—or just people you care about—and see what thoughts they share on a daily basis. Remember, if you don't like what they have to say, unfollow them and go find others who provide you with that WIIFM content.

- Invite others to follow you.

  Be sure to invite others to follow you. They don't know that you are sharing so many pearls of wisdom unless you tell them. Send them your Twitter address, and tweet them often.

- Set up groups.

  Set up groups in Twitter (or platform of your choice) using hashtags. Set up one group for your existing customers, another for your prospects, and yet another for your coworkers. Send different and appropriate tweets to each group.

- Use news feed tweets.

  Set up a Twitter news feed, so that you can get all of the breaking news as it happens—and only that which interests you—whether it's business, lifestyles, finance, gossip, sports, international, health . . . and so on!

- Use tweets for internal communications.

  Try using Twitter for internal communications by setting up separate groups for your coworkers and employees. Send them status reports on the company's stock prices, new product developments, press releases, HR benefit updates, holiday information, or just an occasional atta-boy or pep talk.

Conclusion

Microblogging is a wonderful and interesting way to keep in touch with your family, friends, and coworkers. It's also an imaginative way to send quick updates on news, products, services, legislation, or any content that has a "What's in It for Me?" value to your customers and prospects. Keeping yourself and your company in the forefront of your prospects' minds—by giving them valuable information and updates—will likely convert prospects into customers.

Try it. Set up a free account, follow some like-minded tweeters; invite other tweeters to follow you. Monitor what they say. Evaluate the WIIFM value. Then begin tweeting yourself. Monitor the responses from that. After a short while, you will begin to see the most effective content you can deliver to your followers.

As has been written in almost every chapter thus far, the most important thing to remember is not to get overwhelmed; in fact, whelmed is the state of mind you are looking to achieve. Try using a microblogging platform. Send some tweets or posts. Read some tweets or posts. And enjoy it. If it becomes overwhelming or loses its appeal, back off and unfollow. Like any technology, the key is moderation.

To hear all of the Expert Interviews, go to www.theSocialMediaBible.com.

Downloads

For your free downloads associated with *The Social Media Bible,* go to www .theSocialMediaBible.com,

and enter your ISBN number located on the back of the book above the bar code. Be sure to enter the dashes.

Credits

The ROI of Social Media was provided by:

Joan Koerber-Walker, www.corepurpose.com

Expert Insight was provided by:

Biz Stone, cofounder of Twitter, www.twitter.com

Technical edits were provided by:

Kaila Strong, social media architect, and Arnie Kuenn, CEO of Vertical Measures, www.VerticalMeasures.com

Notes

1. Thanks to Ed Nusbaum for this quote.
2. SMS is the abbreviation for Systems Management Server, which is a communications protocol that allows the exchange of short text messages between mobile telephone devices. In different parts of the world, the acronym SMS is used as a synonym for a text message or the act of sending a text message even if SMS isn't actually being used. With 2.4 billion active users, or 74 percent of all mobile phone subscribers sending and receiving text messages on their cell phones, SMS text messaging is the most widely used data application on the planet. In spite of its wide use, as a cost-cutting effort, on August 14, 2008, Twitter removed SMS access to their U.K. service.

3. Pownce is a good example of the changing landscape of social media. Leah Culver was interviewed just a few months before her company closed its doors on December 15, 2008. Her interview and insights are still as valid as ever, so we left them. Technology will change, some existing players will go extinct, and many new companies will take their place.

CHAPTER 14

Live from Anywhere— It's Livecasting

www.LonSafko.com/TSMB3_Videos/14Livecasting.mov

What's in It for You?

Whether you call it web radio, net radio, streaming radio, e-radio, talk radio, Internet radio, livecasting, lifecasting, webcasting, web conferencing, or webinars, broadcasting information online is all about creating live content that uses the Internet to distribute (or stream[1]) that content. All of these terms refer to the process of producing your own, current content, and then distributing that content live over the Internet. You can actually create your very own radio or television show that will only be as expensive as your production costs dictate. You are the host, the production manager, and the talent. You can speak about nearly anything you wish. You can broadcast your show each day, each week, or only when you feel like it. You can put on a live presentation, perform training, introduce or demonstrate a new product or service, create a preventative maintenance program for your customers, or just talk with a special guest about what's new in your industry. It's easy to do, it's a powerful medium that can reach the entire world, and there's not even a cost.

theSocialMediaBible.com

Think about that for a minute: For the very first time in history, you can actually produce your own radio or television show and distribute it to everyone around the world—live—for free!

Back to the Beginning

This chapter discusses how you can create your own radio show and broadcast it to your prospects, customers, coworkers, and fan base. In the video and television category, the chapter discusses how you can create your very own television show and broadcast that content for free.

Internet Radio

Technologist Carl Malamud first pioneered web radio in 1993. Each week, Malamud would interview a different computer expert during what he called the "first computer radio talk show." The show wasn't really livecasted, as it was prerecorded and distributed one by one to his listeners—who then had to download and play each audio file (an early version of podcasting).

The first groups to actually broadcast audio live over the Internet were existing commercial radio stations that were already producing audio content. The crossover from existing terrestrial radio stations or networks was logical and natural; all that the stations needed to do was take the existing content that they were already broadcasting over the AM and FM radio frequencies and broadcast it over the Internet. The very first rock and roll concert to be broadcast live was the Rolling Stones becoming the "first cyberspace streamed concert." Mick Jagger welcomed his concert's listeners with, "I wanna say a special welcome to everyone that's, uh, climbed into the Internet tonight and, uh, has got into the M-bone. And I hope it doesn't all collapse."

Commercial Internet-Only Radio Stations

The next step in Internet broadcasting was for individuals—rather than traditional radio broadcasters—to take advantage of this new, effective, and free technology. People began creating their own radio show content and transmitting it over the Internet—from everywhere. A new industry was born.

In November 1995, the Minneapolis, Minnesota–based NetRadio Company founded by Scott Bourne and radio veteran Scot Combs began using RealAudio to stream music over the Internet. The company started with only four formats and had expanded to include more than a dozen formats within two years.

Radio audience research company Arbitron (which collects listener data about radio audiences similar to the way that Nielsen Media Research collects information about TV audiences) began rating Internet-based radio stations in 1997. They found that NetRadio continuously held 8 of the top 10 rankings. The Navarre Corporation purchased NetRadio and merged the company into one of its subsidiaries later that year, and NetRadio closed its doors in 2001. NetRadio played an important role in the development of Internet audio streaming and paved the way for other providers.

Livecasting

Livecasting as it is known today was made possible by the evolution of smaller, lighter, more energy-efficient (battery) hardware, which included more portable laptop computers, longer-life batteries, a video camera, and wireless Internet connections. As these technologies became more effective and widely used, more and more people began sharing their lives with the world through the Internet.

The first person to continuously broadcast his life live, in real time—with a first-person video from a wearable camera—was University of Toronto professor Steve Mann. Mann experimented with wearable computers and video cameras, and was streaming video as early as the beginning of the 1980s. His work eventually led to the Wearable Wireless Webcam.

In February 1999, the HereAndNow.net

website, founded by Lisa Batey—or Nekomimi Lisa, as her fans knew her—began livecasting 24/7. Batey and her roommates began to share their college life experiences in live, unedited 24/7 Internet video streams. Unlike JenniCam and other livecasting of their time, HereandNow.net broadcasted their video in higher quality and was the first to stream both full-motion video and audio. HereandNow.net stopped broadcasting in 2001, but Batey's community still exists in a chat room and Yahoo! Group.

In December 1999, Josh Harris (creator of the CBS television show *Big Brother*) introduced "We Live in Public," a formatted, conceptual art experiment in which he placed telephones, microphones, and 32 robotic cameras in the home that he and girlfriend Tanya Corrin shared. Viewers were able to text Harris and Corrin through their website's chat room. Josh Harris is currently founder and CEO of Operator 11 Exchange (www.operator11.com),

a Hollywood-based company that is an Internet-based television studio and online web site.

By 2007, software like Camtwist, Manycam, and WebcamMax allowed livecasts and live video streams to have overlays, commercials, effects, multiple cameras, and more. This expedited the look and perception of livestreams, which allowed a new level of professional-looking live journalism as well as fun shows to fit in.

As more shows joined, livestreaming wasn't solely for livecasting anymore. Walt Ribeiro became an online music instructor who livestreamed to a large virtual classroom. Playcafe became the "first online game show network," and there were presidential campaigns, bands performing live concerts, and even space shuttle launches. The technology was then not only used to broadcast people's lives and webinars, but was creating virtual worlds and businesses—in real time.

Justin.tv

The first person to significantly popularize the concept of livecasting was Californian Justin Kan. While living in San Francisco in early 2007, Justin founded something he called "www.Justin.tv."

While wearing a webcam attached to his baseball cap, Justin began streaming his life in a continuous, live video, beginning on March 19, 2007, at midnight. Justin is actually the person credited with giving this process the name *lifecasting*. He generated a lot of media attention when he announced he would wear his webcam 24 hours a day, 7 days a week and broadcast his life—nonstop. Justin's interview with NBC *Today* show reporter Ann Curry vaulted him into national attention in April 2007.

The credit for Kan's computer hardware goes to Kyle Vogt, one of the four founders of www.Justin.tv.

FIGURE 14.1   Justin Kan—Justin.tv

Vogt created the portable live video streaming computer system that Justin used to broadcast, and he recalls,

I moved to San Francisco so I could be closer to the rest of the team. I mean *really* close. The four of us lived and worked out of a small two-bedroom apartment. I spent my time becoming an expert in Linux socket programming, cell phone data networks, and real-time data protocols. Four data modems in close proximity just don't work well together, so packet loss was as high as 50 percent. I fought with these modems for weeks but finally managed to wrestle them into a single 1.2 megabits-per-second video uplink. The new camera emerged from the pile of Radio Shack parts, computer guts, and hacked-up cell phones that had accumulated on my messy desk. It uses thousands of lines of Python code, a custom real-time protocol, connection load balancing, and several other funky hacks.

FIGURE 14.2   Justin.tv

Enter Justine Ezarik

On May 29, 2007, designer Justine Ezarik became the second livecaster on www.Justin.tv

with a livecast streaming from Pittsburgh, Pennsylvania.

FIGURE 14.3   Justine Ezarik—Justine.tv

Justine changed the format a bit by aiming the webcam at herself, rather than using the host's point-of-view approach that was used before. Another major difference between Justine and Justin is that Justine spent considerably more time interacting with her viewers. Where Justin was more "this is what I am seeing," Justine was "here I am, interact with me." Justine was more conversational through text chat, and watching the feed was almost like being with her and talking face to face.

What You Need to Know

Do-It-Yourself Radio

Do-It-Yourself Radio is another form of livecasting. You are broadcasting live to an audience through the Internet. While more do-it-yourself Internet radio shows are limited to 1 hour and not 24 hours, it's still about communicating with your followers, live.

BlogTalkRadio is an Internet-based audio and radio platform that allows users to host their own, live Internet broadcast radio shows—needing only a telephone, Internet access, and a browser. BlogTalkRadio has been referred to as "a populist force in cyberspace,"[2] and "the dominant player in the latest media trend, one that allows anyone with a web connection to host a talk show on any topic at any time of day. It is the newest form of new media; the audio version of the Internet blog."[3]

Telecommunications executive and former accountant Alan Levy founded BlogTalkRadio, and is now its CEO. After creating a blog to update family members about his ill father, Alan launched BlogTalkRadio in August 2006. He wanted to create a way for bloggers to communicate more directly—and in real time—with their audiences.

Washington Post reporter Howard Kurtz has written many times about BlogTalkRadio in his "Media Notes" column, and claims, "The process is nearly idiot-proof. The host logs on to a web page with a password, types in when he wants the show to air, and then—using a garden-variety phone—calls a special number. The computer screen lists the phone numbers of guests or listeners calling in, and the host can put as many as six on the air at once by clicking a mouse. Listeners can download a podcast version later."[4]

BlogTalkRadio allows up to five callers at any given time to participate in the Internet radio show itself, while the number of listeners is virtually unlimited. The user's radio shows are streamed directly from the host's web page during live broadcasts, and the shows are recorded, archived, and streamed as on-demand podcasts after the initial broadcasts. One can also subscribe to these shows through RSS feeds (see Chapter 17, RSS—Really Simple Syndication Made Simple, for more details on this process). You can post your BlogTalkRadio shows to your Facebook, MySpace, and other social networking web pages. And, since BlogTalkRadio is advertising supported, it's also free to you!

Before podcasting and BlogTalkRadio, there were Satellite Radio stations such as Sirius and XM. Founded in the early 1990s, they promoted a new wave and freedom in broadcasting. By the turn of the new millennium, they grew as fierce competitors to traditional radio stations. Although their talent wasn't DIY, they still managed to take many of traditional radio's personalities off the radio airwaves (which would have perhaps moved to the Internet) and onto a new medium.

Conventional Radio Stations Weren't Happy

The ability to use inexpensive technology to webcast your own radio shows worldwide has allowed independent media to flourish. And as you might imagine, conventional radio broadcast stations weren't very happy with their new, free, global, Internet-based competition, which led to a series of controversial royalty legislation bills, congressional hearings, reforms, and appeals. As this book isn't intended to discuss historical legal aspects, you can learn more about this field by researching the following terms:

- The 2002 Copyright Arbitration Royalty Panel (CARP)

- The 2007 United States Copyright Royalty Board approval of a rate increase in the royalties payable to performers of recorded works broadcast on the Internet
- The 2007 Internet Radio Equality Act (HR 2060)

The good news is that even given the continuous controversy, in September 2008, the Copyright Royalty Board decided to keep the royalty rate the music publishers must pay for each digital track they sell at nine cents per song for companies like Apple and Amazon. However, faced with an industry in transition, with new rules being written constantly, the three-judge panel opted to keep the royalty rate the same for the next five years. Many argue that instead of the per-track fee, the Copyright Royalty Board should have set the rates as a percentage of digital music revenues.

Webinar, Web Conferencing, and Webcasting

As discussed at the beginning of the chapter, the earliest form of webcasting, or broadcasting video live over the Internet, was called *web conferencing.* This particular method used conferencing software that connects two or more people or computers through the Internet, giving them the ability to speak and see one another simultaneously. People were able to conduct live meetings or presentations using this many-to-many two-way Internet video communication.

Webcast: A *webcast* takes place when a live broadcast or prerecorded media file is distributed over the Internet using streaming technology. It is broadcasted or distributed as a single-content source to many viewers simultaneously, or as a one-to-many one-way broadcast. Webcasting has many applications for commercial companies, including investor relations presentations, annual meetings, seminars, and e-learning. The largest webcasters today are existing radio and television stations that either simulcast their over-the-air (cable) broadcasts or provide their content in a prerecorded on-demand type of viewing.

Webinar: The word *webinar*[5] comes from the combination, or concatenation, of the words *web* and *seminar,* and is another form of one-to-many webcasting. Much like a presenter and audience at a live, on-ground seminar, a webinar usually entails one-way (occasionally two-way) communication. Text chat is often part of web conferencing; it allows the audience to communicate, ask questions, and interact with the presenter in real time. The audio portion of the webinar can be technically achieved by a conference call, wherein the presenter addresses the audience over a speakerphone while presenting visual information over the Internet.

State-of-the-art webinar software uses VoIP, or Voice over Internet Protocol (like Vonage telephone service), which allows the two-way audio conversation to also be transmitted over the Internet. This eliminates the need for conference telephone calling, and allows the software to capture both of the activities that are taking place on the screen (the video as well as the audio conversation). The complete webinar capture is able to be distributed and played again at a future date.

Videoblog

The videoblog is the same as the conventional blog, except that it uses short, prerecorded video in addition to text to convey your messages. (See Chapter 6, The Ubiquitous Blog, for extensive detail and explanation on the origin and use of videoblogs.)

Ustream.tv   (www.Ustream.tv)

is a public platform that grants anyone the opportunity to lifecast through live streaming video for free. It was founded in March 2007 and currently has more than 320,000 registered users, who generate more than 350,000 hours of live video content per month. The Ustream site generates more than 10 million unique visitors per month and has received $11.1 million in funding for new product development.

Ustream also won some acclaim during some recent political campaigns for its usefulness in campaigning. While campaigning in the 2008 U.S. presidential election, former senator and presidential hopeful Mike Gravel became the first candidate ever to stream a debate using www.Ustream.tv.

The site allowed Gravel to address a larger number of voters' political questions in real time.

Streaming online was becoming so mainstream, affordable, and accessible, that in 2010, people began streaming through their "smart" cell phones. iPhone apps by Ustream.TV, and many others, used your phone's camera to shoot the video, and VoIP to upload the video in real time. Whereas Justine Ezarek and Justin Kan had to carry around large batteries, huge cameras, and bulky laptop computers, we now had the power to stream in our pockets.

The ROI of Social Media

Social Media as an Effective Medium to Promote Offline Events

Background

Think Big Partners is a business incubation company created to help entrepreneurs find success more quickly. Located in Kansas City, the group was looking for a way to announce the launch of the incubation company and generate as much buzz in as short a period of time. With that purpose in mind, Think Big Partners created a local entrepreneurial conference called Think Big Kansas City.

Strategy

With the idea of "practice what you preach," Think Big Partners set out to establish the premier conference for entrepreneurs, investors, and start-ups. The conference was a one-day event bringing over 30 expert speakers, including Chris Gardner, *New York Times* number one best-selling author of *The Pursuit of Happyness*, the namesake for the blockbuster Hollywood movie with Will Smith, and Joe Calhoon, Stephen Covey's most requested speaker during the 1990s, author of two books and the inventor of 1hour2plan.

The issue facing Think Big Partners was that they had just under 45 days to promote the event and get people to the venue. To that point, not a single shred of promotion had been done for this first-time event. And while the intention was to do the traditional mix of marketing, Think Big wanted to do just that . . . Think Big.

Implementation

Think Big turned to social media to help promote the event. On January 13th, Think Big launched a blog, Twitter profile, and Facebook Fan page for

(continued)

(continued)

the March 3rd event. The idea was to generate brand awareness and help recruit attendees. Since attendees would have to pay for entrance, social media was being used as a lead generator to help with revenue and to sell out the show.

With nearly 30 speakers, Think Big had a tremendous pool of content to pull from. The blog was programmatically tied to both Twitter and Facebook to allow all communication to be shared with each of the platforms. Participating speakers provided unique content for the Think Big blog and helped with the link strategy developed for the event promotion. The partners at Think Big also committed to the effort providing for incentives to be used for recruitment. Signed books from Chris Gardner and scholarships were awarded through Twitter follow campaigns to help generate awareness and engagement. Additionally, a $10,000 business plan competition was created and promoted through a unique landing page developed for the Facebook fan page.

Opportunity

The opportunity was to show the tremendous reach of social media and just how much of an effect it could have on driving not only conversation, but actual people to the event. The viral nature of this medium provided a great chance to test the effectiveness of word-of-mouth advertising and social lead generation.

Conclusion

Think Big KC was able to go from 0 to 1,540 Twitter followers on the day of the event, and just over 15 percent of the traffic to the blog and promotional pages for the event were attributed to social media efforts. Event planners attributed nearly 5 percent of ticket sales to the promotion. Secondary benefits were that several published authors and professional speakers were introduced to Think Big Partners because of the social media campaigns and have requested the opportunity to engage with the Incubator as mentors and contributors.

—Chad Herman
www.thinkbigkansascity.com

Expert Insight

Jody Gnant, singer, songwriter, and community marketer, www.jodygnant.com

Jody Gnant Laptop

Well, first and foremost I consider myself to be a singer/songwriter. That's what I've wanted to do since I was 11 years old; and I kind of always knew I was going to have to do it independently if I did not want to compromise who I wanted to be as an artist. Luckily, I was born and raised in a time when the Internet was being born and raised right around me, and so I kind of grew up with the Internet and the development of it.

I was chatting online at, you know, 13 years old with the nickname of "Scooter," even before the Internet transitioned over to being more of a corporate arena for companies to put up these flashy websites and wow the rest of us with their technical attributes. Now it is actually coming full circle. The Internet has been brought back to the people, so to speak, with social media, and it is really an exciting time to be an independent artist and to be able to promote what I do independently. So that is what I do. I sing, I write songs, and I put them out there for the world to see on the Internet.

Like I said, it seemed as if, when I was a little kid sitting on my dad's lap with the modem, with the rotary phone . . . it would just sit. . . . I don't know the technical term for what modem that was, but it was actually at that point about the people, too. We would sit there and we would chat and we had the monochrome screens; you really could not do anything else. You could play Zork, which was like a great game. Love that game. However, other than Zork and chatting online, the Internet did not do much yet.

Then the companies took it over and I now feel like it is . . . it is being handed back to the people. That is kind of what I am all about as a musician. The entire reason I have decided to be a songwriter and a singer in the first

(continued)

(*continued*)

place was to effect positive change. And I think that is why I like the Internet so much and why I like these tools—like blogging, livecasting—is because it allows us to continue to make that positive change in our own special way. Each of us has our own voice, and the Internet gives us the distribution channel for it. . . .

Lifecasting is . . . I think it is awesome! Wikipedia explains it as a continual broadcast of a person's life through the general media. And basically, a lot of lifecasters actually wear a camera and give the first-person perspective of what they see on a day-to-day basis, and so it's their lifecast. But I wanted it to be viewed as a promotional tool to launch the release of *Pivot,* which was the album that I had recorded and released as part of my "One Red Paper Clip" trade. And so we decided that we would just start broadcasting. And we broadcast the recording, mixing, mastering, and printing of the record . . . the rehearsing of the band for the CD release party; and then we would broadcast the CD release party . . . "Live . . . On the Internet!" with all these multicam systems and then . . . actually I was only going to do it for the six-week feed after the CD release party. But it dawned on me once I had had the CD release party, that really this was becoming the world's longest documentary *The Life and Times of an Independent Singer/Songwriter* (and the struggles that they go through).

So it actually became more of a journalistic process for me, and capturing for posterity what I was trying to accomplish as an artist. And . . . at some point, [it] became less of a promotional tool and more of something that was a personal mission for me to capture. The fact that there were other people along for the ride was just so cool, because people could actually choose to get involved in the process in real time. You know, if they wanted to affect how my music career was going, there was a chat right there; and they could do something about the fact that I was lost in L.A. And they would get on and google and they would figure out where I was and they would say, "Go left down Wilshire!" So here I am having my own personal GPS through the Internet. Or—they could just sit back and watch the show.

And [something else that] dawned on me was that—even though I started using it as a promotional tool—without even knowing it, in just in the way that we were handling the situation, we had started to create a community. And so all of a sudden there were hundreds of people that would just come by on a daily basis to get a smile. People have told me that they were in the hospital coming out of a coma and they genuinely didn't know how they were going to survive the next seven weeks of a car accident; and then stumbled upon my lifecast. And the community is what helps them get through that time; and then they show me their scars and, you know, it is really humbling to know that what started out as a promotional tool ended up being a home and a community that still exists even without me.

Right now I am not lifecasting on the Internet, but there are 36 people on the chat befriending each other and talking about what they are going to be doing in their [lives]. It is very humbling; and it is not just broadcasting if you do it right. . . . [Then] it is actually community building, and probably the most enriching experience I've ever done for myself.

When you are doing a community marketing project, [you have to know] who you are focusing on, and which community you are trying to build. It is integral to know which [group] you are going after and how you want to affect them at the end of the day. What is interesting to me is that [there are] lives being affected. No longer am I just selling a product. You know when I was lifecasting, my response to every single thing that came across my plate was being broadcast and analyzed and, perhaps remixed and copied, or inspiring somebody else. And so as somebody who has—kind of—planned on being in the music business, the concept of living your life in the public eye was not completely foreign to me; but living it in such a way that every single thing you were doing could have an impact (whether it be negative or positive) on somebody's actual life all of a sudden became a huge responsibility . . . even above and beyond the content that I was putting out musically. . . .

Even if you think about trying a new product, you know . . . (laughter) and I was trying a new product live on the air, and somebody would see it either being really great or really bad. And I guarantee (and I'm not trying to jump around here) that what is really interesting is that . . . in, say, trying new coffeemakers in the lobby of my apartment complex, we would go out every morning and we would get this coffee. And because the lifecast also had a chat room attached to it, it was real-time feedback from people that were participating in the chat. And so you can actually count and monitor how many times a specific brand name is mentioned in the chat. And you can then monitor what types of questions are being asked about your brand. You can monitor every time somebody says, "Hey, I bought this specific product because you tried it in your lifecast and you said it was good." And so you become a brand ambassador of sorts, of every single brand that you pick up in your life. And the lifecasting, in that sense, is a really powerful brand-integration model in that sense . . . [something] you will see a lot more of in the coming years in terms of what's being put out there on the Internet.

And community marketing, in general—where the community is actually . . . I don't want to say *celebrities* . . . the community, the spokespeople, the brand ambassadors. And it becomes less about celebrities and more about trusted community members giving their thumbs up, too. We already see it now; but I think even more so as lifecasting and as citizen journalism become

(*continued*)

(continued)

more of the valid form for the rest of the media world to pick up on and embrace, we will see a lot more of that kind of integration in the marketing in general. It's very powerful!

I think if your friend told you to go see a movie because it was the best movie he had ever seen, you would go see that movie over and above and beyond Tom Cruise getting on the television and then saying, "It's the best movie I've ever seen!" Because you have a bond with your friend. . . .

To listen to or read the entire Executive Conversation with Jody Gnant, go to www.theSocialMediaBible.com.

International Perspective

New Zealand

Getting Social in Business—the Kiwi way!

A snapshot of social media adoption and interaction among businesses in New Zealand.

At 91 percent, New Zealand has one of the highest broadband penetration levels in the world,[1] which ranks Kiwis among the most digitally connected people in the online world.

Likewise, the social media phenomenon has gone main stream across the nation, garnering regular usage among professionals and businesses alike. With smartphone penetration fast rising and ultra-fast broadband on its way, it will only increase.

With New Zealand internet user statistics currently at 3,600,000,[2] Twitter still maintains its novelty and growing, LinkedIn adds two new members per second worldwide, YouTube still accounts for half of all videos viewed, and Facebook leads among social networks with 2.1 million users in New Zealand.[3] Business blogs, location-based services (Foursquare) and social gaming apps (Smallworlds.com) are gaining traction and tipped to pick up in 2012.

The first commercial wave hit NZ shores in early 2008, with large local businesses like Air New Zealand, Telecom and Vodafone dipping their toes in social media to maximize customer outreach.

Some early adopters, mainly SMEs and owner-operated businesses, gainfully put social media to work in NZ. Here are their success stories and strategies that found the sweet spot:

- **Bullet PR** (now owned by Ogilvy NZ): A pioneering PR firm that has made a significant contribution to social media in New Zealand by organizing major international social media conferences (Social Media Junction 1 and 2); business networking events (Media Mingle); and founding Social Media Club Auckland in 2010—the local chapter of the popular worldwide movement www.SocialMediaClub.org.

- **Giapo**: a gelato store has created an empire of fans, friends, and followers; organizing marathons, running charity drives, crowd sourcing ice-cream flavors, while making the yummiest gelato in NZ.

- **Urgent Couriers**: a local network built a top brand as NZ's only carbon-neutral courier with a killer reputation for on-time delivery, quality customer service, and speed of response.

- **Real Estate NZ**: achieved a remarkable turnaround as to how a staid business sector got "social media-savvy," going from logs to blogs, and roadmaps to mobile apps.

- **The Wine Vault** via Jayson Bryant, a fine case of a wine business and personal branding working in tandem, leveraging the power of YouTube.

- **syENGAGE**: a specialist social media consultancy focused on creating business value via social engagement. With a reputation as the go-to resource for social media best practice, they deliver solutions in content creation and curation, training and education, and marketing, planning, and strategy.

Apart from salient "social media in business" case studies in 2011 such as Air NZ's Mile-High madness in-flight viral video, ASB Bank's virtual branch on Facebook, and NZTA's "Ghost Chips" anti-drink and driving campaign, social media usage reached its peak in 2011 during the Rugby World Cup and NZ Elections. However, the biggest ever social media stories in NZ remain the earthquakes in Christchurch.

(continued)

(continued)

Top social media influencers in NZ: Giapo, John Lai, Justin Flitter, Linda Coles, and Simon Young.

—Amar Trivedi
amar@syengage.com twitter:@Mr_Madness
LinkedIn: nz.linkedin.com/in/trivediamar
Blog: www.MrSocial1.blogspot.com

Statistics Sources

[1]World Internet Project New Zealand (Jul–Aug 2011)

[2]Internet World Stats (August 2011)

[3]SocialBakers.com

To-Do List

- Explore livecasting.
  Go and explore some of the websites mentioned in the chapter. Take a look at what Justin Kan has done with Justin.tv.

Take a look at Alan Levy's BlogTalkRadio. Sign up for an account. Get to understand what options are out there for when you are ready to create your own radio or television show.

- Get a webcam.
  Go on, get a webcam and try it out. You can buy one for around $25. In fact, some laptops even have cameras built in to the screen. If

nothing else, try a video chat with some friends or colleagues. Become comfortable with the technology. The next time you are on the road, try livecasting with your family, a friend, or a coworker. You will be surprised how different it is when you're able to see the person with whom you're speaking while away from your home or office.

- Try a webinar or your own radio show.

  Produce and perform a webinar. Create one for your prospects. Always keep the "What's in It for Me"? WIIFM content in mind. Present your slides, have some real-time audio, and be sure to have some live text chat. You'll be surprised how differently your prospects will view you and your company.

- Try a web conference.

  Try setting up a web conference the next time you need to meet with colleagues—even if they are only on the other side of town. You can use iChat if you are a Macintosh aficionado, or AOL AIM on either platform. All you need is an inexpensive webcam and a free account. Again—like the sports shoe slogan says, "Just Do It!"

Conclusion

Whether you're someone like Justin, Justine, or Jody, or just someone who wants to build a community of trusted followers—or if you ever wished you had your own talk radio or television show—then you need to explore livecasting. A friend of one of the author's does a weekly show every Friday at noon, and over the past year, he has built a fan base of more than 5,000 people. While that number won't get the attention of the *New York Times,* it certainly is a great personal, loyal, trusted network of potential book buyers for his next novel.

What if you did a weekly radio show in which you interviewed industry experts (like the Expert Insights on www.theSocialMediaBible.com)?

How would your customers and prospects perceive you and your company—even if you only did it a few times?

Invite your prospects to a webinar during which you talk about something important to them (always remember the WIIFM factor). Discuss new legislation, an innovative product or service, maintenance tips, installation, your development or manufacturing team, or a message from the president or CEO. This step will really humanize your company, and put a face on an otherwise faceless corporate entity. The best way to build trust is to talk with your customers and prospects.

And like the other social media tools, it only takes some time and creativity.

To hear all of the Expert Interviews, go to www.theSocialMediaBible .com.

Downloads

For your free downloads associated with *The Social Media Bible,* go to www .theSocialMediaBible.com,

and enter your ISBN number located on the back of the book above the bar code. Be sure to enter the dashes.

Credits

The ROI of Social Media was provided by:

Chad Herman, www.thinkbigkansascity.com

Expert Insight was provided by:

Jody Gnant, singer, songwriter, and community marketer, www.jodygnant
.com

Technical edits were provided by:

Walt Ribeiro, www.ForOrchestra.com

Notes

1. Stream/streaming/multicast occurs when Internet-rich audio or video content is continuously uploaded and fed into your computer as you listen to or watch it. It is the opposite of the typical on-demand file downloading, wherein you have to wait for the entire file to be downloaded to your computer before you can play it. Streaming can deliver live, real-time content, or prerecorded podcast-type files (see Chapters 9 through 13 for more information on these topics). With livecasting, the audio and video content is broadcast live and is playing in real time; the listener/viewer has no control over the broadcast, as in traditional broadcast media.

2. Howard Kurtz, "With BlogTalkRadio, the Commentary Universe Expands," *Washington Post,* March 24, 2008; www.washingtonpost.com/wp-dyn/content/article/2008/03/23/AR2008032301719_pf.html

3. David Levine, "All Talk?" Condé Nast's Portfolio.com, February 26, 2008; www.portfolio.com?/?culture-lifestyle?/?goods?/?gadgets?/?2008?/02/26/Internet-Talk-Radio?page=0 and http://bit.ly/GDZZtP.

4. Kurtz, "With BlogTalkRadio."

5. The term *webinar* was actually registered by Eric R. Korb in 1998 with the United States Patent and Trademark Office, but was too difficult to defend, so the term is in common use today.

CHAPTER 15

Virtual Worlds—Real Impact

www.LonSafko.com/TSMB3_Videos/15VirtualWorlds.mov

What's in It for You?

Any time you can become part of a "trusted network with a million-plus people in it," don't you want to be part of that—especially if you have similar interests?

In an interview, the CEO of Linden Labs, Mark Kingdon, said that Second Life—the 3-D virtual world created by Linden Research Inc.—experiences more than 990,000 logins every 30 days, with more than two billion user-created items stored on the Linden servers. That sounds like the ultimate in *trusted network* and *user-generated content*. Second Life is only one of many three-dimensional gamelike virtual worlds or environments, but it is the largest virtual world without a gaming foundation. And according to Mark, when Google and its many resources create Lively, their own virtual environment—they are "validating the virtual world market." When these types of huge companies are inventing in this type of a social environment, there must be a reason.

In addition to being a fun, entertaining way to pass the time, virtual worlds give you the opportunity to browse new and unexplored domains, visualize and participate in imaginary communities, and do business in a virtual marketplace with real customers and colleagues. With companies like IBM, Coldwell Banker, Dell, Armani, Ben & Jerry's, BMW, Cisco, Coca-Cola, and Domino's Pizza doing business in Second Life, there is most likely a good reason for *you* to be there as well.

theSocialMediaBible.com

Back to the Beginning

Virtual worlds began with simulators, which were three-dimensional graphic representations of a virtual, or simulated, environment. Then in 1968, Internet pioneer Ivan Sutherland developed the first computer-based virtual reality.

During the 1980s and 1990s, the author, Lon Safko, worked independently on his own, commercially available virtual environmental system called SoftVoice (later renamed SenSei when ported from the Apple II to the Macintosh Platform in 1986). While Lanier, Furness, and Wise's system was intended for F-15 fighter pilots and astronauts to perform complex repair without the need of dangerous spacewalks, SenSei was developed to help the physically disabled access computer technology and their environment (see SoftVoice/SenSei, discussed next).

While developing this virtual reality (VR) platform, Safko was lucky enough to spend a day brainstorming with Dr. Furness and William Gates Sr. at the University of Washington; as Dr. Furness put it, he "had to see a system nearly as elegant as my own . . . especially when mine cost 5 million dollars, and yours can be purchased for 2,500 dollars." As a result of this meeting, Dr. Wise became a member of the corporate board of directors and advisors for Safko International Inc. in 1989 and provided a great deal of support and industry knowledge. He and John Williams, the author of the Americans with Disabilities Act, helped guide Safko International through the late 1980s and into the 1990s during the turbulent times of rights for the disabled and by advising on technology applications that helped the severely disabled.

The application of this three-dimensional virtual world I created is the very first as an operating system for the Apple II, then Macintosh computers, and was intended to help the disabled and to teach individuals who had never used a computer before how to access its technology. It's hard to imagine today that during the early-to-mid-1980s most people had never used a computer before. And by definition, a disabled person had never used a computer because of physical disabilities.

I designed the SenSei System so that a user with no computer experience could sit down at a computer, look at the screen, and intuitively know what to do next. If she wanted to type, she selected the typewriter; to place a telephone call, she selected the telephone; to turn on the lights, select the light; to turn off the television, select the television; and so on.

The SenSei System included a collection of world's firsts, such as the fully graphic virtual environment operating system, first voice recognition, environmental control, telephone control, nurse call, all-in-one IR media control, electronic hospital bed control, software version user guides, and even ToolTips, the little window that pops up when you place your cursor over a button and get an explanation of what that button does.

The SenSei System later became the archetype for the Apple Newton (first PDA ever) and Microsoft's "Bob" operating system. The original SenSei operating system code and hardware now reside in the Computer History Museum, in Mountain View, California; Apple Computer Inc., Cupertino, California; the U.S. Library of Congress and the Museum of American History, Smithsonian Institution, Washington, DC; and I am credited as the designer of the first computer to save a human life (http://invention .smithsonian.org/resources/fa_safko_index.aspx).

Figures 15.1 through 15.3 are examples of the SenSei System and the work I did with the first commercially available three-dimensional virtual environment operating system.

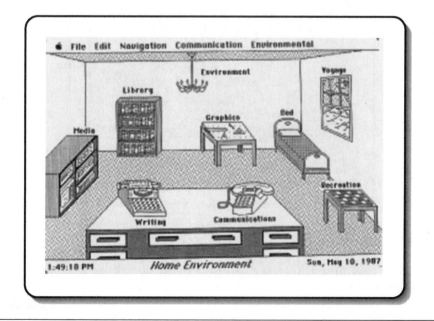

FIGURE 15.1   Lon's SenSei Operating System, 1987

FIGURE 15.2   The SenSei Operating System, 1992

FIGURE 15.3   The SenSei Operating System, 1994

Figures 15.4 and 15.5 are examples of Microsoft's "Bob" OS and the Apple Newton OS.

Figure 15.6, taken from my Sensei Operating System, is the SenSei Library, 1987, and Figure 15.7 is the new Apple iPad Library.

FIGURE 15.4   Microsoft's "Bob" Operating System, 1995

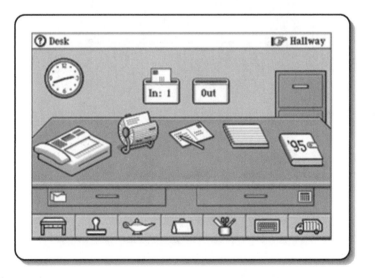

FIGURE 15.5   The Apple Newton Operating System, 1993

FIGURE 15.6 The SenSei Library, 1987

The first three-dimensional MMOG or MMORG (the acronyms for Massively Multiplayer Online Game or Massively Multiplayer Online Role-Playing Game, coined by the developer of Ultimate Online Richard Garriott in 1997) virtual environment was created more than 35 years ago. In these MMOGs, participants would play the role of the main fictional character, and were challenged with obstacles that needed to be overcome in order to advance their status in the game. This first game was called the Maze Game, Maze War—or simply "The Maze." The avatars or representations of the player were eyeballs, and the environment was a

FIGURE 15.7 The Apple iPad Library

three-dimensional wire-frame maze. The Maze was played on the original Internet—a network of computers called ARPAnet—and could be played only on an Imlac computer, which was the first networked graphics workstation, which debuted in 1970.

During an MMOG, a large number of players interact with one another in a virtual world meant to resemble the real world. This game-culture social interaction and competition motivates users to keep coming back. Most of the earlier games were similar to the more traditional Dungeons & Dragons, which remains the best-known and best-selling role-playing game, with an estimated 20 million people having played it and more than $1 billion in related book and equipment sales. The two most popular MMOGs today are Blizzard Entertainment's World of Warcraft and Microsoft's Halo 3 (designed by Bungie Studios).

On October 4, 2007, Microsoft announced that Halo 3 had officially become a global phenomenon, garnering more than $300 million in sales in the first week alone. The critically acclaimed Xbox 360 exclusive, which was released worldwide on September 25, 2004, was "the fastest-selling video game ever—and one of the most successful entertainment properties in history." Microsoft went on to claim:

> Halo 3 is quickly staking its place as the most popular Xbox LIVE game in history with members gathering in record numbers to play on the world's largest online gaming and entertainment network on TV. More than 2.7 million gamers have played Halo 3 on Xbox LIVE in the first week, representing nearly one-third of the seven million Xbox LIVE members worldwide. Within the first day of its launch, Halo 3 players racked up more than 3.6 million hours of online game play, which increased more than eleven-fold to more than 40 million hours by the end of the first week—representing more than 4,500 years of continuous game play.[1]

(You can read more about gaming in the next chapter, Chapter 16, Gaming the System: Virtual Gaming.)

SoftVoice/SenSei

While certainly not the first virtual world, SenSei was the first commercially available virtual environment created to give the severely disabled access to a computer and their environment around them. I created this project back in 1986; it was called SoftVoice, which stood for Voice Activated Software. It later became known as the SenSei System, and it was originally designed so that those with physical limitations could access a computer and other elements of their environment, such as lamps, telephones, and even electronic hospital bed controls. The first system ran on the most sophisticated and widely used computer at the time: the Apple II.

SenSei allowed its users to access all of its functions through voice commands. Once developed, the system was quickly redesigned for the new Macintosh computer. It used its distinctively different graphic operating system to navigate a virtual environment, which allowed access to the software functions of the computer by selecting, for example, a typewriter for word processing, a telephone to make a call, or a lamp or radio to turn on and off electric appliances. The user could control the computer navigation by moving one's head to activate a head-mouse, or simply by speaking the task they wished to perform. This gave the physically disabled—as well as any computer novice—the capacity to use a computer with little or no knowledge of how one operated, which was important in 1985.

Many original technologies spun off from my SenSei's decade-long development, including the first fully graphic operating system, the first PDA, the Apple Newton OS, the Microsoft operating system "Bob," voice-activated environmental control, electronic hospital bed control, infrared television and media control (voice-activated all-in-one controller), the first-ever software user's guides, tool tips by which you place your cursor over a button and a window pops up to tell you what that button does, and more.

I personally had the pleasure of working with Steve Wozniak's post-Apple start-up, Cloud Nine, the company that developed the first all-in-one-controller for infrared devices such as TVs, radios, VCRs, and stereos. Because the device had an RS-232 connection inside its case, crossover into the virtual world of the computer operating system was possible, using the real-life control of media equipment.

As with the wheelchair ramp and other disabled accommodations, many of these inventions—and their significant contribution to society—became mainstream. Eighteen of them and 30,000 of my personal papers are now housed in the permanent collection of the Museum of American History, Smithsonian Institution, in Washington, DC, along with 14 more inventions maintained by the Computer History Museum in Mountain View, California.

Second Life

Philip Rosedale founded Linden Research Inc. in 1999 after conducting some early tests with virtual worlds while studying physics at the University of California at San Diego. Many believe that Neal Stephenson's novel *Snow Crash* inspired Philip to create Second Life (even though Rosedale claims that he had imagined the concept before reading the book).

FIGURE 15.8   Lon Safko in the Virtual World, Second Life
(http://slurl.com/secondlife/pinastri/215/8/21, and http://bit.ly.t8WF3r)

Rosedale set out to develop a VR system that would allow its users to become fully immersed in a 360-degree virtual world experience. He produced the Rig—a large, slow, expensive, and difficult to wear and use system. However, the Rig eventually evolved into the Internet software Linden World, which was designed to allow its users to play games and socialize with other users in a 3-D online environment. Linden World then grew into today's Second Life (SL) software experience.

The key to SL's success came as Rosedale observed participants at an investors' meeting gravitating toward the social, collaborative, and creative nature of Second Life. This inspired Rosedale to see the importance of focusing more intently on the user-generated content and social networking aspects of his project—the very aspects that made Second Life such a success.

Second Life launched on June 23, 2003, and was closely followed by the unveiling of a 3-D virtual world intended for younger audiences, Teen Second Life. While Second Life caters to members over the age of 18, Teen Second Life is restricted to members between 13 and 18. With child online security as important as it is, the age restrictions are closely monitored. Teen Second Life was dismantled in 2010, with 16- to 18-year-olds being allowed onto the main grid, but restricted to areas designated PG. 13- to 16-year-olds are allowed access to the grid but only through an approved third-party organization and registration, and access is restricted to the region or simulator controlled by that third party.

What You Need to Know

A virtual world, or virtual environment, is usually an Internet-based simulated environment inhabited by avatars, or graphic representations, of its interactive users. An avatar can be represented textually, by a photograph, logo, image, or a 3-D cartoonlike person, animal, or object. While not all virtual worlds are 3-D, many began as forums, blogs, and chat rooms in which communities and trusted networks were created.

Figure 15.9 shows examples of two avatars used in Second Life—those of Mark Kingdon, CEO of Linden Labs, creator of Second Life, and Lon Safko. Mark's photo is on the left; his avatar is to Lon's right.

FIGURE 15.9 Kingdon and Safko Avatars. Mark Kingdon, CEO of Linden Labs (Second Life), and Lon Safko (author) avatars discussing social media.

www.LonSafko.com/TSMB3_Videos/Kingdon_Safko_Interview.mov

Virtual worlds are often mistaken for user-immersed games in which players navigate their way through a simulated environment, shooting, fighting, and interacting with other players' avatars (that are controlled either by humans or the game itself) with the goal of winning or overcoming a pre-determined challenge. While virtual worlds may appear similar to and were inspired by these types of games, they are designed to serve a completely dissimilar purpose. There is no game-winning objective in a virtual world. Virtual worlds are designed for people from around the world—and their avatars—to enter into, navigate, and interrelate by engaging in personal, one-on-one communications. The intent of a virtual world is to encourage users to explore, learn, interact, do business, meet, and make friends with new, multicultural people from around the world that they otherwise might never have had the opportunity to encounter. Virtual worlds may appear to be sim-ulated versions of the real world, an accurate re-creation of part of the real world, or even an Alice-in-Wonderland-type fantasyland where reality has no place. Immersing oneself in this virtual world—or *metaverse*—environment is referred to as having a *telepresence*.

Virtual Economy

Most of these worlds have even gone so far as to create and develop their own virtual economic systems. Second Life, for example, has a currency called the Linden Dollar (L$). While Lindens are fictitious and only nego-tiable within the confines of Second Life, the people at Linden Labs have made it possible to put real money into the virtual world and withdraw it as well; the Second Life economy does translate into real-world money. Not all virtual worlds have the same capability. By setting up an account with PayPal or registering a credit card, the Second Life member can transact actual business. You can go to the mall and "buy" clothes, new hair, or even a car using Lindens (L$). Once the transactions have taken place, your credit card is charged (or credited), at the then going rate of Lindens per one U.S. dollar, and you don't need to be a vendor or own a shopping cart; you only need to be a resident with a credit card. Virtual products can include buildings, vehicles, animations, clothing, skin, hair, jewelry, plants, and furniture—almost anything that you can find in that environment. At the time this chapter was written, the exchange rate for buying Lindens was L$249.00 in real-world money and L$184 per dollar at the LindenX Exchange on the Second Life website. Selling Lindens at the LindenX Exchange could be done at $1 for L$258.00 pulled out of Second Life. Linden Labs has even gone to the extent of recording and complying with a value-added tax (VAT) for many European countries.

While an exchange rate in which you can purchase a suit for $5 or new hair for 75 cents may seem small, many people have actually made money in this virtual world. In fact, at least one person became a millionaire. In November 2007, *BusinessWeek* ran an article by Rob Hof entitled "Second Life's First Millionaire," which told the story of Anshe Chung. Hof's article stated, "Anshe Chung's achievement is remarkable because the fortune was developed over a period of two and a half years from an initial investment of $9.95 for a Second Life. Chung (Ailin Graef, Second Life Persona) achieved her fortune by beginning with small-scale purchases of virtual real estate that she then subdivided and developed with landscaping and themed architecture for rental and resale. Her operations have since grown to include the development and sale of properties for large-scale real-world corporations, and have led to a real-life spinoff corporation called Anshe Chung Studios, which develops immersive 3-D environments for applications ranging from education to business conferencing and product prototyping." (To read the rest of this article, go to www.business week.com/the_thread/techbeat/archives/2006/11/second_lifes_fi.html.)

While stories like Chung's make for good press, few people have found this kind of fortune in a virtual world. However, it *is* possible. In Second Life Mainland, prices run about $11.50 per square meter (at the time this chapter was written), and more for island and waterfront property. Properties are around 640,000 square meters on average, 410,000 of which are bought and sold by Groups each day—which equals roughly 1,050,000 square meters, or 16 regions, of Mainland land that is bought and sold daily.

At the time this chapter was written, there were over more than 2,000 square kilometers of virtual land in Second Life, with a sales economy worth over US $4.5 million per quarter.

Enterprise in Second Life

Many enterprises now have a presence in Second Life. Most people still don't completely understand how businesses can make money in a virtual world, but three things are clear: Some are doing it; some will figure it out; and merely having a presence in Second Life can give a company great brand recognition. As CEO of Linden Labs Mark Kingdon states, companies are using the Second Life platform for gauging customer reaction, receiving feedback, and testing prototypes; and—in the case of one of the author's own businesses—Paper Models Inc. has a storefront and 3-D displays showing the models adjacent to the Social Media Bible Beach, www .slurl.com/secondlife/Pinastri/215/8/21,

and selling some "first-life" products. This was an interesting transformation for Paper Models, which is now selling electron-based (PDF) items to real people through the Internet for real profits—versus selling virtual products in a virtual store to virtual avatars that simply represented real people. This kind of engagement in Second Life gives companies a significant competitive advantage. (To listen to the entire Mark Kingdon interview, go to www.theSocialMediaBible.com.)

Some businesses are also using the metaverse as a meeting place as well—for customers, prospects, and even employees. IBM has utilized Second Life on a regular basis as a forum for their engineers from around the globe to meet, exchange ideas, or see PowerPoint presentations—while never having to leave their respective offices. During a project in 2007, Lon used Second Life to meet with paper model developers from Ukraine.

FIGURE 15.10   American Cancer Society's Memory Tree in Second Life

In fact, the first time in scheduling a call with developers—to discuss the American Cancer Society's Kiosk Design—it came as such a surprise to the author to actually hear the voice of Roman Vasilev, a developer with whom the author had been working for over two years through e-mail and the Internet. Up to that point, they had been able to only speak with each other virtually and exchange ideas and concepts in real time—and for free.

Sun Microsystems is another example of a company that has created its own island in Second Life dedicated solely to employee use. Their virtual island is a place where employees can go to seek help from colleagues, exchange new ideas, or advertise an innovative product. The American Cancer Society has its own in-world presence with its help island, which was established to raise awareness and provide support for this widespread, life-threatening illness. Paper Models was honored to sponsor and participate in ACS's Island Dedication in the fall of 2007 (http://maps.secondlife.com/secondlife/American%20Cancer%20Society/128/128/25; http://bit.ly/GBB8EI),

an event that accompanied the free distribution of a 3-D model of its landmark in-world Memory Tree, a virtual tree that is surrounded by small flashes of light (see Figure 15.10). Each flash of light represents the memory of someone who has passed away from cancer. While on the island, you can download a PDF, print it, and—with a little glue and scissors—re-create the virtual ACS Memory Tree in real life. (To download your free ACS Memory Tree, go to www.papermodelsonline.com/acstree.html.)

Lon was also given the chance to work with ACS member Steven Groves (Estaban Graves in Second Life) and ACS in sponsoring an International ACS Donation Kiosk Design Contest. Second Life developers from around the world competed in creating the most imaginative freestanding kiosk through which residents within Second Life could pledge donations to help fight cancer (see Figure 15.11). Dozens of entries were submitted; the winner was announced at the 2008 ACS's Second Life Relay for Life Launch Event. (Go to www.papermodelsonline.com/amcasodokiin.html

to download your free copy of the ACS Kiosk winner paper model.) Two monumental events took place at this event, in addition to presenting the winner of this contest. First, in anticipating a good turnout for the event, Linden Labs agreed to assign additional servers to accommodate the high level of computation and distribution of data needed to bring

FIGURE 15.11   The ACS Kiosk Design Finalists in Second Life

so many avatars together at one time. Even with this precaution, so many avatars (residents) participated in this event that Linden Labs' servers were taken down and Second Life shut off until they were able to reboot. The second phenomenal occurrence was that the American Cancer Society raised more than $200,000 in real cash for its research at the 2008 Relay For Life in Second Life, up from $120,000 in 2007. (Be sure to visit the American Cancer Society's Island for this year's events.) Besides making some history and raising a significant amount in donations for a great cause, Paper Models had fun, garnered a great deal of publicity, and is now branded as having a presence in both first-life and Second Life.

At the time this chapter was written, other companies that were utilizing Second Life to conduct their business were 20th Century Fox, Armani, Avnet Inc., BBC Radio, Ben & Jerry's, Cisco, Coca-Cola, CNN, Coldwell Banker, Creative Commons, Dell, Disney, Domino's Pizza, IBM, ING Group, Mazda, MTV, Reuters, Starwood Hotels, Toyota, Wells Fargo, Paper Models Inc., and John Wiley & Sons. As an example, Wiley has a bookstore in Second Life in which you can go, sit, and meet other book lovers. Many of the companies mentioned here pay someone to represent them 24/7/365, so when you walk into their building, an avatar (with a real person operating them) will greet you and answer any questions you have about their product or service.

The Social Media Bible in Second Life

You guessed it. *The Social Media Bible* has oceanfront property in Second Life. Pinastri, 215/8/21—http://slurl.com/secondlife/Pinastri/215/8/21

—is what is referred to as a Second Life URL, or "SLURL." It can be typed/ pasted into a standard web browser, and if you have a Second Life account, it will take you and your avatar there right away. This makes it easier to connect a Second Life location to the 2D web browser. *The Social Media Bible* gives away a virtual device here that is called a HUD (Heads Up Display) at the back of the garden, where you can take it and listen to any of the Executive Conversation podcasts while continuing to explore the garden— or anywhere else in Second Life. *The Social Media Bible* will continue to build the content of the Social Media Garden so it becomes a virtual world resource for all things social media. Just go to the SL address given earlier and select the SLURL; or go in-world in Second Life and look for the group "Social Media Bible Evangelists."

Your Own Second Life

Second Life appears as an example throughout this chapter since it is the most popular virtual world platform in use today. Even Google had decided to compete in this space, as mentioned earlier, with their newest virtual world, Lively. To understand how a virtual world works, Second Life will remain as an example. See *The Social Media Bible* in Second Life (Figure 15.12).

To participate in Second Life, you can simply visit Second Life.com and download a program that allows you to enter this virtual world. This program, client, or viewer is free. Once you create your account (also free), you become a resident of Second Life. Now you are able to explore, interact with other residents, participate, learn, create, buy, socialize, and network.

Second Lifers refer to their world as *the grid*, which is divided into 256-by-256-meter areas of land called *regions*, or *sims* (short for simulators).

FIGURE 15.12   *The Social Media Bible* Headquarters in Second Life
(http://slurl.com/secondlife/pinastri/215/8/21)

Each region is created and housed on a single computer server and is assigned a unique name and content rating—either PG, Mature, or Adult. While in SL or on the grid, your avatar can get around by walking, running, jumping, or riding in vehicles. Your avatar can also fly and quickly jump from one region of the grid or one place to another, or you can teleport—TP—directly to that location.

The ability to create virtual objects such as chairs, clothes, and even buildings from primitive shapes called *prims* is also built into Second Life. A scripting language called LSL (Linden Scripting Language) is similar to C++ programming language. LSL allows Second Lifers to add behaviors to these objects, like having avatars cross their legs when sitting on a chair. Other options to create more complex 3-D virtual objects are sculpties, mesh, textures, and animations. A *sculptie* is short for *sculpted prim*, which is a prim whose shape is created by an array of x, y, and z coordinates. Sculpties are used to create more complex, organic shapes for virtual goods.

Figure 15.13 shows an example of cows and horses created using sculpties.

FIGURE 15.13   Sculpties Design Elements in Second Life

A mesh is a more traditional wire frame 3-D model created in applications such as Blender (http//blender.org)

allowing more versatile models to be introduced to the grid.

The Avatar

The Second Life avatar often has a cartoonlike, yet slightly human appearance and may be male, female, or androgynous—in the case of an avatar being a boat, mythical creature, or even a pile of rocks. Avatars may be casually dressed, in a tuxedo, or wearing wildly ornate costumes that users can change at any time. You can even pay a service to take your photograph and create a skin that looks exactly like you do in real life, but many residents just choose to display themselves as their alter ego. An avatar's real identity is anonymous; you cannot access any personal details about an avatar's identity (a precaution that was implemented to provide age verification and to protect children).

Avatars can communicate through instant messaging (IM)–type text chat. They can alternately use a voice chat component that allows users to actually speak aloud to a computer's microphone using Voice over Internet Protocol (VoIP)[2] to transfer the two-way voice in real-time communications. Avatars are also able to send and receive e-mail, and their instant messages will roll over to an avatar's real-life e-mail when they log off if they choose to select this option. (See the Mark Kingdon Executive Conversation video at www.theSocialMediaBible.com.)

Expenses in Second Life

Even though this book continually touts the low- and no-cost benefits of social media, Linden Labs has adopted—as have most companies in the social media ecosphere—a freemium business model. (If you want to just browse and explore, however, your account is completely free.) Second Life offers a Premium Membership for $9.95 per month that entitles its users to own a small amount of land up to 512 square meters without additional fees, or a prebuilt house. It provides extra technical support and a salary or stipend of L$300 per week. If you own larger areas of land, you will incur additional rent or a land use fee. Most members refer to this fee as a *tier*, since this is the manner in which it is charged—tiers that range from $5 per month or more depending upon the amount of land you own. As a member, you can choose to purchase land from another member or resident directly.

You can also purchase a different type of land that is known as a private estate. This usually consists of one or more private islands or regions, and has a completely separate set of regulations and pricing policies. A private region is 65,536 square meters (about 16 acres), and costs $1,000 to purchase with a $295 per month maintenance fee. Included in the ownership of a private estate is the member's ability to alter the terrain of the land.

Second Life Stats

Second Life had a banner year in 2008. There were 16,785,531 registered Second Life residents spending more than US $100 million on virtual goods and services, and participating in more than 397 million hours in the world. The residents bought and sold more than 43,965,696 square meters of land with a total of 1.76 billion square meters of land owned by its residents, and as many as 76,000 residents logged on at any one time. See http://bit.ly/oI67Pn,

www.secondlife.com/whatis/economy_stats.php,

or go to www.theSocialMediaBible.com for "clickable links."

The Viewer

You can browse SL using many browsers . . . the original one, the new viewer 3.0, the open-source official snow globe, and the very popular Phoenix/Firestorm, and others. . . . It is hugely worthy of mention that Linden Labs has provided open source code and allowed developers to improve their viewer—and that they have implemented those improvements into the official viewer with regularity.

The ROI of Social Media

Take It to the Social Media Streets: How Infusionsoft Builds Brand, Buzz, and Super-Sizes Serving Customers through Social Media

Background

Infusionsoft has a very robust combined e-mail marketing, CRM, and marketing automation application that nearly 20,000 users rely on to power their marketing activities. The Gilbert, Arizona–based company is poised to grow to support hundreds of thousands of small business users and desire to expand their footprint through social media. Key motives to leverage social media include brand awareness, participate in industry discussions, provide non-linear support, and introduce lead-generation opportunities for the business.

As a growing business in a highly competitive small business market, we addressed the challenge of raising industry awareness on a lean marketing and communications operation. Social media has delivered results to yield serious merit and mojo to Infusionsoft's marketing, lead generation, and brand-building abilities.

Strategy

Infusionsoft's social media efforts began with its roots in community forums. After facilitating user forums that invoked many discussions across its user base and employees, the company in late 2008 decided to expand their efforts to outside social networking applications such as blogging, Twitter, LinkedIn, YouTube, and Facebook.

The company discovered the Infusionsoft blog experienced limited growth due to frequency of updates, lack of hard-hitting topics, and lack of variety of authors and content. Faced with the clear-cut opportunity to grow and utilize the blog as a communications hub that could engage customers, prospects, and market influencers in a dynamic way, the company's executive leadership gave the community manager the green light to launch a focused and sustained social media–centric effort. This was the turning point for the company to focus on the merits of social media more seriously than before.

Foci of the social strategy included presence throughout industry conversations and emerging as a thought leader on the topics of e-mail marketing, customer follow-up, and marketing strategies. Target demographic included solo entrepreneurs, small businesses with 25 or fewer employees and who were already using the web to drive their marketing activities. Valuable content and unique perspective was a key component to its success. One requirement of the strategy is to give room for flexibility and agility to monitor and address topics prevalent in industry discussions and pertinent to the brand itself.

Implementation

We established our blog as the hub of our social media execution. Later, [we] expanded our Twitter and Facebook presence. We continued to identify social media outposts such as LinkedIn, Mahalo, YouTube, and other social network profiles.

To make our social media activities and practices known, we educated all employees about our social media program and have a very open policy for how employees engage in social media. We believe cross-division engagement is key to the level of participation the company has in social media.

Opportunity

Listening to and engaging in the conversation happening online around small business growth and e-mail marketing presents a huge opportunity for Infusionsoft, both internally and externally. Our activities in social networking enable market research, competitive intelligence, and lead generation just by listening to what people are talking about on key topics. We view Twitter and Facebook as key sites where the conversation is abundant and the opportunity to listen and engage is limitless. There's a real opportunity to showcase Infusionsoft's expertise and knowledge as thought leaders in e-mail marketing, CRM, and small business growth in an authentic way. Additionally, we leverage sites like Twitter and Facebook to enhance customer service and support so users receive killer service and have their needs met in ways other than simply phone support.

Conclusion

Social media has yielded impressive benefits for Infusionsoft, its users, and the industry at large. We have launched affordable brand-building activities

(continued)

(continued)

that helped gain visibility and relevancy among top industry bloggers, including Anita Campbell, Starr Hall, and our industry competitors, including Aweber, 1ShoppingCart, MailChimp, and the popular marketing community at Warrior Forums. This has positioned our company to be a viable candidate for the growing small business who doesn't have needs—or can afford—midsize platforms like Netsuite or ExactTarget, but has outgrown their current separate e-mail marketing and CRM solution.

We've leveraged the live video streaming service, Ustream, on a number of occasions as a part of our annual user conferences and online educational sessions, attracting several thousand online viewers at our live events. These community engagements attract prospects and satisfy customers from across the globe, giving them a window into Infusionsoft—giving them a sense of exclusivity that recorded videos don't have.

Through continued focus on quality content and sustained quantity, our blog has grown from a Google PageRank of 2 to 5, attracting over 100,000 page views annually. We have tracked revenue from visitors who visited the blog first to becoming active paying subscribers to be over several thousand monthly. Content from the Infusionsoft blog has been featured by top bloggers [leading] to engagement with an ever-increasing amount of customers and prospects.

We monitor our brand 24/7 on Twitter and provide instantaneous support, rapid responses, and manage critical situations with the utmost of care and diligence. We attract more of our prospects toward our Twitter presence. In addition, our Facebook fan page has grown successfully and has a higher affinity with our users on it.

We listen and participate but not facilitate our user-driven groups on LinkedIn. We continue to have lively discussions on our community forum and are mentioned frequently within our industry by thought leaders, analysts, and our loyal users.

—Joseph Manna, community manager, Infusionsoft, www.infusionsoft.com

Expert Insight

Mark Kingdon, chief executive officer, Linden Labs, creators of Second Life, www.SecondLife.com

Mark Kingdon

There's something like 2 billion items in the databases; you know, content and scripts that Second Life residents have created. It's really a powerful platform for co-creation, for collaboration, and just for [generating] amazing things. . . . We do a lot of our meetings *at* Linden Labs inside of Second Life. I would say that I spend anywhere from one to four hours a day in Second Life and—as you can imagine because folks at Linden Labs are so involved in the Second Life experience—we have an amazing array of creative avatars. You can have jellyfish, tugboats, beagles, piles of rocks; it's just an endless array of crazy avatars. It's a blast!

Second Life is a platform and a set of content-creation and collaboration tools that members use to populate this incredible three-dimensional environment—this virtual reality—with immersive experiences. So Second Life is a destination, but it's [one] that's really created by the residents using the platform tools that we provide. And we have had—over the past 60 days, I think—1.2 million logins, as people come to Second Life. So it's a really rich and vibrant community with members from literally every country in the world. . . .

Well, the amazing thing about Second Life is, kind of, the breadth of the use-cases, right? Just like the real world, [Second Life] is incredibly diverse; [and] the audience—or the user base—is incredibly diverse [as well]. So the use-cases are as broad in Second Life as the experiences would be in the real world. People use Second Life to go to a live music venue and hear a concert in an intimate setting. They use it to go shopping with friends. They use it to create a personal space, like their own home, that they can enjoy in the virtual world. They use it to connect with other people around a common interest, a common concern, a common problem they share. Companies use

(continued)

(continued)

it to work together to create products in a rapid-cycle product-development process, or for virtual meetings, for virtual learning. . . .

It's companies like IBM, Sun, Intel, Dell, Orange, British Telecom, Arcelor Mittal, CIGNA; lots and lots of companies around the world are using Second Life in their business. I saw Arcelor Mittal having a shareholders' meeting in SL. Whether it's CIGNA creating a help island where their customers can connect with health information in a unique way, [or] Cisco doing a developers' conference Q&A in Second Life—the use-cases are really, really broad. [And] it's an amazing way to experience a product before it's built. I think that we've only just started to scratch the surface on the "possible"—right? [Because] up until now I think that we were very much in [an] exploratory phase in the virtual world space. But what we're seeing now is companies who come back a second and third time, trying new ideas, and new approaches to doing business. . . .

One of the things that I can tell you is that we're really working hard to listen to our user base and to understand what our core customers are looking for in the platform. One of the really important customer segments that we want to develop further is the enterprise customer segment; so we've been listening to enterprise customers very closely to understand what their specific needs are. So, as we make adjustments and changes and improvements to the core Second Life platform, it's more supportive of enterprises and educational institutions. I think you should keep your eyes peeled, because as of next year [2009], there are going to be a lot of things that we do with and to the platform to enable business in a substantial way as we continue to support our core audience around the world.

To listen to or read the entire Executive Conversation with Mark Kingdon, go to www.theSocialMediaBible.com.

International Perspective

Cyprus

The importance of Social Media for Cyprus Airways.

The explosion of social networks last decade could not leave Cyprus unaffected. Social media has gradually won over the youth population in Cyprus, who in turn passed the trend on to the rest. Facebook is the most well known and most widely adopted social network in Cyprus. Currently, there are over 500,000 Facebook users in Cyprus.

Social media has gained a significant importance in businesses and has proved to be an effective online medium for marketing strategy, business development, and customer service. Businesses gain visibility and brand credibility to a great extent with this online advertising tool.

Cyprus Airways, keeping up with the market trends and the changes in consumer behavior, have created their own pages on Facebook, Twitter, and YouTube. We are currently concentrating our efforts on Facebook, which is the most popular social media in Cyprus.

We have approximately 8,500 fans and Cyprus Airways' Facebook page is ranked at No. 8 of the most popular Facebook pages in Cyprus.

The importance of social media for Cyprus Airways is tremendous and our aim is to:

- Build a two-way communication with our audience
- Build a strong customer base
- Increase our website traffic
- Enhance brand awareness
- Advertise and market our services, through interactive strategies, i.e. competitions, quizzes, etc.
- Provide up-to-date information on our services (new destinations, new cooperations, and so on)
- Create customer engagement
- Take advantage of a free word of mouth publicity

The fact that we currently run a Facebook competition has helped us to increase our fans approximately by 4,000, in only two weeks. We succeeded

(continued)

(continued)

in making people talk about Cyprus Airway and share with their friends their experience.

—Kiki Haida
Cyprus Airways
CyprusAir.com

Source: www.socialbakers.com

To-Do List

- Try out a virtual world.

  Take a look at a few of the many available virtual world websites, and become a member of one yourself. Sign up for a free membership and use it to explore. Don't be discouraged by the initial difficulty in navigating your way around. It isn't always intuitive, but you can become a pro in no time. The principal skills you need to focus on to have a satisfactory first experience is movement, communication, and how to find things to do that interest you.

- Explore other company's successes.

  Take a look around. Google some of the companies listed throughout this chapter and read about some of their successes. Get ideas about what has worked from them. After researching several companies, you will begin to formulate a plan about what will work for you and your company.

- Explore selling.

  Can you sell your products or services in a virtual world? Should you set up a virtual store? Can you partner with someone who already has a strong presence in a virtual world? Can you cross-promote between first-life and your virtual life? Think about how you might get started marketing and selling in a virtual world to see if it's right for you and your business.

- Explore meetings and training.

  Investigate the idea of holding your next design, sales, or marketing meeting in a virtual world. You must realize that there will be an initial learning curve for everyone, but once you bridge that curve, it's fairly easy from there on out. Maybe HR would like to present; maybe it's a new product or service you want your satellite offices to see. You can even do a PowerPoint-like slide presentation within the virtual world.

- Join the community.

  Take a look at the search menu options, and look for groups with whom you might have common interests within the virtual world of your choice. Find a group that shares a similar interest to yours and meet with them, share ideas, make friends.

Conclusion

The concept of doing business in a virtual world is still new. There is a tremendous opportunity for enterprises to participate in a huge trusted network of like-minded participants—in which many may be prospects. As with most technologies, it's the early adopters that get the home-team advantage. You won't know if marketing in a virtual world is right for you and your company until you explore the concept. Pick a virtual world, sign up for a membership, visit a few in-world businesses, talk to the business owners, talk with their customers, meet other avatars, follow and meet with groups within the community—and better understand how virtual worlds work.

To hear all of the Expert Interviews, go to www.theSocialMediaBible.com.

Downloads

For your free downloads associated with *The Social Media Bible,* go to www .theSocialMediaBible.com,

and enter your ISBN number located on the back of the book above the bar code. Be sure to enter the dashes.

Credits

The ROI of Social Media was provided by:

Joseph Manna, community manager, Infusionsoft, www.infusionsoft.com

Expert Insight was provided by:

Mark Kingdon, chief executive officer, Linden Labs, www.SecondLife.com

Technical edits were provided by:

Ray Robinson, Graham Dartmouth (Second Life),
www.slurl.com/secondlife/Builders%20Brewery/25/196/23

Notes

1. Source: HuliQ News, "Halo 3 Records More Than $300 Million in First-Week Sales Worldwide"; www.huliq.com/36851/halo-3-records-more-than-300-million-in-first-weeksales-worldwide.

2. VoIP, or Voice over Internet Protocol, is the technology used to digitize voice into discrete packets of digital information and transfer or transmit that conversation over the Internet. Vonage is an example of a VoIP long-distance telephone service.

CHAPTER 16

Gaming the System: Virtual Gaming

www.LonSafko.com/TSMB3_Videos/16Gaming.mov

What's in It for You?

Online gaming is another one of those Internet phenomena that just keeps gaining popularity. The trusted networks of the MMORPG—or Massively Multiplayer Online Role-Playing Game—communities are in many cases, in the millions. In fact, Blizzard Entertainment, creators of World of Warcraft, announced recently that the MMORPG game World of Warcraft in October 2010 "now exceeds 12 million players worldwide. World of Warcraft is currently available in eight languages and is played in North America, Europe, mainland China, Korea, Australia, New Zealand, Singapore, Thailand, Malaysia, Indonesia, the Philippines, Chile, Argentina, and the regions of Taiwan, Hong Kong, and Macau."

As of January 11, 2010, Xbox LIVE reached a new milestone, with 30 million active Xbox LIVE members. In fact, a new member joins Xbox LIVE every two seconds. See www.xbox.com/en-US/Press/archive/2011/0112-BiggestYear, and even Barack Obama purchased advertising in the online racing game Burnout Paradise during his 2008 campaign

theSocialMediaBible.com

for the presidency: www.gamepolitics.com/2008/10/09/report-obama-ads-burnout-paradise.

Many people tend to view online video games as an activity with no business value—a waste of time in which only teenagers participate. However, any time you have 50,000 to 8 million people in the same place with the same interests in a trusted network, a business opportunity exists. In fact, only 25 percent of online gamers are teenagers; the average MMORPG player is approximately 26 years old. Fifty percent are employed full-time, 36 percent are married, and 22 percent have children. They include high school and college students, professionals, homemakers, and retired individuals.

On average, they spend 22 hours per week playing these games, and there is no correlation between hours spent playing and age. Sixty percent of all players report that they have played for 10 continuous hours at one time or another. Eighty percent of MMORPG players also play on a regular basis with someone they know in real life such as a romantic partner, family member, or friend. In fact, MMORPGs provide highly social environments in which new relationships are forged and existing relationships are reinforced. Many players report feeling strong emotions while playing, and a recent statistical study showed that 8.7 percent of male and 23.2 percent of female players have even had online weddings. The average MMORPG player is by no means average.

(For more information about online gaming, be sure to also read Chapter 15, Virtual Worlds—Real Impact.)

What You Need to Know

An MMORPG is a genre of computer or Internet games in which a large number of players interact with one another in a virtual world on the Internet. In an MMORPG, players assume the role of a fictional character, often in a fantasy world. This first-person play allows the participant to control the character's actions in an ongoing virtual world—usually hosted by the game's publisher—that continues to exist and evolve. Worldwide revenues for these types of games exceeded a half billion dollars in 2005, with U.S. revenues exceeding $1 billion in 2006.

Features that are common to all MMORPGs are themes, progression, social interaction, culture, and customization of the player's character. Most MMORPG's themes are based on fantasy and science fiction, such as the genre's two most popular games: Lord of the Rings Online, and World of Warcraft. Another subgenre of online games is called FPS, or First Person Shooter, such as Halo 3.

All MMORPGs have some kind of progression for the main character's player, or avatar. You can earn points or capabilities, gain inventory or wealth, or be challenged with more difficult levels. The reverse is true as well; if the main character fails at the challenge—such as combat with another player's character, or with the character generated by the game itself—points are taken away, inventory is lost, and the main character is often forced to go back to the beginning or simplest level. This play/challenge/replay cycle is called the *level treadmill*, or *grinding*.

In an MMORPG, characters are encouraged to communicate with one another, and often team up. By doing so, individual players can offer their skills to other players, which results in many players becoming members—or even leaders—of that particular group. In many MMORPGs, a player's specialized abilities can be categorized as a *tank* (one who absorbs blows and

FIGURE 16.1 World of Warcraft

protects members from the enemy), or a *healer* (who keeps the members of the team healthy). Then there's the *DPS—Damage per Second*—who inflicts damage; the *CC*, or *Crowd Control* character, who temporarily controls the opponent. There is also the *Buffer* or *Debuffer,* who use their abilities to affect opponents. Most players can have one, none, or many of these characteristics. All of these characters interact with the *NPC* (*Non-Player Character*), which is the computer-controlled entity that operates under limited artificial intelligence, or scripts. Some are quest givers, others are Mobs (the enemies that players defeat). Most MMORPGs have a *Game Master,* or *Moderator (GM)*—who is either a paid employee of the publisher or a volunteer from the game. The GM's job is to supervise and manage the game world.

Much like Second Life, MMORPGs run on the publisher's server 24/7/365, which means you can access and play any time of day or night. To play, participants download client software that's able to run on their PCs. The player then connects to the game's world by using the software and the Internet. This software can be made free—as with Second Life—or for purchase, as with World of Warcraft and EverQuest. Some MMORPGs require a monthly subscription, while others are moving to what is called a *thin client,* through which the game can be played without the use of client software, using only a web browser.

Back to the Beginning

As mentioned in the previous chapter on Virtual Worlds, a very fine line exists between participating in online gaming and a virtual environment. Nearly every successful MMORPG today is a role-playing, full-immersion, three-dimensional virtual world scenario. This type of game play dates back to the early 1990s, while the earliest online game—called MazeWar, or the Maze—which was much like the later Pac-Man, in which you maneuvered through a maze while being chased by objects that would harm you—began back in the 1970s (again, see Chapter 15, Virtual Worlds—Real Impact, for more information). The first fully graphical multiplayer game, Neverwinter Nights, a role-playing game (RPG) set in a huge medieval fantasy world of Dungeons & Dragons, hit the Internet in 1991 and received promotion from then-president of America Online (AOL) Steve Case. Then there were MMORPGs from the Sierra Network—the first online multiplayer gaming system—that became popular in the early 1990s, like The Shadow of Yserbius (released in 1992), The Fates of Twinion (1993), and The Ruins of Cawdor (1995).

There are basically three MMORPG business revenue models: pay-to-play, free-to-play with in-game advertising and merchandising, and buy-to-play. Pay-to-play is when the player sets up an account and pays what is usually a monthly subscription to have access to the game. Free-to-play is when a player can log on and just play for free. And buy-to-play is when the player first buys the game, and can then play online for free. Holding the largest pay-to-play MMORPG market share is Blizzard Entertainment's World of Warcraft, followed by Fantasy Westward Journey and Perfect World; see www.forbes.com/sites/velocity/2010/06/10 /top-moneymaking-online-games-of-2009/?partner=yahootix. Titles with large market shares in the free-to-play category are Dungeons & Dragons Online, Maple Story, Rohan, and Blood Feud, with the most popular buy-to-play game being Guild Wars.

Social Impact

Nick Yee (www.nickyee.com),

a research scientist at the Palo Alto Research Center, studies online games and immersive virtual reality. Yee has created something called the Daedalus Project, which he explains as "an ongoing study of MMORPG players. MMORPGs are a video game genre that allows thousands of people to interact, compete, and collaborate in an online virtual environment. Over the past six years, more than 40,000 MMORPG players have participated in the project."

Yee's Daedalus Project has generated some interesting articles, such as "Superstitions: Exploring Superstitions in MMOs and How They Develop" and "Social Architectures in Virtual Worlds: How Do the Rules in Virtual Worlds Encourage Certain Social Behaviors?" Yee makes the following statement in his "Social Architectures" article:

> We tend to think of altruism and gregariousness as personality traits. Some people are more helpful; other people are more chatty.

One reason why I'm fascinated with MMOs is because it seems that game mechanics also change how communities and individuals behave. For example, when people had to ask casters for "binds" (i.e., set their respawn point) in the original EQ, it seemed to help create a cultural norm of asking for help in general. In a way, altruism was not only an aspect of individual players; it was also partly fostered by the game mechanics. This "social architecture" of virtual environments is interesting because it hints at the possibility of shaping community and individual behavior via game mechanics.

Yee sees a potential for human behavior in the real world to change because of the types of behavior that are becoming more acceptable in virtual gaming worlds. By participating in an online world, players can more easily develop and embrace these particular traits and attributes once they've moved from their gaming interactions to those in their everyday lives.

British writer and game researcher Richard Bartle studied multiplayer RPG players and classified them into four primary psychological groups: explorer, socializer, killer, or achiever. Erwin Andreasen (www.andreasen.org)

then expanded Bartle's classifications and developed this concept into the 30-question Bartle Test—which more than 521,112 gamers have taken and which is available on the Gamer DNA website at www.gamerdna.com /quizzes/bartle-test-of-gamer-psychology.

Bartle's and Andreasen data include more than 200,000 of the original responses that Andreasen recorded between the years 1996 and 2006. Originally designed for MUD (multi-user dungeon) participants, it remains relevant to new virtual worlds and MMORPGs. Scoring is interesting and entertaining. The original wording of all questions has not been changed, except to modernize certain terms (such as replacing MUD with the more encompassing MMORPG).

The CDC in MMORPG WoW

Although MMORPG participants invent imaginary characters to play in what are usually considered make-believe games, one particular incident took place that proved to be great practice for a real-life disaster. On September 13, 2005, the Corrupted Blood epidemic hit (www.wowwiki .com/Corrupted_Blood; see Figure 16.2).

Upon engaging the demon, players were stricken by a "Corrupted Blood," which would periodically sap their life. It inflicted 250 to 300 points of damage (compared to the average health of 4,000 to 5,000 for a player of the highest level at that time) every few seconds to the afflicted player. The disease would also be passed on to other players who were simply standing in close proximity to an infected person. Originally this malady was confined within the Zul'Gurub instance, but made its way into the outside world by way of hunter pets that contracted the disease. Within hours, Corrupted Blood had infected entire cities because of their high player concentrations. Low-level players were killed in seconds by the high-damage disease. For days, carpets of skeletons riddled the highest-populated towns and were rendered uninhabitable by the persistent plague.

This was a temporary programming error that created a virtual plague that infected and spread rapidly from character to character throughout

FIGURE 16.2   Corrupted Blood Screen

Blizzard Entertainment's World of Warcraft—and resembled a real-life disease outbreak. This virtual plague attracted the attention of psychologists and epidemiologists across North America. The Centers for Disease Control and Prevention actually used this incident as a research model to study both the progression and transference of a disease and the potential human response to large-scale epidemic infection.

Virtual Economies

Like Second Life, MMORPGs also have thriving virtual economies. Virtual money can be earned through game play, items can be bought and sold, and wealth can be accumulated. And these virtual economies can have an impact on the economies of the real world, as demonstrated by Anshe Chung's ability to become the first real—or first first-life—millionaire generated from

Second Life's virtual land. (See Chapter 15, Virtual Worlds—Real Impact, for Chung's full story.)

Edward Castronova (www.mypage.iu.edu/~castro/home.html)

—one of the early researchers of MMORPGs—demonstrated that a supply-and-demand market that exists for virtual items often crosses over to the real world, or first life. This crossover assumes that the players have the ability to sell or barter items to each other for virtual currency, and that the currency translates—and exchanges—into real-world currency.

This real/virtual world currency connection is having a profound effect on players, the gaming industry, and the courts. When Castronova first studied the trend in 2002, he found that a highly liquid—and often-illegal—currency market existed. At one point, the value of EverQuest's in-game currency exceeded that of the Japanese yen. Some players—referred to as *gold farmers*—make a living by using these virtual economies. A few of the game publishers prohibit the exchange of real-world money for virtual items, whereas virtual worlds such as Second Life and Entropia Universe support and profit from this system. This link between currencies is common in virtual worlds, but rare in MMORPGs, where it is generally accepted that this kind of exchange is detrimental to game play. When real-world wealth can influence greater rewards than skillful game play, the incentive for strategic role-play and real game involvement can become diminished.

This blurred boundary between the various currencies has also led to the proliferation of in-world gambling. Because gambling is illegal or controlled in so many areas of the world, Second Life was forced to remove and prohibit gambling within its virtual world.

Raids

A fast-growing segment of the MMORPG is the *Raid*, which is an adventure or part of the parent game designed for specific groups of players—often 20 or more. Raids are copied from the parent game and allow that particular segment to be separated from the rest of the game world. This reduces competition, provides for faster game play downloads, and lessens screen-refresh lag times.

Single Player

Even though the MMORPG is designed for multiple players and social interaction, many games allow the user to interact solely with the game itself. As a result, many of the most popular MMORPGs have now developed single-player play options. Even the older Dungeons & Dragons Online was retrofitted to allow for single play. This change has increased the popularity of the MMORPG, because many of the gamers prefer to play while interacting with the computer only or offline. One of the authors recently tested an MMORPG car race game called FlatOut 2. While the racing interaction and competition with others from around the world is exciting, sometimes just taking the car out for a spin or against the computer can be a lot of fun as well.

User-Generated Content

More and more MMORPGs are encouraging user-generated content. Ultima Online provided a 30-page book that instructs players on how to collect, trade personal libraries, and build houses. In fact, any noncombat-type MMORPG relies on user-generated content—including textures, architecture, buildings, objects, and animations—much like the two billion user-generated items on the Linden Labs server. (Listen to the interview with Mark Kingdon, CEO, Linden Labs—Second Life, at www.theSocialMediaBible .com.)

Console-Based MMORPGs

Again—although the MMORPG is intended to be played on the Internet by large numbers of players at any given time—two major video game manufacturers are releasing console-based MMORPGs, including The Age of Conan for the Xbox 360, which will allow the user to play these online games on their Xbox consoles or their PC while online.

The Largest MMORPG: World of Warcraft

World of Warcraft—commonly known as WoW—was designed by Rob Pardo, Jeff Kaplan, and Tom Chilton, developed by Blizzard Entertainment, published by Vivendi Universal, and released on November 23, 2004. WoW is considered a fantasy MMORPG, and is the fourth game released by Blizzard (the first was Warcraft: Orcs & Humans in 1994). World of Warcraft differs from other MMORPGs in many ways. Players complete quests and experience the world at their own pace, whether it be a few hours here and there or entire weeks at a time. Also, their quest system provides an enormous variety of captivating quests with story elements, dynamic events, and flexible reward systems. World of Warcraft also features a faster style of play, with less downtime and an emphasis on combat and tactics against multiple opponents. World of Warcraft is currently the world's largest MMORPG, with more than 12 million monthly subscribers, and holds the Guinness World Record for the most popular MMORPG ever with an estimated 62 percent of the MMORPG market in April 2008. While most online MMORPGs have peaked or flattened, WoW is still really "wow!"

The management of Blizzard Entertainment "didn't see the connection between WoW and social media's 'trusted networks'" and declined to participate in *The Social Media Bible*. To read their response, visit www .theSocialMediaBible.com.

Halo 3

Halo 3 is a first-person shooter, or FPS, video game. It was developed by Bungie Software exclusively for the Xbox 360 video gaming console. Halo 3 is the third edition in the Halo series, and concludes the trilogy story that began in the original Halo game. The game's themes are based on an interstellar war between twenty-sixth-century humanity—led by the United Nations Space Command—and a collection of alien races known as the Covenant. The MMORPG player assumes the role of the Master Chief, a cybernetically enhanced super-soldier, as he wages war in defense of humanity assisted by human Marines as well as an allied alien race called Elites, which is led by the Arbiter.

On September 25, 2007, Halo 3 was released in Australia, Brazil, India, New Zealand, North America, and Singapore; in Europe one day later; and on the following day in Japan. There were 4.2 million copies of Halo 3 in retail outlets on the day before its debut, and the game grossed more than $300 million during the first week following its release. Within the first 24 hours, more than 1 million people played Halo 3 on Xbox Live. By January 3, 2008, Halo 3 had sold more than 8.1 million copies and was the best-selling video game of 2007 in the United States.

At the time this paragraph was being written, there were 68,064 Halo 3 players online, with 604,821 unique players and 1,342,417 battles logged in the last 24 hours, and a UNSC Campaign Kill Count of 6,737,856,503.[1]

In-Game Advertising

As discussed in Chapter 15, Virtual Worlds—Real Impact, in-game advertising is growing in popularity. The following article from TechCrunch shows the level of interest of many of the Fortune 500 companies regarding in-game advertising.

FIGURE 16.3   Halo 3

FIGURE 16.4   Halo 3 Screen

FIGURE 16.5   In-Game Ads

The ROI of Social Media

Universal Studios Home Entertainment's Public Enemies Blockbuster Social Media Campaign

Background

The critically acclaimed gangster saga *Public Enemies* (www.publicenemies.net)

has been described as "explosive . . . thrilling . . . suspenseful," "one of the best of the year," and "like no other." Those same descriptions accurately reflect the success of the wildly popular Facebook game, Zynga's *Mafia Wars* (www .zynga.com/games/index.php?game=mafiawars),

that launched an unprecedented social media campaign to promote the film's high-profile December 2009 Blu-ray and DVD release. Mafia Wars enables social gamers to start a Mafia family with friends, run a criminal empire and fight to be the most powerful family in New York City, Cuba, and Moscow. For those who don't know, Mafia Wars is played by more than 25 million monthly active Facebook users!

Strategy

The campaign, led by appssavvy (www.appssavvy.com),

a direct sales team for the social media space, in partnership with the Los Angeles office of Ignited (www.ignitedusa.com),

a marketing innovations agency working on behalf of Universal Studios Home Entertainment (www.universalstudioshomeentertainment.com),

celebrated the home entertainment release by launching this first-of-its-kind integration reaching tens of millions of consumers.

(continued)

(*continued*)

The strategy was to maximize awareness of *Public Enemies* in the face of larger releases through unique opportunities that created viral buzz.

Implementation

During *"Public Enemies* Week" on *Mafia Wars,* players completed various jobs so they could unlock *Public Enemies* Loot—items such as John Dillinger's wooden gun, prison stripes, and *Public Enemy Number 1* newspaper, among others.

Additionally, special *Public Enemies*–featured jobs were offered for a limited time. After completing jobs (playing the game), players were able to view clips from the movie and read John Dillinger factoids.

Opportunity

Mafia Wars was an incredibly dynamic environment to seamlessly integrate the *Public Enemies* property and to effectively engage a significant and relevant audience. The opportunities for marketers to engage with people in social media are vast and must be done in ways that are relevant to consumers— *Public Enemies* did just that.

Conclusion

To demonstrate the success of the campaign, *Public Enemies* Jobs were played nearly 45 million times by 19 million unique users and Loot garnered nearly 55 million interactions during the week-long campaign. Not only did the game reach millions of players, but it also overdelivered by a multiple of 13, which ultimately supported the film's Blu-ray and DVD breakout during the busy holiday season.

Outside of Loot interacted with and Jobs completed, as one would expect, the integration was a viral success. Loot and Job interactions were posted to players' Facebook's news feed more than 7.6 million times delivering nearly a million (992,000-plus) viral impressions. Lastly, 1.5 million trailers were watched to completion. Meanwhile, the campaign generated nearly 25,000 likes and more than 26,000 comments on the *Mafia Wars* Facebook fan page.

—Appssavvy
www.appssavvy.com/publicenemies

Expert Insight

Scott Clough, avid online gamer, www.facebook.com/sclough68

Scott Clough

Actually, I was playing a tabletop role-playing game, since probably the early 1980s. I started with tabletop games like Dungeons & Dragons.

I then moved into playing computer games, especially ones that had elements of role-playing games in them. . . . Zork was a very early one, very simplistic. Then I moved up to playing games such as Ultima, Might and Magic, Bard's Tale . . . and then they started making some of the Dungeons & Dragons into computer games. I got involved in the online role-playing at about 1996 when I went through a divorce and had suddenly lots of time, and in 1997 Ultima Online (the first of the genre) came out. And it gave me something to fill up my time.

I played Ultima Online until EverQuest was released, and that was probably the online game that probably really made the whole genre successful, because the numbers became staggering . . . how many people were playing.

It had graphics that were just amazing; it had a world that was realistic, and I think all the current big games owe a lot to EverQuest.

I used to play games with almost all my free time, but in later years I've learned to limit my playing. I also try to make sure it doesn't dominate my life, and I stopped playing particular ones when I realized I'm not being entertained. But I always look for something else to move on to.

I became interested in fixing up computers for myself and then I was building bigger and more powerful machines for friends and family. One day I was online in Everquest and said I was looking for another job. A guy who I was gaming with, never met, asked, "Would you be willing to relocate?" And I said, "Yeah, sure, as long as it was Arizona."

The next day I had an interview set up, and since then I have been working in computer support and eventually ended up at Hewlett-Packard. . . .

(continued)

(*continued*)

Well, [MMORPG] was a term coined by Richard Garrett, creator of Ultima Online. It means, "Massively multiplayer online role-playing game."

Well, yeah, it gives an explanation of what it is. The term was kind of coined to differentiate the different kinds of games that were out there at the time. You've got to realize, this kind of game was an evolution that's still in process. What had happened is back in the day, people were playing the very games I spoke of, such as Ultima, some of the Dungeons & Dragons games, and they were very active. The thing they kept saying they wanted to do was to be able to have a friend come over, like you with our brother, and play head on head or in the same world with it. And it was just a natural interest to say, "Hey, if we can make it so you can play with two, four friends, why not do it over the new medium called the Internet," back at that time. And as you know, Richard Garrett's Ultima . . . was the first big one. And actually it was interesting because they had eight different versions of their stand-alone game before they came out with Ultima Online; and amazingly enough it's still out there! . . .

Yes, but it also has some drawbacks, because whereas a bot or mob is going to react in a set mode based on the programming (and that has been developed more each year), some players that you get out there can be unethical. And they use cheats, hacks, exploits (as it's called out there) to get the edge on you rather than by skill. . . .

Well, it's really interesting. It's people in all the demographics, I would say. This is a hobby that has no separation by race, sex, religion. . . . You know a lot of the people out there try to classify the online player as a teenage boy, you know! But I've run into family groups that play, moms, dads, and the kids. I have met professionals who play everything, from computer engineers to lawyers to police officers, to soldiers sitting over in Iraq. . . .

You know the biggest appeal is the ability to be another person, or another entity. You can be a hero or a villain, just depending on how you want to play or the aspects of the game. There are some people out there who are dedicated to the role-playing aspects, and it's interesting because the games have started to have to modify to get there.

So they have dedicated role-playing servers, where everything you say or do is supposed to be in character. There are other servers who are dedicated to player versus player, and that's a real big growth area currently. And I would say most of the arguments in the games are about character balance in player versus player. In case you weren't aware, but that's where other players kill or defeat real players in the game, and usually you get some type of reward.

But I think the real attachment in the games is the community aspect. Usually, most of the games allow you to form up a group, usually called a guild.

And while you're doing this, you chat and you develop friendships. I've even known people to get married and divorced as a result of playing this game. . . .

It's something to watch because it's a new and developing technology, and games such as World of Warcraft have shown the worldwide appeal of such games. But you know, it's not just the game itself that is being sold. There's now a thriving industry on the items that are in the game . . . virtual items.

There's a third-party market on games guides, there's help websites. There are even companies out there that are selling online money, gold, and characters for real-world cash. Now many of the games are like, trying to shut this down, this behavior, but others have started to embrace it for themselves. Most players do not like it and deride those who buy their gear and stats. And also some of the games are based on the current entertainment industry. There's a Star Wars game, Lord of the Rings game, and there's even a new Star Trek game based on the recently released movie out there now. . . .

Yeah, there's online money. Actually, since most of the games are fantasy, it's gold or credits, but there's also items in the game that people desire. Say for instance, a really powerful sword that's a very rare find. There's an organization out there that goes and they do what's called "camping." They sit there and wait for the mob that has it, they take it, and then when they get it, rather than using it for that character, they turn it over to their company that sells it online. I've seen items sell for hundreds of dollars. . . .

Actually if you're interested in statistics, there's a great site, http://www .mmosite.com/, and they actually track how many people are playing in certain games, the basic activities.

If you're more casual and you just want to know what your kids are getting involved in, you can go on the Web and look for sites like wow.allakhazam.com;

you can go to the manufacturer of World of Warcraft and get information off of those. You can also buy magazines such as *PC Gamer*, which is only one example. And you can always tell them apart because they will have screen shots of the various games on their cover, usually.

(continued)

(continued)

But really, if you just want to know about the games, just go to any place that sells the software, such as Best Buy Electronics, and you'll see they have their own sections, their own shelves, and you can look at the game boxes and read what they're claiming that their world gives to you. You can actually buy even game guides that tell you how the game is played.

To listen to or read the entire Executive Conversation with Scott Clough, avid online gamer, go to www.theSocialMediaBible.com.

International Perspective

Turkey

For Turkish companies, competition is moving beyond the physical market into social media such as Facebook and Twitter. Today, 1.7 million people on Facebook like and follow Avea. Turkcell's corporate webpage has over 1.25 million fans. In the competition on social media it is fast moving consumer goods, banking, automotives, and information technology companies which come to the fore. The budgets allocated to these media are growing all the time. The amount that Intel Türkiye allocates to social media accounts for 30 percent of its total media expenditure. Doğa Koleji in education, Pfizer Türkiye in pharmaceuticals and Favori in jewelry use 20 percent of their media investments in social media.

Socialization is Accelerating

Turkey is stunning the world through its effective use of social media. The number of Facebook users in Turkey has now reached 30,963,000, ranking the country fifth worldwide. The number of people using this medium has increased by 1,313,000 in the last six months. Similarly, according to a survey conducted by ComScore, Medya in March 2011, Turkey ranks eighth in terms of use of Twitter, the number of whose users is expected to reach 500 million worldwide in February. Twitter and LinkedIn have penetration rates of more than 16 percent of Internet users. In the light of all of these data, Turkish companies are conceptualizing the importance of actively using social media. For all of the sectoral leaders, competition is moving beyond the physical market into social media such as Facebook and Twitter. In addition to profiles on Facebook, Twitter, and Friendfeed, they are regularly following and responding to the content related to them on blogs, websites and search engines.

Which Areas Are More Effective?

Companies are making their presence felt in social media both in the corporate arena and through the accounts that they have opened in the names of their brands. Naturally, the companies which are most effective here are in the sectors which need to form the closest links with consumers. The companies which are competing with each other to communicate with customers through social media networks are headed by Avea and Turkcell in telecommunications, Ülker and Avon in fast moving consumer goods, Oxxo and Mavi Jeans in clothing, and Garanti Bankası and Akbank in finance.

On Facebook, Avea's and Turkcell's corporate pages have more than a million "likes" from people. Avea is the leader in Turkey in this field with nearly 1.7 million "likes." Avea Digital and Direct Marketing Department Manager Omer Lütfi Diri says: "The number of people who 'like' us on Facebook represents over 10 percent of our 12.5 million subscribers. . . . Tens of people are being added every day. We regard this as an indication of the trust in our brand." Turkcell reaches 1,263,000 people through its corporate Facebook page. Turkcell Deputy General Manager Koray Öztürkler believes that the data they receive from social networking sites is very valuable because the quickest and most easily accessible way to measure customer satisfaction today is through social media.

Different Methods for Different Media

Facebook provides companies with the opportunity to promote their goods and services, whether through multimedia games or promotional campaigns, on a broader platform. In Turkey, it is the banks which are most actively taking advantage of this. . . . Galip Tözge, who is Deputy General Manager Responsible for Retail Banking at Akbank, says that they first entered social

(*continued*)

(continued)

media in July 2010 by opening a Facebook page. He explains how they have benefited from these media as follows: "Today we manage 16 different accounts in the social media. We support our existing marketing campaigns and communications channels on Facebook in particular."

Of course, differences between the nature of different media mean that they each need to be managed in a different way. Twitter provides short, succinct messages of 140 characters, primarily reflects the viewpoints and ideas of popular people and leading thinkers and is focused on the topics of the day. Philips Türkiye CEO Willem Rozenberg says: "From a corporate perspective, we regard Twitter as a very simple platform and it is used less for brands. We use Twitter to announce events, provide information about products and to hold new little competitions." For THY, interactivity is mostly through Twitter. The company sees it as a forum for comments and criticisms from consumers and an opportunity to develop itself. Yıldız Holding Digital Marketing Director Nevgül Ambarlılar says that they also try to produce special content for Twitter and highlights another factor. "We regard Twitter as an alternative means of interaction. But unfortunately Twitter still doesn't provide profiles of followers. Even though the number of Twitter users in Turkey is rising rapidly, it still doesn't provide the same level of access when we compare it with Facebook. On the other hand, we believe that the opportunities it provides for instant communication mean that it stands out from other communications channels in terms of its cost advantages."

The Share of the Budget Is Increasing

One of the areas in which social media is used most effectively is in offering rapid solutions to consumer problems. Teknosa General Manager Mehmet Nane says that they regard both Twitter and Facebook as effective means of resolving complaints. Banks are pursuing the same strategy. TEB Deputy General Manager for Retail and Private Banking Gökhan Mendi says the following: "Whereas we use our Facebook wall and webpages for competitive purposes, we instantly respond to the suggestions, request and comments that are received on the TEB Priority Customer Line. These are given priority compared with demands coming from many other channels. When necessary, we are able to translate user complaints into thanks by contacting them by telephone."

Companies are increasing the proportion of their media investments they allocate to these channels in order to strengthen their presence in social media which offer all of these advantages. Emre Başkaya of Intel says that they allocated 30 percent of their media investments to social media in 2011 and that they will increase these investments in 2012. In the same way, Ömer Lütfi Diri notes that they increased their investments in social media channels by 33 percent in 2011 compared with 2010.

Pfizer Türkiye, which is one of the giants of the pharmaceutical sector, is the first in its field in this area. Deputy General Manager and Corporate Relations Director Şebnem Girgin says: "We opened our Facebook and Twitter accounts in April 2010 and became the first pharmaceutical company in the social media. We can say that 20 percent of our resources are allocated to social networks." Volkswagen Türkiye Passenger Vehicles Marketing Manager Çağrı Öztaş says that they have been continually increasing their digital marketing investments since 2009, approving projects that will provide value for the brand and the target market, and that they have allocated 10 percent of their communications budget to social media. Favori Board Chair Dr. Selami Özel says that five people in the company are responsible for these media and that they account for 20 percent of the annual advertising budget.

The Most Up-to-Date Way of Finding a Job

It Is Becoming Increasingly Effective

Today, many companies in Turkey, such as Microsoft and Yıldız Holding, are using social media to recruit personnel. Yıldız Holding HR General Manager Ege Karpınar says: "We are evaluating applications via social networks for 15 to 20 percent of entry positions and 5 to 10 percent of middle-level and high level posts. We shall increase our use of social media in 2012. I can say that 2 to 3 percent of recruitment is done via social networks."

Just Getting Used to It

The Turkish company that has made the most effective use of social networks for recruitment is Microsoft Türkiye. Indeed, HR Director Cavidan Özdemir says that that over the last six months they have recruited 70 percent of first-time employees via social media networks. But it is very difficult to find another example like Microsoft in Turkey. . . . The white goods giant BSH is planning to start recruitment over LinkedIn this year.

—Elçin Cirik
ecirik@capital.com.tr
http://capital.com.tr/AnaSayfa

To-Do List

- Visit the occasional MMORPG site.

  Go look at the most popular MMORPGs, and choose one to play. This is the perfect opportunity to buy an Xbox and Halo 3 as a tax deduction under market research (see your tax professional for advice about this first, of course!). Experience it firsthand. Look for in-game advertising. See how it's used. Understand its application. Maybe it isn't right for you, your product, or your service, but what if it is?

- Read MMORPG articles.

  Read some articles about MMORPGs. MMORPGs are popular and have a very strong fan base, but the size and influence of the market can be staggering if you are unfamiliar with it. Study a few MMORPGs so that when the Fortune 500 companies have figured out how to effectively monetize in-game advertising to its huge loyal user base, you will be there.

- Understand in-game advertising.

  Read a few articles about in-game advertising. If all of the major online advertisers are buying and building companies that provide in-game advertising, maybe there is a reason. Encourage others to follow along until everyone understands the application and potential of this powerful new media.

Conclusion

The moral of the story is to remain open to all of what's going on around you in the world of social media and advertising. MMORPGs provide a huge base of trusted networks. When you have people with the same interest who participate in trusted social networks that are more than 600,000 members strong in any given 24-hour period—and eight million participants in one game alone—you might want to be aware of this as a businessperson. As you can see by the number of existing games, numbers of participants, and the rate at which this marketing opportunity is growing, companies like Microsoft and Google will figure out how to effectively monetize it. You need to be aware, informed, and there when it happens.

To hear all of the Expert Interviews, go to www.theSocialMediaBible.com.

Downloads

For your free downloads associated with *The Social Media Bible,* go to www .theSocialMediaBible.com, and enter your ISBN number located on the back of the book above the bar code. Be sure to enter the dashes.

Credits

The ROI of Social Media was provided by:

Appssavvy

Expert Insight and technical edits were provided by:

Scott Clough, avid online gamer

Note

1. UNSC Campaign is the Brute Infantry Specialist Kill Count within the Halo 3 game. At the time this chapter was written, according to the

UNSC Campaign Report, the total number of Enemies KIA (Killed In Action) was 6,737,856,503. This in-game "killed" number is now nearly as high as the world's estimated population at 7 billion. Bungie, the developers of Halo 3, monitors and reports statistics on the their game's usage. Bungie's servers record all manner of statistics when you play, all of which are used to track players across all of their Halo 3 games, multiplayer and campaign alike.

CHAPTER 17

RSS—Really Simple Syndication Made Simple

www.LonSafko.com/TSMB3_Videos/17RSS.mov

What's in It for You?

For the first time in Internet history, you can syndicate or distribute your original website content worldwide for free. That's right. No longer do you have to subscribe to a news service or be part of a large media organization to send your news or receive news from any other website from all around the world.

RSS—or Really Simple Syndication—is a one-click solution that allows your readers to subscribe to your content and receive updates the moment you publish it. The reverse is also the case; you can have each of your preferred blogs and news stories sent to you automatically without having to take the time to search all of your favorite websites every day for new content and updates. Simply adding a syndication button to your blog site lets your followers click your Subscribe button and instantly receive your latest breaking blog.

But what exactly does RSS have to do with building an online following for your business? Let's start with some basic information, so that you can see how this really simple concept can be easily applied to your own company.

theSocialMediaBible.com

Back to the Beginning

The early RSS formats date back to 1995, when computer scientist Ramanathan V. Guha and several of his colleagues developed the Meta Content Framework (MCF)[1] at Apple Computer's Advanced Technology Group between 1995 and 1997. Dan Libby is responsible for improving the first RSS by incorporating Dave Winer's "ScriptingNews" format, which he dubbed "Rich Site Summary" (see more on Winer next). Winer is a pioneer of RSS as Really Simple Syndication, and his Scripting News is one of the oldest blogs on the Internet, having been established in 1997.

Winer continued to develop and release improvements to his RSS project, the most significant of which came in 2000 when he introduced a version that could enclose audio files. This technology made the still-new process of podcasting (see Chapter 9, Talking about the Podcast (Audio Create)) much easier and more user-friendly. Then, in December 2001, RSS-DEV Working Group—which by now included Guha and O'Reilly Media—developed RSS 1.0. Winer released his newest major revision of his RSS—2.0—in 2002, which then took on the name Really Simple Syndication.

Atom was born out of this controversy in June 2003. Atom was a ground-up redesign of the RSS delivery system that was adopted by the IETF, or Internet Engineering Task Force, Proposed Standard RFC 4287 (see the following for more details about Atom's creation and development). The Atom Syndication Format is similar to the RSS format and uses the Extensible Markup Language (XML) employed for web feeds. The Atom Publishing Protocol (AtomPub or APP) is a simple HTTP-based protocol for creating and updating web resources. Web feeds allow software programs to check for updates published on a website.

Atom

In June 2003, IBM software developer Sam Ruby created a wiki to discuss the deficiencies of RSS and to solicit ideas about syndication. Ruby wanted to come up with a better system than Blogger API or LiveJournal API—the ones that were currently being used. More than 150 developers and prominent members of the online community came out to support the development of Atom, including Jeremy Zawodny of Yahoo!, Brad Fitzpatrick of LiveJournal, Glenn Otis Brown of Creative Commons, Timothy Appnel of O'Reilly Network, Mena Trott of Six Apart, David Sifry of Technorati, Jason Shellen of Blogger, and others. Even RSS originator Dave Winer gave Atom his full support. By July 2003, the project code names "Necho,"

"Pie," and "Echo" had become known as Atom 0.2. Google added Atom to its Google News and Google Blogger in December 2003—an event that marked the full support of the syndication community.

In June 2004, the Atompub Group was formed by Paul Hoffman and Tim Bray (co-developer of the XML specification), which moved the Atom project to the Internet Engineering Task Force (IETF). In December 2005, the IETF accepted the Atom Syndication Format as the industry standard. Even

FIGURE 17.1   RSS

though Atom 1.0 is an IETF standard and widely supported by many podcasting applications such as iTunes and Google, RSS 2.0 still remains the most widely used and accepted format. Many websites, such as those of the *New York Times,* CNN, and the BBC, will publish their feeds only in the RSS 2.0 format.

What You Need to Know

RSS is a way to feed (or web feed) your web pages, blogs, audio, video, and photographs automatically to people who subscribe to your content through a feed. In other words, every time you create something new on the Internet and hit Publish, a feed goes out to everyone who has subscribed to your updates. Your followers are automatically notified through e-mail, mobile texting, or tweets (see Chapter 13, Thumbs Up for Microblogging), and your content is automatically added to their feed reader or aggregator page (such as iGoogle, etc.). You can also subscribe to feeds from others' websites or content, and have news headlines, stock quotes, blogs, and other frequently updated information automatically sent to your reader page or feed reader—which can be either desktop- or browser-based. The only requirement for you to subscribe to a feed is to go to your favorite website, blog, or news site, locate the Subscribe button or the familiar orange RSS Subscribe button, and select your feed reader (or paste the link into your Add Subscription box). That's it! Now each time that web or blog page publishes new content, your reader page will be notified and provided with a copy of that new content.

Reader or Aggregator

A reader, or aggregator, is a program or website that will check and continuously search all of the blogs, news sites, or other websites to which you have subscribed for new content (see Figure 17.2). If fresh material is identified, the reader page will show a summary of that information with a link to that page. This way—instead of having to visit all of your favorite websites, news sites, and blogs—the newest content comes to you, and is aggregated—or summarized—in one reader page. Some web pages allow you to subscribe in RSS, Atom, or both formats.

iGoogle Reader (Aggregator): These reader pages or aggregators are designed as a stand-alone software program or as a web page (browser-based), such as iGoogle. Web-based or browser-based feed readers allow the user to access aggregated content from any Internet browser.

Social Bookmarks

Social bookmarks are small icons found on nearly all blogs, websites, news sites, sports sites, or any pages that provide fresh, updated content on a regular basis. By selecting your feed reader or aggregator icon, the content feed is automatically added to your specific reader page. Most of these social bookmarks are a one-click addition. Some feed readers might require

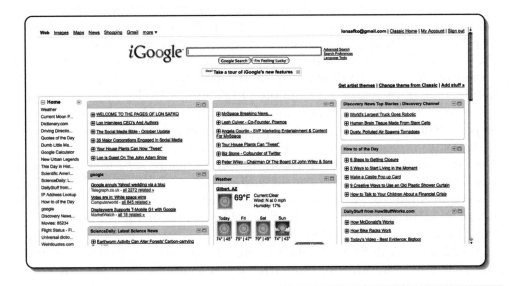

FIGURE 17.2   iGoogle Reader

you to copy and paste the URL of your favorite news or blog page into an Add Subscription textbox. It's easy, and requires only one step. (Most readers provide a bookmarklet that you can add to your browser to easily subscribe to sites as you are visiting them.)

FIGURE 17.3 Social Bookmark Chiclets

The ROI of Social Media

The Utility of B2B Twitter

Introduction

This chronicles the first three weeks of a successful experiment to evaluate the utility of Twitter as an adjunct to traditional B2B marketing and promotion.

Background

The company in this case is a medium-size firm [that] provides products and services based on the technology of major partners, all of whom had well-advanced social network strategies. Its normal methods for promotion are web, newsletter, banner ad, trade show, purchased lists, press release, and published case study or white paper.

(continued)

(continued)

Strategy

Since the major partners all had an active social media presence, it seemed a strategy to follow and comment on these established social media blogs, and tweets might give some early visibility.

Implementation

A Twitter account was opened in the company's name. The account followed one of the major partners and retweeted relevant messages. Where appropriate, a Bit.ly

URL (shortened URL) was added to the tweet, which included Google Analytics tracking code to the company's website. All other web and newsletter promotions were tracked with Google Analytics in this way, to allow comparisons of effectiveness over the period.

Opportunity

This program was timed to coincide with some major product releases from one of the major partners. This means potential customers were searching for just-announced product names and following the major partners' social media tweets.

Conclusion

Since the nature of this B2B relationship is long-term, the practical measurement ROI is difficult. We use ROO (Return on Objective), where Twitter can be compared to other media based on cost effectiveness for a specific objective. Objectives are *exposures,* meaning brand name exposed to target audience; and *access,* meaning audience follow-up—in this case, click through to a web page.

Exposure of the company's name went way up. Exposures are the way magazines and banner ads are sold, and for a company seeking to build brand, exposures is a reasonable objective. By this measure, Twitter may mature to be a silver bullet.

By multiplying the company's tweets times the average number of followers, we calculate something like 10,000 exposures—to a fully opt-in audience. The cost for this is quite reasonable compared to exposures from banner ads or purchased e-mail lists, neither of which is opt-in.

Access to the company website went up, too. In this case, Access means the number of times a person led by Twitter came to the company's website.

Thirty-eight web visitors is not a lot, but it is more than could be expected from a typical 10,000-name e-mail distribution to a blind list, say, a list rented from a magazine.

What is most relevant is the comparison to other channels. During the test period, people were brought to the site by participation in a very popular sponsored blog site of a partner, and a mention in another partner's newsletter. Clearly, Twitter was more effective.

This effort was determined to be cost effective. Twitter was found as effective as the company newsletter, and more effective than other media.

—Lawrence Ricci
www.EmbeddedInsider.com

Expert Insight

Krista Canfield, public relations manager, LinkedIn, www.linkedin.com

Krista Canfield

Basically, what LinkedIn does is help professionals accelerate their success. They can do that in a number of different ways, whether it be looking for employees and trying to get a bit more background information on them in terms of what they've done in the past and who they've worked with. We've even had companies that have acquired other companies through the website. Small business owners are using the answers portion of LinkedIn to get advice on building their business and taking it to the next level. So, it really depends on what success means to you, but LinkedIn can definitely help in a variety of different ways.

One company actually got acquired by the Weather Channel, and LinkedIn helped facilitate that whole process. There was [someone who] knew that his company was going to be the perfect fit for the Weather Channel. He just wasn't sure how to get in front of the right person. So what he did was search for the person on LinkedIn that might be the right contact at the Weather Channel, sent him an e-mail and began an e-mail dialogue; and within a few months his company ended up getting acquired by the Weather Channel. So this is a demonstration of how LinkedIn can get you in touch with the right people and to make sure you are getting your business ideas, your own personal brand in front of the right people.

It's very cool! And, you know, it's all about leveraging your relationships. I think the whole idea of creating LinkedIn in the first place was to keep in contact with all the different people that you've worked with in the past: friends, family members, coworkers, all those sorts of people. You know, a lot of times if you get someone's business card and you want to get in touch with them three years later, and you do need that reference or you need that recommendation . . . a lot of times that person has switched roles and they're at a different company . . . and that e-mail address and phone number may no longer be of use to you. So, first and foremost, [the site] was meant to be a way to stay in touch with all of the people that you have worked with in the past, even if they have changed positions or switched companies. But the other thing that it really enables you to do is to find the right person who is going to be the right contact for you, no matter *what* company they may be at.

Chances are that one of your contacts works at a totally different company in a totally different world from you; so they have a whole different network of people that you could probably utilize that might help you accomplish your goals. It's all about working off of those relationships. . . .

We do offer premium accounts for those members that are looking to reach out to more people outside of their network; but for the most part, that free version can actually help you get a lot done. Some people either jump in there with both feet and try it out, without having to worry about something you need to pay on a monthly basis, until you are ready for that level of commitment. . . .

The average user is around 41 years old, and has a household income of just over $110,000. But we also have everybody—from high-level CEOs . . . Bill Gates is on LinkedIn. We have professional athletes, like Yao Ming, who has a profile on LinkedIn. Both presidential candidates have profiles on LinkedIn. But we also have over 600,000 small business owners. So there's really a wide range of people that are on the website, and certainly professionally from every single industry. Yes—over 25 million people across the world!

We also have an API[2] that a number of different sites use. So, if you go to, say, *BusinessWeek*'s or the *New York Times*'s website—or if you go to CXO Media (which owns cio.com)

—there is another site called "Simply Hired" that's using our API. What's really cool about the API is it will show you—if you are reading an article in *BusinessWeek*—the first company that appears in the headline of the article. And if you give it permission to log in to your account simultaneously while you are looking at that article, it will show you—if, say, the article

(continued)

(*continued*)

is about Volkswagens—who you know in your network that knows someone who works at Volkswagen. So it is very powerful to a professional who may be looking at an article and saying, "Wow, my company's a great fit for Volkswagen." Or, "I think Volkswagen would be the perfect client for us." Or, "Wow, gee, I'd love to work at Volkswagen." To be able to sit there and say, "Oh, my friend, Joe, is connected to Susan who works at Volkswagen." So, it definitely makes the world a smaller place, and it really helps you get business done much more efficiently. . . .

To listen to or read the entire Executive Conversation with Krista Canfield, go to www.theSocialMediaBible.com.

International Perspective

Bulgaria

Bulgaria is undoubtedly a social media country. This is true not only because it is ranked 55th among the world's countries on Facebook with almost 2.5 million users, but because Bulgaria is full of young, intelligent, very enthusiastic, and quite ambitious people.

The characteristics of the market—relatively stable, with an extremely attractive tax policy and good niches for business—mean that many ideas and sales initiatives are able to find customers and places to thrive.

At least 80 percent of Bulgarian businesses currently online—mostly consumer goods and retail—use Facebook. Among the top businesses represented there are one of the leading discount coupon sites, the most popular disco club, and tourism and fashion sites, as well as a chocolate brand produced by a large international company. Commercial Facebook pages average about 100,000 fans, while media and entertainment pages have at least 35 percent more.

The most successful strategies involve implementing Facebook applications, such as creating "like/dislike" games, but the commercial effect is definitely still below expectations. The main reason is the low level of understanding that direct promotions and marketing tools work in a completely different way on social media. Some have also attempted to use Twitter commercially to improve their branding or to create business interest, but up to now, although "140-character media" is quite popular in the country, its primary uses are to provide news or as a mood-sharing instrument.

Lately Foursquare has been getting more and more business customers in Bulgaria, and may soon become a very successful marketing tool for retail and entertainment businesses. One of the leading local banks, First Investment, provides excellent information on the network about its branches, and also gives awards to the mayors of its branches. The top computer seller, Plesio, provides special discounts for mayors and regular visitors, and many restaurants and shops have also taken over their places on Foursquare and provide attractive incentives for users.

Vbox7, Bulgaria's YouTube-style website, provides a lot of commercial opportunities and is actively used by show business, while Google+ is still being scrutinized and is used by almost no business customers in Bulgaria.

Bulgaria is generally a very well-connected country, and the more Internet users it gains (57 percent of the population in late 2011), the more businesses will start to rely on online sales, primarily based on social media promotions. This is a stable, growing trend that will surely develop in the coming years.

—Maxim Behar, Social Media Expert
CEO and Chairman of the Board
M3 Communications Group, Inc.
www.m3bg.com

To-Do List

- Sign up for a feed reader.

  Go to one of the many websites that provide a feed reader, such as iGoogle. This way, every time you open that page, all of the freshest content from the entire web to which you subscribed will be there waiting for you.

- Go forth and subscribe.

  Go to your favorite websites, blog sites, and news sites and hit the Subscribe button. Follow the directions, copy and paste the URL in the Add Subscription text box—and you're ready to go.

- Be sure your site has social bookmarking.

  Make sure that your company's web and blog pages have Subscribe and social bookmarking buttons, so that your customers and prospects can be easily, instantly, and automatically updated on all of your business's news.

Conclusion

The two most important items you need to know about RSS are as follows:

1. You can provide a one-click solution to any friend, family member, associate, customer, or prospect that will allow them to automatically view any new content the moment you hit your Publish button. You don't have to e-mail, call, or text message them; simply by hitting your Subscribe button, they are part of your syndication.

2. Be sure to subscribe to all of your favorite web, blog, and news sites. This way, all of the updates that you care about will be instantly sent to your reader page, and you'll never have to search the web, site after site, to see if new content and updates have been published. It all comes to you!

To hear all of the Expert Interviews, go to www.theSocialMediaBible.com.

Downloads

For your free downloads associated with *The Social Media Bible,* go to www
.theSocialMediaBible.com,

and enter your ISBN number located on the back of the book above the bar
code. Be sure to enter the dashes.

Credits

The ROI of Social Media was provided by:

Lawrence Ricci, www.EmbeddedInsider.com

Expert Insight was provided by:

Krista Canfield, public relations manager, LinkedIn, www.LinkedIn.com

Technical edits were provided by:

Lynne D. Johnson, www.lynnedjohnson.com

Notes

1. Meta Content Framework (MCF) is a specific format for structuring meta data (behind-the-scenes information that the web browsers and search engines look at) about websites and their data.

2. An API is the acronym for Application Programming Interface, or sometimes referred to as an *app*. An app is a specific software application that allows one software application to talk to communicate and often exchange information with another.

Spotlight on Search (Search Engine Optimization)

www.LonSafko.com/TSMB3_Videos/18SEO.mov

To some experienced members of the social networking community, search engine optimization (SEO) may seem like an old-school process. However, it is still the very foundation of how search engines index all of your website's pages—and therefore, how your customers eventually find you. SEO is incredibly important and relevant to any business. In fact, some people have only two pieces of information on their business cards: their name and their web address. At least one person has gone one step further: only the image of the Google Search Bar with his name in it printed on the face of the business card.

Websites have become such an important marketing tool nowadays that they essentially serve as the foundation for everything that's done in business. The processes of SEO and search engine marketing (SEM, the focus of the next chapter) are all about being sure that when people are trying to find you, your company, your product, or your service—they can.

FIGURE 18.1   Google Search Bar

What's in It for You

Search engine optimization (SEO) and search engine marketing (SEM) are techniques by which you optimize your web pages, photos, blogs, social media profiles, and even videos to maximize search engine rankings. They are practices that almost everyone has heard of, but that few people understand. Search engine marketing requires implementing the optimization of your web pages and a keyword-sponsored link advertising program, or SEM. While SEO and SEM are two completely different functions, they are equally important; both refer to your website's ability to be recognized by the major search engines. This chapter discusses search engine optimization.

More and more customers are searching on social media portals like Twitter, Facebook, and LinkedIn. When people are conducting an online search for the type of product or service you provide, they will use their favorite search engine—Google, Yahoo!, MSN, Bing, Ask, or some of the many others available today. They will type in one, two, or three words that they think best describe what you do, and hit Enter. How well you have completed your SEO will determine your position on the search engine results pages. If you did a good job, you will rank high—if not in the first position, then at least on the first page of results. Ensuring that your page appears on this first page, referred to as an *organic listing* or *organic search,* simply means that you are optimizing your web page(s) so you have the best ranking possible as determined by the search engines.

A plethora of books can teach you the specifics of all of the SEO techniques you can perform to guarantee you always have the highest ranking in the organic listings, but that's not what this chapter is about. Rather, this chapter explains the dozen or so techniques that anyone can perform that will probably attain 95 percent of everything you need to do to get your company's web pages or personal web pages listed in the top 10 search engine results for any given keywords.

Back to the Beginning

SEO has been around ever since the first search engine searched for the first computer file. Surprisingly, Google and Yahoo! were not the first search engines; Gerard Salton, a professor of computer science at Cornell University, beat them by nearly a half-century. His search engine, and the use of Hypertext (see the following), were actually developed in 1965 to locate and retrieve files from the earliest computers.

Hypertext and the 1960s

In 1960, Ted Nelson developed Project Xanadu.[1] He coined the term *hypertext* in 1963 from *hyper* (meaning motion) and *text* meaning . . . well, text. This moving text then led to the development of the term *HTTP* (Hyper Text Transfer Protocol)—which are the first four characters of every web page address; and *HTML* (Hyper Text Markup Language), which is the language used today to create web pages. And of course, *WWW* stands for "World Wide Web."

Here's an example of how a typical web address would read if spelled out completely:

- Original: www.theSocialMediaBible.com/Index.html
- Spelled out: World Wide Web.theSocialMediaBible.Commercial/Index Page.Hyper Text Markup Language

Enter the Military and ARPAnet

Salton's and Nelson's work eventually led to the 1972 creation of ARPAnet (Advanced Research Projects Agency Network), the predecessor to today's Internet. The very first official search engine emerged in 1990. It was called Archie—from the word *ARCHIvE*—and was created by McGill University student Alan Emtage in Montreal, Canada. By 1993, there were only a few hundred websites to index, most of which were owned by colleges and universities.

Search capabilities allowed early Internet users to access a file. They didn't come, however, with the ability to share files back and forth. For this application, Tim Berners-Lee developed FTP (file transfer protocol), a program used in place of HTTP for uploading and downloading files directly from a server.

The Internet has come a long way from the inception of HTTP, HTML, FTP, and Archie. SEO is an incredibly important element of Internet marketing that requires you to create a web page in the most efficient manner possible to facilitate its retrieval by a modern-day search engine.

What You Need to Know

A typical Internet search has three components to it. The first is a huge database that contains every word from every page from every website in the world. This database can be searched and matched very quickly against any word(s) that you enter into a search engine. For example, at the time this chapter was written, a query of the term *social media bible* in Google (see Figure 18.2) returned "Results 1–10 of about 2,320,000 for social media bible. (0.21 seconds)."

Thus, Google was showing the first 10 results—or matches—of 2.3 million possible matches; and it found all 2.3 million records in just about 0.21 seconds (see Figure 18.3 to see results of my name). Pretty impressive!

The second component of a search engine is its spiders, robots, or just bots. These terms are metaphors for automated computer programs that go out and creep around on the Internet—find a website, and crawl from

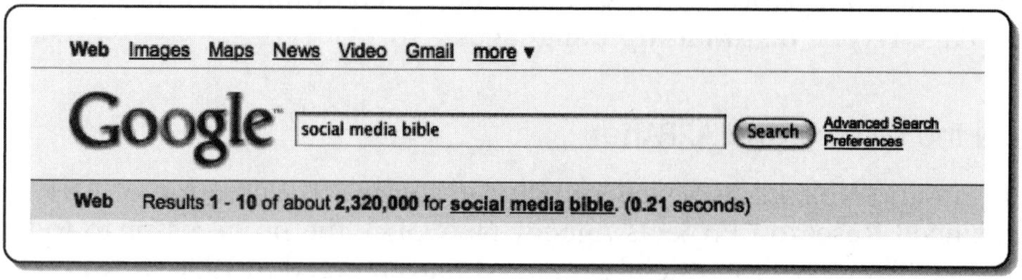

FIGURE 18.2 Google "Social Media Bible" Search

Google
Go to Google Home

"Lon Safko"

Advanced search

Search   About 54,600 results (0.32 seconds)

Everything

Images

Maps

Videos

News

Shopping

Books

More

Gilbert, AZ
Change location

All results
Sites with images
Visited pages
Not yet visited

More search tools

Lon Safko - Google Profile
https://plus.google.com/109303254942390082831
Gilbert - Author, Speaker, Entrepreneur at Innovative Thinking
LonSafko - The Social ... - lonsafko
Edit profile

Lon Safko
www.lonsafko.com/
Lon Safko is The Social Media Strategist who speaks and consults with Fortune 2000
companies across America. Learn how Lon's social media tactics, tools, ...
You've visited this page 123 times. Last visit: 3/18/09

The Social Media Bible - Lon Safko
www.thesocialmediabible.com/
"**Lon Safko** and The Social Media Bible address the key questions -- Why should I take
part in Social Media? How should I take part? How do I reap the greatest ...
You've visited this page 5 times. Last visit: 6/17/11

Lon Safko (@lonsafko) on Twitter
twitter.com/lonsafko
Sign up for Twitter to follow **Lon Safko (@lonsafko)**. Innovator & Author.

Lon Safko | LinkedIn
www.linkedin.com/pub/lon-safko/0/9/943
View **Lon Safko's** professional profile on LinkedIn. LinkedIn is the world's largest
business network, helping professionals like **Lon Safko** discover inside ...

Lon Safko | Fast Company
www.fastcompany.com/tag/lon-safko
Apr 11, 2011 – Are you voracious for video, but not fascinated by photos? Bonkers for
blogs, but not titillated by Tweets? Fanatical about Facebook, but not ...
You've visited this page 5 times. Last visit: 7/20/11

Lon Safko - Member Profile Page | Fast Company
www.fastcompany.com/user/lon-safko
From One Comes Many Are you voracious for video, but not fascinated by ...
⊞ Show more results from fastcompany.com

Images for "Lon Safko" - Report images
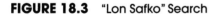

FIGURE 18.3   "Lon Safko" Search

page to page indexing and cataloging each page's content. Sound creepy?
In reality, the search engine's computer simply opens a home page, captures
the content, and goes onto the next page, and does the same thing. And the
reason that that activity usually takes place at night is that Internet traffic
is at its lowest.

James Burnes of MediaSauce describes it this way: "Because search
engines are constantly indexing sites across the web, it is imperative that

business's content be updated as soon as possible online to increase the relevancy and likelihood that your content will appear the next time someone searches for content. The reality is that bots and spiders run 24/7/365. The sooner you add content relevant to a user's search terms, the quicker you have a chance to be in front of them."

The third part of the process is your typical search interface, which is what you see when you go to Google or Yahoo! when you enter your query and see the results.

Search Engine Optimization

Let's first look at SEO, or organic listings. You can do many different things to your website to achieve a high SEO ranking. While many are ethical, some are not. Most of them are fairly simple to execute, however, once you know how they work; nearly all of them are time-consuming. Everything you do in terms of SEO is meant to satisfy the search engine's algorithm (pronounced "Al-Gore-Rhythm"; you can insert the joke of your choice here).

The truth be told: Al Gore never actually meant to say that he invented the Internet. The joke was somewhat misleading and out of context, related to a statement Gore made during an interview with Wolf Blitzer on CNN's *Late Edition* in 1999. When asked to describe what distinguished him from his challenger for the Democratic presidential nomination, Senator Bill Bradley of New Jersey, Gore replied, "During my service in the United States Congress, I took the initiative in creating the Internet. I took the initiative in moving forward a whole range of initiatives that have proven to be important to our country's economic growth and environmental protection, improvements in our educational system."

Source: www.snopes.com/quotes/Internet.asp;

http://articles.cnn.com/1999-03-09/politics/president.2000_transcript.gore_
1_21st-century-american-people-shadow?_s=PM:ALLPOLITICS; www.bit.ly/GI76Mt

The Infamous Algorithm

An algorithm is just a mathematical formula that each search engine uses to determine how well your page matches against the user's query. Remember, Google or Yahoo!'s only real purpose is to return the most relevant match. The more sophisticated the algorithm, the more relevant the match is; the better the match, the more you will use that search engine. The incentive for a Google or Yahoo! is that a search engine will make more revenue from their advertisers every time it's used. When you consider Google's 2007 revenues were $17.91 billion, a lot is riding on the quality of its algorithm.

If you want to see how your website is listed in the search engines, go to either Google or Yahoo! and type "site:www.yourdomain.com" (no spaces) into the search box. This will pull up all of the pages that have been indexed by that search engine. If an important page of yours isn't listed, it's not indexed—and you need to find out why.

Everyone—including the author of this book—wants to know exactly how each of the search engines works. But the fact is that no one except for the search engine developers knows. As you can imagine, anything that helps generate $18 billion in revenues is a closely guarded secret. So how do you find out what you can do to get that competitive edge? You test, test, test, and add a little common sense. The good news is that certain techniques will get your web page ranked top in the search engines. Don Schindler, digital strategist at MediaSauce, www.MediaSauce.com, said:

The search engine algorithms are based on trust and search engine language. They want to trust your website, they want to trust that what you say you are is what you really are. They want to trust your relevance on the subject the searcher cares about. The search engine language is keywords, tags, and text. Right now, it is all a search engine can read. If your website is relevant but can't be properly understood, then it can't be ranked properly. When it comes to trust—the age of your site is important as well. If the URL is new to search engines, it is not trusted as much. If it is older and has had content on it for a long time, then the search engines trust the site more than new. This doesn't mean that site is put up and forgotten. Old content does not help drive SEO unless it is very meaningful to the audience.

The Key to Keywords

The most important criterion that a search engine examines are your keywords. These are the words that you (or your web programmer) have told the search engine are the best possible words to describe the content on your web page. These terms are placed into something called *meta tags,* which are the first thing you will see when you look at the code for your web page. Here is some of the HTML code text for *The Social Media Bible* website:

```
<!DOCTYPE html PUBLIC "-//W3C//DTD XHTML 1.0 Transitional//
EN" "www.w3.org/TR/xhtml1/DTD/xhtml1-transitional.dtd">. . .
<title>The Social Media Bible</title>
<meta name="generator" content="WordPress 3.1.2"/>
<!—leave this for stats—>. . .
. . .<link rel="alternate" type="application/rss+xml" title="The
Social Media Bible RSS Feed" href="theSocialMediaBible.com/
feed/"/>. . .
. . .<meta name="description" content="The home of The Social
Media Bible Published By John Wiley & Sons, Inc."/>
```

<meta name="keywords" content="social media, social media bible, lon safko, marketing, pr, sales, innovation"/>
Note that because of keyword abuse, which is often called *keyword stuffing* or *keyword spamming,* through which web developers jam every possible keyword into every possible keyword meta data line, Google has discontinued looking at the keyword meta data line altogether. See

http://googlewebmastercentral.blogspot.com/2009/09/google-does-not-use
-keywords-meta-tag.html or Bit.ly shortened link: http://bit.ly/3SdTa1.

Take a thorough look at your meta tags. There is a chance that your web page is missing an important component in regard to your keywords, and this is where you look to find out. The missing components may have happened because the technical person programming your page didn't know what the meta tags should be and didn't bother to ask, whereas your marketing person knows your keywords, but might not be quite sure what a meta tag is. That's why you need to find out!

Content Is King

This industry has a saying: "Content Is King." The content of each of your web pages is critical. Evaluating that content—and choosing the most appropriate words to describe it—are an important part of SEO. You can read the page several times, or go to www.theSocialMediaBible.com

and find the downloads for this chapter. A fun little macro there will help you. Copy the text from the page that you want to analyze, and paste it into a Word document. Run the Key Word macro, and it will tell you every word you used in that text and the exact number of times you used them. Look at the list, and disregard words like *at, is, a,* and *the.* Look at the main words, and determine which are the most important. This will help generate a list of keywords.

Once you've created your list, either place those words in your metadata line using a web page programming tool such as Dreamweaver, or give it to your technical person to do. It will take less than five minutes, so don't pay an exorbitant fee.

One of the most important pieces to SEO is the URL. Having proper keyword terms within the URL can really help your search engine results page (SERP) position because of algorithm. Search engines put much emphasis on the URL. Not only is it good to have keywords in the main URL but also in the subdomains like http://articles.cnn.com/

and make sure you use dashes and not underscores as some search engines have problems reading underscores as separations.

Next is the Title tags. Title tags should be your keywords but they should also match the content. If the Title tags are not matched for the content or they are duplicated for multiple pages, the search engines will downgrade the Title tag emphasis in indexing. Using fewer than 70 characters in the Title tags helps the search engines focus on what the page means to the site.

Meta-descriptions are important not for keywords but for users to understand what the page is. If you do not have a description for each page, the search engine may not know what to use for the description of the site and will either pull content from the page or pull a description from its database that can be written by a directory web editor. The main thing you should take from here is that it is important if you want users to hear your message. This shouldn't be longer than 150 characters.

Finally, you can add meta-keywords. Only use 7 to 10 keywords in this section. Any more are wasted and considered unnecessary by most SEO experts.

"MediaSauce frequently uses the free tools from Webconfs.com to analyze the keywords. We like them because it automatically disregards words that the search engines don't see and it picks up the title tags, keywords, navigation, and alt tags on the page," recommends Don Schindler, digital strategist for MediaSauce, www.webconfs.com/keyword-density -checker.php.

The Fresher, the Better

The next most important criterion is the notion of *content freshness.* Think about it. Many of our company's web pages haven't been changed since the year of the flood! If your job was to return only the most relevant results from a search, and two pages came up—one from 2003, and one that was updated yesterday—which page would you return to the customer?

The search engine assumes that the fresher the content, the more relevant the web page will be, which is where common sense comes in. You need to keep your content current. This is why all search engines put such a high priority on blogs, because blogs (see Chapter 6, The Ubiquitous Blog) by definition are new and fresh.

Don't ever try to fool the search engines into thinking that your content is fresh by changing a word or two and resaving. They know, and they penalize. Search engines actually compare, page for page, the difference between your new page and the one they last indexed. If it isn't considerably different, then you don't get the index points. "Some ideas for fresh content could be newsletters, latest customer success, product and/or your opinion on the latest news in your industry," says Sandy Rowley of Megastarmedia.com.

This doesn't mean you need to change your entire home page content every week. Just do what you can to keep the content fresh.

External Reputable Links

This crucial topic applies to web pages and blogs. An external reputable link is the place where another website links back to yours. The more external websites that link back to your website, the better. And the more reputable the website is that links to yours, the more weight it holds. Think about the logic behind this. Let's use two hypothetical websites again—yours and your competitor's. Say that the search engine sees that 25 other websites are linking to your competitor as a resource, and no one is linking to yours. Which one of you gets the higher ranking?

Of course, people have attempted to figure out how to try to beat the system. One group sold placement on a website that consisted solely of web page links to other websites. Sites like these are called *link farms*—don't use them! (This is where the word *reputable* comes in.) Search engines look at the content of the referring websites to see if there is any similarity. If another website is linking to yours, there is probably a reason; and there should be some similar words. If the referring website is only a bunch of links . . . you get penalized. Again, think about the search engines' responsibility and interest in returning the best possible matches.

A very simple test can show you how many other websites are linking back to yours. Go to Google and type "link:www.yourdomain.com," or go to Yahoo! and enter "linkdomain:www.yourdomain.com." You will immediately see how well you are doing. It used to be possible to drive your website higher on the search engines if you had at least 20 or so links to your site. We used to create a link exchange campaign. This is when you search the Internet for complementing but not competing websites, contact them, and pitch them on the notion that if they link to your site from their site, you will do the same for them; however, since the 2009 Google Caffeine switch, this practice is no longer considered a white hat practice and will no longer help your site with its ranking. Search engines are now looking for one-way links. This tends to take a lot of time and follow-up, but it's worth it in the end. Sandy Rowley, social media marketer and developer, says, "It is also a good idea to perform this search on sites ranking for your keywords. Use this list to find out who is linking to them, helping their rankings."

When searching for relevant sites to have links to your site, do a search for "no follow" blogs. Some blogs have in their code a no follow, meaning they will not pass on points from the back link you post in your comment. So your link will not get SEO credit, but you do get to share your opinions and build relationships with the community, which is very important for your online reputation.

One more tip: Always check to be sure that each of your web pages has a unique page title, as discussed earlier in the chapter. All too often, websites contain many untitled pages. This is a foolish oversight, and it's easily corrected. Name your pages, and ask your technical person to simply type the name in and save the page. That's all there is to it! It's a little bit of effort that can have a significant effect. A quick and free way to check which pages within your website need unique title tags is to use xml-sitemaps.com. You have several options after your sitemap is completed. One is to use an html version to display on your website to help your viewers find information they need. A second is to use an XML site map, which is automatically generated, which you should upload to your server. This will help search robots index the pages within your site. A third option is to scan through the site map to find any pages that have duplicate titles or worse, Untitled.

Last, read (or reread) Chapter 3, It's Not Your Father's E-Mail, and understand the importance of WIIFM (What's in It for Me?), because no matter how high your page ranking is—or how many potential customers you get to visit your website—if they don't find something of value, they are out of there!

Don Schindler, digital strategist at www.MediaSauce.com,

said:

> This is actually very, very important. External links mean more than almost all other pieces. This is also why black hat SEO guys can be successful quickly. They use unethical linking strategies to build networks and link sites together to push a site up to the top of a SERP for a specific keyword. But these sites quickly fail because search engines are getting better at discovering these sites and blacklist them.

Every site has "voting" capability for any other site. If site A is linking to site B, then site A is passing along some of its PageRank to site B. If site A links to a lot of sites on the same page, then its voting relevance, or link juice, is degraded. If site A and site B are just linking back and forth to each other, then both sites might be degraded.

The higher the site's PageRank, the more voting power it has. You want quality links from sites with high PageRank but that are also relevant to your content. If the search engines see that the two sites do not have anything in common, then the link juice will be degraded.

Some of the highest-ranking sites are sites where links cannot be purchased, like .edu or .gov sites. There are many ways to link your site to other sites, especially through social media. Blog commenting is one of the most popular.

Practices to Avoid

Keyword Density: There is also an aspect of **SEO** known as *keyword density*. Search engine spiders check this by analyzing your list of important keywords and checking the number of times those words are actually used on your web page. This helps to prevent a process called *hijacking,* which occurs when someone lists important words such as "presidential election" for a website that sells shoes so that it garners traffic for the site. Think about how much traffic you might generate with keywords that aren't true. It's actually *none,* because search engines check and penalize for this kind of dishonest keyword stuffing. Four to 7 percent density is good for any given keyword. Go to the download section of www.theSocialMedia Bible.com

for your free Word Density Analyzer Macro.

A quick word of caution on websites that have Flash web pages: because they don't have text content and keywords, getting a high ranking on such pages has been impossible in the past with a standard Flash design. Flash sites can now be optimized through web objects to showcase content. URL, title tags, description, and keywords are all available to use. Building an alternative HTML site specifically for the search engines is not only possible but is widely used and effective.

You Can't Hide Cloaking: A practice called *cloaking* is also worth mentioning. No, it doesn't have anything to do with *Star Trek*'s Klingons' ability to go invisible. It's about trying to hide your stuffing keywords—the ones that really have nothing to do with your content, and are only there to hijack web traffic—in plain sight. How might one do this? By loading your page's content with those unrelated words in a text color that is the same as the background. What would you see? Nothing!

However, the search engines are wise to this, and can spot it quickly—and if you get caught trying to cheat a search engine, you will be banned from that search engine for up to five years. Imagine learning that your web page will never be listed in a search again for the next half a decade. Try explaining that to your supervisor or to your board of directors.

Tips, Techniques, and Tactics

Here is a quick list of some of the techniques mentioned in this chapter, and some that weren't addressed:

- Don't flood or stuff keywords with words not found in your pages' content even though Google doesn't look at it. Other search engines may.
- Don't bury or cloak text with the same color as the background or in margins.
- Don't participate in link farms.
- Don't use redirects, URLs, or web addresses that don't have pages, but only redirect the browser to another page unless you use a 301 redirect to permanently direct traffic to another site. You also need to make sure you redirect your www.domain.com to domain.com—search engines see *www* and your *domain.com* as two separate sites. A permanent redirect on the *www* is a must. A quick call to your domain registrar can help you determine if this is set up correctly.

- Do have at least 25 reputable external links back to your site from other reputable and related content sites—it's a good start. Much more are required today to get significant SERP ranking movement. Remember, they must link from other high-traffic or high-impact sites within your industry.
- Do use vortals or Vertical Web Portal, directories (hubs), and blogs for link backs. See Chapter 4, The World of Web Pages, or search Google for more information.
- Do integrate a blog into your website and add content to it regularly.
- Do rearrange your keywords to create keyword phrases.
- Do be sure that the keywords in your metas match your page content.
- Do create unique titles containing your most important keywords.
- Do include your keywords in your meta description.
- Do create good content (which contain your keywords).
- Do have at least eight keyword hyperlinks (internal, external, anchor).
- Do have at least eight keyword alt tags.
- Do place your keywords in your anchor code (see your programmer for this).
- Do research-related keywords and try to rank for them. This process never stops on successful SEO campaigns. You're either growing or you're dying.
- Do place your keywords in your file names: .jpg, .gif, .asp, .php.
- Do link PDFs and text documents with keywords in actual content of those documents.
- Do create comprehensive site maps. There should be two site maps: one for users, which can be a straight HTML page, and one for Google, which should be XML. This is very helpful for search engines. www .xml-sitemaps.com is a free resource.

- Do place your keywords in captions and headings. H1 headings have the most emphasis, followed by H2, H3, then bold.

- Do use bullets, bold, and underlined (hyperlinked) text, for emphasis for both your viewers and the search engine spiders.

- Do keep your pages fresh, with at least 15 to 25 percent change. While there is no time limit on freshness, the fresher the better!

- Do use subdirectories: for example, with www.yourdomain.com /alligator/yourpage.html, the best solution is to use www.yourdomain .com/aligator/your-page and eliminate the ".html." Also, never go over four slashes total, and never use variables or "?" in the html.

- Do use subdomains: www.alligator.yourdomain.com, in which you create a folder with a keyword name. See your IT person to learn if and how you can do this.

- Never use iframes to build a website. Search engines cannot read websites that are inside iframes.

- Keep navigation out of JavaScript with dropdowns. This is also harder for search engines to read.

- Do choose a handful of popular social media sites, join, be an active and helpful member.

- Do post comments on related blogs. Be honest, helpful, and follow the rules for that blog.

- Do post an update daily on your social media profiles. Need help finding content? Search for latest news in your industry and tweet, blog, or post about it. Share it with others.

- Do be patient. SEO is an ongoing process. Not something you try. This is vital to your company's success.

- Do integrate SEO into your daily routine. Set aside one hour a day to blog, post, comment, and share and add content to your websites, social profiles, and online groups.

- Do be a friendly neighbor. Remember, everything you do online stays online forever. Customers will be reading your statements for years to come.

- Do keep up to date on what is considered White Hat SEO versus Black Hat. Visit www.theSocialMediaBible.com to keep up to date on what is now considered good SEO.

- Do share your resources. Volunteer for great online organizations like www.Kiva.org.

One reason is you get a quality back link; a second is that you're helping your fellow man; and a third is that it is great public relations and something you can blog about.

- Do protect all of your company names online in the major social networks. Choose your company name as your user name on social sites to protect them from competitors and would-be fake employees.

- Also, if the keyword you are targeting is available as a user name, scoop it up. The future of search is in social media sites. So when someone searches in Twitter for social media, having your user name match this keyword will help you rank high.

- Do hold on to those old domain names. If you change your website name, keep the old one and do a permanent redirect with all the pages within the site.

- Do keep the same URLs that are indexed. If you update your site, make sure to keep the same URLs for the pages.

- Do start a podcast and add to it at least monthly; weekly is best. You can rank quickly for keywords using free radio or podcast-like portals like www.blogtalkradio.com.

- Do write articles and submit to online PR sites linking back to your websites, blogs, *and* your social media profiles.
- Do remember to post back links to your social media profiles.

Dozens and dozens of search engine criteria are used nowadays. Every time you score in a particular area, your web page gets points. Once the search engine's algorithm has tested everything and has awarded all of the possible points for each category, the algorithm then computes an overall *page rank*. You can see every page's ranking in the Google menu bar as a progressive green bar. The greener your page gets, the higher it's ranked. (Side note: The term *page rank* was first used by one of the founders of Google, Larry Page. Perhaps it's more than a coincidence that it's called "page *rank*.")

The ROI of Social Media

Blogging and BlogTalkRadio Really Made a Difference

Introduction

The PI social media network includes the *Procurement Insights* and *PI Window on Business* blogs, the *PI Window on Business* show on BlogTalk Radio, and the PI Inquisitive Eye and TV2 Young Entrepreneurs Internet TV Channels. The *PI Window on Business* is a featured show on BlogTalk Radio.

The combined syndicated reach through affiliations with social media sites such as BlogTalkRadio (which has more than 7 million listeners each month), [and] Evan Carmichael (500,000 visitors monthly) as well as various

(continued)

(*continued*)

social networking groups and forums has enabled the PI social media to connect with an ever-expanding audience of readers, listeners, and now viewers.

Background

The PI social media network's origins began with the launch of the *Procurement Insights* blog in May 2007. The blog was created as a means of providing various magazines and publications with a single site access to our articles and reports.

Procurement Insights is today the top sponsored blog in its industry sector in terms of the number of total sponsors.

As a means of building upon and expanding the reach of the *Procurement Insights* blog, the *PI Window on Business* show was launched. Within three months, it was a featured show across the entire BlogTalkRadio network.

The *PI Window on Business* blog was launched as an adjunct support for the show. Within the first six months, the total number of site visitors cracked the 10,000 mark on a monthly basis.

Based on the cross-pollination between venues both within and external to the PI social media network, the *Procurement Insights* blog realized an 1,100 percent increase in blog visitors in the past 30 days, while both the *PI Window on Business* show and blog have seen equally impressive growth.

The PI social media network recently launched two Internet TV channels as well as corresponding blogs.

Strategy

The hive, or cross-pollination concept, or theory, is based on the observation that individuals will likely choose at most one or two primary social networks as their preferred platforms. That is, they will spend the majority of their social networking time interacting within these main hives.

While they may venture out into the vast social media/social networking world visiting countless other networks, [just like] the honey bee, these forays are ultimately geared toward gathering information and insights to bring back to the hive to share with their established community of contacts.

Simply put, while static, single sites (blogs, websites, and so on), that limit their cross-pollination activities to providing somewhat passive links to other similarly myopic single site blogs or websites, have failed to recognize that market dynamics change, and that you have to connect with the audience through their preferred venue points.

Implementation

The PI social media and its service offerings provides our clients with an ability to transition from the traditional and largely ineffective broadcasting model of yesterday, to the relationship-centric conversational marketing world of social media.

Opportunity

The opportunity afforded the PI social media network, through its services both in the present as well as in the foreseeable future, has been proven by the steady and sustained growth in readership, listener, and viewer base.

Through this expanded and diverse reach that leverages venues such as blogs, Internet radio, Internet TV, and social networks, the company's increasing revenue base reflects the model's effectiveness—even during a slow economic period.

Conclusion

The company's revenue forecast is $250K US. The *PI Window on Business* blog was launched, and the *PI Window on Business* blog's overall Alexa rank was 1,014,248 with a U.S. ranking of 627,904. The *PI Window on Business* blog's overall Alexa ranking was 855,686. In terms of the new U.S. ranking, the March numbers showed that we are now at 328,775, which is a 299,129-position improvement over the 627,904 from two weeks previous.

The *Procurement Insights* blog took two and a half years to break the 100,000-reader mark while the *PI Window on Business* took only nine months to hit the 50,000 mark.

In its first year, the *PI Window on Business* show on BlogTalkRadio had more than 35,000 listens/downloads, and became a featured show within three and a half months of launching.

—Jon W. Hansen, http://piwindowonbusiness.wordpress.com/book-resource-center/jon -hansen-host-pi-window-on-business-show; http://bit.ly/mUex9b

Expert Insight

Marc Canter, CEO of Broadband Mechanics, www.broadbandmechanics.com

Marc Canter

I'm the CEO of a company called *Broadband Mechanics*. The product enables any community to build and run their own social network. Most people use it to create their own Facebook kind of experience. But there are LOADS of other ways it can be utilized.

My past is that I have been in the software business for about 29 years. I started a company called *MacroMind* that became *Macromedia*, so I'm a toolsmith by trade, and watched the blogging world and the world of what I call the *open mesh* evolve over the past few years; open social networking, and structured content, and what I call *digital wide style aggregation*.

It all leads to saying basically, *open* is the new black. . . .

. . . I mean, certainly in the world of expression and blogging, that is kind of obvious. But the other thing is where the user's data, their profile record, their social graph, should be owned by them. We shouldn't be locked inside of *Facebook* or *MySpace*. So we are starting to see the standard, like *OpenID*, and a new effort from Google called *OpenSocial*, which they are using to build lots of great solutions with.

All these are standards that are emergent. We are even seeing Microsoft opening up, believe it or not! . . .

. . . Facebook's recent moves are showing that it very much wants to "take over the entire web." What people need to do is play along with those 850 million people and have a great time, while at the same time realize that THEY control their own destiny, not Facebook. So now—more than ever—open social networking is important. . . .

. . . I'm a toolsmith and we've been trying to build some tools to help solve that. We call one of them a *persona editor,* which helps to stay on top of managing all of your different personas. Okay?

The other thing is we are seeing a big trend going from giant, centralized social networks, these kinds of horizontal networks, to tens of thousands of niche vertical networks. Right? And a typical person will be in a membership of one or two horizontal networks, or maybe even five or ten niche networks. So whether that's the school you go to, or the after-school activities of you dealing with your friends and kids, the affinities like Reggae or Chocolates.

So the trick here is to have a world, have a blueprint, and a world within, that can practically adapt to the fact that Microsoft is going to do live mesh and Google is going to do this, and Yahoo! is going to have their own thing, and after a while we have to leave some crumbs on the table for a smaller-software guy. We want to get involved and we want to mesh into this huge world, and perhaps build our own ecosystem.

All those poor people locked inside of Ning—need to get out—as soon as possible! . . .

. . . And we see more and more consolidation over the years. I mean, this is where us old-timers can tell you, "Back in the '80s, when it was between *Microsoft* and *Apple*," right.

That world has changed now. So, along the way the other thing we've seen the rise of is *international*, and maybe the governments of Singapore or Dubai want to do some of this stuff and they do not want to use Yahoo! or Google, right! And maybe you see innovation coming out of Russia. I mean, this is no longer just a game that is played off of Silicon Valley or Lafayette, Louisiana.

. . . Oh, by the way, needless to say, both the Chinese and Russian governments are tightly coupled to these cyber-terrorists. Whether it's an attack on Google or an attack on Estonia or when they invaded Georgia, we're seeing the power of online technology being used in all sorts of ways. Right? So we are starting to see the realities of technology and politics, virtual economics. When the oil industry is attacked and they claim that they are making too much money, they can turn and say, "Well, look, the software business. They make even higher margins than we do." As if that matters, right? This is somehow supposed to deflect the attention.

You know, we are finding the technology to be intrinsic and embedded everywhere. It's no longer, "You can keep your head in the sand." And so, the issues of all software being about people and open standards, if users want to control the rights to this general notion of social media, as we move forward, it will affect everything. . . .

. . . When I saw the web first and it was simple HTML graphics, I felt as if we were going backward, because we did have graphics and video on our screens in the early '90s. They were coming over the wire; they were coming off of a CD-ROM. And it took about 10 or 15 years for the world to catch up.

(continued)

(continued)

Just now, with *Flickr* and *YouTube*, we now have a full media on our machines, right? And so we are seeing a number of different factors. One of them I call *persistent content.* So, like the BBC or NPR, are going to put up all of this content into the clouds and it's going to be there, available, full time. And we've got *Hulu* and we've got *iTunes,* and it's all there and we are competing in all this knowledge and it's sitting there in the clouds waiting for us.

So whole new kinds of applications and services will be born that rely upon that stuff, you know, and then to be able to rely upon storage and computing grids and all this incredible stuff that, even five years ago, was only a dream and a glimmer in our eyes.

So if we jump forward four or five years in a natural helix, of course there will still be normal people who still just use e-mail. You know, it takes a long time for stuff to disseminate through society.

Check out news regarding OAuth 2.0 and XAuth—timestamp—spring 2010. . . .

http://www.readwriteweb.com/archives/oauth_2_draft.php; http://rww.to/9uR9Ez.

Another is a large media company called *Radio One,* so they have a site called www.radio-one.com.

And they have a bunch of sister sites, because we also have an aggregation engine in the CMS publishing system. So, we have a bunch of sister sites that we also built for them.

GT Channel is a great kind of niche network for car enthusiasts, people who are into drifting. Then there is what we call a *Meta* network, called www.socialworld.com.

These are for people who put on events, who produce concerts, and so they can get their own network and we built it for our customer called *Acteva*. So they sell tickets, and do ticketing online.

To listen to or read the entire Executive Conversation with Marc Canter, go to www.theSocialMediaBible.com.

To-Do List

- Understand your keywords for every page.

  Be sure that every individual page is analyzed for its own keywords. You want to bring your customer to the exact page at the exact time they are ready to convert. (See Chapter 4, The World of Web Pages, for more on this.)

- Check your page titles.

It's an easy thing to do, and to overlook. Open your pages and look in the Title Bar. Come up with a title that includes your most important keywords, and remember to do so for every page. Use free tools like www.xml-sitemaps.com to check for untitled pages.

- Check your meta keywords.

Open your page, select View, then Page View, and look for your meta keywords. If they don't reflect your content, then you won't get ranked highly.

- Build your external reputable links.

Type "site:www.yourdomain.com" into Google, and see how good you are doing. If you don't have 20 external reputable links, then go get some. When getting back links from sites, ask them to use one of your keywords to link to you.

- Never try to trick a spider.

Never, ever, try to trick a search engine spider. It might work for a while, but they always will catch you. If they do, you could be banned from search engines for up to five years.

- Always have a strong WIIFM.

This is always the most important commandment. Whether it's SEO, SEM, e-mail, web pages, or a hard copy brochure, your marketing message *always* has to have a strong "What's in It for Me?" (See Chapter 3, It's Not Your Father's E-Mail, for more information on this.)

Conclusion

What does SEO have to do with social media? A lot! It's all about having a presence on the Web. It's about being found exactly when your customers are looking for you. It's about being found before your customers find your competition. It's about always showing up in a listing no matter what your customer types in when they're trying to find your product or service—despite where they are in the buying cycle, or whatever keyword they think is relevant. And it's about being part of the World Wide Web with integrity.

To hear all of the Expert Interviews, go to www.theSocialMediaBible.com.

Downloads

For your free downloads associated with *The Social Media Bible,* go to www .theSocialMediaBible.com,

and enter your ISBN number located on the back of the book above the bar code. Be sure to enter the dashes.

Credits

The ROI of Social Media was provided by:

Jon W. Hansen, http://piwindowonbusiness.wordpress.com/book -resource-center/jon-hansen-host-pi-window-on-business-show

Expert Insight was provided by:

Marc Canter, CEO of Broadband Mechanics, www.broadbandmechanics .com

Technical edits were provided by:

Michael Donato, managing partner at National PC Solutions, www .nationalpcsolutions.com

Note

1. Project Xanadu was the very first hypertext project, founded in 1960 by Ted Nelson. "Today's popular software simulates paper. The World Wide Web (another imitation of paper) trivializes our original hypertext model with one-way ever-breaking links and no management of version or contents."

CHAPTER 19

Marketing Yourself (Search Engine Marketing)

www.LonSafko.com/TSMB3_Videos/19SEM.mov

Search engine marketing (SEM) is one of the most effective ways you can market and advertise your website on the Internet. There is nearly no financial risk; the costs are incredibly low when compared to any type of conventional advertising; and, unlike any other advertising, it's based on performance. There is, however, a great deal of risk involved if you don't understand that everything you say and do is part of your online brand.

People forget that you can't separate one from the other and it gets them in trouble. When was the last time you've heard a newspaper, radio, television, or magazine tell you that if your ad doesn't generate calls, you don't have to pay for it? Never.

Although it's possible for this chapter to be read and implemented without reading Chapter 18, Spotlight on Search (Search Engine Optimization), you are strongly recommended to also read that chapter. The two are complementary; one is the yin to the other's yang. And although either can be executed without the other, the synergy of doing both well can put you at the top of the rankings.

What's in It for You?

As discussed in Chapter 18, Spotlight on Search (Search Engine Optimization), when you take the time and follow the simple guidelines to making your web page appealing to the search engine spiders, you will rank the highest on the organic or nonpaid listings. When you add a well-thought-out SEM keyword advertising campaign, you will own the sponsored listings. When SEO and SEM are combined on one web page, the rankings are unstoppable.

SEM Stands for Search Engine Marketing

When someone is looking for the type of product or service you provide, he will use his favorite search engine—be it Google, Bing, Yahoo!, Ask, or one of the countless others available today. He will type in one to several words that he thinks best describe what you do or offer, and will then hit Enter.

SEM in part means marketing your web page(s) through a paid CPC (cost-per-click) or PPC (pay-per-click) marketing plan. You still have to consider your blog (see Chapter 6, The Ubiquitous Blog). If you are running an SEM campaign and are paying for PPC, the relevance of your online advertisements to the search query a user performed, how much you are paying per click, and what you are spending each month for that campaign, will determine where you show up on the sponsored links section of the search page. This is referred to as a *paid listing*. When you use Google, Bing, or other search engines to perform a search, you will usually see the organic listings in the left column, and the paid listings on the right column (or sometimes in the top several rows on the left above the organic listings).

Back to the Beginning

SEM Is Named and Introduced

The SEM advertising system first appeared in February 1998, when Jeffrey Brewer presented the pay-per-click concept at the TED8 conference in California. http://adwords.google.com

founder Bill Gross is given credit for conceiving of PPC while working at IdeaLab in Pasadena, California. Gross's 25-employee start-up became Yahoo!'s Overture, which is Yahoo!'s Search Engines' pay-per-click system.

Google offered its own, impression-based form of search engine advertising in December 1999, based on CPM, or cost-per-1,000 impressions (or views). They introduced AdWords in October 2000, which allowed their users to create their own ads for placement on the Google search engine result pages. In 2002, Google switched to PPC, the then-successful Yahoo! advertising model.

What You Need to Know

Assuming that you have read Chapter 6, The Ubiquitous Blog, and have begun blogging, and read Chapter 18, Spotlight on Search (Search Engine Optimization), and have performed your SEO, your pages are gradually being ranked higher in the organic listings. It's now time to work on your SEM—or simply, your pay-per-click advertising.

PPC advertising requires that you decide which keywords or keyword phrases you used in your SEO campaign are most important—the ones that best match those that your customer will type into a search engine when trying to find your site. It's also the words and phrases that come directly from your website's content—the words you will be able to pay for when a potential customer clicks on your link.

The definition of SEM used in this chapter is relatively generic, because the best way to experience the ease and excitement of creating and managing an SEM campaign is by actually *doing* it. Also, each search engine is a little different in regard to how you go about creating an account, adding funds to your budget, and reporting on its success.

While there are many providers of PPC, banner advertising, and other pay-for-performance advertisers, Google is by far the largest. According to VentureBeat Digital Media, the top five search engines in market share at the time this chapter was written were as follows: Google 68 percent; Bing/Yahoo! 27.4 percent; with 70 other search engines sharing 4.6 percent. Even with an algorithm and sponsored advertising merger between the two largest players below Google, Yahoo!, and Bing, Google still represents the strongest market share. What does this mean? That it's probably best to start your SEM campaigns with Google AdWords, as it already owns over two-thirds of the market share, or two-thirds of your potential customers.

Start Your SEM Campaign

To launch your SEM keyword campaign, you should begin with two- to four-word keyword phrases. These keyword combinations are significantly more specific than a single word and will help you connect with a more targeted and specific audience. Go to the SEM provider for your search engine of choice, such as Google AdWords, Yahoo! search engine marketing (formerly Overture), or Microsoft's AdCenter, and sign up for an account; you can do this with a credit card or a PayPal account (Figure 19.1). Then follow the easy steps to complete your registration and set up a keyword campaign.

After you select your keyword, you'll want to see what others are willing to pay each time someone clicks on the word from the sponsored links section of that search engine. The more generic the word, the more expensive the CPC (cost-per-click) is. The keyword you like best is often one that other advertisers desire most as well. This can drive the CPC up to a point at which you may want to consider using a more specific—and less expensive—keyword.

While most keywords can cost under $1, many are as high as $5 per click, and they can even go as high as $80 for terms like "Austin DUI," for example. Once you've done several keyword campaigns, you will find the *sweet spot*—the word that generates the most traffic at the lowest CPC.

What Are You Willing to Pay?

The next step is to indicate how much you are willing to spend on each click. It's a bidding system, and even though the last CPC was 50 cents, you may want to raise the stakes and claim that you're willing to pay $1 for that same click. By bidding higher, you have the opportunity to be placed higher on the search engine's list of paid sponsors. Remember: The reason and purpose in life for a search engine is the theory of relativity—that is, they must always return the most relative search results. The same is true for paid sponsors; the victory doesn't always go to the highest bidder. Your relevance—and how often your sponsored ad has been clicked in the past—all determine your position.

Now that you have selected a keyword and know how much it will cost you each time someone clicks on it, the search engines will ask for your monthly budget: How much you are willing to spend each month on clicks for your entire advertising account. Start with a small amount—say, $100—and watch the keyword's progress over the next 30 days. That's all there is to it!

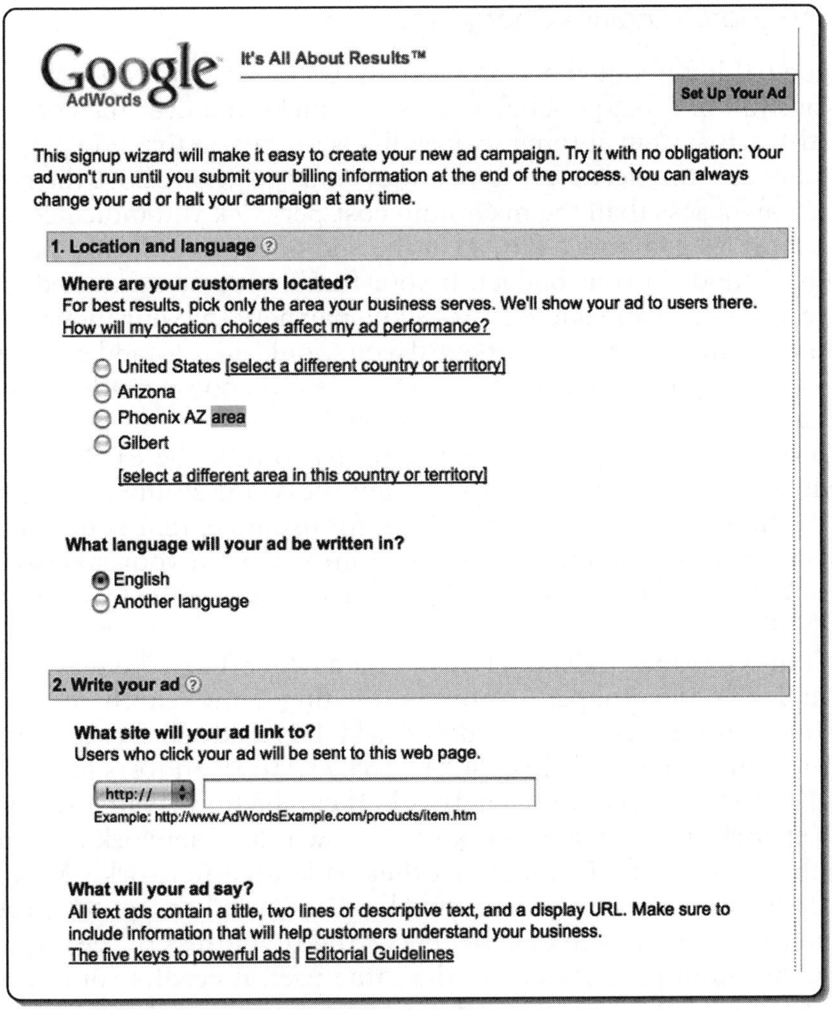

FIGURE 19.1 AdWords Wizard

The next time you go to that search engine and type in your keyword or keyword phrase, you will be listed in the sponsored link section. If someone is listed above you, it means that they are willing to pay more than your maximum bid, or that they historically had a good click-through rate (which means that people clicked on them more often than the competing sponsors).

How the Search Engines Charge You

The good thing about the search engine's bids is that you don't have to pay your full bid cost-per-click if someone picks you over the competition. The AdWords system automatically adjusts pricing so that you pay only the minimum amount necessary to maintain your position above the next ad— which may be less than the maximum cost-per-click you indicated you bid. This continues 24 hours a day, so at the end of the month, you may have a surplus of funds in your budget. If your funds become exhausted, you will receive a notice from your search engine partner that your money is about to run out, and you will be asked if you would like to add more money. If you do, everything continues normally. If you choose not to, you simply no longer appear in the sponsored listings.

Just as there is always someone trying to beat the SEO system with techniques like link farms, cloaking, and keyword stuffing, people try to beat the SEM system as well. Suppose, for example, that your competitor hires someone at minimum wage to sit and click on your sponsored link all day. Within a short amount of time, she would have cost you your entire SEM budget!

Things like this really did happen for a while. Then the search engines got wind of it and stopped it from happening. Now search engines track your Internet Protocol, or IP address, which is a number assigned to your computer that looks like this: 74.213.164.71. An IP address is unique and identifies each computer on a network. It can be for private use on a local area network (LAN, like at work or your wireless network at home), or for public use on the Internet or other wide area network (WAN, a network that interconnects geographically distributed computers, LANs, or the Internet). The search engine checks the IP address of the clicker, and if there are multiple clicks from the same user, it credits your account— and even bans that user from clicking in the future. (Don't you just love this stuff?)

Once you see the return on investment (ROI) on your SEM keyword campaign, you will want to go back to the search engine and create additional campaigns for new keywords and phrases. While teaching at a conference in Portland, Oregon, the author met someone who manages 165 keyword campaigns every month! He said that he spends a lot of money on them, but that they usually return 350 percent of what he spends in sales— and generates new customers. This alone is worth the cost of customer acquisition.

Tips, Techniques, and Tactics

To get started on your own SEM campaign, take the following steps: Go to www.theSocialMediaBible.com

and download your Key Word macro.

- Use the macro to determine your most important keywords.
- Use the keyword finder in Google or Yahoo! to gauge what others are paying for the keywords that you have selected.
- Determine how much of an initial budget you are willing to spend on each of your keyword campaigns.
- Consider two- and three-word keyword phrases, because they are often less expensive and significantly more specific—and can return more effective results.

The ROI of Social Media

Turning a Fun Hobby into an Internet Business

Background

Paul Petty, the creator of rcFoamFighters, dreamt of a way to escape the average everyday work routine. During a scheduled business conference in Miami, Paul attended a presentation by Lon Safko. The presentation and casual talks with Lon inspired Paul to try to turn his hobby of RC Airplanes into a part-time side business, with an eventual goal to free himself from

(continued)

(continued)

the everyday cubicle work environment. rcFoamFighters was created on January 1, 2009.

Strategy

Paul's strategy was to harness the power of social media to promote his new idea and spread word of his business, rcFoamFighters, across the globe. By using all the available free advertising through social media, there would be no substantial start-up costs.

Implementation

The primary method was to use YouTube to create a large viewer and fan base. This large fan base would eventually lead to large quantities of traffic [to] the independent rcFoamFighters blog site. The blog was set up with minimal costs for server space, and the freeware program WordPress was used as the blog software. Other social media sites such as Facebook, Twitter, and MySpace were also used to get the message out. Social media ideas also included using the many RC forums that thousands of people use daily to share information about RC-related topics.

Opportunity

One opportunity was to become a YouTube partner, which allows for revenue sharing with YouTube. The blog site would host many affiliate ads to generate income from ad clicks and affiliate sales [and the] possible opportunity to land sponsors, which would provide free product and/or monetary compensation [and the] opportunity to sell actual products and digital products, such as PDF plans.

Conclusion

rcFoamFighters' level of current success has been all due to the use of social media to build a large fan base. Currently, the YouTube site has had nearly 500,000 views and 1,400 subscribers. rcFoamFighters is now a YouTube partner and receives monthly income from YouTube. The YouTube traffic is constantly growing and the revenue increasing. The independent blog site has been visited by over 30,000 unique visitors from 148 countries. Affiliate ad clicks and product sales are constantly increasing. rcFoamFighters is now associated with two sponsoring partners. One of them is one of the largest online hobby stores that provides compensation and free sponsored products.

The original goal to be free from the typical cubicle work life is seen on the near horizon.

—Paul Petty, founder of rcFoamFighters
www.rcFoamFighters.com

Expert Insight

Linh Tang, coauthor, *Launching Your Yahoo! Business* and *Succeeding at Your Yahoo! Business*, www.LinhTang.com

Linh Tang   Yeah, virtual-electronic-retailing—or V-E-Tailing—is about selling products that are digital. And what I mean by that is you could have [any kind of product]. Ours is paper models; and our Paper Model Inc. is three-dimensional advertising, creating corporate specialty products, and school projects. We specialize in replicas of buildings and monuments and even . . . cars. Our main customer is the education market; one model that made our site popular is "California Missions." We've had a lot of fourth-graders who have to come in and build that for their school projects; they come to our website, download it, print it out on a computer, and within 30 minutes to an hour they have a replica of that particular model. . . .

(*continued*)

(continued)

That's the beauty of electronic retailing. Once you create the product, it's there! People continuously come and purchase your product—unlike eBay, [where] you continuously have to take pictures, upload to your store, and—once you've sold that particular item—go find new products.

Well, SEM marketing first started with optimizing your website and doing link building. But with social media, it has taken . . . I believe it has taken the corner. What I mean by that is now it incorporates blogs, videos, RSS, social networks, alerts. Now, with the limited time people have, they don't want to come visit your site every day. But what you can do is feed out your information to all these other networks. I call it "The Mall." Why do you want to be at "The Mall"? Because everyone else is there. . . .

Now everybody can get traffic to their website. You can do a little bit of search engine marketing, but what happens when they're there? Now social media tools, such as video and blogs, give your potential customers added value, added information. For example, one of the websites I'm working on is Office Chairs Outlet built on the highly recommended Volusion shopping cart platform. We did a product demo of one of the chairs, just as if you were walking into the showroom and getting a demo from a salesperson. Now, all the other websites out there have a little description, which they all get from the manufacturers, anyway. But here, we are actually doing a demo for you. So you don't even have to sit and read the page of descriptions; you could actually just sit there and watch a 30-second video of how that chair works, how that chair operates, how it's ergonomic, and why it's the best. . . .

You can now put your link, your URL, your website information on YouTube. So, if anybody went to YouTube, [they could be sent] back to your site for further information. The beauty of YouTube is you can often embed that video onto your website or blog. So you don't have any expensive streaming or hosting fees. . . .

The social media ecosphere is huge. There's a lot of tools out there, and what you should really do is sit down with a social media strategist to see, "What's your first step?" Is it doing video, or just doing a blog? We've seen success by just doing that. You can blog about anything. It doesn't have to be just about your product only—and that's what was going on with search engine optimization, was that you were just optimizing using your website for your information, your keywords.

To listen to or read the entire Executive Conversation with Linh Tang, go to www.theSocialMediaBible.com.

International Perspective

Germany

Flying High with a Global Approach—Lufthansa Takes off with Social Media

Germany-based global air carrier Lufthansa Group is flying high with social media. Their global approach is a success model for any business looking to take off and grow.

Lufthansa has over 50,000 employees, serves over 250 cities in over 100 countries and has over 10,000 flights per week. Their customers travel everywhere—to over 200 countries—and so all this could get out of hand quickly without great strategy, planning, and execution.

Strategy: Customer-Centric

A customer-centric strategy is much easier to say than do, and Lufthansa has pulled it off. A key to their success is embracing the very real target of global travelers looking to have their life simplified with technology. Lufthansa did much more than embrace them, and they thought beyond just their own customers. They researched how global travelers think and tested what would be valuable for them. They began seeking to become the "most linked airline brand in the world," providing passengers access to social networks, information, and applications to make their life easier and frankly more fun. An important step was to allow in-flight Internet access with FlyNet. Then the information sharing and fun really began!

(continued)

(continued)

Planning: Add Value

Lufthansa has been planning and introducing useful social media applications starting with MySkyStatus. It allows passengers to communicate their flight information through social media. Frequent flyers keep others informed instantly about their schedule, including delays.

MySkyStatus works with any airline, and so whether you fly Lufthansa or not, you can always be powered by Lufthansa. It's simple, easy-to-use, and viral since friends see their friends' status via tweets from MySkyStatus. In the first three months there were over 35,000 tweets and a half million page views.

Another application success from the most linked brand is the award-winning Cloudstream, allowing passengers to tuck videos, games, and other entertainment onto a phone, laptop, or notebook for reading later without an Internet connection. It integrates seamlessly with social media and is ideal for flights and other places in-between available Wi-Fi areas.

The cost? Totally free! The value? Passengers say yes!

Execution: Be Local

Lufthansa rapidly implemented MySkyStatus and Cloudstream through their global network. This network thinks globally and acts locally. This is a key lesson: if you're global, be local.

The company maintains dozens of Twitter and Facebook accounts with specific country and language focus. They are staffed by locals on the lookout for information that can assist travelers anywhere in the world.

Lufthansa's local approach hits the ground in China with Renren (similar to Facebook), Youku (similar to Youtube), and Weibo (a hybrid of Twitter and Facebook). Across these social media sites the company quickly broke through 100,000 fans because they operate the sites effectively with local people. Now there's no looking back, because Lufthansa has already gained mindshare country-by-country, city-by-city.

Being local improves the ability to go viral, too. An example is a Lufthansa social media campaign that encouraged people wanting to fly somewhere special to tell their social network. If enough of their friends responded and liked Lufthansa, the company gave the participants travel discounts. The passenger got a discounted ticket and a great trip, the friends found out more about Lufthansa, and the company filled a seat and more in the future. Everybody won!

Summary

Some of these ideas are translatable to your social media strategy, plan, and execution, and most don't cost an arm and a leg. While you're rolling down the marketing runway, fire up your social media engines and reach your targets by being customer-centric, value-adding, and local.

—Doug Bruhnke, CEO
Growth Nation
www.GrowthNation.com

To-Do List

- Perform SEO.

  The most effective way to win at SEM is to perform your SEO first. Even though you are paying to be placed in the sponsored links section, your position will depend on your page ranking (see Chapter 18, Spotlight on Search (Search Engine Optimization)), and how many times your link is clicked. If no one clicks your link, you will move lower and lower in the sponsored links until you disappear. You will be dropped, even if you are willing to pay the most.

- Understand your keywords for every page.

  Be sure that every individual page is analyzed for its own keywords. You want to bring your customer to the exact page at the exact time he is ready to convert. (See Chapter 4, The World of Web Pages, for more on this.)

- Check your meta keywords.

  Open your page, select View, then Page View, and look for your Meta Keywords. If they don't reflect your content, then you won't get ranked highly.

- Always create good content.

  Never, *ever* try to trick a search engine. It might work for a while, but they always will catch you, and possibly ban you from their sites for up to five years.

- Focus on the WIIFM.

  This is always the most important commandment. Whether it's SEO, SEM, e-mail, web pages, or a hard copy brochure, your marketing message *always* has to have a strong "What's in It for Me?" (See Chapter 4 for more information.) Even with paid or sponsored links, you have to have a strong WIIFM to hook your searcher to first read the subject line, and then to read your description. If each of these is written well, the searchers will click on you—and not your competition.

- Search engine market through pay-per-click.

  Try it; it's fun. And while it's nearly the only place you need to spend any money while marketing on the Internet, it has the potential to return more than 300 percent of what you spend.

Conclusion

What does SEM have to do with social media? As much as SEO does—in other words, a good amount. Again, it's all about having a presence on the web, building community, and generating revenue. It's about being there when your prospect is in the buying phase of her cycle, ready to click on the Purchase button. You have to be found when someone is looking for you—whether it's on your web pages, in your photos and videos, on your podcasts, or on your blog. The combination of SEO and SEM is the most cost-effective way to achieve this goal.

To hear all of the Expert Interviews, go to www.theSocialMediaBible .com.

Downloads

For your free downloads associated with *The Social Media Bible,* go to www .theSocialMediaBible.com, and enter your ISBN number located on the back of the book above the bar code. Be sure to enter the dashes.

Credits

The ROI of Social Media was provided by:

Paul Petty, founder of rcFoamFighters, www.rcFoamFighters.com

Expert Insight was provided by:

Linh Tang, coauthor, *Launching Your Yahoo! Business* and *Succeeding at Your Yahoo! Business,* www.LinhTang.com

Technical edits were provided by:

Michael Donato, managing partner at National PC Solutions, www .nationalpcsolutions.com

CHAPTER 20

The Formidable Fourth Screen (Mobile)

www.LonSafko.com/TSMB3_Videos/20Mobile.mov

What's in It for You?

Mobile phones are the epitome of both digital convergence and social media, and have probably done more to advance social media than any other single digital device. One of the first major breakthroughs after the Internet was created was cellular technology. Today's cell phones allow people to download music; read from and write to a blog; surf the web; receive their e-mails; take and share photos and video; Jott speech-to-text messages to themselves and others; tweet to groups in excess of 6,000 followers; capture a photo of a billboard with an embedded link that takes the user to a product website; have a five-star rating of all Italian restaurants within walking distance of your cell phone; get coupons to those Italian restaurants delivered by text directly to your phone; get step-by-step directions on how to get from here to there; access maps, art, and encyclopedic information; watch a movie; take a high quality photograph; post that photograph to a social, web, or blog site; text message; update your website; listen to a podcast; organize your address book and calendar; record your notes . . . and, oh yeah—you can even make a telephone call.

theSocialMediaBible.com

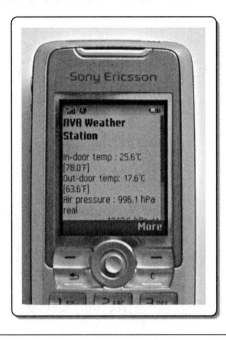

FIGURE 20.1   Mobile Weather on a Mobile Phone

Key Global Telecom Indicators for the World Telecommunication Service Sector in 2010 (all figures are estimates)									
	Global	Developed nations	Developing nations	Africa	Arab States	Asia & Pacific	CIS	Europe	The Americas
Mobile cellular subscriptions (millions)	5,282	1,436	3,846	333	282	2,649	364	741	880
Per 100 people	76.2%	116.1%	67.6%	41.4%	79.4%	67.8%	131.5%	120.0%	94.1%
Fixed telephone lines (millions) (	1,197	506	691	13	33	549	74	249	262
Per 100 people	17.3%	40.9%	12.1%	1.6%	9.4%	14.0%	26.6%	40.3%	28.1%
Mobile broadband subscriptions (millions)	940	631	309	29	34	278	72	286	226
Per 100 people	13.6%	51.1%	5.4%	3.6%	9.7%	7.1%	25.9%	46.3%	24.2%
Fixed broadband subscriptions (millions)	555	304	251	1	8	223	24	148	145
per 100 people	8.0%	24.6%	4.4%	0.2%	2.3%	5.7%	8.7%	23.9%	15.5%
Source: International Telecommunication Union (October 2010)								via: mobiThinking	

FIGURE 20.1.5   Key Global Telecom Indicators

According to a press release from the research firm IDC's Digital Marketplace Model and Forecast (http://www.idc.com/home.jsp?t=1332356335030; http://bit.ly/GExeN2):

- Nearly a quarter of the world's population—close to 2 billion people—were using the Internet regularly in 2010. This number is expected to surpass 2.7 billion unique users—or almost 40 percent of the world's population—in 2015.

- China passed the United States in 2007 to become the country with the largest number of Internet users, and the country's online population is predicted to grow from 275 million users in 2008 to 375 million users in 2012.

- Nearly half of all Internet users will make online purchases in 2010. In 2012, there are more than 1 billion online buyers worldwide making business-to-consumer (B2C) transactions worth $1.2 trillion. Business-to-business (B2B) e-commerce has increased 10-fold, totaling $12.4 trillion worldwide in 2012.

- Global online ad spending was expected to hit $81.1 billion by the year 2011, says a report released by the research firm Piper Jaffray & Co., more than 10 percent of all ad spending across all media. This share has reached 13.6 percent by 2011.

- Roughly 40 percent of all Internet users worldwide currently have mobile Internet access. The number of mobile Internet users reached 546 million in 2008, nearly twice as many as in 2006, and is forecast to surpass 1.5 billion worldwide in 2012.

- The most popular online activities today are searching the web, finding information for personal use, using Internet e-mail, accessing news and sports information, and accessing financial or credit information. In addition to these activities, more than 50 percent of online users worldwide are using instant messaging and playing online games. The fastest-growing online activities include accessing business applications, creating blogs, online gambling, accessing work-related e-mail, and participating in online communities.

- The most popular online activities among mobile Internet users include searching the web; accessing news and sports information; downloading music, videos, and ringtones; using instant messaging; and using Internet e-mail. In 2012, downloading music, videos, ringtones, and apps has become the number one activity among mobile Internet users worldwide.

According to John Gantz, chief research officer at IDC:

> The Internet will have added its second billion users over a span of about eight years, a testament to both its universal appeal and its availability. In this time, the Internet has also become more deeply integrated into the fabric of many users' personal and professional lives, enabling them to work, play, and socialize anytime from anywhere. These trends will accelerate as the number of mobile users continues to soar and the Internet becomes truly ubiquitous.

Given the recent advances in mobile technology, the one tool that you must have to access this wealth of social media is a good cell phone. As Kakul Srivastava of Yahoo!'s Flickr said, "There are three cell phones for every human being on the planet. Get one, learn how to use it, and participate!"

Mobile Applications

The most common data service used on mobile phones today is SMS text messaging.

More than 92 percent of the more than 322.9 million mobile phone users in the United States are actively using text messaging on a regular basis. According to a June 2011 CTIA report, Americans sent more than 196.9 billion text messages each month with more than 2.12 trillion SMS text messages sent in 2011. Mobile telephone usage has surpassed cable TV, web access, and home PCs. More than 95 percent of all new mobile phones, now referred to as smartphones, sold today are web enabled, and more than 100 million U.S. consumers use them regularly.

Many companies have claimed to have sent the very first SMS text message. According to a former employee of NASA, Edward Lantz, the first message was sent by one simple Motorola beeper in 1989 by Raina Fortini from New York City to Melbourne Beach, Florida. Fortini used upside down numbers that could be read as words and sounds. The first commercial SMS message was sent over the Vodafone GSM network in the United Kingdom on December 3, 1992, from Neil Papworth of Sema Group using a

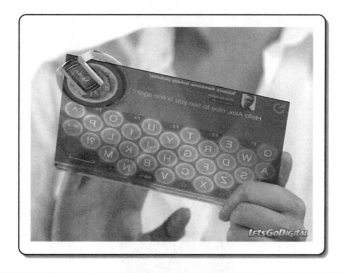

FIGURE 20.2   The Morph Mobile Phone

personal computer, to Richard Jarvis of Vodafone using an Orbitel 901 handset. The text of the message was "Merry Christmas." The first SMS typed on a GSM phone is claimed to have been sent by Riku Pihkonen, an engineering student at Nokia, in 1993 (www.wapedia.mobi/en/Text_Messaging).

Go to www.theSocialMediaBible.com for clickable links.

FIGURE 20.3 Text Message

The next most common use of mobile data services is for music. Music file downloads generated more than $31 billion in revenue last year, with the next in line being ringtone downloads.

In the year 2000, Finnish telephone company Radiolinja (now Elisa) introduced the first mobile news service, delivered by SMS text messaging. After that came video games, jokes, horoscopes, TV content, advertising, and other content downloads. Mobile product sales for ringtones, games, and graphics are displacing the money that is spent on traditional youth products such as music, clothing, and movies.

Other mobile data services range from conducting a job search or seeking career advice from Monster.com;

to transferring up to $1 million in cash from one mobile account in one country to another overseas; to paying your utility bills in one city and a parking ticket in another. Mobile devices and applications are seen as remote controls for the web, or, as Director of Strategy for Crayon Marketing Adam Broitman puts it, "The mobile phone is our remote control for our lives!" (See Broitman's Expert Insight later in this chapter, or listen to Adam Broitman's Executive Conversation by going to www.theSocialMediaBible.com.)

Rich Media

More and more content is being developed for the mobile telephone, as it has quickly become a mass media device—and even commonly called "the Fourth Screen" (with the other three being movie, television, and the PC). With the advent of the iPhone, Android, and other similar smart phones, movie distribution companies are taking new rich media distribution seriously and making it possible to download full-length movies from your PC and transfer them to your phone (in addition to downloading them directly from your mobile device).

Mobile technology is becoming so prevalent, in fact, that it has elicited the creation and inclusion of new words to our everyday vocabulary, one of which is *mobisodes*. A mobisode is a short episode of a popular television show that is specifically intended for mobile device viewing. Radio, television, and satellite TV broadcast media all require us to tune in at a very specific time (same time, same channel) to catch a given program or breaking news, unless you record it using a DVR or TiVo. If you aren't able to get to your TV set in time to view or record it, you either miss the program altogether, or you have to wait for the next broadcast time. Subscribing to a mobile news feed, however, enables you to receive this information anywhere, at any time.

What You Need to Know

Over the past several years, the mobile phone has become increasingly more important to one's participation in social media. With popular networking sites such as Facebook, LinkedIn, and Twitter; photo-sharing sites like Flickr, SmugMug, and Photobucket; video sharing websites such as YouTube and Vimeo; and information sites like Wikipedia, mobile telephone web access is more important than ever. Even personal publishing platform WordPress (see Chapter 4, The World of Web Pages) has plug-ins now that give mobile phone users the ability to view their blog sites on the go. (See Downloads at the end of this chapter.)

Twitter

Twitter has also made a huge impact on texting, microblogging, and communicating through the use of a mobile phone. Please read Chapter 13, Thumbs Up for Microblogging, for a more in-depth description of Twitter and tweets.

Real-Time Social Engagement

The portability of the mobile phone promotes real time, living in the moment, or life presence for its user. The device allows users to participate in an event and share their reactions and ideas with others instantly.

In 2000, this interaction might have been as simple as holding up a cell phone toward the stage at a concert and letting the person on the other end of the connection hear a song. Today, from a mobile telephone one could photograph the concert, videotape it, blog about it, tweet it, and share it with friends, family, and colleagues even before the show ends! Being able to share these important experiences in real time creates strong social bonds.

In one case, a stolen mobile phone was even returned to its owner based on photographs that its camera took and automatically uploaded to the web. And as far as sharing your experiences in real time, Twitter is a great way to post instant, up-to-the-minute news about what you are doing and thinking. (See Chapter 13, Thumbs Up for Microblogging, for more information on microblogging and Twitter.)

Reviews

Mobile user-generated content creates a powerful trusted network, whose recommendations can have a significant impact on your decision making. If a restaurant review comes from someone you know—whether it's a friend or just someone from your hometown—you're likely to receive that review with much more trust than one from a paid critic.

A great enterprise example of this is Yelp.com,

a website that you can access through your computer or through your mobile phone. Connecting to Yelp allows you to check out reviews for any kind of business just by typing in your zip code, or simply allowing your GPS-enabled mobile phone to tell Yelp where you are located. So, for example, if you are looking for a great pasta restaurant near the corner of Main and Broadway, Yelp will show you a half dozen or more restaurant reviews from people who live in that area and who have actually eaten at those restaurants. (To hear or read the Executive Conversation interview with Stephanie Ichinose, the director of communications for Yelp, go to www .theSocialMediaBible.com.)

Mobile Marketing

The popularity of marketing to mobile phone users has grown steadily since the rise of SMS in Europe and Asia in the early 2000s. During this time, businesses began collecting mobile phone numbers to send both wanted and unwanted (spam) advertising messages to their users. Because of global government regulations, SMS has become a legitimate form of advertising. Unlike the public domain in which the World Wide Web exists, mobile carriers control their own networks and have set guidelines and best practices, monitored and enforced by the CTIA (Cellular Telephone Industries Association, the international association for the

FIGURE 20.4 Mobile Gaming

wireless telecommunications industry) and CSCA (Common Short Code Administration), for the entire mobile media industry.

The Mobile Marketing Association and the Interactive Advertising Bureau (IAB) have established strict guidelines and are evangelizing the use of mobile phones for advertisers. This initiative has been very successful in North America, Western Europe, and several other regions.

Another issue with which some countries are dealing is mobile spam advertising messages that are sent to mobile subscribers without an explicit opt-in (see Chapter 3, It's Not Your Father's E-Mail, for more information on opt-ins). This is due to mobile carriers' sales of subscribers' telephone numbers to third parties. Legislation often requires permission, or an opt-in, from the mobile subscriber to advertise to them, which has seriously delayed the growth of mobile advertising and marketing. The mobile carriers require a double opt-in from the subscriber and the ability for the consumer to opt out at any time by sending the word *STOP, END, CANCEL,* or *OPT-OUT* by SMS or text messaging. These guidelines are very similar to the 2004 U.S. CAN-SPAM Act and are established in the MMA Consumer Best Practices Guidelines (see further on). All mobile carriers in the United States voluntarily follow these guidelines. (For more information on the CAN-SPAM Act, see Chapter 3, It's Not Your Father's E-Mail.)

In 2002, Labatt Brewing Company ran the first successful cross-carrier SMS advertising campaign. Since then, mobile SMS advertising has gained recognition as a new advertising channel and a way to communicate to the mobile consumer. Due in part to the 97 percent read rate on SMS messages, large consumer brands have accepted SMS advertising, and have created mobile domain names that allow their consumers to text message their brand name while in a store or at an event. Motorola's ongoing campaign at the House of Blues venues is another example of well-designed mobile advertising. The House of Blues allows their patrons to send their mobile photos to the LED display board and their online blog in real time.[1]

Mobile Web Marketing

For online mobile advertisers, the Mobile Marketing Association (MMA) provides a set of guidelines and standards that specify recommended formats for ads and mobile presentations. Google, Yahoo!, and other major mobile content providers are selling mobile advertising placement as part of their advertising services.

Bluetooth Connection

Bluetooth began in 2003 as a wireless radio protocol technology called *frequency hopping* or *spread spectrum* that chops up the data being sent and transmits chunks of it on up to 75 different frequencies. This allows data transmission using short-range communications from fixed or mobile devices, creating a wireless personal area network or PAN. Bluetooth provides access and secure information exchange between devices such as mobile phones, digital cameras, telephones, personal computers, microphones and headsets, printers, GPS receivers, and video game consoles. Since Bluetooth provides secure high-speed transmission of data, it is an appropriate technology for mobile advertising and marketing. Companies like ProxiBlaster.com,

bluetoothmagnet.com,

and bluecasting.com

are providing Bluetooth marketing solutions. Using Bluetooth, companies can automatically send media files to all Bluetooth-enabled devices, such as mobile phones, PDAs, and laptops within a range of around 100 meters. This is commonly referred to as bluecasting, bluetooth broadcasting, or proximity marketing.

Location-Based Services

Location-based services (LBS) are a great way to send geographically specific advertising and SMS messages to a mobile phone subscriber based on GPS—or radiolocation—or trilateration location for those not equipped with GPS. Radiolocation and trilateration are methods by which a cell phone's location is determined based on its signal strength to the closest cell phone towers. You may have heard of the woman stuck in her car in a blizzard at night who was saved by rescuers who used radiolocation and trilateration to find her car in the snow bank. LBS can even be used to locate a stolen phone or kidnapped person.

Day-to-day uses for LBS might include locating the nearest type of business or service that a customer is looking for—such as an ATM, restaurant, or doctor; determining meeting room schedules; executing turn-by-turn navigation to a specific address; locating friends on a map displayed on your mobile phone; receiving personal alerts, such as notification of a sale on gas and traffic updates that can include warnings of traffic jams and bad weather; finding taxis, people, employees, or rental equipment location; fleet scheduling, identifying passive sensors or RF (radio frequency) tags for packages and railroad train boxcars; or using an E-ZPass, toll watch, or other geographically targeted mobile advertising.

Mobile LBS marketing has also been used for mobile coupons or discounts that are sent automatically to mobile subscribers who are near advertising retailers, restaurants, cafés, or movie theatres. In 2007, Singapore mobile carrier MobileOne initiated an LBS advertising campaign that involved many local marketers that was widely accepted by its subscribers. Companies offering location-based, geo-targeted advertising, or geo-messaging include Loopt.com,

and Hopstop.com.

Mobile Gaming

Mobile gaming takes place when a video game is played on a mobile phone, smartphone, PDA, or handheld computer. The first game that was factory-installed on a mobile phone was called Snake, which came equipped on certain Nokia models in 1997. Snake has actually become the most popular mobile video game on the planet, and is regularly played by more than one billion people worldwide.

Mobile games can be factory installed, installed by memory card or Bluetooth, or—in most cases—downloaded from the carrier for a fee or for free as a mobile app for smartphones. They can include both stand-alone and networked multiplayer games. (See Chapter 15, Virtual Worlds—Real Impact and Chapter 16, Gaming the System: Virtual Gaming, for more information on virtual worlds and gaming.)

One of the most popular gaming applications for mobile technology today is online mobile gambling. In 2005, PokerRoom, a poker software application, was developed by Ongame in which the player can play poker in a single-player or multiplayer mode for real or play money.

MMORPG

In addition to ordinary mobile gaming, MMORPG—or Massively Multi-player Online Role-Playing Games—have become very popular with mobile phone users. (See Chapter 16, Gaming the System: Virtual Gaming, for a complete explanation of MMORPG.) The first of these for the mobile audience were called TibiaME and were developed by CipSoft SmartCell Technology. The company is also working on a gaming application for the first cross-platform MMORPG called Shadow of Legend, which is designed to be played on both PCs and mobile devices.

Location-Based Games

There are even games that one can play on mobile phones that use geographic location technology such as GPS. These are called location-based games, and they integrate the player's position into the game play, making the player's coordinates and movement the main elements.

The best-known example of a location-based game is a high tech treasure hunt game called Geocaching, which is played throughout the world by adventure seekers equipped with GPS devices. The basic idea is to locate hidden containers—called geocaches—outdoors, exchange a hidden gift, and then share your experiences online. Geocaching has become popular with all age groups—especially for people who have a strong sense of community and support for the environment. (You can learn more at www.geocaching.com.)

Mobile In-Game Marketing

There are five popular categories of mobile gaming: interactive real-time, 3-D games, massive multiplayer, social networking, and casual games (the most popular kind). Casual games like Angry Birds are single-player and very easy to play. In addition to many old favorite video games such as Space Invaders, Tetris, and Solitaire, many of the big video game companies have scaled down their computer and console games and have created mobile divisions such as PlayStation Portable and Nintendo DS. Many companies have developed their games directly for mobile phone play.

Large brands are now delivering advertising messages within those mobile games, and often even sponsoring an entire game to drive brand, sales, and consumer engagement. This type of advertising is known as mobile *advergaming* or *ad-funded mobile gaming*. Puma running shoe brand developed a comprehensive engagement marketing campaign by creating a racing game that coincided with the Shanghai F1 race. Their advergame was called F-Wan, which sounds like F1 for Formula One racing and means *play* in Chinese. The racetrack was designed in the shape of their Puma logo, a jumping wild cat with its tail extended. F-Wan was a multiplayer game, allowing up to four gamers to race against one another. The top three best scores each week would win Puma merchandise.

Mobile Viral Marketing

Mobile viral marketing is similar to the e-mail and Internet variety. Its distribution and communication rely on customers to transmit a particular company's content—known as *mobile viral content*—by mobile SMS to other potential customers in their trusted network, and encourage these contacts to pass the content among themselves. To begin a viral marketing campaign, the enterprise *seeds* (or sends) content to first-generation key customers—also called *mavens* and *influencers*—who become *infected* with this information. These individuals, or *communicators*, then forward the message to recipients, who are encouraged to do the same and keep the message moving. The better the "What's in It for Me?" content, the more effective the viral spread of this message will be. In one case, the Italian Passa Parola (Spread of Mouth) [this actually is the literal translation. The correct translation is *word of mouth*] campaign reached 800,000 users solely by using viral marketing.

Mobile Marketing Future

A recent survey stated that approximately 89 percent of major brands are planning to market their products through SMS text and multimedia mobile messaging. One-third of those brands are planning to spend about 10 percent of their total annual marketing budgets on mobile marketing. According to Andrew Koven, president of eCommerce and Customer Experience at Steve Madden, New York, "We'll likely see the continuing shift of dollars out of traditional media into mobile specifically, which is an exciting trend." Within five years, more than half of all major brands are expected to spend between 5 percent and 25 percent of their total annual marketing budgets on mobile marketing. Of the companies that responded to this survey, 40 percent of them have stated that they have already begun mobile marketing to their audiences because of their ability to reach a specific target audience, in a specific geographical location, with a very specific marketing message. For more information, go to www.airwidesolutions .com/press2006/feb2106.html.

Messaging Convergence

Multifunctional services are becoming more popular with mobile phone users because of the ability of these services to integrate SMS text messaging with voice—such as *voice SMS*, in which voice replaces text. One such company is called Jott.

To sign up for Jott's service you simply create an account with your name, group names, and telephone numbers. Once this is complete, you call an 800 number and talk to the answering machine, which asks, "Who do you want to Jott?" You could give your own first name, and Jott replies with your full name. After a confirmation and a tone, the user leaves a standard voice message. Within moments, that message is transcribed from voice to text, and sent to both the user's cell phone as a text message and to a designated e-mail account.

Jott is a great service when you get an idea, remember something, or need to be reminded of something. You can simply *Jott* yourself. This is particularly good when you're driving 60 miles per hour on the freeway, walking down the street, eating at a restaurant—any place where finding paper and a pencil is inconvenient. It's also great to be able to Jott people to tell them you are running 10 minutes late while driving in the car.

To listen to the Executive Conversation with John Pollard, the founder of Jott, please go to www.theSocialMediaBible.com.

The Mobile Marketing Association

The Mobile Marketing Association (MMA, found at www.mmaglobal.com)

is the premier global nonprofit association that strives to stimulate the growth of mobile marketing and its associated technology. The MMA has more than 600 global member companies that include agencies, advertisers, handheld device manufacturers, carriers and wireless operators, retailers, software and service providers, aggregators, technology enablers, market research firms—as well as any company focused on the potential of marketing to mobile phones. The MMA's primary focus is to establish mobile as an indispensible part of the marketing mix. The MMA works to promote, educate, measure, guide, and protect the mobile marketing industry worldwide.

Mobile Phone Technology

The Apple iPhone: As a certified developer for Apple from the mid-1980s to the mid-1990s, the author had a front-row seat to the advent of the many

FIGURE 20.5   iPhone Mobile Phone

innovations that paved the way in the world of technology. Twenty years later, Steve Jobs was still at it. This chapter would be incomplete without mentioning Apple's iPhone because of the impact this single product has had on social media (see Figure 20.5).

On January 9, 2007, Apple announced their version of the smartphone: the iPhone. The iPhone connects to the Internet, plays multimedia, and of course, is a fully functioning mobile phone with text messaging and voice-mail capabilities. The iPhone has a touch screen that replaces a mobile phone's conventional keyboard. It includes both still and video cameras, plays MP3-formatted music and other audio file formats, and proudly represents the fourth-screen category with a fully functioning video player similar to Apple's iPod. The iPhone allows its users to create, upload, share, and view audio, photographs, and video.

With the iPhone's ability to connect to the Internet, you can browse a website, read a blog, access traffic reports, view your stock portfolio, or do anything that you can do with a standard PC and an Internet connection.

After repeated attempts to encourage Apple to participate in *The Social Media Bible*, it unfortunately declined.

Google Android: The Android is Google's answer to Apple's iPhone. It's a smartphone mobile device built on an open-system platform in cooperation with the Open Handset Alliance (OHA), which is a business alliance of 34 firms, including Google, HTC, Intel, Motorola, Qualcomm, Samsung, LG, T-Mobile, Nvidia, and Wind River Systems, which have joined together

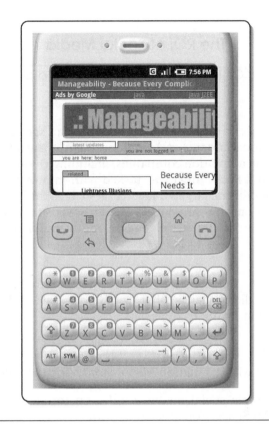

FIGURE 20.6 Android Mobile Phone

to develop open standards for mobile devices. The Android can function with any mobile carrier and features Google Search, Google Apps, Gmail (Google's e-mail system), and Google Chat (Google's instant messaging application). Google's entry into the mobile advertising market is both welcomed and viewed as the company's intention to dominate the mobile-based advertising market as it did with the desktop.

As with all open platforms, a rush of high quality developers are currently building the very best and most advanced applications possible. Similar to the advance in market share that computer technology has enjoyed over the past three decades, this open platform will create more applications, features, and benefits, and will dramatically increase Android's market share. With Google's dominance in web-based advertising combined with the relatively untapped mobile advertising market, the company's revenue potential for dominating mobile marketing is huge.

The ROI of Social Media

Improving Online Visibility Using Social Media Properties

Background

Animation Mentor is an online animation school that specializes in advanced character animation. Students at Animation Mentor learn from professional animators from top animation companies, including Dreamworks, Industrial Light & Magic, and Pixar. Anvil was tasked with improving online visibility for Animation Mentor for targeted keywords such as "animation school" and "character animation," but Animation Mentor's website was built entirely in Flash, leaving little room for search engine optimization efforts.

Strategy

Anvil developed an optimization and promotion strategy for Animation Mentor's social media properties that would both drive traffic to the properties and rank well in search engines.

Implementation

Anvil collaborated with Animation Mentor to pursue the following tactics:

- Created multiple social media profiles on top-tier social media sites Facebook, MySpace, YouTube, and Twitter.
- Launched Animation Tips and Tricks ebook and advised on the development and promotion of Animation Mentor's blog.
- Created a StumbleUpon campaign to direct traffic to the blog, home page, and social media properties; directed paid search traffic to blog, site-hosted webinars, and social media properties.
- Anvil interlinked all social media properties, directing new friends and fans from Facebook and MySpace to the blog and webinars. Anvil also created a blog roll of social media sites for www.animationtipsandtricks.com

and directed users to various social media properties with Twitter.

Opportunity

The opportunity was to capitalize on social media properties created to reach users in the communities in which they feel comfortable.

Conclusion

Animation Mentor's Facebook fan page rose quickly in the rankings, ranking in the top 10 for "character animation," "best animation school," and "online animation school" and ranked twelfth for "animation school" queries. Social media accounted for over 4,000 visitors to www.animationmentor.com.

Since Anvil has started working on social media with Animation Mentor, Animation Mentor has witnessed a substantial increase in accepted students:

- 60 percent YTD increase in enrollment
- 40 percent increase in enrollment since last quarter
- 700 percent increase following term YTD enrollment
- Increased conversion rate by 315 percent

—Mike Nierengarten, account executive
Anvil Media, Inc., www.anvilmediainc.com

Expert Insight

Angela Courtin, Senior Vice President of Marketing Entertainment and Content, MySpace, www.myspace.com

Angela Courtin

You know, I think the beautiful thing about MySpace is that it's different things to different people. We consider ourselves a premier lifestyle portal that connects friends discovering popular culture, and making a positive impact on the world. We really look at it through a different lens. It really is about the experience . . . your personal experience on the space.

We also have a global community, so we are connecting people both domestically as well as internationally. We are in over 30 territories now; and again, I go back to the idea that it is about the fabric of what social media is: the profile of blogging, instant messaging, e-mailing. And then you also get to stream music and watch videos. You get to upload your own photos. At MySpace, you can go into classified listings. We've just created a new business for small businesses in order to advertise their own wares. You can check out events in your neighborhood, in the state, or in the country. You can join groups. You can blog on forums and communities. You can search and befriend celebrities as well as bands, TV shows, your high-school and college friends, your fellow mommies—anyone in your network. So it really is what you want it to be and what you make it. . . .

There's really no typical demographic on our site. Our user base is expanding every month, and I think it's a misconception (as you say) that this is a young person's site. We're more than 85 percent over the age of 18, in terms of our user base. And there are 70 million users in the United States alone that have a profile. And if you think . . . one of my most favorite demographic nuggets to share with people is that 40 percent of all moms that are online are on MySpace. . . . That's a huge number, and they are not going there to spy on their kids; they are actually going there to engage in the tools that make social networking so powerful, as well as the discovery of content. . . .

I [always] go back to this: You can personalize it the way you want. If you want to have a very robust page, you can. If you want to keep it simple, you can do that as well. If you want to build a playlist of your favorite music that you like to listen to, or you just want to have a single track, there's that capability to expand and contract. It's really up to the user. . . . First and foremost, I think it's all about connecting and communicating—regardless of whether you are contacting your friends or community, or your favorite band or celebrity; but it also takes the next step. So it's *how* we communicate through e-mailing and instant messaging, connecting with people of similar interests, uploading photographs, commenting on photographs, sharing photographs. We make it very easy to stay in touch and maintain connection with your family or community of friends. And so this goes back to the analogy of scrapbooking. . . . It is a way to have a one-to-many conversation if you want to keep it that way . . . like, if you want to upload your baby's photos and send those to your friends and family, you can do that with the touch of a button.

So you can blog and you can share on a daily basis what your musings are on everything from politics to music, to your favorite cupcake joint in the neighborhood, or just whom you connected with. It may be an old high-school friend and you want to share that with your other high-school friends.

And then, of course, we're now creating a portable experience; and now you can take that online experience in MySpace and take it directly to your mobile phone. So you can connect whenever you want to, wherever you are, as long as you have your mobile phone . . . which is incredible for someone who is just an average user, connecting with their friends; but even extrapolating beyond that . . . for a band (whether you're signed or independent) the ability to be able to push out communication to 1,000, 14,000, 140,000, 1.4 million, now became very acceptable.

To listen to or read the entire Executive Conversation with Angela Courtin, go to www.theSocialMediaBible.com.

International Perspective

China

China will see "one-stop shop" convergence of microblogging, social networks, and information portals.

The explosive growth in social media has had undoubted worldwide repercussions, least not in the world's most populous country, China. Though Facebook is officially delisted, social media thrives under the umbrella of local alternatives like Ren Ren and Kaixin, both overwhelmingly used by locals. With a keen desire to broadcast and share opinions, bloggers (over half of Internet users were purportedly *active* bloggers according to the China Network Information Center (CNNIC) in 2009) migrated towards the user-friendly environment of the Social Network Sites in which to provide personal musings.

That tide, however, is turning fast—as is ever the case in China—with the advent of microblogging (the most popular being Sina.com's Weibo). Weibo is fundamentally different from Twitter and offers multi-functions that essentially make it a simplified version of a Social Network Site. In China, where recreational time is a premium, this is critical. Weibo, for instance, offers visual, audio, and video facilities and enough character spaces (140) to give substantive feedback. Layouts are basic, easy to follow and users can split interfaces into different categories, themes, and threads.

The allure of Social Network Sites is now, from this angle, statistically on the wane. According to CNNIC, in 2010 the penetration rate of Social Network Sites among Chinese Internet-goers was 51 percent and in 2011 this has fallen to 47 percent. From December 2010 to the end of June 2011, Weibo usage has grown 200 percent. Weibo is fast usurping other Social Network Sites as the place to broadcast. 2012 will bring about the effects of integration and how to manage consumer expectations on news, communication, and information sharing. Portals (who want a piece of the action), microblogs, and Social Network Sites will converge under one umbrella to offer users an integrated one-stop shop.

—Chris.Maier, Director of Digital and Media Solutions for Greater China
Millward Brown ACSR
MillwardBrown.com

To-Do List

- Learn more about mobile marketing.

    Read some mobile marketing blogs. Watch how some of the big players are branding, selling, and interacting with their customers and prospects through mobile marketing. Give this commandment 15 minutes two or three times a month. Follow mobile marketing to see when it's the right time for you to jump in.

- Understand the technology.

    Understand the technology's capabilities. No need to go totally geek, but just understand the main features and benefits of the major players. Before reading this chapter, did you know you could do that much with a simple smartphone? Spend a few minutes to see how the iPhone and Android work. The more you understand about how the technology functions, the better you will understand how to apply it to your own marketing and advertising concepts and campaigns.

- Set Google Alerts.

    Set some Google Alerts for the terms *mobile marketing, mobile advertising, mobile marketing* [fill in your industry terms]. See what others are doing in your industry with mobile marketing. Most important, remember to keep an eye out for the competition by including their company, product, and service names in your alerts.

- Try mobile applications.

    Set up a Jott account and see how you quickly cannot live without it. Get a few of your customers and prospects to opt-in on receiving your company updates in their e-mails and their mobile phones. Try Twitter for communicating with your employees. Capture a photo or, better yet, a two-minute video at your next conference and send it to a few key prospects who could benefit from that "What's in It for Me?" content.

- Try the mobile web.

    Try accessing your favorite sites with your mobile phone. Go to Yelp the next time you're out and want a good restaurant recommendation in your area. If you are GPS-enhanced, try getting directions the next time you're lost (especially you guys out there). Important: See what it takes to get your website mobile ready. If it's WordPress, you need only a plug-in (see the following Downloads).

Conclusion

Wow! Mobile phone technology is advancing at breakneck speeds while new features are being added every day. The mobile telephone is truly social media in a box that includes nearly every social media tool in one device. Today's smartphone lets you take pictures; upload them to your blog or photo sharing site; send them to friends, colleagues, and customers; or view others' photographs. And you can do the same with audio, music, and video.

You can surf a website, get tweets, and send and receive text messages. You can receive up-to-the-minute news and stock quotes, traffic reports, and weather. You can listen to music, watch a full-length video, have it wake you on time in the morning, give you turn-by-turn directions, let you know the best pasta restaurant closest to you . . . and even make a call.

As the smartphone continues to develop and become part of everyone's "remote controls for life," more and more companies will understand how to better serve you with demographically specific, geo-targeted, trusted network, permission-based information and advertising.

Mobile marketing is relatively inexpensive and has one of, if not the highest, return on investment (ROI) of any marketing channel available today. Companies and providers have only begun to understand how to best serve information to trusted customers using this technology. While mobile marketing might not be a viable solution for every business right now, it likely will be soon. You owe it to yourself and your company to monitor this industry. Watch the technology, and follow the players in this field so that when it is the right time for you to begin mobile marketing, you will recognize the opportunity.

Downloads

For your free downloads associated with *The Social Media Bible,* go to www
.theSocialMediaBible.com,

and enter your ISBN number located on the back of the book above the bar code. Be sure to enter the dashes.

Credits

The ROI of Social Media was provided by:

Mike Nierengarten, account executive, Anvil Media, Inc., www .anvilmediainc.com

Technical edits were provided by:

Jay Veniard, cofounder, ChaChing Mobile Marketing, www.Cha Ching411.com

FIGURE 20.7   Couple Sharing an iPhone

Expert Insight was provided by:

Angela Courtin, Senior Vice President of Marketing Entertainment and Content, MySpace, www.myspace.com

Note

1. "Motorola is making mobile music access seamless for music lovers—in their homes, at work, on the road, and now at the premier live music venue—the House of Blues," said Kathleen Finato, senior director of marketing for North America Mobile Devices, Motorola, Inc. "It's a true marriage of entertainment and mobility as the music lifestyle fan receives the ultimate concert experience long before the

first song is played. House of Blues is an innovator in the live music category. By combining our expertise with a mobile leader such as Motorola, we are able to create new interactive opportunities for our artists and customers," said Paul Sewell, senior vice president, sponsorship House of Blues Entertainment, Inc. "Together, Motorola and House of Blues will power the enjoyment for the growing tech savvy music generation."

CHAPTER 21

Let the Conversation Begin (Interpersonal)

www.LonSafko.com/TSMB3_Videos/21Interpersonal.mov

What's in It for You?

Interpersonal refers to the many applications and websites in the social media ecosphere that allow us to communicate live and in real time between individuals, small groups, or large groups. Choosing an interpersonal tool starts with two questions: What do you want to communicate, and with whom do you want to communicate it?

Talking to people in your social network easily and naturally is fun, and helps develop deeper relationships between people—most of the tools here are free for personal or small group use. When people are in business settings, there are significant productivity benefits to be gained from real-time communication, and investment in tools to help build relationships is well worth the price. Many of these tools can significantly reduce or even eliminate expenses like long-distance telephone calls, airfare, and hotels for companies. Also, with the emergence of mobile devices, people can now communicate at their desk or on the go with the same application and the same individuals.

theSocialMediaBible.com

Since the first edition of this book was published, video has exploded onto the social media scene and is now powering many new innovative video conferencing applications, and sharing applications are also gaining popularity as ways to collaborate with your social network. We've redrawn the categories in this chapter to reflect those changes. We look at a range of applications from free to enterprise-level, and from the well known to some of the latest up-and-coming ideas.

Messaging examples include AOL Instant Messenger, Google Talk, Apple iChat, Microsoft Windows Live Messenger, Yahoo! Messenger, Twitter (covered in depth in Chapter 13, Thumbs Up for Microblogging), and LivePerson. In video examples, we look at Skype, Apple FaceTime, Logitech Vid, VSee, Polycom RealPresence, Cisco umi, ooVoo, Vidyo, fring, OpenTok, and Spreecast. Sharing examples explore GoToMeeting, WebEx, Adobe Connect, ON24, Persony, FuzeMeeting, Salesforce.com, Doodle, Trumba, Jive, Convofy, and Frenzy.

Of course, this list is by no means complete; it's simply intended to provide a sampling of some of the wide variety and broad range of social media interpersonal tools. As with all of the other chapters' content, useful tools, applications, and innovative companies in the space are continuously changing. Many are being added, and some are becoming extinct. For example, the first edition of this book featured Jott, a speech-to-text tool which has since been acquired by Nuance Communications (www.nuance.com).

We're hoping the companies featured here meet with success over the next few years—that's in large part up to you, the people who will select and use these applications.

To help with the constantly changing nature of this field, the website accompanying this book will be constantly updated with the latest information on social media techniques, tools, and strategies, and updates to *The Social Media Bible*. So visit www.theSocialMediaBible.com often, and contribute to the future of social media.

What You Need to Know

As you might suspect, this chapter's format needs to be a little different. A section like *Back to the Beginning* really isn't appropriate. Instead, this chapter provides you with some facts about the features and benefits based on a few hand-selected, highlighted companies, and introduces you to some extraordinary tools in the social media ecosphere. You will also see that many of these selected companies and services—although listed in a particular section—can be used in a variety of ways, and a good number of the applications actually fit into more than one category. With that, let's dive in to our three categories.

Messaging Applications

Messaging was one of the first social communication applications, usually built around a chat metaphor through which people connected one to one with "buddies" or coworkers in a list. Conversations are opened by clicking on a name in your list, and typing a message to that person. As these tools have become extremely popular, often with millions of users, features have expanded to provide better integration with e-mail and applications such as Facebook, audio and video chat capability, and more ideas—but the core of these applications remains as a quick way to message another person directly, usually for free.

AOL Instant Messenger: AOL Instant Messenger (AIM, www.AIM.com; see Figure 21.1)

is a free online service that lets you communicate in real time. Using the AIM Buddy List window lets you see when your buddies are online and chat with them. Chatting and sharing with your friends, family, and colleagues is more fun than ever using this application. You can send text messages, share photos and URLs, make a PC-to-PC voice call, create an online personality, and more.

FIGURE 21.1   AOL Instant Messenger

AIM Buddy List   AIM now includes instant messaging, talk and voice chat, video IM, e-mail, and text messaging. Additional features of the AIM software include AOL Radio; file transfer for pictures and documents; a buddy list;

address book; integration of address book with Plaxo, the industry leader in web-based contact management; IM forwarding to mobile phone; AOL alerts and reminders; and browse or search the web through AOL Explorer. AIM is downloadable for Windows, Mac, Android, iPhone, iPad, and BlackBerry.

Google Talk: Google Talk (www.google.com/talk; see Figure 21.2)

features include instant messaging, which allows you to chat with all of your Google Talk and Gmail contacts in real time, and free PC-to-PC

FIGURE 21.2   Google Talk

voice calls, which lets you talk for free to anyone else who is online and is equipped with the Google Talk client. Google Talk allows you to send and receive voicemails and provides unlimited file transfers that lets you send and receive files to your contacts without file size or bandwidth restrictions.

The Google Talk gadget does not require any download; you can start chatting immediately from any computer with a browser. You can also create a group chat and invite multiple people to join an online conversation. Google Talk also has media previews that allow users to cut and paste video and slideshow URLs from sites like YouTube, Google Video, Picasa Web Albums, and Flickr into your chats, and view them in your chat window.

iChat: With Apple's iChat (www.apple.com/macosx/features/ichat .html; see Figure 21.3)

FIGURE 21.3 iChat

feature, you can text, audio, or video chat from anywhere—as long as you are using a Mac. iChat offers crystal-clear audio quality using Apple's wideband codec AAC-LD—which samples a full range of vocal frequencies—and sounds great with any voice. iChat also offers text messaging that includes Tabbed Chats, Multiple Logins, Invisibility, Animated Buddy Icons, SMS Forwarding, Custom Buddy List Order, File Transfer Manager, and Space-Efficient Views, and it works with AIM as well.

iChat screen sharing allows you and your buddy to observe and control a single desktop—a feature that makes it a cinch to collaborate with a colleague, browse the web with a friend, or pick plane seats with a family member. And iChat automatically initiates an audio chat when you start a screen-sharing session, so you can talk things through while you're at it. iChat also allows users to save audio and video chats for posterity with iChat recording. When the chat is done, iChat stores the audio chats as AAC files and video chats as MPEG-4 files—so that users can play them in iTunes or QuickTime.

Yahoo! Messenger: Friends are only an instant away on Yahoo! Messenger (www.messenger.yahoo.com; see Figure 21.4).

It includes a wide range of features, including text messaging, photo and file sharing (up to 2 GB), webcam video, chat rooms, and more. Yahoo! Messenger provides Phone In and Phone Out features, to get a phone number for Messenger and allow inexpensive PC-to-PC calls.

Yahoo! Messenger supports many personalization features with skins, fonts, emoticons, ringtones, and IMVironments backgrounds. It also integrates with other Yahoo! applications such as Mail and a set of games, and now allows chatting with Facebook friends directly. There are versions for Windows, Mac, Android, iPhone, and BlackBerry.

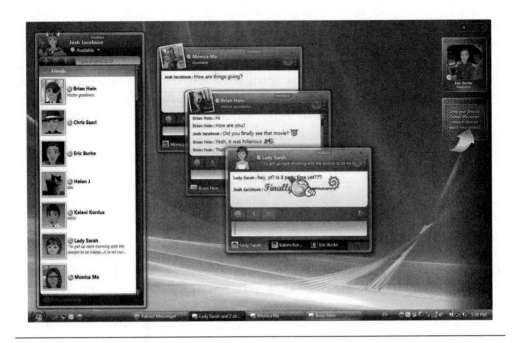

FIGURE 21.4   Yahoo! Messenger

Microsoft Windows Live Messenger: Much like the other messaging tools mentioned so far, Microsoft Windows Live Messenger (http://explore .live.com/messenger; see Figure 21.5)

allows you to connect and share with contacts—anywhere. Like the other tools we've discussed, it supports text and video chat, and photo and video sharing. It also provides a Hotmail account, which allows you to stay connected anywhere with your web e-mail account.

FIGURE 21.5   Microsoft Live Messenger

Messenger is part of Windows Live, which provides SkyDrive, a password-protected online file storage feature; Spaces, the best place to share your world online; Photo Gallery, where you can get creative and share your photos and videos; Writer, where you can easily publish pictures, videos, and other rich content to your blog; and Events, where you can plan your next meeting or gathering, send invitations, and share photos. Microsoft Windows Live Messenger is available on Windows, Windows Phone, iPhone, Android, Symbian, and BlackBerry. Learn more on the latest Microsoft Windows Live Messenger in our Expert Insight later in this chapter.

Twitter: The most popular one-to-many communication tool today by far is Twitter (www.Twitter.com; see Figure 21.6),

Home   Profile   **Messages**   Campaigns

New Message

Send Support a message

Message   support   ×

Hey Support! Thanks for your help.

105   Send

tip: you can send a message to anyone who follows you

FIGURE 21.6   Twitter

the microblogging platform. As you've heard by now, Twitter is a microblogging and social networking service that allows its users to send and receive brief (140 characters or less) text-based, micropost instant messages that are called tweets. Your tweets are received by anyone who has chosen to follow your profile, or views your profile directly, or searches for a topic in a search engine and finds your tweet content.

Twitter also offers two ways for more direct communication between individuals. First, you can reply to an individual by beginning your tweet with @username as the first characters. You, the individual you replied to, and anyone following both of you will see the reply in their home timeline. For more private conversation, Twitter also has a direct message feature, where you send a tweet directly and only to @username. The individual sees this as a direct message and can reply with a direct message only to you.

For a complete discussion on Twitter, please see Chapter 13, Thumbs Up for Microblogging.

LivePerson: One innovative way organizations are connecting with customers using social tools is an application called LivePerson (www.live person.com; see Figure 21.7).

FIGURE 21.7 LivePerson

Many websites offer the "Click to Chat" feature using LivePerson, which connects you immediately to a customer service representative. No more e-mailing and hoping for a response, or dialing a number and waiting on hold. When you click a LivePerson box, you get a live person at the other end you can start talking with, either through messages in a chat box or with voice, depending on how the website has implemented the solution.

Say it's Cyber Monday and you're trying to place a gift order online, but you have a question or a problem. Clicking the LivePerson Chat box opens a chat screen in which you can type your questions and get answers, interactively, instantly from a knowledgeable customer service representative who is looking at the same web page. Both you and the representative can multitask and look at other things while chatting to help work together to reach a solution. LivePerson also offers a voice service, in which you enter a phone number and the representative calls you, instead of making you wait in a phone queue. Or, the customer service rep can escalate your session from a chat to a call.

Video Conferencing Applications

Many applications started out as audio calling tools, using voice-over-IP (VoIP) technology to replace phone technology with free computer network connections. As network bandwidth and processing power has increased, most of those applications have evolved into more complete audio and video communications platforms, and are now adding group conferencing capability. People connect better when they can see faces and hear conversations in sync, and the advent of high-definition video and clearer, delay-free audio has helped people feel more comfortable with using video calling. Again, the rise of mobile devices has empowered users to use more video, either at the desktop or on the go.

Skype: The web audio calling revolution was started by Skype (www .skype.com; see Figure 21.8),

FIGURE 21.8 Skype

and it's the most widely used calling application today. Skype-to-Skype calls are free, and Skype-to-phone calling is inexpensive. You can also now use Skype from your home phone and platforms running Windows, Mac, Linux, iPhone, Android, and Symbian. (It should be noted that Microsoft acquired Skype in May 2011.)

With millions of users, Skype has now added video calling capability to computers, mobile phones, and even TVs with Skype applications. The latest version, Skype 5.3, supports one-to-one and group video calling and allows people with mobile devices to join these group calls through voice. Video calls can be recorded using a product like Pamela (www .pamela.biz).

Skype audio and video calling are free, while group video calling is part of Skype Premium.

Apple FaceTime: Apple products are fully video-call enabled, and you can call a friend with an Apple ID on her Mac, iPad 2, iPhone 4, or iPod Touch using Apple FaceTime (www.apple.com/mac/facetime/;

see Figure 21.9). FaceTime epitomizes Apple's core design values: it's simple to use, and provides a very personal, up-close video experience. It's simple to use, and focuses on the person you're talking to—click on a name in the Address Book, the call begins, and the application frame and controls fade away leaving you with a large view of the other person, and a smaller view of how you look to them. That's it; you both are talking.

FIGURE 21.9 Apple FaceTime

Mac users get a full high-definition experience in 720p video. iPad, iPhone, and iPod users have a smooth experience using either the front or rear-facing camera, and can rotate their view in either portrait or landscape. Mobile users are connected by Wi-Fi, which avoids costs of mobile minutes and provides a reliable connection with enough bandwidth for the experience—this is one consideration when users are on the go: they need to be in a location with Wi-Fi.

Logitech Vid HD: On the PC side, where many machines don't have built-in high-definition cameras, Logitech has both the camera hardware and their Vid software to enable a personal video-calling experience (www .logitech.com/vid; see Figure 21.10).

FIGURE 21.10   Logitech Vid

Vid HD works with a variety of webcams, including ones built in to laptops, and also works with the Google TV system, so you can make a video call from a PC to their connected TV.

Vid HD claims simplicity, through which invites are made with only an e-mail address. Once a friend accepts an invite, their picture appears in your Vid "Who would you like to call?" list. It presents a very simple interface bar, and, like FaceTime, shows a large picture of the individual you've called along with a smaller picture-in-picture view of how you appear to your friend. It's simple, person-to-person video calling without any extra features.

VSee: Compared to Skype, which grew from an audio call base, VSee started out as a video-calling tool (www.vsee.com; see Figure 21.11)

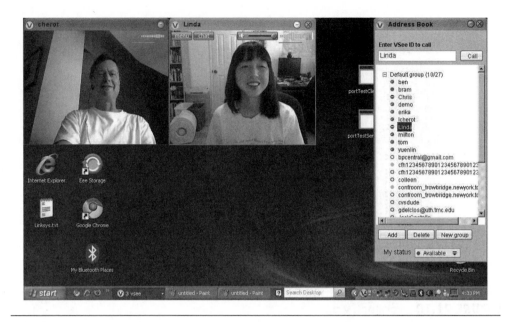

FIGURE 21.11   VSee

and rethought a couple of important features. Desktop users usually have a very high bandwidth wired network connection, which supports a smooth HD video experience. What if all you have is a wireless connection, or you're on a busy corporate wired network? VSee has been designed around a proprietary technology which uses half the network bandwidth of competing products, which makes calls on Wi-Fi or even a cellular network as smooth as those experienced on a wired network connection. VSee also tunes itself to network conditions, and uses AES encryption of video so calls are secure—something enterprise IT departments often look for. It's also a peer-to-peer connection without a server involved.

VSee also incorporates desktop or application window sharing, concurrently with video, and there's also drag-and-drop file sharing capability. All call participants can annotate the shared window—draw lines, circles, make text comments. To make that point again—your video view is still available to other callers even when you share an application window, something VSee says contributes to increased trust. VSee claims to have 11-way calls running smoothly, which is outstanding. VSee currently runs on Windows, and they are working on versions for Mac and Android. It's free for personal, noncommercial use, and is fairly inexpensive for commercial use.

Polycom RealPresence: Corporate video conferencing types are very familiar with the Polycom brand. Video conferencing used to mean going to the specially outfitted conference room with the video conferencing equipment, and the other participants in the video conference had to be at a similar location with compatible equipment. Now, there are growing numbers of mobile users armed with laptops and tablets who need to conference, but don't want to sacrifice video quality. Polycom's RealPresence (www.polycom.com/realpresencemobile; see Figure 21.12)

integrates room based, desktop based, and tablet based multipoint video calling into a single, smooth environment. RealPresence Mobile supports applications for Apple iPad 2, Samsung GALAXY Tab, and Motorola XOOM tablets.

Polycom is continuing to create more interoperable environments as well. On the technology front, they've started the Open Visual Communications Consortium, seeking to get different video conferencing solutions to

FIGURE 21.12 Polycom RealPresence

work together. On the social front, their first partnership for RealPresence is with Jive Software (www.jivesoftware.com),

which we'll look at briefly in the Sharing section of this chapter.

Cisco umi: Another well-known corporate telepresence vendor is Cisco, and they are making a platform for home video conferencing called umi (www.cisco.com/umi; see Figure 21.13).

umi is one of several attempts to bring the connected TV into focus, along with things like Google TV, game controllers from Sony and Microsoft, and social applications being integrated directly into advanced TV sets. umi is a small box that connects to your TV through an HDMI port, and connects to either your home Wi-Fi or wired Ethernet network.

umi turns your living room into a stage, connecting you through your TV to video calls with anyone with either another umi box, or a computer with a webcam and Google Talk's video chat plug-in (mentioned earlier in the Messaging section of this chapter). umi supports call screening, call blocking, and a privacy shutter, and supports video messages—similar to voice mail, but with video content. umi videos can be captured and shared on Facebook, YouTube, or e-mailed. Videos can also be viewed on mobile apps for iOS and Android.

ooVoo: Similar to Skype and VSee, ooVoo (www.oovoo.com; see Figure 21.14)

FIGURE 21.13   Cisco umi

offers video calling in a free chat app that they claim supports six people. ooVoo also offers a video chat room service, where a widget can be embedded on your website or blog which anyone can access. Chat rooms can be open, or require a password. This gives a way for someone in the community to reach you and discuss a topic they saw immediately.

ooVoo also offers premium paid features such as file transfer and desktop sharing capability, along with recording of calls, and 10-minute video messages. ooVoo supports Windows and Macs, and there are also free apps for iPhone, iPad, and Android devices so mobile users can participate in group video calls.

FIGURE 21.14   ooVoo

Vidyo: One big challenge for corporate video conferencing is quality. Personal video calls tend to be one-to-one or small groups, but corporate meetings tend to grow quickly and it seems there's always another person that needs to be added. Vidyo (www.vidyo.com; see Figure 21.15)

is looking to compete with Polycom and Cisco higher-end telepresence solutions by using a technology called H.264 Scalable Video Coding.

In short, traditional video conferencing systems have a single video stream that serves everyone connecting from room-based to desktop to mobile users, and then rely on the device to perform what's called *transcoding* to get the video displayed. This allows more devices to connect,

FIGURE 21.15   Vidyo

but can chew up a lot of processing power on a laptop or mobile device and dramatically affect call quality. Scalable Video Coding (SVC) optimizes video for each type of device connecting to the call, so that each person connecting sees the conference with less delay and better quality. Vidyo offers this technology in higher performance room-based systems, paid desktop solutions for Windows, Mac, and Linux systems, and free mobile solutions for iPad and Android.

fring: The mobile revolution has caused many people to completely ditch their desktop or laptop machines in favor of a smartphone or tablet. fring's tagline is "Get together, mobile" (www.fring.com; see Figure 21.16).

Without the constraints of supporting desktop machines, fring has optimized its solution for mobile users of iOS, Android, and other platforms.

FIGURE 21.16   fring

fring offers free mobile group video chat for up to four users at a time, free calls to other mobile fring users, live text chat to friends on fring and AIM, GoogleTalk, Yahoo! Messenger, and Microsoft Windows Live Messenger. For calls to non-fring numbers, fring offers a calling plan to any number starting at 1¢ per minute.

OpenTok: If you're looking to develop video chat applications, OpenTok from tokbox (www.tokbox.com/opentok; see Figure 21.17)

is a cloud-based service that allows video stream sessions to be created flexibly. Some of the applications they've created: video embed, with live group video chat; TokShow, which is a one-to-many video broadcast; and

FIGURE 21.17   OpenTok

Co-Viewing, which invites friends to a viewing party for a game, concert, movie, or other video.

OpenTok is based on sessions in a publish-subscribe model. For example, one person can broadcast to 2,500, or 50 people can be connected to everyone else in a video chat. The OpenTok application programming interface (API) is free, so any developer can use it and the prebuilt applications to create video conference capability on a website. TokBox is planning to make money by offering premium services such as archiving, through which streamed events are recorded and played back.

Spreecast: Social networking is as much about creating content as it is viewing it. Spreecast (www.spreecast.com; see Figure 21.18)

FIGURE 21.18 Spreecast

is backed by the founders of StubHub and has a different model: the social video platform that lets people broadcast together. Spreecasts are completely integrated live video programs with chat and social sharing to Twitter, Facebook, and Google+. You can watch a spreecast without creating an account, but with a spreecast account is where the fun starts.

   With a spreecast account, you can chat with others viewing. You can submit a comment or question that the producers of the spreecast you're watching review, and can choose to display for everyone. You can request to join the spreecast on camera (up to four people can be live on camera simultaneously), and the producers can chat with you privately and put you in a queue to go live. You can also RSVP for a future event. Producers can create branded content and control participation. Programs are organized into channels, broadcast live, and recorded immediately. Spreecasts are the talk show metaphor, now live with video and social networking features working together.

Sharing Applications

Sharing tools help teams collaborate with a variety of content, beyond just chat or video, exchanging information and ideas in a way that many people can see and instantly participate in. Sharing applications range from simple scheduling tools to commenting platforms to sophisticated corporate presentation and collaboration tools, even a new category called social business software. Sharing helps viewers absorb information better, because they're participating in a discussion as if they were actually there—they see and hear material, can ask questions or discuss it, and can use social networks to comment and invite others to join the discussion. Sharing also can have a huge impact on corporate travel costs; running a webinar on one of these platforms can eliminate the need for travel for hundreds of people.

GoToMeeting: GoToMeeting (www.GoToMeeting.com; see Figure 21.19)

is a web conferencing service which allows up to 15 users to meet online rather than in a conference room. It's a screen sharing tool that allows meeting attendees to take control and share webcams, application windows, and documents. Attendees can connect to a meeting from Windows, Mac, iPhone, iPad, or Android devices. It allows unlimited meetings for a low monthly fee.

Meetings are secure, with passwords and encrypted content, and there are a set of scheduling, invite, and meeting-attendance-tracking tools to help get people organized. If you need to reach a larger audience or want additional marketing tools such as polls, surveys, and reports, GoToWebinar offers unlimited webinars with up to 1,000 attendees, plus the collaborative online meeting capabilities.

WebEx: WebEx (www.WebEx.com; see Figure 21.20)

FIGURE 21.19   GoToMeeting

is also a web conferencing service for online meetings, with document and screen sharing and video. WebEx allows the impact of live events by holding large, scalable online proceedings—such as all-hands meetings, shareholder presentations, and webinars—with interactive and dynamic multimedia presentations.

Professionals can use WebEx Training Center to deliver interactive world-class training and reach more people than they ever thought possible by offering on-demand and live, online classrooms. Students are seated in a virtual classroom where instructors can present on a whiteboard, marking up documents and shared views of applications. Students can respond to polls, and figuratively raise their hand to ask questions. WebEx Event Center

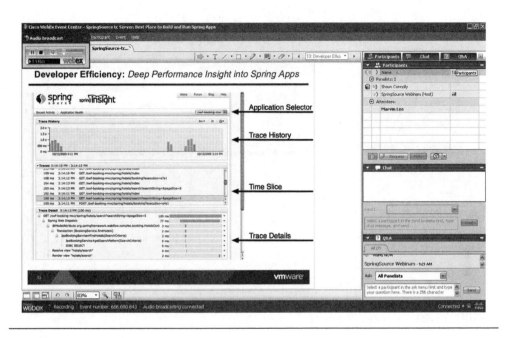

FIGURE 21.20   WebEx

allows meetings with up to 3,000 people. WebEx also supports Windows, Mac, Linux, Android, BlackBerry, and iPad and iPhone platforms.

Adobe Connect: Another web conferencing service is Adobe Connect (www.adobe.com/products/adobeconnect.html; see Figure 21.21),

which also supports screen and document sharing, audio and video, and features like whiteboarding and chat, which facilitate training applications. It's extremely flexible in how meetings are supported, including a scenario of a 24/7 meeting room for mission critical operations. There are pay-per-use and monthly plans, with the basics supporting up to 25 attendees.

Besides the robust collaboration and training features, there are extensive customization features in Adobe Connect. The user interface presents

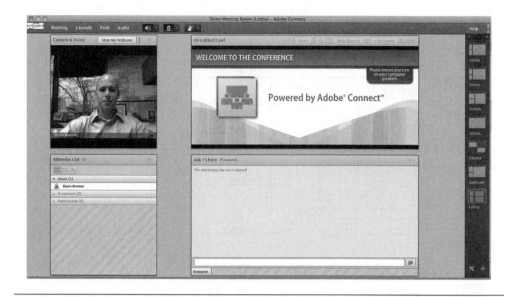

FIGURE 21.21   Adobe Connect

information in pods that can be resized and reconfigured. APIs are available for developers who want to write extensions to the platform. Mobile device support includes Android, iPhone, iPad, and BlackBerry PlayBook.

ON24: When it comes to fully integrated webinars with social media capability, ON24 (www.on24.com; see Figure 21.22)

continues to innovate with their platform. The latest release of ON24 Webcasting Platform 10 is a complete solution for webcasting. Viewers can join events using just a web browser, live or archived. Content sources include shared presentations, recorded video, live webcam, and telephone audio.

The newest features to the ON24 event delivery is social integration. Viewers can choose widgets that they want to use onscreen, and besides the

FIGURE 21.22   ON24

primary widgets for presentation and video, content can include Twitter, Facebook, and LinkedIn, and there's further integration with Yammer and SocialCast. There are over 50 prebuilt widgets a viewer can configure. ON24 supports robust viewer registration pages and provides extensive analytics on viewers of both the live and on-demand events.

Persony: For companies looking to offer customized web conferencing, Persony (www.persony.com; see Figure 21.23)

offers Web Conferencing 2.0, which supports a wide range of meeting features including presentation, whiteboard, and webcam sharing to as many as 250 attendees. The solution is web-based, with only a browser required

FIGURE 21.23 Persony

to join a meeting. Persony allows companies to create hosted meetings on your own website, with your branding, instead of using a third-party web conferencing service.

Persony supports either voice-over-IP or audio conferencing, along with meeting recording features. There are attendee management features to help organizers view attendee profiles and manage messages from attendees. It supports impromptu or scheduled meetings, sends meeting invitations, and provides full reports on event participation. There's also a Parallels APS Package for cloud-based deployments.

Fuze Meeting: Much like other sharing tools we've already mentioned, Fuze Meeting (www.fuzemeeting.com; see Figure 21.24)

FIGURE 21.24   Fuze Meeting

is made for web conferencing, but it's built around native applications for Apple, BlackBerry, and Android devices. And not just viewing the meeting, but hosting it, and collaborating with HD content—from a mobile app. Fuze is designed to let remote users with mobile devices not just see and hear the video conference in a browser, but share documents and images.

Fuze Meeting also supports desktop users with a browser. It handles up to 100 attendees, and allows meetings to be recorded with the premium version. Documents can be displayed and marked up using easy annotation tools, and there's an integrated instant messaging network that supports contacts from the tools mentioned in the Messaging section earlier.

salesforce.com: Automating the customer relationship management (CRM) process is essential to managing today's mobile sales force and growing business. For organizations looking to track customers and help sales teams, salesforce.com (www.salesforce.com; see Figure 21.25)

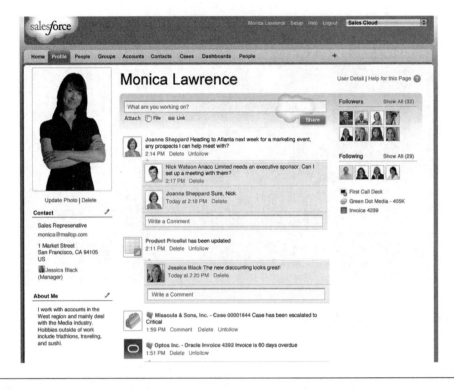

FIGURE 21.25   Salesforce.com

offers a comprehensive set of browser-based applications. Accounts can be created with sets of decision-maker contacts, then assigned to sales representatives, who can create outbound e-mail campaigns with proposals and quotes. Orders can be received and integrated into an approval workflow, and reports run on revenue in a myriad of ways.

But besides being a powerful tool for sales automation and CRM, salesforce.com has two social tools that integrate with it. Chatter is exactly what it sounds like: a way to post status messages, and replies, directly within the salesforce.com application. Radian6 (www.radian6.com)

is a sophisticated social media listening tool that can help organizations identify influencers, see what they are saying, and react. It's now part of the salesforce.com Social Hub capability.

Doodle: Doodle (www.doodle.com; see Figure 21.26)

is an online coordination tool that makes it easy to find a date and time for a group event by helping to determine common availabilities among all parties involved. The basic services are free, requires neither registration nor

FIGURE 21.26   Doodle

software installation, and allows users to schedule events like board meetings, business lunches, conference calls, family reunions, or movie nights.

Doodle's tabular display shows the time slots and the availabilities of all participants. The meeting organizer can immediately spot a suitable time as soon as all participants have cast their votes. Doodle also offers a one-click reminder feature for the organizer to further accelerate the voting process. The tool integrates into all major calendar systems like Microsoft Outlook, Google Calendar, or Notes. Doodle also features a mobile-ready version, iPhone and Android apps, scheduling across time zones, and is available in 30 languages.

Trumba: For developers looking to build scheduling capability into websites, and manage the promotion of events including spreading the word with social media, Trumba Connect (www.trumba.com; see Figure 21.27)

FIGURE 21.27   Trumba

is a web-hosted content management system. You create events, publish them, promote them, and monitor how visitors find and interact with the event pages.

Trumba Connect uses what they call *spuds,* which are calendars, event lists, date tables, and similar ways people like to view events. Those spuds are placed on your website, and the information can also be broadcast to an e-mail list or on Twitter or Facebook. Visitors can add events to their favorite personal calendar—Microsoft Outlook, Apple iCal, and Google Calendar included—with an easy click. Trumba's hosted solution relieves developers of having to create event calendar functions from scratch.

Jive: What's social business software (SBS)? Social networking, collaboration tools, and community software combine in Jive (www.jivesoftware .com; see Figure 21.28). Jive has also combined three key audiences in one approach: Employees, customers, and the social web are blended into a rich user experience. Instead of building around the existing tools—conference calls, e-mail, and intranet—Jive goes after grabbing organizational intelligence, internal and external, and putting it at everyone's fingertips.

FIGURE 21.28   Jive

Jive has modules for collaboration and communication, for social marketing, for sales enablement, for customer support communities, and for social media monitoring. It's a transformative tool that really acknowledges that a large business is communities of employees serving communities of customers and a larger community of potential customers, and making information from all of those communities as transparent and readily available as possible increases in productivity.

Convofy: Reinventing the comment seems to be a mundane goal, but it's exactly what Convofy (www.convofy.com; see Figure 21.29)

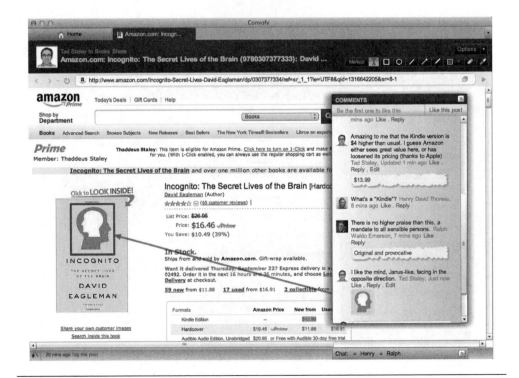

FIGURE 21.29 Convofy

has set out to do. There are collaboration tools, but they're often built around document sharing and viewing. They support annotation, but unless someone captures those annotations, and connects them in context, the ideas can be lost.

Convofy is browser based, and uses lists of employees with verified company e-mail addresses to set access policies. Documents are uploaded for sharing, and permissions are set for "My Followers," a group name, or a user name. When you create comments, you mark up images, files, and text—even on web pages—and embed a link. Documents can be just about anything: PDFs, Microsoft Word and Excel files, and images. Comments are editable at any time. The original, uncommented version of the document is also stored for reference.

Frenzy: Frenzy (www.frenzyapp.com; see Figure 21.30)

calls itself "the Dropbox powered social network." Dropbox (www.dropbox .com)

is a popular file sharing tool, which stores versions of uploaded documents and keeps everyone with access working on the latest copy. Frenzy builds on this, creating a "feed" which notifies everyone in the group what's new and gives them a chance to comment.

Frenzy is simple and minimal. It shows in your feed when someone has posted a document to the Dropbox, and allows you to post a reply to the group regarding that document, or a question about lunch, or whatever.

FIGURE 21.30   Frenzy

It's a bridge between an instant messaging tool that doesn't synchronize files across a group, and a file sharing solution that's not conversational. Frenzy is currently supported only on Macs, with an iPhone version coming soon.

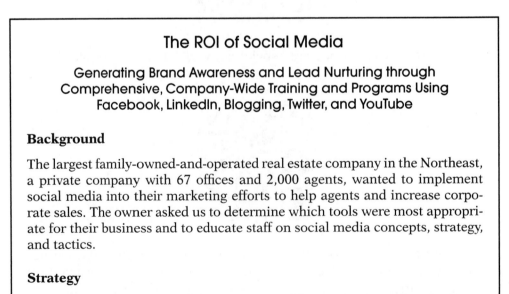

The ROI of Social Media

Generating Brand Awareness and Lead Nurturing through Comprehensive, Company-Wide Training and Programs Using Facebook, LinkedIn, Blogging, Twitter, and YouTube

Background

The largest family-owned-and-operated real estate company in the Northeast, a private company with 67 offices and 2,000 agents, wanted to implement social media into their marketing efforts to help agents and increase corporate sales. The owner asked us to determine which tools were most appropriate for their business and to educate staff on social media concepts, strategy, and tactics.

Strategy

Assessment and recommendations: We started by monitoring and evaluating competitor activities and best practices in the marketplace. We presented data on what was happening in real estate in the Northeast, as well as nationally, what the best tools are to use, and a preliminary strategy for the company.

Our research showed that very few, if any, RE firms in the Northeast had integrated, systematic programs in place companywide, which provided excellent opportunities for the company to make a mark and stand out from their competition.

Implementation

Executive education: Presented social media primer to top leadership (120 managers) at monthly sales meeting.

After manager buy-in, we developed social media guidelines, which spell out the company's expectations for agent behavior online.

Social media primer webinars: Delivered webinars for all sales agents to educate them on the value of social media and to walk them through the guidelines.

Train the trainer program: Recruited social media consultants from each office (67 people). Delivered train the trainer program in two locations (Connecticut and Massachusetts) to train them and support them in training others. Topics: Facebook, Twitter, YouTube, LinkedIn, and blogging with specific industry tie-ins and how to [manage] information.

Agent blog program: Developed turnkey WordPress MU back-end system that allows agents to set up a blog with the click of a button on their intranet site. With our WordPress template, the agent's data is pulled in with preloaded blog roll and SEO tools. The blog is set up within minutes.

Agent social community: Set up a private social media resource center community on Ning to post educational information and field questions, provide support to agents companywide.

Corporate blog program: Redesigned, optimized, and created content strategy for company.

Social networks: Set up Twitter, Facebook business page, YouTube channel, and audio feeds from blog. Trained internal staff to manage them.

Opportunity

The opportunity is to show the company's expertise and knowledge in the real estate marketplace and provide multiple communication channels via posts, photos, audio, and video, for agents to interact with prospects and clients.

Conclusion

To date, there are over 1,000 Facebook fans on company business pages; 200 agent fan pages; 1,100 sales agents have profiles on LinkedIn; [and] more than 200 have a feed from the company blog on their profile.

(continued)

(*continued*)

More than 60 agents have set up blogs and received blog training as part of the agent blog program.

Since the program's inception, agents and corporate officers report the company's social media strategy along with their presences in the social sphere, have made a significant impact on netting new customers, and increasing close rates.

—Catherine Weber
Website: www.webermediapartners.com

Blog: www.impressionsthroughmedia.com

Expert Insight

Dharmesh Mehta, director of product management, Microsoft Windows Live Messenger, www.get.live.com/messenger/overview (http://explore.live.com/messenger)

Dharmesh Mehta

Microsoft Windows Live Messenger has been around a little over a decade now. We originally launched it back in 1999, and it was pretty much focused on just being an IM text solution. What you've seen over the years is, as we continue to grow, we've turned that from text chat and added voice and video. We then added photo sharing and games. We've added a ton of personal expressions so you can change your display pictures and record videos with your webcam. We allow you to have both those real-time conversations, but also a synchronous offline instant message. Today Windows Live Messenger is actually used by more than 325 million people worldwide. So it's come a long way, and we hope to see that growth continue. . . .

So you have your contacts in your Messenger's main window, and you can start a chat with them—and it's not just about chat. You can share files, just drag them right into there. . . . One of the latest things we've just added is a really rich photo sharing. If you drag photos in, you can look at a set of photos with one of your buddies; or you can, at the same time, change what photo you are looking at while you're commenting and chatting about them. You can save them to [the] cloud and have them permanently shared out where others can see them. Again, you can share that just with your contacts or you can open it up to the whole Internet. . . .

Whether you're in IM or you're up on the web, or you're on your mobile phone, we want to make sure you can get your stuff. Whether that's photos or bios or being able to have real-time chat; we want to bring that context to you wherever you happen to be. . . .

So we offer a couple of different things on mobile phones. The first is for our PC users . . . when you're there chatting with someone and all of a sudden they go offline because they are no longer on their PC. The fact of the matter is many of those people are actually online on their phone and they can receive alerts. So we have connections from the PC and the web messaging experiences straight to your phone. And that's the first one.

But the one that I'm more excited about and continues to be growing really rapidly is about the fact that when you are on your mobile phone, you now actually have far more phones that are data-capable. And so whether that's browse services for IM'ing or photo sharing; whether that's doing little microblogging and updating your status; or even on some of the higher-end phones . . . actually having rich client application.

Obviously you have to design those slightly differently; the context is different. There's different user experiences because of the fact that you're always reachable on your phone, but you may not always want to be reachable. But it's actually really exciting what's happening on the mobile phone, and it's really two things. It's bringing the things that people have been doing on PC and the web and extending them to the phone. But then in some countries you just come online on the phone and you may never, ever get on a PC. They may never get download apps onto a Windows PC, but you want

(continued)

(continued)

to make sure that you have as great a mobile experience that's served from their phone. . . .

Mobile is actually a real exciting space for us, just for the amount of growth and the amount of different possibilities that are coming. . . .

On Windows Live Messenger today there are 325 million people who span the world, and so we are actually more of an international company than just being U.S.-focused, like some of the other instant messaging companies, and in terms of demographic, it spans everyone. So it's all the way from young teens to even younger than that, all the way up to adults and seniors.

We recently did some reports looking specifically at a fast-growing demographic of the 70-plus population that's starting to come online and wanting to chat with their grandkids and share photos and talk to them. And it's actually really interesting how IM, which once upon a time was really just restricted to, almost, college students and very young age ranges, really brought in all people on the planet. . . .

You know, often sitting here in the United States, we get very U.S.-focused and we often think that a lot of technology starts here in the U.S. and spreads to other parts of the world. But going back to that discussion that we had on mobile, some of the most interesting things in mobile are actually happening in Asia; whether that's Japan and South Korea or in India and China, where users are coming online on mobile and may never use a PC.

Think of this from a global perspective. We're learning and discovering from other players, other competitors, and companies, just around the world. . . .

To listen to or read the entire Executive Conversation with Dharmesh Mehta, go to www.theSocialMediaBible.com.

To-Do List

- Explore.

  This is the only commandment for this chapter, because it is so incredibly important. Go look at a few of the applications discussed in this book. Read some of their online literature, download their trials, and try them out to see if they are right for you and your business. Decide which ones work the best for your purposes, and really hone in on your use of those applications. Knowledge really is power; and we are in the midst of the Age of Knowledge. For the first time in human history, nearly the entire accumulation of human knowledge is at our fingertips and accessible in an instant. The more you know about social media and its tools, the more capabilities you will be able to access; the more you can reduce expenses; and the more competitive you can be. And isn't that what everyone is looking to do for our businesses: Reduce expenses and increase revenue?

Conclusion

As with all of the other chapters, the advice is to go explore. A lot of great social media applications allow you to better communicate with your customers and prospects, which is really the essence of social media. And surprising as it may be, many tools mentioned in *The Social Media Bible* are either free or very inexpensive. Unless you investigate and try out the various services that you've read about here, you won't know what incredible tools are available to help grow your business, build your community, and develop trust within that community.

To hear all of the Expert Interviews, go to www.theSocialMediaBible .com.

Downloads

For your free downloads associated with *The Social Media Bible,* go to www
.theSocialMediaBible.com,

and enter your ISBN number located on the back of the book above the bar
code. Be sure to enter the dashes.

Credits

The ROI of Social Media was provided by:

Catherine Weber, www.webermediapartners.com

Expert Insight was provided by:

Dharmesh Mehta, director of product management, Windows Live
Instant Messenger, www.get.live.com/messenger/overview

Technical edits were provided by:

Don Dingee, Left2MyOwnDevices LLC, www.l2myowndevices.com

PART II

STRATEGY

The Five Steps to Social Media Success

Introduction

Over the next five chapters, I am going to get more hands-on; show you more practical examples, and how to develop a step-by-step plan using the Five Steps to Social Media Success. After consulting and speaking with many of the United States's Fortune 1000 companies on down to the individual entrepreneur, and from governmental agencies to nonprofits, I am always asked the same thing: "Now that we have a Facebook page and sent out some tweets, where do we go from here? How do we integrate and implement a complete social media strategy into our existing marketing, sales, and communications strategy?"

Here are five easy steps (chapters) that explain how and why social media needs to be integrated into your marketing strategy.

Chapter 22—Analyze Your Existing Media

Chapter 23—The Social Media Trinity

Chapter 24—Integrate Strategies

Chapter 25—Identify Resources

Chapter 26—Implement and Measurement

 theSocialMediaBible.com

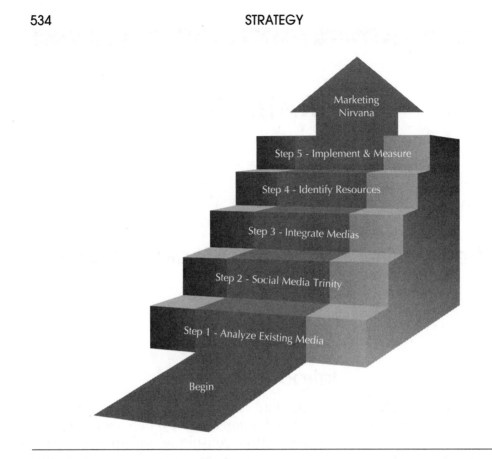

FIGURE 22.1   The Five Steps to Success

Fundamental Shift in Power

We are in the middle of a Fundamental Shift in Power that is taking place across the world in media and advertising that is having far-reaching effects in industries that used to dominate the businesses of marketing, public relations, advertising, media buying, television, radio, newspapers, magazines, billboards, and even the music and film industries. Newspapers are collapsing at an alarming rate, magazines are shutting down, radio stations are going syndicated to reduce costs and to amortize their ad revenues over a national area and no longer regional, and the music and movie industry is trying to cope with technologies such as iTunes, Netflix, and peer-to-peer distribution.

The Fundamental Shift in Power is shifting the power of the corporate messaging, the power of the news agencies, and the power of the ad agencies into the hands of the cyber-citizens like you and me. Our customers are now controlling our brands and our messages.

We are no longer in control of the media, the news, or the advertising, but our customers are. More and more and nearly exclusively, people are turning to peers for product and service recommendations. Facebook, with its 845 million members, is where most people now go to find out about how one automobile compares to another, or how good was that movie, or what is the latest news on, or what's the truth behind such and such.

CNN, Fox, ABC, the *Wall Street Journal*, and the *New York Times* are being replaced by the Internet, blogs, aggregators, Facebook conversations, and tweets. When the commercial jet landed in the Hudson River in New York in January 2009, it was a private individual who broke the news from the wing of the plane, with his cell phone and Twitter. When we watched the elections in the Mideast, it was Twitter again, coupled with a mobile phone. Unlike Desert Storm, when everyone, including the military, was watching Wolf Blitzer bringing us the play-by-play actions of the war on CNN, today it's we who are telling the story through our own technologies and social media.

TechNewsCrunch reported "More People Around The World Get Their News Online From Google News Than From CNN." We are getting our news from social networks, Twitter reports, and blogs, while the social networks are getting their news from us!

A recent poll showed that:

37 percent of Americans regularly go online for their news

27 percent picked up a newspaper on any given day

39 percent turned to cable television

Those who watched a nightly news bulletin on TV fell from 34 percent to 29 percent over the past four years.

There is a 30-second video from the Federal Trade Commission (FTC) that I use in my keynotes that really summarizes this shift. While the video wasn't designed to address this shift, it certainly recognizes the implications. Here is a transcript of that video.

Mary Engle, Associate Director, Bureau of Consumer Protection, Federal Trade Commission (FTC)

Mary Engle, Associate Director Bureau of Consumer Protection

Mary Engle

There's been a lot in the news about the FTC Endorsement Guide, "What's the story?" Well, the FTC cares about protecting consumers. We know that nowadays when consumers want information about a product or service they are thinking of using, they often go online to see what other consumers have to say. Don't you want to know if the reason the consumer is giving a rave review is because they're being paid by the advertiser to say it or they're getting a steady stream of free products from that company? We just want to bring some transparency to the process, so that when there's a relationship between the advertiser and the reviewer, the reader knows about it.

www.LonSafko.com/TSMB3_Videos/Mary_Engle.mov

"Transparency, Sincerity, and Authenticity," is what people are looking for in product recommendations and in advertising.

The primary cause for this shift is we are moving away from the age-old tradition of pontification and moving toward two-way communication. We are more interested in what a peer thinks about a particular product than what the company has to say about it. It's now peer perspective, not sponsor perspective.

For the first time in history, people are spending hundreds of dollars to buy and install technology that can remove or at least fast-forward through companies' commercials. In my presentations, nearly half of all attendees have purchased and installed a TiVo box so they can skip our messages. In many ways, we brought it on ourselves. For all of our lifetimes, we have been bombarded with commercials' hidden agendas and psychological hot buttons that make us react to the advertisers' commands. There're hidden messages and psychological hot buttons?

There better be! The average 30-second television commercial costs about $250,000 to produce; some more, some less. To play that commercial nationally just one time, prime time, costs about one and a quarter million dollars. So, if you were producing a commercial for your company and just spent one and a half million dollars, you had better get people to react, convert, and buy your products. Otherwise, you'd be out of a job and should be.

We, as consumers, are no longer falling for this. We have moved from being *con*sumers to *pro*-sumers. We are professional consumers and don't want to be sold, tricked, or manipulated.

We now listen to commercial-free radio shows on our computers and mobile phones, watch live mobile phone TV, aggregate the news we want without advertising on our Google or Yahoo! home pages, watch live streaming video on Ustream, and get our editorials from people we trust on blogs and Twitter.

The other reason for this Fundamental Shift in Power is because nearly all of the social media tools and implementation are free; no hard costs. And . . .

It's Word of Mouth at the Speed of Light . . .

CHAPTER 22

Analyze Your Existing Media

www.LonSafko.com/TSMB3_Videos/22ExistingMedia.mov

In this chapter, we are going to get into the weeds with what you have been currently doing with your traditional marketing. As I refer to marketing, I am also referring to public relations, communications, sales, and marketing.

We are going to look at all of your efforts and determine return on investment (ROI), cost of customer acquisition, and determine the overall effectiveness of how and how much you are spending on communicating your message to your customers and prospects.

When I speak about entrepreneurship and always start with the business case, I say, "Plan your work and work your plan." Then I say, *"Yuck!"* The purpose of preparing a business plan isn't as much as planning your work as much the value of a business plan lies in the process. When you get into the details necessary enough to produce a good business plan and understand the customer, the competition, the expenses, the SWOT (strengths, weaknesses, opportunities, and threats) to your business, then and only then do you understand your business well enough to start building it.

The same is true for this exercise. You need to go through the process described in this chapter so that you will understand how effective what you have been doing is, understand it enough to know how to integrate

social media marketing into it, and finally understand it well enough to know what and how to measure it.

Identifying Your Existing Media

To start off, you need to look at *all* of your existing traditional media, whether it's print ads, newspapers, trade journals, trade shows, radio, TV, telemarketing, billboards, door hangers, direct mail, whatever. Lock yourself in your office, turn off the phone (and your cell phone), and start making a list.

Analyze Your Existing Media Strategy

Now that you have a complete list of your entire marketing media, let's take a look at what has been effective and what has not? I am sure you have some feelings about what has been effective, but we need something more tangible than that. Have you been accurately measuring your traditional media?

If not, don't feel bad; nearly no one does, or can, for that matter. In traditional marketing, we almost always use impressions. If you ask any newspaper how they measure the effectiveness of their medium and my advertising dollars, they tell you that for each ad placed, two and a half people per newspaper will view that ad. Do you actually believe that?

In my opinion, half of all printed newspapers go unread. And when read once, they either go into the landfill, the recycle bin, or at the bottom of a birdcage. I don't believe that two and a half people read each newspaper.

The same is true for magazine, radio, and television impressions. When was the last time you sat through and comprehended a television commercial or listened to a radio ad, or studied, let alone reacted, to a newspaper ad?

The next step is a valuable one and takes a little detective work. You will need to go to your accounting software or ask your accountant or accounting department for some numbers.

Expense/Conversion (ROI)

You need to get two numbers: the total amount your company spent last year on sales, marketing, and public relations (PR). Be sure to include all of the hidden costs beyond just what you paid for the media. Include all of the indirect costs such as payroll; add 32 percent for indirect costs associated with payroll such as taxes, sick days, vacation, and so on. Add in all of the travel costs for trade shows, visiting clients and prospects, and other sales and marketing-related activities. Add your lease and rent, telephone, automobile allowances, airfare, hotel, meals. . . . You're getting the picture. Another way of looking at it is to take your total expenses for last year and simply deduct the administrative (and manufacturing if applicable) costs and do not include any social media marketing in this number.

The next number you need is the total number of new customers you acquired last year for each marketing campaign. Next, divide the new customers into the total expenses for each marketing campaign. Now, when you regain consciousness and look at that number, you will realize how incredibly expensive it was for you to acquire just one new customer. This is referred to as the cost of customer acquisition. It is the best way to determine the effectiveness, or ROI (return on investment), of your traditional marketing. (Now clear, crumble up, or erase that number before anyone sees it!)

Who Is Doing It?

The next step is to take a serious look at how your marketing is performing, whether it's being executed in-house or out-house. If you're a small entrepreneurial company, you're probably doing it all. If you're a Fortune 1000 company, you probably use an outside agency. Take some time right now to seriously question the effectiveness of who's doing it. Is your time better spent on different activities, building your business, other marketing-related projects? Is the marketing and PR company the right choice? Have they done a really good job at a really good cost? Are there activities they are doing that should be brought in-house?

Analyze Your Many Demographics

In this next step, we need to look at *all* of your demographics. Oh, I know, you know your demographic. I am suggesting that you might not. First off, if you refer to it as your demograph*ic* and not in the plural, you don't know who your customers or prospects are. When using social media marketing, one size doesn't fit all. You can try to make one size fit and your customers will look like they're wearing their parents' clothes.

Social media is most effective when you listen to the conversation and participate appropriately. The conversation you have at night with your kids is different from the conversation you had that day with coworkers. The conversation you have with your parents is different from the ones you have at church or hanging out with your friends. Social media conversations are the same.

Identify Your Demographic Groups

If you defined your demographic as male and female between the ages of 25 and 54 with a combined annual income of more than $50,000, that's a *huge* demographic and needs to be treated differently. What will motivate a 25-year-old is completely different from what motivates a 50-year-old. Men and women are different. You've heard of the whole Mars and Venus concept, and different income households buy differently.

They are different because they think differently. Their motivational psychological hot buttons are different and where they participate on the Internet and in which social networks they interact with are different.

There are also different ways that different people communicate. Which of your different demographic groups prefer audio? Which prefer text? Which are using text messaging and Twitter? Who hangs out on Facebook or LinkedIn? Who loves watching videos? Maybe some, maybe all, maybe different groups prefer different forms of communication, and maybe they overlap. Do they learn through text, audio, visual, or kinesthetic stimuli?

How Many Groups Are There and What Are They?

Take some time to calculate each group. I want you to understand them psychologically. What are they doing right now? What do they do after dinner and on weekends? Do they text? Do they watch video on the mobile phone, their computer, their laptops? Do they listen to podcasts at the gym? Do they even go to the gym?

Break them down into as many categories and subcategories as you can. You will see a pattern emerge. You will see several distinct groups appear. Now, you will better understand how to effectively reach each group with both traditional and social media marketing. Again, it's in the process.

You may discover that you have a category of customers who really do like to participate on Facebook or maybe LinkedIn. Some, if they're older, might still respond best to direct mail. Keep in mind that the fastest-growing single demographic population in social media is the 54-plus baby boomer age group. They also still have the greatest amount of disposable income. You may also have a very mobile 25-to-35 age group that does everything on their mobile phones.

By determining the ROI on each of your different demographic groups, you will suddenly see which form of communication is the most effective for each. When Bill Marriot, the second-generation head and CEO of the

Marriott Hotel chain, was asked about why he loves to blog, he said, "I get to communicate directly with my customers. I find out what we are doing right so we can keep doing it, and what we are doing wrong so we can stop it." What terrific wisdom; listen to your customers, keep doing what's right, and stop doing what's wrong.

Determine what you are doing right and keep doing it. Find out what isn't paying off and stop it.

Who Are You?

The final step in this chapter is to closely analyze your communication strategy. Analyze each demographic group, and ask, "Who are you?" What persona are you or your company portraying? Answer the following questions for each demographic group:

- What is the description for the demographic group (for each)
- Who is your persona? (for each)
- What is your style? (for each)
- What is your message? (for each)
- What is your frequency? (for each)
- What is your call to action (conversion)? (for each)

Your persona is important. When you participate in an online conversation, who are you? Are you being authentic, sincere, and transparent, because if you aren't transparent, your customers will see right through you. You can still represent your company by being yourself. Someone would much prefer building a relationship with a person rather than a corporation. Most people would prefer buying something from a person and not a corporation.

You may have to change your style of communication with each demographic audience. I significantly change my use of *dude* according to who my audience is. I like using it and it's part of who I am, and I use it more or less freely, depending on my audience.

What has been your persona? If it's been all about features and benefits like we were taught in the 1970s, let it go. If it's been a corporate message, no one is listening, If it's been one of sell, sell, sell, you've been TiVo'd. It's about listening, participating, and being trusted. Then they will buy.

Let's go to the next chapter, Step 2—The Social Media Trinity.

The ROI of Social Media

Exploding Book Sales through LinkedIn

Background

With my social media effort, I needed to attract interest in my book without being a pushy salesman, in a short amount of time with little or no expenses. As a first-time author and unknown brand, the challenge was to gain attention and in the process generate interest in my book. Using LinkedIn to penetrate my market created no hard costs, only time.

Strategy

Sale without selling. Be visible, be controversial, be friendly, be open to get noticed. The target group was pretty wide, a book on creativity can reach across many niches and overall interests. The largest two target groups were business leaders and creative people. Being visible was achieved by answering questions on LinkedIn, posting questions that would draw combative or heated discussion postings by other posters. Being visible was also achieved by being friendly whenever I was able to help someone make a connection, by giving personal advice not posted to the public forums. Being visible was also achieved by being open with answers. The intuitive thinking would be to not give away the store when answering a question publicly but to give them just enough so readers would want to hire you, at which point you give a whole answer to the question. I found that the more advice I gave, the more I became visible and had an increase in connection requests.

Each tactic was taken without selling my book, but providing an opportunity for someone to discover my book when reading my posts.

Implementation

Online shops were set up on the publisher's site, my site, and major bookseller sites. I joined or created groups for members who might have an interest in my book.

Opportunity

To present me, the author, as legitimate, caring, and forthright, which makes post readers comfortable enough to relate that to how my book might be and be worth buying.

Conclusion

Within two months, there was a 15,000 percent increase in hits to my website, Amazon could not keep the book in stock and major booksellers like Borders and Barnes & Noble could not get the book reordered fast enough to keep up with demand. According to Alexa, my site is rated in the top 14 percent of all globally tracked websites. By the end of the fourth month, my site had a Google ranking of four. There was a peripheral relation as well. One guest blog post I did for a site generated a 1,000 percent increase in traffic to their site.

Traffic generated: 40 percent of all traffic generated now is direct traffic, which means they go straight to my site because visitors either know the URL or have it bookmarked. Thirty percent of traffic is generated by referring sites, which means other sites are linking to mine from theirs. Thirty percent of traffic comes directly from search engine searches for things related to me or my book.

—Gary Unger, Author
garyunger.com

Expert Insight

Chris Pirillo, geek and technology enthusiast, www.chris.pirillo.com

Chris Pirillo

(continued)

(*continued*)

. . . Every year something new pops up onto my radar; and a couple of years ago, it was the ability to livestream without really paying anything other than your ISP, so I thought, "Hey, why not!". . .

. . . [Usually in the beginning of the interview, I'll just say, "Can you tell us a little bit about yourself" but I wanted the listeners to get a full appreciation of who Chris Pirillo is. So I threw out a few statistics: "You've recorded over a thousand videos in the past year, you cracked the Top One Hundred Most Subscribed throughout the whole of YouTube, your live stats are more impressive, with five million unique video viewers watching Chris do his thing in 2007 with a total of two-plus million live viewer hours with an average viewing of 25 minutes per visitor. This past August, your live video feeds recorded 279,000 viewer hours with over a million viewers; 827,000 unique viewers; 395 average viewers, and 707 hours of live broadcasting! In addition, in the first seven days of launching your Web community for geeks, you logged in 587,000 page views. I mean, this stuff is unbelievable and here's one that is just totally cool because it's so simplistic; you are the Number One hit on Google for the word "Chris." Now how cool is that?]

. . . Mostly that particular statistic will hold true for the duration of my life, I don't know. . . . There's only one place to head, and that's down, after you're [the] Number One "Chris" on Google; although I haven't had it happen yet. I'm praying that they never change their algorithms or another more important "Chris" potentially comes along and usurps my position. . . .

. . . I turned a personality disorder into a career, as I have been prone to say. There's really no one thing that I do. I'm an omni-geek, so some might call me; someone who has just always been attracted to technology, much like a bug may be attracted to a light hanging on the porch in the middle of summer.

Sometimes it works pretty well for me and other times not so much. Umm, but I'm a content publisher, I help other people publish content and now have gotten more and more into increasing and sharing my own video experiences when they're live or, of course, recorded on YouTube.

The direction that I have been going is just largely just being myself. I enjoy talking about technology during the sharing of information; and when that's directly with people like myself, or specifically in talking directly to companies either on a sponsorship level, or specifically, a consultancy. . . .

. . . When I started online, there really weren't a lot of pools to facilitate community building; it hadn't really grown. Today, those tools are plentiful. There are plenty of ways that you can build communities and draw people in to the things that you are interested in, and help build their interest and their experiences with you. The hope in community building is that you feel less and less alone in this world, and no matter your background and the chances of some other people sharing your similar interests, or similar enough, are pretty strong.

You know, the Internet is a big place and community ebbs and flows, but certainly the one thing that you're obviously going to have going for you is yourself. So as long as you are honest with yourself and with your friends and the people who are not yet your friends, the chances of you maintaining a level of integrity on an ongoing basis (no matter if the tools are not where you're at) are pretty strong.

It's all about being honest and direct and that really is. . . . It's not so much in the area of community building; it's just more in being (I guess) a good communicator in general. . . .

. . . Well, you can't talk about something if you don't know what you are talking about. . . . When people do that it's pretty obvious that they are just either a hired gun, hired talent, or shouldn't be doing the things that they are supposedly doing. . . .

. . . People come and opportunities come in a multitude of directions; and certainly I started cultivating a lot of it back in 1992, but unofficially (at least in the commercial path) in 1996. From that point forward, you know, it was kind of an uphill battle because I was left to my own devices. This was long before social networking was a word and we had other services like Facebook and MySpace and Twitter; and you name any one of those services that are really there to help give anybody a voice to share with the rest of the world. And, of course, that came not long after blogging.

I've surveyed the landscape of these services efficiently. There is always something new to look at. And so I look at all of these resources and being able to leverage my own knowledge and passions against these resources to reach the same people or potentially new people, is really kind of key to, I think, any success for community building.

It's not just being there, it's really getting what the tool is and where it fits, specifically in your modus operandi. I was doing all this stuff before I had started to work on a radio show as a host; and before I had done a stint at Tech TV. Some people believe that I got my start at Tech TV and they really don't know me at all [Laughter], if that's the case. And it usually is. They seem to believe that everything came because of Tech TV, but . . . Tech TV only happened because of everything that was done before that, including writing books, sending out newsletters, and doing community building a lot on my own. . . .

. . . I've been working with CNN.com, doing a live segment every week, and carte blanche in terms of the content part, but I'm looking to involve myself a little deeper with CNN.com as the tech expert. And that only came

(continued)

(*continued*)

about because of everything else I am doing. So one thing builds on top of another, on top of another, on top of another. . . .

. . . If something couldn't be entertaining, why would anybody watch it? I mean that it should be informational and entertaining at the same time. I approached the classroom in much the same way when I was student teaching. I am a teacher by degree, but never actually became one in any kind of school.

Even if I've got my livestream going and nothing's going on and all that the people are doing is staring at the back of my head or listening to whatever I'm listening to, or whatever . . . then at least I've got a chat room that's integrated with the experience.

So even if I cannot be entertaining, well maybe I can be informative. . . .

. . . The airline safety instructions was the first video I uploaded to YouTube and it made it to the front page of YouTube. . . . It was three months into it, but it made it to the front page.

You know, I've been recording video since I could. I used to record videos, I'm pretty sure, on a Sony Mavica here and used a later series to actually record videos onto a floppy disc.

. . . And I was like, "Oh wow, I can record videos! This is so cool!" Of course, they were stamp-sized but they were still good. . . .

. . . Umm, you know, in respect, to livestreaming, I seldom move the camera. I usually play the Xbox 360. I just started to bring my laptop in there and then I switched the stream over to that. But usually I only keep one camera on, and I can leave the room at any time and not feel obligated to take the camera with me.

Umm, and because of that, I have set out that particular boundary. Some people violate that particular boundary, you know, whether they share personal information about myself that I would rather not have shared, like a phone number or what-have-you . . . anything like that, you know. But for the most part, I'm in control. My wife Ponzi can now watch . . . keep an eye on me throughout the day. Hey, you know, what wife would not want that? . . .

. . . It's all about sponsorship and those kinds of partnerships. And certainly other things come from it as well. Whether it's me, or Valunet . . . that's just the direction I've followed and that kind of stuff follows me.

Certainly sponsors have been extremely supportive in the things that I try to do and that's . . . not an uphill battle, necessarily, but since my model is usually a little different I have to, kind of, ride the cusp between what they're used to and what I think the next step is going to be. You know, it usually works out pretty well. . . .

. . . Usually I come up with a wacky idea that works and then find a way to underwrite it with the sponsor, and that's how it goes. I have never been asked to go out and speak on community building by any one of those companies. I would certainly welcome it, but I've never had the opportunity.

If it's kind of how my career path is going, and an opportunity will come up, and do I have the time and it's something that I'm interested in and will it be fun, . . . then I will give it a shot. . . .

. . . I love saving money and, more importantly, I love helping people save money, which I've done over and over and over and over again; and everybody loves to find a good coupon . . . and so now people will e-mail me and say, "Hey, I'm thinking about buying Product X. Do you have a coupon for it?" and I go find one. And then just sharing it with them, I share it with the rest of the world.

And so because of that, I'm able to close that loop between myself and the community and also create a value-add for everybody else. So, yeah, I like posting a lot of coupons on the blog. . . .

. . . Locker Gnome is what started it all on LockerGnome.com and that's still around. Now, well I guess, trying to build it into a blog network and a community and beyond. But unfortunately a lot of the platform choices out there are really limiting. I tried a lot, but unfortunately they're really, really expensive or really, really impossible to work with. So I try to find the "sweet spot" in the middle that I can give people a voice and give them a chance to get paid for what they know, like blogging. . . .

To listen to or read the entire Executive Conversation with Chris Pirillo, go to www.theSocialMediaBible.com.

Conclusion

We discussed in this chapter the process of really analyzing your existing media, what you are currently doing to touch your customers, the definition and importance of ROI, and the cost of customer acquisition. We also discussed your persona, how you communicate with your customers, the frequency, your message, and your call to action or conversation strategy.

Determining your ROI and cost of customer acquisition is more than an exercise. This process will be critical when you get to Step 4, Chapter 25, Identify Resources. The answers you get in this chapter will identify what you are currently doing that is effective and is returning a good ROI and what isn't. As Bill Marriott, the CEO of Marriott Hotels, says about his blog, "It will tell you what you are doing right so you can keep doing it and what you are doing wrong so you can stop."

Credits

The ROI of Social Media was provided by:

Gary Unger, author, GaryUnger.com

Expert Insight was provided by:

Chris Pirillo, geek and technology enthusiast, www.chris.pirillo.com

CHAPTER 23

The Social Media Trinity

www.LonSafko.com/TSMB3_Videos/23Trinity.mov

We discuss in this chapter the importance of the Social Media Trinity: blogging, microblogging (Twitter), and social networks. Chapter 6—The Ubiquitous Blog, discusses blogs quite thoroughly, while Chapter 13—Thumbs Up for Microblogging, discusses Twitter and other microblogs (mobile text message communication that is limited to 140 characters), and Chapter 2—Say Hello to Social Networking, discusses social networks. Here, I want you to understand the importance of these three chapters and their associated technologies. If you understand the Social Media Trinity, you will have a good understanding of 90 percent of everything you need to be successful using social media in your marketing strategy.

At the risk of being redundant, I am going to list many of the particular features of each of these three technologies so you can go back and read or learn more. Let's start with blogs.

Trinity Number One—Blogs

As I discussed in Chapter 6, blogs are an integral component to social media marketing. Blogs help you and your company build a trusted following, allow you to brand yourself in a strong environment, get you and your

brand in front of your audience automatically, and frequently, set you up as a perceived industry thought leader.

Get to know the Five Ws of blogging: the Who, What, Where, When, Why, and How. The *Who* is twofold: Who within your organization is the right person to blog on your company's behalf? Who likes to communicate through the use of text? Who would be willing to take the responsibility of blogging for your company? The second Who is who else is blogging about your industry out in the blogosphere?

The *What* is what are they blogging about? What should you blog about? What does your customer want to read? The *Where* is where will your blog reside? On another's website, such as Blogger.com,

or on your own URL with a blogging platform like WordPress. (Hint: The answer is on your server.)

The *When* is when are you going to blog? How often will you post new material? The *Why* is in Chapter 6 and this chapter; and the *How* is how will you find the time to do this? You'll learn more about this in Chapter 25—Identify Resources.

Understand the Terms

If you want to be successful at integrating blogging into your existing marketing strategy, you need to understand the jargon of the genre. Get familiar with terms such as: posting, publishing, RSS feeds (Chapter 17—RSS—Really Simple Syndication Made Simple), tags, and so on. The more you become familiar with these terms, the better you'll understand how to take full advantage of all of the benefits of blogging.

Identify Your Tools

You will need to decide where your blog is going to reside. You can use other people's platforms to base your blog on because they're free and easy to use, but you don't get SEO (search engine optimization) advantages.

I discuss more about this further on. Choose an easy-to-use platform such as WordPress and have it installed on your root directory directly on your website. WordPress is free. It's open source, so many developers are working on it from around the world, there are more widgets and plug-ins (which give it additional capabilities), and it takes about 15 minutes to download from WordPress.org, and ftp upload it to your website. Whatever ISP or web hosting service you use, such as GoDaddy or BlueHost, they will do it for you while you are on their tech support phone line.

Identify Your Content

If you want to be successful at blogging, the first thing you must have is a strong What's in It For Me angle, or WIIFM, or you can add, IDKT (I Didn't Know That). You've heard me preaching about this throughout this bible. So now that we have established that, you need to consider how you will best convey those thoughts. Of course, there will be text, but also consider the photos you will use. What touches the psychological hot buttons of your reader? People love to look at photos, so give them some. Include one, two, or three photos in your blog, and if you have more photos that your readers can look at, give them a link. Put your photos up on a photo sharing site such as Flickr and share them with your blog readers.

Create and add links to podcasts and video. This adds interest and good content. Your readers would much prefer looking at you in a video explaining your thoughts than just reading them. Make it fun, interactive, and rich in content.

Identify Plug-Ins and Widgets

Take a look around at the plethora of plug-ins and widgets that can be added to your blog site to give it more capabilities. It really is amazing. If you can think of it, there probably is a plug-in or widget for it.

For my TheSocialMediaBible.com

website, I wanted to add a countdown timer to when the book would be released. There was a plug-in for that. On my LonSafko.com

website, I wanted to add an unlimited number of my personal quotes, which would rotate randomly. I found a plug-in for that. A WordPress blogging platform is in many ways much more versatile and component rich than a standard HTML web site, and it's easy, and it's free.

SEO Advantages

By running your blog directly off your own website (in your root directory), you can take advantage of a great deal of SEO perks. The two I like the best are Google Juice and Link Love.

Google Juice is a fun term that means the number of links to web (or blog) pages that Google has indexed in its search engine that refer to you, your company, and your website. In the world of SEO, there are an estimated 140 different tests that each search engine performs on every web page to determine where in the rankings that website or web page should reside. Each test is weighted and some math is applied and your web page gets a ranking from one to nine. Google Juice, or the number of links to your web pages along with the page rank, will push you higher on the SERP, or search engine reply pages.

By creating a lot of blogs, you are creating a lot of different web pages for the search engines to find and to index. Also, blog pages get a significantly higher priority than does a standard HTML web page. Here's the reason.

The only purpose for a search engine is to return the most relevant results for your query. The better the results, the happier you will be using that search engine. The Google indexing algorithm is the best in the industry. It's what gave them the advantage over Yahoo! even though Yahoo! has a few years' head start in the search engine business.

So, when you ask Google (or any search engine) for the most relevant pages to your query, should it return blog pages, which by definition are new, timely, and fresh, or web pages that probably haven't been updated in two years? It's the blog pages.

When I was first doing the research for the blog chapter back in 2007, I wrote a blog about when Subway sued Quiznos for defamation of sandwich. See my blogs for the story. I wanted to see how Google indexed my blog page. With a strong background in SEO, I knew that a standard web page could take as much as 12 to 14 days for Google to find and index my new page.

Thirty minutes later, Google sent me a Google alert that my blog page had been indexed. Thirty minutes instead of 12 to 14 days! I then wanted to see how well it was indexed. I chose not to use my name in the search query. I am the only Lon Safko there is and already have about 158,000 references to me personally on Google. I went to Google and entered the terms *Subway, Quiznos,* and *social media.* I wanted to see if those terms would deliver good results.

The term *Quiznos* had about 1,160,000 SERPs, while *Subway* had 24,700,000 (mostly because of the underground rail system), and *social media* had about 185,000,000, none of which should have taken you to my page. In December 2007, I ranked first place, second place, and fourth place on the Google search results. And the last time I checked, I still held first, second, and fourth position for the terms.

As a result of this occurrence back in 2007, I formatted my website hard drive (completely erased), all 102 pages, and recreated my entire website using only the WordPress blogging platform. Now, any time I create a new blog, a new page, or just update a page, I get priority search engine rankings.

I don't recommend that you erase your entire corporate website, but I do strongly recommend that you add a WordPress blog for the same results.

RSS and Readers

There are a lot of other technical reasons for creating and maintaining a blog. Having your blog pages automatically delivered to your customers and prospects every time you create a new blog is priceless. By providing an RSS button so your followers can click and have your updates delivered to their reader or an e-mail notification be sent within seconds of your new blog post is unbelievable.

Interconnection

And with many of the new tools such as Google Buzz, HootSuite, and others, you can directly interconnect your blogs with your Facebook, e-mail, Twitter, and social bookmarking sites.

Blogging Conclusion

Determine your strategy, your conversion, your persona, develop a strategy for your content, frequency, and type of interaction. Make your blog posts full of hyperlinks to interactive rich media, with photos, audio, and video, and interconnect with all of your other community social networking sites.

Trinity Number Two—Microblogging (Twitter)

Everyone is talking about Twitter. Lady Gaga has more than 18.5 million followers and Justin Bieber has nearly 17 million followers. That's more followers than the combined populations of Ireland, Norway, and Panama, each. Oprah has more nearly 9,000,000 followers. This is all reason enough to take Twitter's capabilities seriously.

If you don't fully understand microblogging (Twitter), and have begun using it, now is a good time to go back and read Chapter 13—Thumbs Up for Microblogging. As with the previous Trinity category, you need to get into the Five Ws: Who, What, Where, When, Why, and How, again.

The *Who* is who in your organization will be tweeting and managing your Twitter account. Microblogging also has a second who and that is, who is out there in your industry who is tweeting? Identify some of the thought leaders in your industry and follow them. See what they have to say. Look at the number of followers they have. Look at how many people are following them. Look at the frequency and the content of their tweets. Are they providing their customers with a good WIIFM or IDKT?

The *What* is, what are those leaders tweeting about? What do your customers want in their tweets? The *Where?* The Where is any place you can tweet: the office, the coffee shop, the airport, at home, but *not* while driving. . . .

The *When* is as often as you have good content. If you are going to use Twitter for business, please don't tell me your plane is late, or you're having bacon with your eggs, or the sunset is pretty. I will unfollow you as fast as my thumbs can move. On my personal account, that's okay. On my business account, not so much.

The *Why* is because I want you to amass as many customers and prospects as Oprah and Justin. The *How* is right here.

Coming to Terms

You need to understand the basic vocabulary of microblogging: following, followers, tweets, retweets, direct, hash tags, and so on. Hash tags are particularly useful, so be sure to understand them.

You will also need to identify the right tools. Twitter is the most popular microblogging platform, while there are others, such as Yammer, which can be used behind your firewall for internal use only; Tumblr, which combines microblogging, blogging, aggregation, and social network integration; and Twitpic, which lets you upload a photo and post the shortened URL for that photo you tweet.

Manage the Tweets

Part of the responsibility of participating on Twitter is its management. Once you begin to play, it's good to stay in the game. You need to do some cyber surveillance. This sounds all CIA-ish, but just means monitoring what's being said about you and participating in that conversation. People *are* talking about you; it's not the schizophrenia talking. People are having conversations about you, your company, and your brand.

There are quite a few really good tools out there to manage the tweets. Applications such as Tweetdeck and Seesmic Desktop are great. You can download them for free and they all work on the Windows, Mac, and Linux operating systems. Either of these apps will let you see all of the tweets from every one of your followers, see all of your direct messages, allow you to send messages, and provide a great search capability much like Google Alerts and SocialMention, in which you can set up search terms such as your name, your company name, product names, and so forth. Then, anytime, anywhere in the world, someone tweets about you, you get a copy of the message at the same time the recipient does.

There are other helpful tools such as URL shorteners such as Bit.ly. These allow you to put in a large URL and it assigns a small, usually four-character URL to paste into your tweet so as not to hog up your 140 characters with one URL.

Determine Your Strategy

As has been stated before, you need to determine your strategy. Are you going to use Twitter to sell, educate, add value for your followers, create personal interaction to build trust, or the always-present brand awareness? The answer is "all of the above" and more.

As with all communications with your customers, you have to provide that strong WIIFM content and be the cognoscenti of your frequency. As long as the content is good, the frequency on Twitter is better high, unlike e-mail, in which if the frequency is too high, people will unsubscribe. This is because it's only 140 characters, about 5 seconds to comprehend, which is a small investment of time.

Here's another friendly reminder: Do not sell on Twitter. Don't spam Twitter. Build trust, let your customer get to know you, stay in front of them, and when they are ready to buy, they will.

Trinity Number Three—Social Networks

The third and last part of the Trinity of Social Media is social networks. Now is a good time to reread Chapter 2—Say Hello to Social Networking.

Once again, it is in your best interest to understand the Five Ws—Who, What, Where, When, Why, and How. The *Who* is you, or someone who can manage the social network site. That person needs to stay active, participate, kick out advertisers and spammers, post new content, and have a social presence.

The *What* is your content. You are building a friendly website that uses you as the representative of your company. Understand what persona you are going to use. It should be much different from the persona you use when you are interfacing with college classmates, or the teen you dated in high school.

The *When* is now. The earlier you get a presence and a following the better. The *Why* is because any time you have a watering hole (a marketing term for a place that like-minded customers and prospects gather), with 425,000,000 members, you need to be there. You need to be available to participate in that conversation. If Facebook were a country, it would be the third-largest country in the world, exceeding the 309,409,364 total population of the United States. For the *How*, reread Chapter 2 and read on.

What Are the Terms

Again, with each of the three technologies described in this chapter, you will need to understand the vocabulary. You need to understand what a profile, group, fan page, in-mail, questions, and so forth are. That's your homework assignment.

Identify the Tools (Sites)

You really need to have a profile on most every social network site you've ever heard of. Why not? It's free and if you don't sign up for your account, someone will eventually take your name, either because it's also theirs, or on purpose to sell back to you later when you realize the importance of it. It's easy to do. Use Open Social and with one click, your new profile is completely filled in using the information from an existing social networking site.

Facebook—Largest U.S. network, with more than 800 million members

Google+—Fastest-growing U.S. network

LinkedIn—Professional network

MySpace—More of an entertainment network

Ning—Usually themed within a niche or interest

Plaxo—Large alternate to Facebook

Others—Which are the right ones for your demographic? If you've heard of it, go sign up.

Determining the Strategy

As with the other categories, you will need to develop your strategy for interaction. Play with each network to help you understand the culture of that network and how the members interact. Each network is different, with a different basic purpose: Facebook to interact on a personal basis; LinkedIn to provide an online individual directory; MySpace, music and entertainment; Ning, to create your own vertical niche social networking site. Then refer to all of the strategy advice from this section; determine the frequency of participation, listen before you speak, provide strong content, and never sell.

The ROI of Social Media

Adobe Asks Students, "Is It Real or Fake?"

Background

College students are a vital audience for the long-term success of Adobe. These are the future creative professionals who will buy Adobe products like Photoshop and Illustrator. It's essential that they be exposed to them when they are young, so they will want to use them when they enter the workforce. They also happen to be incredibly skeptical of marketing. Adobe engaged Traction to break through to this challenging target.

(continued)

(*continued*)

Strategy

Create relevant value. Clever advertising wasn't enough for Adobe to successfully reach this challenging audience. They had to provide relevant value—relevant to the audience, relevant to the brand, and relevant to the medium through which our message would be delivered. The Millennial audience was the first to grow up with technology as a ubiquitous part of their lives. They were not afraid of it and we had to respect them. The brand's flagship product was Photoshop—a tool that gives users powerful capabilities to manipulate photos. The medium was Facebook, where our audience was spending an average of 22 minutes a day at the time. It was an entertaining diversion for our target and the value we would provide would be an entertaining diversion as well.

Implementation

Seizing upon the cultural insight that Photoshop was famous for faking photos (think Sarah Palin in a bikini holding an assault rifle), Traction created a Facebook game called "Real or Fake?" that challenged users to guess if a series of images were real or fake? If the answer was "fake," a tab popped up that provoked users to "See how we did it" and showed them a brief tutorial of how to use Adobe products to create the effect in the image.

Opportunity

The opportunity was threefold. One was to provide a simple, yet compelling brand experience that would re-engage audiences again and again. The second was to educate while we entertain—the potential to make players feel like experts and thus have a greater emotional investment with the brand. Finally, there was the opportunity to drive sales. Adobe had terrific student-only pricing offers for this audience designed to make their products affordable to future customers. By engaging audiences again and again, we were able to expose them to offers again and again.

Results

Adobe "Real or Fake?" garnered results on all three opportunities. First, 40 percent of people who played the game returned to the site to play again.

Twenty-one percent of game plays resulted in players experiencing a tutorial and another 6 percent clicked to check out the offer.

—Adam Kleinberg
CEO, Tractionco.com

Expert Insight

Michael Naef, CEO and cofounder, Doodle, www.doodle.ch/main.html

Michael Naef

Doodle takes the pain out of scheduling. It helps people find a common date and time for their next conference call, project meeting, business lunch, family reunion, barbeque—any group event. It focuses on delivering a very simple and usable service, which is free to end users. . . .

The service was conceived and implemented in 2003 and the idea for it was born from my personal need. I wanted to schedule dinner with some friends. The process of finding the right time was very inefficient, involved a great number of e-mails. So I concluded that there has to be an easier, more efficient way, and implemented Doodle. The service attracted a large and growing user base quickly. In 2006, I decided to professionalize the service, so Paul Sevinç and I decided to found the company that still runs Doodle. . . .

(continued)

(*continued*)

We launched the service in Switzerland, but our biggest growth is outside Switzerland. Doodle is used in many countries worldwide and is translated into 30 languages. What's interesting is that almost all of these translations are the work of volunteers from these various countries. . . .

Translations are important to our users. We provide a very simple service, and one could think that it's okay to have it in English only, but it's important to have it in the local language of the people who are using it. Our target audience is not only the Internet professional, but everyday people who might not be familiar with an English application. . . .

Localization is very important and I think that as a Switzerland-based company we are in a perfect position for that, considering that Switzerland is a country with four official languages. We are quite used to providing just about everything in several languages. . . .

People are using Doodle for all kinds of use cases, both for business and private events like family reunions, ski weekends (in Switzerland, obviously), et cetera. Our users appreciate Doodle's simplicity, high usability, and low entry barrier. They don't have to download anything or even register for the service. These factors have contributed to our high number of users; we're currently reaching way more than five million each month. . . .

The typical use case is that the event organizer visits our site and creates a poll of sorts, which offers a number of dates to choose from. Then the organizer receives a unique web link provided by Doodle, which he or she can send to the event participants. The participants use that link, then, to access the poll and indicate their availability. The organizer uses the same link to monitor the poll's progress and determine the best option at the end. That's it, in a nutshell. This explains that Doodle is a scheduling service . . . not a calendar. It connects with calendars, however, providing the missing link between people who use electronic calendars, paper-based, or none at all. . . . Many of our more experienced users connect Doodle with their calendars to help them schedule even more efficiently. They can set up and participate in polls in the context of their calendar information, and they can book tentative and final appointments directly to their calendar. . . .

Because Doodle itself is not a calendar, we are not competing with companies like Google or Microsoft or Notes and their respective calendars. We help them coordinate the process of finding the dates and time. . . .

We have loads of user success stories and some of them are listed as testimonials on our web site. I just had a call from one user who said that, "My work is driven by conference calls, and it is a pain to arrange an appropriate time among several parties. We have ended this heartache and trouble with this brilliant polling system." This is the type of feedback that we get. There are also people telling us that they're using Doodle to schedule a meeting with people at seven different hospitals where they need a hundred percent attendance, and they're very happy with our service because it allows them to schedule a meeting and coordinate and accommodate the time usually within minutes. . . .

We offer . . . time zone support, which is easily activated when creating a new scheduling poll. If activated, Doodle will display the times in the time zones of each participant so they get their time correct automatically. . . .

We also offer users some social media tools. Doodle integrates with all major calendars like Microsoft Outlook, Google Calendar, Lotus Notes, iCal. Integrating Doodle with your calendar will make your scheduling experience even more efficient and seamless. It will help you determine your available times easily, book your appointments automatically, and help you prevent double bookings. We also offer integrations into a number of social networks and portal sites like Facebook, Xing, and iGoogle. And we provide a number of APIs to help developers implement their own extensions or integrations. . . .

So how do we monetize all this? We currently have three revenue streams: One is based on advertising and monetizes the free service. The other two are based on paid services. One is called *Branded Doodle*; it allows an enterprise or other forms of organizations to run their own Doodle, hosted on our servers, with their branding, additional features, and security options. The other one is called *Premium Doodle* and offers a similar feature set to private individuals. Both paid services are subscription-based. . . .

To listen to our interview or read the entire Executive Conversation with Michael Naef, go to http://www.doodle.com/main.html.

Conclusion

We discussed in this chapter the importance of the Social Media Trinity. If you know these three categories, you know enough to really make an impact for you and your company's marketing and brand recognition. These three categories are the most effective way to build a following and build trust. It may require a little homework, but the juice will be worth the squeeze.

Credits

The ROI of Social Media was provided by:

Adam Kleinberg, CEO, Tractionco.com

Expert Insight was provided by:

Michael Naef, CEO and cofounder, Doodle, www.doodle.ch/main.html

CHAPTER 24

Integrate Strategies

www.LonSafko.com/TSMB3_Videos/24Integration.mov

Integrate Your Existing Strategy into the Trinity

The third step in your Five Steps to Social Media Success is integration. This is when you take all of what you learned from Step 1, Analyze Your Existing Media, filter out what is ineffective with a low ROI, what you learned in Step 2, the Social Media Trinity, and combine the two into one integrated cohesive marketing strategy. Remember, social media isn't a stand-alone set of tools that must be dealt with as a separate strategy. It has to be integrated.

I am often asked when consulting with Fortune 1000 companies, "Does my company need to do social media marketing?" or "How much should my company spend on social media marketing?" I say, remove the term *social media* and ask those questions again: "Does my company need to do marketing?" or "How much should my company spend on marketing?" When put that way, it sounds like a silly question, doesn't it? Just like in the previous chapter, you will now need to develop an integrated strategy that includes your existing conventional marketing and the new digital tools.

theSocialMediaBible.com

Selecting the Best of Both

When you develop your integrated marketing strategy, you will need to identify the best media for each demographic. Sometimes it will be conventional marketing tools such as selling RVs to the retired; direct mail might still be the best way to reach your targeted demographic. Sometimes it might be a combination such as selling RVs to the retired. The fastest-growing demographic is the 54-plus-year-old. Or sometimes it might be just social media such as selling RVs to the retired, as Facebook's fastest-growing and most active population is the 54-plus-year-old.

Remember that when you craft your message, it will be different for each medium you use. The copy in a newspaper article will be significantly different from a tweet or what you post in a blog. They're different audiences even if they are the same people. When we're hanging out drinking a beer, I would expect your language to be different from when you come over for Thanksgiving with the family. Remember your audience, the platform (be it conventional or social media), the culture, and the rules within that environment.

Develop Clear Individual Goals (Conversions)

When you craft your message, it has to have a clear call to action: clear goals, or conversions. The whole reason you are participating in that conversion is to build trust to sell. Be sure each message meets a predetermined definition for conversion. Here are some examples:

- Increase revenue through e-commerce
- Collect user-generated content
- Increase web traffic
- Product or service awareness
- Loyalty and peer support
- Collaboration
- Innovation (ideas)
- Promote events
- Sale or closeout
- Reduce tech support
- Increase e-mail subscriptions
- Drive telephone sales
- Build brand awareness

Develop one call to action (conversion) per message, especially when using e-mail. More than one call to action per message will confuse and weaken your conversion.

Quality Content, Not Quality Production

As I mentioned in the earlier chapter, you, me, and your customers have become pro-sumers, professional consumers. We know that if a company spends a quarter-million dollars to produce a television commercial, there has to be a hidden agenda, some psychological hot buttons being pushed to get us to do something, which is convert. As a result, we subconsciously tune out polished expensive advertisement productions. We, the people, want content, not polished agendas.

Our messages still need to be professional-looking without typos, but the overall quality can and should be lower. Even a hi-def video uploaded to YouTube (regular account), looks pretty bad once YouTube uploads and degrades it for distribution. We are accustomed to it. A blog should be 400 words without typos, and an image or two, with a few hyperlinks. Most videos on YouTube are shot with inexpensive video cameras and flip phones. That's what we want. The days of the glossy one-sheet and B-roll are over. Embrace it.

Integrate Existing Conventional and New Digital

I have been talking so far about integrating the two technologies: conventional media and social media into different demographic groups. Now I need you to take it one step further by integrating each of them into each other.

This is the subject of my newest book, *FUSE! Fusion Media Marketing.* Here are some examples:

- Place all of your major social network links on your stationery, your sales literature, and your business cards. Use the little chicklets (small avatar-type icons that represent those companies).
- Put your Twitter account on your business card. If you want people to follow you, you have to tell them how. A few years ago, if you wanted people to call you, you made it easy for them. Do the same thing with social media.
- Create a social media interactive e-mail signature. Put all of your social media addresses in your e-mail signature. Or, if you think that looks too cluttered, put all of them in your Google profile and put the link to

your Google profile in your e-mail signature. I am surprised (shocked) at how many people still don't use an e-mail signature, let alone include their social addresses. Are you trying to keep them a secret?

- This is one where I get everybody, is your web address on your return mailing label? Why not? The post office doesn't care. They ignore it. Do name, street, city, state, zip, and URL. Put your web address everywhere.
- Is your Twitter web address in all of your print advertising?
- Is your blog address on your brochure and business cards? You do want people to read them and follow you, right?
- Do you tell your customers your web address in company voicemail? They are on hold, they have one hand free, tell them to use it to go to your website while they are waiting.
- Is your URL and Twitter account watermarked on your videos? Do you mention them in your podcasts?
- Do you mention your blog address in your podcasts and videos? Is it in your e-mails?
- Do you print your web address on your brochures and in your direct mail pieces with a "Visit Us at . . ." or "Follow us on @YourName"?
- Is your blog address with a hyperlink in every one of your e-mails?
- Do you mention your Twitter address in your blogs in which you microblog tweets with the address to your social networks that display your web address, where they can download your product PDF that contains your telephone number, from which they can call you to find out your address? I think you're getting the picture.

Is all of this making you think a little differently?

The ROI of Social Media

Hotels Use Twitter to Increase Revenue, Customer Service

Background

Provenance Hotel Group owns and operates five boutique hotels in Portland, Seattle/Tacoma, and Nashville. Because of the economic conditions in late 2008, the hotel was looking for additional sources of revenue and traffic. Social media was the quick answer, as it was a hot new buzz/trend that didn't carry huge startup costs. The barrier to entry was minimal because there were few hotels doing anything noteworthy or extraordinary, so there was an opportunity to jump on Twitter and create a name for Provenance and its hotels, Hotel Lucia (Portland), Hotel de Luxe (Portland), Hotel Max (Seattle), Hotel Murano (Tacoma), and Hotel Preston (Nashville).

Strategy

Anvil was to create Twitter accounts and provide Twitter training to the key contacts at each hotel so they understood what it was, how to use it, and why we were using it. Once they understood the potential, each contact began creating tweets based on events, deals, packages, free giveaways, random thoughts, and so forth for their respective hotels. We quickly noticed two big opportunities. The first was folks looking for hotel recommendations. These folks were immediately tweeted back, offering a special Twitter rate to stay at a Provenance hotel in that area. This started a conversation and established credibility for the hotels. The second opportunity was more of a customer service/concierge role in which guests were asking questions about the hotel, restaurants, dog parks, and so on. Anvil worked directly with the hotels to provide answers to these people as well. Many times it helped solidify a booking, or made the difference between a great stay and an okay stay. Customer service will always win over guests.

Implementation

Anvil worked with a design company to create unique Twitter accounts for each hotel, as well as include social media icons on each hotel's website to increase visibility. Anvil then worked with each hotel to create a process for Twitter, which included an editorial calendar and a process for reviewing tweets.

> twitter.com/hotel_deluxe
>
> twitter.com/hotel_lucia
>
> twitter.com/hotel_murano
>
> twitter.com/hotel_preston

Opportunity

The opportunity was to drive increased revenue through a special Twitter follower rate, increase the credibility of the hotel among the social media community by building trust, and providing top-notch customer service.

(continued)

(*continued*)

Conclusion

Since the Twitter strategy was rolled out, Anvil and Provenance saw huge success, coming in many different forms. Each hotel is consistently booking rooms through Twitter (and a special 15 percent Twitter rate code) on a monthly basis, as well as building credibility for working so hard to engage and communicate with the Twitter community. Provenance has been recognized for its efforts, with Provenance getting mentioned in a CBS News Travel article (and CBS *Early Show* video). Provenance has also received mentions on industry-relevant blogs like *Hotel Interactive* (specifically for their Facebook campaigns) and *Hotel Marketing Strategies* due to activity on Twitter (Anvil helps cross-promote blog posts and Facebook through Twitter).

—John McPhee,
hoteldeluxeportland.com
hotellucia.com
hotelmaxseattle.com
hotelmuranotacoma.com
hotelpreston.com

Expert Insight

Tony Mamone, CEO and founder, *Zimbio*, www.zimbio.com

Tony Mamone

. . . We keep growing; it's just a fun thing to be a part of and definitely infectious here in the office just to watch our stats every month going up and up.

I think we did about 13 million unique visitors last month, so . . . I guess we need to change the tag line to "more than 10 million readers a month." . . .

. . . *Zimbio* is an interactive magazine. We focus on topics in popular culture, so we cover things like style and entertainment and sports and current events.

My background . . . I guess there's a long story and a short story; I'll go somewhere in the middle. I'm an engineer by training, but have now moved more into a business role. I have an interest and passion for Internet content and have been involved with it for quite a while now, starting off with a project that launched the site FindArticles.com, which was a poor man's version of Lexis Nexis, so it was a way to search magazine archives and look up full-text articles of popular journals and magazines.

I loved that project, really enjoyed working on it, and the site was ultimately sold to CNet. And a few years ago, I decided I wanted to get my hands back into an entrepreneurial effort and create something from scratch, and as I thought about opportunities with my partner we saw real opportunities to do something interesting and innovative in the magazine publishing space.

So, hence, *Zimbio*. And a big part of what we do here at *Zimbio* is we are trying to create the most popular and influential magazine published in the world. We start with our flagship property in Zimbio.com. It's quite different from traditional print magazines. In a lot of ways from a reader's perspective, it's not too dissimilar from what you would find in a *People* or *Vogue*, or *Elle* or *Newsweek*, but the way we create it is fundamentally different.

We try to leverage technology to automate a lot of the publishing, and we tap into our members and our readers to actually write and create much of the content. . . .

. . . [I]t's hard to get specific stats, but our best guess is that we're one of the 10 most popular magazines on the Internet right now. There are definitely a few that are above us. . . . *People* and *Time* and *Newsweek* still trump *Zimbio*, but we've passed a lot of great brands.

We are more popular than *Entertainment Weekly*, or *Sports Illustrated*, or *US Weekly Online;* and so we focus heavily on digital distribution. We don't have a print version right now. It's not necessarily something that we're going to want because as we look forward and look at what magazine publishing needs to be in 10 years, we believe that the core focus will be digital; and [it] will . . . strip away the need for paper and ink and will sort of move toward the digital distribution model. And so we've just really focused our efforts there and we're doing quite well. . . .

. . . I think the Internet is the core focus and it will be the growth engine for the industry. At the same time, I think that print has a place, especially

(continued)

(continued)

with magazines. There's just something fun about flipping through the glossy pages of *Rolling Stone* or checking out photos on the beach. I think there will be a place for print; I just believe the core focus of the industry and the growth engine for the industry will be digital. . . .

. . . When we started, the demographic . . . was a very, sort of Internet-savvy user—people that were surfing and finding these social media sites. And, as we've grown, as you approach 10 million-plus readers a month, you start to look a lot more like a mass media play; so at this point our readership is really a broad spectrum of folks who tend to be in the 18- to 34-year-old range. That's where our core concentration is, but they are really evenly spread between males and females and they're also a worldwide audience.

About 50 percent of our audience is here in the United States, but we also have an awful lot of readers in Canada and the U.K. and India and Australia, and other English-speaking markets.

Our aspirations are that hopefully in the not-too-distant future we will start to offer other languages as well and we'll truly become a global brand. So it's a pretty big spectrum of folks that check out *Zimbio* and for different purposes. It's really a consumer magazine and consumer destination site. An awful lot of people are checking it out. . . .

. . . We've got lots of folks in Ireland and all over Europe. And it's kind of fun for me as an employee of the company. I get to come in every day and check out what the most popular stories were. And a lot of times it's a rugby player in Australia, or it's an actress who's quite famous in a different market that I haven't heard of. So it's sort of a neat way to stay up to date, not only on popular culture here in the United States but popular culture worldwide. . . .

. . . I think the magazine publishing industry, and really publishing in general, is such a robust industry; there are so many publications out there and most readers tend to have many different magazines that they like to read. It's not a one-stop shop. It's not quite as cutthroat as other industries can be. There are plenty of people who read *Zimbio* and they also read a handful of other online magazines, and they subscribe to print; and so there's a little less of the sort of cutthroat nature that you might find if it were a conventional publication.

That said, you know I think many of the print magazines and the magazine publishers are starting to look at new media companies as a wave of growth that they're not seeing in their traditional business.

So as folks like the *New York Times* and *Time* start to evaluate their businesses and see that certain profit margins are going away and certain lines of their business aren't growing, you know they're a big company and they're looking for strategic areas of growth. Hopefully *Zimbio* boils up on their radar screen as an example of something that's working. . . .

. . . For my day-to-day job, when I come into the office I don't think about what the exit strategy for *Zimbio* is. I think about what we're trying to build. And that is a longer-term view; it's not this year, it's five to ten years from now. What do we want the company to be and what do we want the brand to represent and how are we going to build an audience and how are we going to attract a readership and a contributor base that's going to volunteer and continue to work on and improve the site and the content?

And that's just such a fun project that I'm not at all anxious and not in a rush to find an exit for the company. I'm really just having a great time building it. . . .

. . . If you walk up and down the magazine aisle at your supermarket and check out the headlines on the covers, it's a pretty good representation of what you'd find on *Zimbio*. We . . . actually cover a very broad spectrum of topics. You can find things on home décor, pets, and health topics and business topics. But our core focus is on four main categories: style, entertainment, current events, and sports.

And if you look into each of those categories on *Zimbio*, one thing that's unique about the way we cover this is that we tend to cover very specific and niche topics within those categories. So instead of covering celebrities, we cover very specific celebrities. Instead of covering sports, or even certain teams or leagues, we cover the actual athletes.

And what we try to do when you come to an athlete's section on *Zimbio*, is we try to show you a very diverse perspective, so you get a collection of photos and articles about a specific person or specific athlete, or a specific actress, a specific politician . . . and it allows you to deep drill and deep dive into one person who is making the news and making headlines, or that you're interested in. . . .

. . . There's a real craft to this and there's a history. If you look at the history of media, there are many different publications that have discovered that people like to read about other people. That's where it really gets interesting, and especially for a magazine where it's mostly reading and you're sort of just browsing because you've got some time and you're interested in a topic. It's just great to get into the details of how people make decisions, and which people are involved in which stories. That's an angle that we like to take and it's really worked for us here at *Zimbio*. . . .

. . . Let me tell you a little story about the history of *Zimbio* and how we started, and sort of lead up to how we generate our content today.

When we first started, we really fully embraced user-submitted content. That was the core and 100 percent focus of the site as we launched. And we were encouraging people to submit articles and photos and write polls, and

(continued)

(*continued*)

so forth. And for the first six to twelve months of the company's history, we continued to just focus on user-generated content.

It allowed us to grow and allowed us to get started, and the nice thing about starting a company that's focused on user-generated content is you don't need a lot of front cash, or capital, in order to get started; and so you can begin to build a community and nurture that community . . . and it starts to take shape.

And as we started to grow, we really started to reach out to some of our readers and try to get a better sense for what value they were finding in the site. And as we talked to folks and as we watched them use *Zimbio*, we discovered that . . . they were indifferent to the source of the content. What they were interested in was high-quality content and they wanted to see diverse perspectives on each story. So one thing that we offered that other folks didn't was that if they came to read the story about Obama street art and the graffiti artists that were drawing these amazing pieces of art about Barack Obama's candidacy, they saw three or four or five, or even more, different authors writing about it. And that was intriguing to them and was something that they liked. As we dug under the covers and peeled back what was going on there, we discovered that sometimes user-generated or user-submitted content was the best source. But other times there were traditional media sources out there, which we could license or find that would add to the mix.

And so where we have evolved to is we now offer a hybrid between citizen journalism and traditional media. So on *Zimbio* you'll find articles written by everyday people just like you, who want to share their opinion and have taken the time to write an article, or submit pieces of content that they feel are important and noteworthy. And you'll also find licensed articles from traditional sources, like *The Guardian*, or Associated Press, or Reuters, or *BusinessWeek*. And we try to mix the two, so that for each reader who comes to the site we can offer them the best of content that we have at our disposal. And that includes professional photography, it includes articles and news, and it includes opinion pieces by our membership. . . .

To listen to or read the entire Executive Conversation with Tony Mamone, go to www.theSocialMediaBible.com.

Conclusion

We are now three for five. By now, you should have a good strategy or at least a good idea about how to develop one. Look at your existing media, determine what's working and keep doing that. Figure out what's not and stop doing that. Take the time to understand the three most important tools in social media: the Trinity—blogging, microblogging, and social networks. Take the time to really identify all of your demographic groups. Integrate your conventional marketing into social media marketing. And develop a strategy for each using the most appropriate tools for each group. If you do this, you will win.

Now that you see the amount of work ahead of you, how are you going to get it all done? Where will you find the resources? Read the next chapter to find out.

Credits

The ROI of Social Media was provided by:

John McPhee, HotelDeluxePortland.com

Expert Insight was provided by:

Tony Mamone, CEO and founder, *Zimbio*, www.zimbio.com

CHAPTER 25

Identify Resources

www.LonSafko.com/TSMB3_Videos/25Resources.mov

The three previous steps (chapters) are mostly your responsibility to implement. Now that you have a comprehensive integrated marketing strategy developed, you have to figure out who is going to be responsible for implementing and maintaining all of these new tools and efforts. I'll bet right now it seems like it would take a team of people to execute your plan. Don't worry; here's how we'll get it done.

The past few years have been tough ones for businesses around the world. The economy affected all businesses from the Fortune 500 down to the one-person sole proprietor. It had the same effect on nonprofits and governmental entities as well. Marketing budgets and personnel were cut, fewer people had to do more work, and now in the middle of all this, we have a whole new way to market using social media.

This is actually good news. While all marketing takes human resources to implement and social media is no different, social media is free and doesn't require huge media buys, creative, and production. Here's some of your resources right here.

Going through the process in the first step showed you what marketing efforts were effective and what weren't. Now is the time to make a list of all of the efforts you are going to put on hold in place of using social media. Grab your yellow pad or erasable whiteboard and start making a list.

List all of your previous activities that didn't return the return on investment (ROI) you had hoped for. List print advertising, your direct mail, your trade show sponsorship. Next to each category, list the number of hours it took for each activity and subactivity associated with that effort. Now make three columns: one for hours; one for the cost of those hours, which will include the base hourly wage plus 32 percent for indirects; and in the third column, list the hard costs.

Right away, you can see extra hours or money to purchase outside assistance or to bring someone in, and more money from the hard costs that can be added in. This can become substantial even if you are a one-person team or had a relatively meager budget to begin with.

In my companies, I pretty much do it all with the exception of hiring outside help on a project-by-project basis. What I found was that there were many marketing activities I simply don't do anymore. When I did my analysis, I realized I would never have to do a direct mail campaign again. This pleased me. They're expensive, time consuming, and the national average conversion is one-half of 1 percent. That's 0.005 percent conversion. This freed up a chunk of time and a chunk of money that I can now spend on other social media–related activities.

I also found that print ads weren't generating the type of ROI I expected, so I am much more cautious where, when, and how much I advertise. And finally, trade shows and conferences were another place I cut budgets without any noticeable reduction in sales from those activities.

Once you see the inordinate ROI of using social media in your marketing strategy, you are going to want more resources than just the ones you saved. That leads us to upper management. I do realize that you may be one of the more than 21 million entrepreneurial companies in the United States and there may be more outside the country, in which case upper management just might mean your spouse.

Management Buy-In

One of the more frustrating conversations I have been having with Fortune 1000 companies across the United States is that while the folks in marketing, PR, and communications get it—they understand the ROI of using social media in their marketing strategy—the corner office folks don't get it, which is unfortunate. For the most part, the "C Suite": CEO, CFO, COO, CIO, and so on, are over 50, and we didn't grow up with this technology. It was handed to us after college. We've had more than three decades of success without using the newfangled social media.

I joke in my keynotes that when my granddaughter was a baby, I gave her a rattle: one of my old cell phones. She was figuratively weaned on technology. It comes easier to the Generation Xs, Ys, and Millennials. For those of us over 50, not so much, but hey, I'm over 50 and I wrote the book on it, so get over yourself and get into this century.

The hard facts are that you need upper management's buy-in for you to secure human and financial resources. Now that you have your plan, go to work on them. Here are a few tips to help win them over.

Give them a copy of this book. I know it sounds self-serving (which it is), but it's effective. Just buy another copy and leave it on their chair when they are out of the office. Put a yellow sticky on this chapter so they can read the Over-50 Speech I just gave you. Also, they will thumb through the book and not be embarrassed by asking for answers to all of the questions they didn't already know the answers to and felt that they should have known.

Next, give them some ROI case studies. There are 27 of them in this book. Nothing pleases the C Suite more than success stories. They feel it limits their liability for trying something new and untested.

Next is third-party credibility. For some reason, even though you've been telling them about social media for some time now, they will believe it more if it comes from an outside source. Again, a consultant's recommendations sound better than an internal recommendation. So hire me to come and say what you've been saying all along (too self-serving?). Then hire someone, but be really careful. If anyone calls himself a social media expert, ask him to leave your building. It took me more than 500 pages to explain social media. If I wasn't forced to understand all of the many facets of this technology well enough to write the book on it, I would never have become an expert.

If you want my 10-Question Social Media Expert Test, go to TheSocial MediaBible.com (aka www.TSMB3.com)

and download your free copy. If your expert can correctly answer 7 out of the 10 questions, she might know something about social media, but that won't mean she's an expert or a guru.

Reputation Management

Another reason to engage in social media is that you have responsibility for reputation management. As I stated earlier, people are talking about you, your company, your products, and your brand. You need to be aware of those conversations and you need to engage in them. You need to encourage good behavior (to get good press) and you have responsibility to defuse negative press.

If someone writes something good about your product or service in his blog, don't you want to know that? Don't you need to know that? Don't you want to encourage that? Drive customers and prospects to that unsolicited rave review?

If someone says something negative, don't you want to know that, too, and feel a responsibility to engage with that person? Unlike conventional media (press), it's okay to engage. It's preferred. Many times the author of the negative press is only looking for engagement, but your customer doesn't know that.

Rule Number One: Always take the high road. Never condescend, get snarky, use inappropriate language, or belittle the writer. Everyone has a right to one's own opinion, even if it's an idiotic one.

Engage with "I understand your point of view, however, . . ." and state your case. If you do it correctly, the reader will side with you and discredit the writer. Set the book aside for a moment, think about this, and let it permeate your thoughts. This is a completely different wisdom from what we've used in the past. It works.

The same is true for Twitter. Retweet good tweets; disarm bad ones. Use this opportunity to drive customers away from having this conversation on Twitter, where you are limited to 140 characters, and drive them instead to your blog or your Facebook Page. The same is true if the confrontation erupted in a social network. One more note: Never, ever, delete a bad comment on your blog. If it used inappropriate language, though, delete it. If it hurts your feelings, don't. Post it and address it.

Successful Campaigns

The next effective solution to upper management buy-in is success. For example, run a Twitter campaign to build your e-mail list or create a giveaway on your Facebook page. Closely monitor and measure (next chapter) your before-and-after result. Set a benchmark, implement measurement tools, run a small campaign, measure the results, create a small white paper, and slip it on to the CEO's desk along with your request for a new hire or budget increase.

This test campaign, along with most of your social media strategy implementation, can be executed with you and some existing staff or just you. It's about managing your time and reappropriating resources to activities with a greater ROI. The great feature about social media is there are no hard costs and it delivers an inordinate ROI. Upper management loves this kind of talk.

Identify Resources

If you weren't previously convinced about the effectiveness of social media before running one or two simple test cases, you will be. You will want to begin testing different tools in different ways and you will eventually need or want help.

In-House

Existing Staff

Even if you are just a one-person show, there might be others within your organization who would love to help. Is there someone passionate about your company who likes to write? Invite her to write your blog. For someone else who is a social butterfly and loves his own Facebook page, have him manage your Facebook page. If there is another who likes to tweet, then you've got yourself your new Twitter rep.

In most cases, they will require only a little guidance to get them started. Have your blogger write a blog (only 400 words or so), look it over for grammar, punctuation, legal perspective, intellectual property issues, and if it's on corporate message. Remember that if you are a publicly traded company, there are a lot of SEC rules about what you can and cannot say in your communications. Guide them without a heavy hand, as they are volunteers, and let them go. It should require much less effort to manage than to do it all yourself.

Outside Staff

If there just isn't anyone you can recruit, then look for help outside that you can bring inside. There are interns, college students, temps, craigslist, eLance, and so on.

I know that managing interns is like herding cats, but once you get them pointed in the right direction with proper training, they're pretty good, and in most cases, they're free. College students are awesome and inexpensive. The best way I have found to identify the brightest and best is to call the dean of communications or marketing at your local university. Ask the dean to recommend their best student. They know who's best and will get kudos for getting them employment.

When I was building my computer company in 1986, I did just this and the student I hired eventually graduated, worked full time for me, became my vice president of engineering, and worked with me for more than 10 years.

Craigslist and eLance are two other places to find great inexpensive help. I found one person on eLance who did 24 hours of interviews for the Expert Insights for this book entirely through eLance. She was half the cost of even getting translations done in India, and English is, of course, like a native language to her.

Warning: I mentioned Generation X, Y, and Millennials earlier. Just because they understand the technology doesn't mean they understand marketing, communications, sales, and public relations. They may have a Facebook page and use text messaging, but don't assume they understand how to communicate on a corporate level. Guide them or provide them with the content and let them execute.

Changing the Mind-Set Challenge

Overall, we have to realize there is a different mind-set when using social media. Not all uses are intuitive, especially when we've had two or three decades of doing things differently and having success without the new ways. Some techniques are the same and some are different. The key to your success is knowing the difference.

Out-House

Marketing and Public Relations Firms

I get teased about using this descriptor. I have worked with a lot of outside agencies in my career. Some were good, but most knew about as much as I did and often less. Please be wary of service agencies and marketing and public relations firms selling social media services. Most companies know less than you do by now (unless they also read this book).

I can't tell you how many times I have been asked to present and talk about social media with some of the world's largest firms only to find out that they know less than average and have been selling social media services to their clients for several years now. Have them take the earlier-mentioned test as well. Make up a list of questions you have.

Consultants

The same goes for consultants. Within the past two years, almost everyone is now calling herself a social media expert or guru. She's not. If you are going to hire a consultant, please interview her extensively. Quiz her on specific IDKT (I Didn't Know That) moments you had when reading this book. If she can't answer most of your questions, invite her to leave and you should try again with someone else.

Warning: Out-house firms don't want you doing your own marketing, social media or otherwise. If you do it yourself, they get no billable hours. They will often obfuscate the execution and insist you leave it to the experts. You are the expert here. No one knows your company, your product, and your services the way you do.

The ROI of Social Media

Exclusive Blogger Event Results in Widespread Social Media Buzz

Background

Moving away from the big box, sterile office supplies world, OfficeMax is targeting women with stylish, affordable private brand lines that encourage creativity, productivity, and efficiency. To support its new positioning, OfficeMax and nationally renowned organizational expert, Peter Walsh, partnered to boost organization and innovation in the workplace with the launch of a new product line—[In]Place System by Peter Walsh.

Strategy

To introduce Walsh's line and bring his workspace organization expertise to life, OfficeMax and Peter Walsh selected to host a sneak preview web event with influential women's interest bloggers. OfficeMax chose to inform and educate women's interest bloggers about office organization and give them special access to celebrated organization expert Peter Walsh. Taking place at the start of spring, OfficeMax also leveraged the timeliness of the announcement during spring when organization and spring cleaning are common interest areas to engage its social media audience and offer them useful tools and advice.

Implementation

To generate anticipation and excitement leading up to the product launch, OfficeMax selected 250 influential women's interest bloggers to participate in a sneak preview of Peter Walsh's new product line and attend a live event titled "Work Life Organized Blogcast." The bloggers were selected for their readership and focus including parenting, professional women and moms, organization, and product reviews. One week before the blogcast, the women's

(continued)

(continued)

interest bloggers received product samples of [In]Place System by Peter Walsh, product brochures, and an introduction letter.

Peter Walsh and OfficeMax's VP of marketing and advertising, Julie Krueger, met the women's interest bloggers online for a 40-minute blogcast live from a Los Angeles studio. During the blogcast, Peter and Julie shared organization tips and strategies for addressing clutter, answered live blogger questions and demonstrated Peter's new organizational system in relation to common workspace organization challenges. To facilitate real-time conversation, a TweetChat room was arranged using the hashtag #OfficeMax, where hundreds of bloggers discussed workspace organization and the new product line on Twitter.

Following the blogcast, the bloggers received Peter Walsh's "Work Life Organized" tip sheet, product images, and links to the recorded blogcast and [In]Place System microsite.

Opportunity

To offer bloggers high quality content they can leverage for their blogs in combination with the introduction of a new workspace organization product line.

Conclusion

OfficeMax's "Work Life Organized Blogcast" with Peter Walsh attracted over 200 live participants, including some of the highest-ranking women's interest bloggers in social media. The web event resulted in more than 125 favorable blog posts about office organization and [In]Place System by Peter Walsh with a total of 2.75 million audience impressions. Furthermore, its hashtag, #OfficeMax, became the number 2 trending topic on Twitter and secured over 1,000 tweets with a total of 2.3 million impressions. The social media coverage eventually led to traditional media coverage from 15 news outlets with a total of 2.1 million audience impressions. In sum, the web event contributed to a successful product launch at OfficeMax with widespread social media and traditional media coverage focused on the product line and its many uses for home and business office organization.

—OfficeMax PR team, OfficeMax.com

Expert Insight

Gary Vaynerchuk, Wine Library director of operations and host and founder of Wine Library TV, www.WineLibrary.com

Gary Vaynerchuk

In October 2007, I decided to start videoblogging under my name—GaryVaynerchuk.com—to kind of talk about the business behind *Wine Library TV* and just business in general—something I'm obviously very passionate about as well. I wanted a platform for that; and so that's been quite successful for me and has led to a lot of speaking engagements, consulting, and opportunities on that level.

So being very entrepreneurial, that's been fun; being artistic with the wine stuff, that's been fun. So I've been, kind of, scratching multiple itches. . . . I come from the lemonade-stand world, and the baseball-card world, and the snow-shoveling world . . . so I've been very, kind of, entrepreneurial my whole life. What's great about social media and where the world's at now is [that] you have the ability to build much bigger brands much quicker and at much lower price points; and that's a very big change in the way business is done in America.

The gatekeepers are [slightly] out of control . . . have *lost* control, actually. No more editor/producer telling you what you can or cannot be, or deciding whether you can speak to the American people or the people of the world, actually. We now have tools that allow us to communicate our message, whatever that may be, with zero cost; just the time and effort we put into the community. That is the fundamental shift of what we're living through right now. . . .

And commitment to our community. I think that's really . . . that's the real equalizer to money for somebody small, like myself, compared to the *Wine Spectator,* or a comedian compared to a top-notch comedian who's on Comedy Central. Whoever leverages their community and whoever builds a community better is in a position to win, whatever that may be. And so time, once again, continues to become important; time has become more valuable

(continued)

(*continued*)

than ever, and I've already cited that people who care and give back are going to win. And I think that's a very powerful message, a very good message, and a very big opportunity for a lot of people. . . .

I think it's one step at a time. I think a lot of people ask me, "What was the tipping point: when you got on Conan, or you were on Leno, or *Nightline,* or in the *Wall Street Journal?*" And I think when you don't focus on tipping points and just focus on pumping out good content—and you focus on hustling every day and answering your e-mail and caring about your community, putting out good content . . . I think you start realizing that you don't need a tipping point and that that's not really what fundamentally separates a victory from a loss. I think that for me it was just pumping out good shows every day and becoming part of the community; leaving comments and blogs and answering my e-mail and creating accounts in things like Facebook and Twitter; you know, just working it. And I think that that is the way to success; it's always been. And the only difference is that now your fans and consumers and the people who care about you have the ability to build you quicker and easier and better because they have tools. Word of mouth has changed; not the way you build a brand. . . . Yeah, I mean, I think the message is the whole game. I think the less polished it is sometimes, the better. I think that the lighting or the mike or the camera you use is so irrelevant and just such a stumbling block by many producers. Many people who want to get into the game spend so much time on trying to figure that part out and that part has no value . . . none! I really think zero. Some of them, you know I mean . . . it's got to be watchable, you've got to be able to hear it, but outside of that, that's the threshold. . . . I think authenticity of the message is what really attaches people to the product, to the service, to the individual. And I think it's quality of message, not quality of the way we consume it, or the video or the sound. So I think it's very obvious what works.

You know, people like tradition, and commercials didn't need to get into million-dollar budgets; they just did because they had the money and people weren't making smart decisions, really! I really believe that. So I think that, you know, you've got to really take a step back and understand what people react to; and people react to things that are authentic, real, transparent, and deliver. And listen . . . some people really love watching something in HD; I get that! But I don't think that's going to be the differentiator from victory or defeat. I really don't! . . .

Building community is about giving a crap! That's where I separated myself from everybody else, or whoever else. . . . I mean, those other people do a great job, but to me it's about really caring about your user base: listening to them, making them involved, letting them participate, caring about their thoughts, letting them have their say in molding the direction of what you do. And so to me, it's just about caring. It's about taking the extra effort to read your e-mails, to respond to them, to meet them in person, to send them little gifts. To just care. I mean, it's a very simple process. It's just one that's costly of time and money and that's something people aren't willing to invest.

To listen to or read the entire Executive Conversation with Gary Vaynerchuk, go to www.theSocialMediaBible.com.

Conclusion

The reality is, if you want to incorporate social media into your marketing, sales, public relations, and communications plan, you can. The resources are there. You may have to be a little creative in where you find them. You may also have to educate upper management to the effectiveness of the combination of conventional and social media marketing. You may have to reprioritize your activities and you may have to look at marketing a little differently. When you do finally implement your phase one strategy and realize the ROI and effectiveness of adding social media, you will be hooked like I am.

Let's go to the final step and talk about implementation and measurement.

Credits

The ROI of Social Media was provided by:

The OfficeMax PR team, OfficeMax.com

Expert Insight was provided by:

Gary Vaynerchuk, Wine Library director of operations and host and founder of Wine Library TV, WineLibrary.com

CHAPTER 26

Implement and Measurement

www.LonSafko.com/TSMB3_Videos/26ImplementMeasure.mov

Implementing Your Strategy, Metrics, and Analytics

Dr. W. Edwards Deming has been incorrectly credited with saying *"You can't manage what you don't measure."* No truer words were never spoken. If you want to measure your return on investment (ROI) and determine your conversion rate, you do need to have measurement tools in place.

I wrote earlier that nearly every newspaper claims that every printed copy of their newspaper is read by two and a half people. Not likely. That's been the problem with measuring conventional marketing. If we learned anything from the late-1990s-to-early-2000s dot-bomb era it's that impressions may add to additional brand recognition, but had little measurable value beyond that.

Measuring ROI, or responses using conventional marketing, has always been difficult. We used multiple post office boxes to track ads, we've used coupon and discount codes, and we've used different telephone numbers. At one time, Hewlett-Packard maintained more than 4,000 different telephone numbers just to track the responsiveness to all of their different advertising.

theSocialMediaBible.com

The problem has been that there wasn't a way to run the responses through an automatic counter until the advent of the Internet.

Because the Internet is managed by computer systems and networks, everything that passes through the system can be measured. Over the past 10 years, we even used the Internet and unique landing pages to measure immeasurable conventional responses. Today, there is a myriad of tools, mostly free, that can help us measure and manage all of our marketing efforts.

Determine Your Measurement Tools

There are a ton of different tools for every category of social media distribution and communications channels. Unfortunately, there just isn't enough space to go through all of them with their features and benefits in this book. You will have to accept their research as a homework assignment. I will discuss some of the more popular and feature-rich tools and their advantages, but do your homework. I will be calling you shortly to grade you.

Web, Blog Page, and Tweet Measurement—Check the Pages

The easiest and freest way to monitor every web page and every blog page in the world is through Google Analytics. If you aren't using Google Analytics, you need to. Go to Google and google Google Analytics. You need to have a Gmail e-mail account, and you should have one anyway; it's free.

Once you have access to all things Google, select Google Analytics and set some up. You create a new Google search term by typing "whatever you want Google to notify you about." I have Google notify me of every occurrence of "Lon Safko," "*Social Media Bible*," my other companies and products, my partners' names, and more.

This way, any time there is the use of that exact text on any web page, any blog page, anywhere in the world, I get a notice with a clickable link that allows me to view that page. Think about that for a minute. Any time anyone mentions me anywhere in the world, I get a notice and a link within 30 minutes of it happening.

Being the first to know about my mention gives me the opportunity to maintain my reputation as I discussed earlier. I am often the first to comment on the blog either thanking the author for the good mention or offering my point of view.

Listen for the Tweets

While this takes care of nearly all of cyberspace, there still is the **SMS** text messages, or tweets. What if you could monitor every tweet sent from anyone on Earth who mentions you, your company, your products, or services and actually get the exact tweet at the same time the recipients get it? You can with Seesmic Desktop or TweetDeck.

Both of these products are free, easy to set up, amazingly powerful for managing your brand, and even have mobile versions so you can manage your brand from your mobile phone. You set up searches the same way you set up searches in Google, using text within quotes.

You can also read all of the tweets from the people you are following, read all of the tweets and replies you send out, and all of your direct messages without having to log on to Twitter. Every minute or so, the screen refreshes and there is all of your company's Twitter activities right there on one screen, and it runs in the background.

A quick way to check every tweet worldwide is Search.Twitter.com. Here's an example of a quick search for "Social Media Bible":

> marconabu: Espero q n la office el boss entienda q si me llevo el social media bible pa la choza es porq quiero q me pasen al dpto de redes sociales!!
>
> about 5 hours ago from TweetDeck · Reply · View Tweet
>
> marconabu: yo sé q hoy s jueves pero cómo yo nunca sigo las reglas! mi #librorecomendado de la semana será Social Media Bible!!
>
> about 5 hours ago from TweetDeck · Reply · View Tweet
>
> njhogan: @Sarah_Tweeds I was unaware social media was in the bible!:P
>
> about 6 hours ago from web · Reply · View Tweet · Show Conversation
>
> lilymafiette: Nerd-out bedtime reading with The Social Media Bible. This book is my new religion. @nguyener0127 Thought you'd appreciate this!:)
>
> about 15 hours ago from HootSuite · Reply · View Tweet

If you don't read or speak Spanish, I will let you look up the first two in iGoogle Translator.

More Sophisticated Surveillance

If you want more sophisticated analysis, you can opt for a pay service such as Radian6, which with one piece of software, will do all of the Google Analytics and SocialMention, all of your Twitter tweets, all of your Facebook and other social network comments and wall writings, and . . . look for trends, both negative and positive, for your keywords and notify you of any negative trend or discussion taking place about your company or brand. This service does have a price tag associated with it, but it's well worth the price.

If you are using video sharing as part of your strategy, which I highly recommend, and are posting videos on YouTube, wouldn't it be great if you could see how many times the video was downloaded and viewed? What if you could know the number of views per day your video received, where those viewers are in the world, how popular your video is compared to other videos in a given period of time, popularity by country, by U.S. state, track the life cycle of videos, including how long it takes for a video to become popular, and what happens to video views as popularity peaks, and a lot more metrics? You can, for free; it's called "YouTube Insight."

Video Sharing

If you post your videos to more than one video sharing site (and you should), there's TubeMogul, which allows you to view statistics from all of your video sharing websites. Now YouTube has great analytics, also.

Traffic Analytics

If you really want to monitor your web traffic (and you do), then Google Analytics and Alexa are the tools you need to become familiar with.

Google automatically generates an analytics code that can be placed in any HTML website or blog site, and the amount of data that is now available to you, in real time, in incredible detail, is amazing. Try it to see for yourself. Honestly, it's worth the effort.

Alexa is known for its data collection and reporting on browsing behavior. Alexa uses toolbars on Firefox and Internet Explorer that collect the data and report back the web pages' popularity as measured against all of the web pages in the world with similar keywords and other metrics, including page views, bounce rates, and time onsite.

External Reputable Links

As External Reputable Links are one of the most important and heavily weighted criteria search engines used, it might be good to know how many external links there are coming in to your website. Interested? Then just go to Google and type in "links:www.yourdomain.com," and there they are! Here is every website that has ever linked to yours.

You may want to go back to Google and type in "site:www.yourdomain .com." This tells you every page that Google has indexed for your entire web or blog site. This way, if you have an imported page or pages, you want to be sure they are getting indexed.

Cyber Surveillance

All of these tools are used for reputation management and what I call Cyber Surveillance. Tools that allow you to monitor your brand. There are many other tools, including Spyfu.com for PPC (pay-per-click) monitoring, a general Google search, Google universal search, Google blog search, Google social search, forum search, and even Flickr and YouTube search.

Know Your Competition

Here's something that most people don't think of: You can use all of the preceding tools to monitor and surveil your competition. Yes, monitor everything they are doing in cyberspace. By using the same tools, you can know every minute of every day what social media tools they are using, where they are engaging with their customers (Facebook, blogs, Twitter), where they are advertising, read their blogs, their tweets, and follow them in the Google shopping search.

Analyze Each Marketing Channel

Once you have set up all of your tools with the appropriate keywords, be sure that you do this for each campaign and not just overall. This way you can monitor specific keywords and the ROI for each campaign and for each activity. Your ROI will be different: some good, and some not so good. As in the previous chapter, either change the way you are performing the activities with the lowest ROI or just stop them altogether. This will allow you to relocate resources to the activities with the best ROI.

Once you have them working for you, lather, rinse, and repeat. Keep perfecting what's working. Also remember that even the activities with a lower ROI are generating a great deal of brand awareness and recognition. It's also building a good reputation and trust in those areas.

Note: I would love to know which genius wrote those three amazing words: *lather, rinse, repeat,* which doubled his client's shampoo sales from just this marketing message. If anyone can tell me who was responsible, I will give any free product that person wants from my www.PaperModelsInc.com store.

Managing Your Expectations

Manage your expectations and the expectations of upper management. While social media is an amazing set of technologies, they still take time. Trust isn't something you can buy or trick someone into giving you. It's earned. Total success will not be measured overnight. Like all marketing, social media marketing is a long-term strategy that needs to be coupled with your conventional long-term marketing strategy. Social media is inordinately effective and in most cases nearly free. Keep at it and it will pay off.

Putting the Pedal to the Metal!

Keep your enthusiasm. Don't give up. Stay current on the technology by setting some time aside each week and looking around on the web. Read some of *Tech News World*'s articles. Renay San Miguel writes some great stories on all of the cutting edge technologies. Look at theSocialMediaBible.com,

and my ExtremeDigitalMarketing.com

for how-to videos on everything I discussed here in this book.

The most important element of a Five-Step Social Media Success Plan is Commitment!

The ROI of Social Media

Increasing Attendance and Revenue to Peabody Rooftop Parties

Background

We needed to increase our attendance and revenue for a series of 16 hotel rooftop parties lasting from April to July. We also wanted to target a younger demographic. Social media was a cost-effective way to promote all the parties in a short amount of time. Because our target audience had begun to adopt the technology, social media provided an efficient channel for us to tap the market.

Strategy

Visibility on the social networks of our target audience was our main focus. We created episodic content to gradually grow our audience week by week. Our two platforms were Facebook and Twitter. Facebook served as more of a weekly publication of invitations, party information, photos, and video. Twitter served as a real-time broadcast of updates, links, and stories our rooftop audience would find valuable. We created the hashtag #pbodyroof for all rooftop-related content.

Implementation

We created a Facebook group, The Peabody Memphis Events and Rooftop Parties. The landing page featured this year's prices and music lineup. We ran a two-week Facebook advertisement in April 2009 about the group. Clicking on the ad brought the viewer to our group. We created 16 rooftop party events and sent invitations to each party on a weekly basis. During the parties, we took photos and recorded video. Photos were posted the next day to the group. We tagged all of our friends, radio station hosts, DJs, and bands and encouraged [that] they tag their friends and share content with their fans and listeners. A rooftop recap video was posted each month that highlighted the month's music lineup.

On Twitter, all of our posts included the hash tag #pbodyroof. We posted party updates, including last-minute band additions and weather updates. We answered questions from our followers about the parties. We also posted twitpics of the parties in real time.

Opportunity

The opportunity was to establish the Peabody Rooftop Parties as the premier social event in Memphis throughout spring and summer. It also built credibility with our online audience because of our engagement on Facebook and Twitter. The Peabody Memphis also earned credibility in the industry as an effective social media marketer, being featured in trade magazines such as *Hotels* magazine and *Hospitality Technology*.

Conclusion

We increased our attendance by 113 percent. Beverage revenues also increased 83 percent. Before Twitter, 700 people would be considered a huge turnout for a rooftop party. Today, the average number is 1,000 to 1,200, with upward of 1,700 in attendance. Our group page grew from 800 members in April to

(continued)

more than 2,200 members by the end of July. The rooftop parties were featured in local blogs as being a successful turnaround from the previous year. Local bloggers and community influencers also praised the Peabody for listening to the community putting on the acts people wanted to see.

You can currently find the Peabody Memphis on the web at:

peabodymemphis.com
facebook.com/peabodyducks

twitter.com/peabodymemphis

The Facebook group is "The Peabody Memphis Events and Rooftop Parties."

—Jonathan Lyons, marketing and PR coordinator, The Peabody Memphis

Expert Insight

Rishi Chandra, product manager, Google Enterprise, www.google.com /apps/intl/en/business/index.html

Rishi Chandra

The Google Apps is a set of business applications, which are hosted on the Internet, or . . . on Cloud. The idea is—if you have heard of some of Google's more famous consumer products like Gmail, Google Calendar, and Google Talk—[that] we actually take those consumer technologies, package, and bundle them in a way that enterprises and businesses can actually use.

So, for example, instead of having a Gmail.com e-mail address where you use the Gmail product, you can use your own company's e-mail address, and access the power of your company's e-mail infrastructure. . . .

So, as I said, there are two core components to Google Apps. There is a messaging component, which includes Gmail, Calendar, and Contacts. And on the collaboration side—the other element of Apps—includes Google Sites, Google Docs, and a new product we have just recently launched, called Google Video for Business . . . the difficult thing is that we launched [it] only two to three weeks ago [September 2008]; and [again], we are really excited about taking this idea of Google's Consumer Technologies—in this case, YouTube—and being able to apply [them] to a business setting. So being able to allow companies to upload their own video content and within their company—just as you see YouTube do in the consumer world for them. . . .

We have done a couple of things that . . . work in a business environment. . . . Businesses love the fact that we have very easy-to-use and powerful tools [that] can be hosted on the Web. They get all the benefits of Google hosting it for you. You do not have to worry about it; [and since] it works in a browser, you do not have to install or maintain any type of hardware or software. At the same time, businesses have a higher level of expectation around certain features than [consumers do]. You need to have more control, more

(continued)

(*continued*)

security, and more functionality targeted for specific business-use cases. And that's actually what we have done with the video product, for example. We actually have it at higher resolution; it's more secure because you can actually share it with a set of people; and only a small set of people so that they will be the only ones to have access to that information. And we have administrative controls in there, so that your administrator can administer the product just as you could with any other product. . . .

That is really one of the key benefits of Cloud computing . . . this idea that you have a single place for your information—in this case, it is on the Internet—[that] most people can access from [wherever they are in the world]; whatever company they are a part of, or whatever device they are accessing it from, whether it be a mobile device or a computer or a laptop. . . .

That is one of the great benefits: anyone can access [the information] at any point in time. The other benefit—as you [pointed out]—is this idea of collaborating with multiple people in different places. You know, the biggest challenge we heard from both businesses and consumers is this idea of collaboration through e-mail is a pretty broken process. . . . So, for example, if four or five people wanted to work on a document today, most people actually just e-mail that out to five different people; each of them downloads an individual copy of that document, work off their own copy, and send it back. Now [the original] person has to recompile those different changes; and if multiple people are working off of it with different revisions, you can see yourself getting into a pretty easy nightmare, pretty quickly . . . and so, . . . we are thinking of a new way for people to interact with each other and actually share information and collaborate on information.

That is really one of the key benefits of Cloud computing. . . . And what that product does is actually a wiki. A wiki is [a document or web page] that anyone can edit a piece of . . . and you can easily create multiple pieces of data in one single place. So, for example, if I have a Project Team, I can embed a Google Calendar in that Google Site; I can embed a document associated with that Project Team; I can associate videos with that Project Team. You can bring together all of these different types of rich, social information into one single place and have people collaborate on it in a very easy way. . . .

It is a monumental change with how people interact with web pages today. [When] most people hear the word *web page*, they get really intimidated. It certainly makes them think of things like HTML and how complicated those are. Google Sites wants to make it as easy to edit a web page as it is to use *edit* in a document. Anyone who has permission to that site can go do it, and it is as straightforward as editing a document. You can edit text, you can pull different pieces of information in very quickly and easily, and with one button you can publish it to the set of people you want to share that information with. That's the real philosophy behind Google Sites. . . .

It is a great product, because it brings together a lot of different places that use information; and really highlights to business users in particular. There are certain technologies that they are just not used to using, but it really does enable much richer collaboration. Video is a great example of this. You will find in the consumer world [that] video is actually very pervasive. Lots of people interact with video content all the time, but somehow it never made the transition to the business world. And we believe that there are a couple of reasons for that. . . . One is that it is just not simple and easy to do so. . . . That is where Google can really change the game there with our simple user interfaces, which are incredibly powerful, to enable much richer collaboration. But at the same time it is incredibly expensive for most business to do something like that, because video is a very intensive application and most companies do not have the time, the bandwidth, or even the costs to actually make it work for them. And that is really where Google Apps can change the game. We can bring these really great, compelling, new social technologies into the enterprise and do so in a way that is very cost-effective for most businesses. . . .

It is pretty amazing actually, when you think of what's happened in the consumer world, where storage has become much and much less of an issue for most users. In the business world, it actually still is a really big problem. One of the greatest examples and what really highlights that is, if you go to Gmail.com, for free you can sign up for a 7-gigabyte e-mail storage on your inbox . . . and most companies today still only give 500 megabytes to their users; even though they pay lots and lots of money to actually make the technology work for their employees. Somehow, we have gone completely backward. . . . And that is why Google technology can really change the game here. With the premier edition of Google Apps, we give our users 25 gigabytes of e-mail storage—which is just monumental compared to what most businesses already give their users. So we can really change the game by giving more storage at a better price and giving more tools that actually incorporate these new social technologies in an easy way for the end user.

To listen to or read the entire Executive Conversation with Rishi Chandra, go to www.theSocialMediaBible.com.

Conclusion

Developing an integrated conventional and social media strategy isn't difficult. It will take a little time to go through the steps. The toughest part is changing the way you think about marketing and finding the time and support to implement your effort.

You still have to focus on the message. That is the reason you are communicating. Never sell or you will get flamed. Remember, it's like walking into a networking event; there is a room full of small groups between three and five people all talking, all holding the tiny wines. If you walk up, push in, and start telling everybody that you sell such and such and the next time someone needs one and that you are the person to call, you will get slapped in the lips. That is inappropriate behavior. You know that.

The same goes for online. Listen first, and when it's appropriate to add something to the conversation, slide it in. After that, you are part of that group and will be treated as such.

Listen, Participate, Trust. Authentic, Sincere, Transparent. Lather, Rinse, Repeat.

That's all there is to it!

Credits

The ROI of Social Media was provided by:

Jonathan Lyons, marketing and PR coordinator, The Peabody Memphis

Expert Insight was provided by:

Rishi Chandra, product manager, Google Enterprise, www.google.com/apps/intl/en/business/index.html

608 INDEX